JAVA ACTUALLY

JAVA ACTUALLY

A First Course in Programming

Khalid A. Mughal, Torill Hamre and Rolf W. Rasmussen

THOMSON

Australia · Canada · Mexico · Singapore · Spain · United Kingdom · United States

Java Actually

Khalid A. Mughal, Torill Hamre and Rolf W. Rasmussen

Publishing Director	**Publisher**	**Development Editor**
John Yates	Gaynor Redvers-Mutton	Laura Priest
Production Editor	**Manufacturing Manager**	**Marketing Manager**
Fiona Freel	Helen Mason	Mark Lord
Typesetter	**Production Controller**	**Cover Design Controller**
WordMongers Ltd	Maeve Healy	Jackie Wrout
Cover Design	**Text Design**	**Printer**
Jackie Wrout	Design Delux, Bath, UK	C & C Offset Printing Co., Ltd

ISBN : 978-184480-418-4
First edition published 2007 by Thomson
Learning.

While the publisher has taken all
reasonable care in the preparation of this
book the publisher makes no
representation, express or implied, with
regard to the accuracy of the information
contained in this book and cannot accept
any legal responsibility or liability for any
errors or omissions from the book or the
consequences thereof.

Products and services that are referred to
in this book may be either trademarks
and/or registered trademarks of their
respective owners.
The publisher and author/s make no
claim to these trademarks.

British Library Cataloguing in-
Publication Data
A catalogue record for this book is
available from the British Library.

To my one and only Chachaji, a.k.a. Mohammad Amin, for always inspiring to discover wonders in the written word.

– K.A.M.

To my mother Anna and in loving memory of my father Hallstein.

– T.H.

To my brother Knut Henrik and my sister Elisabeth.

– R.W.R.

OVERVIEW

CONTENTS

4 Using objects 75

5 More on control structures 99

LIST OF PROGRAMS

LIST OF FIGURES

LIST OF TABLES

About the book

This book provides a coherent coverage of topics relevant for a first course in programming using Java. It is ideal for a one-semester course at college and university level. Techniques for problem solving on the computer are emphasised, and the Java programming language is used for implementing the solutions.

The book assumes no prior knowledge of programming beyond the basic skills required to use a computer. It is also both platform- and programming-tool independent. The book is backed by a web site that offers lecture notes, source code for every programming example in the book, links to Java-related resources and more.

The topics covered in this book are up-to-date with Java technology as of JDK 1.6. The aim is *not* to cover every Java-based technology under the sun, but to teach the fundamentals in programming and build a foundation that the reader can use to move on to the more specialized and advanced technologies that use Java.

Our approach is to introduce enough structured programming concepts to write meaningful examples, and then quickly proceed to object-based programming (OBP) for working with objects. The book emphasises testing of program behaviour using assertions, and includes common sorting and searching algorithms. It covers the way in which programs interact with their environment via the terminal window, text files, and through simple GUI dialog boxes.

Basic UML (Unified Modelling Language) diagrams are used to illustrate Java language constructs, basic program design and programming concepts.

Book audiences

The book should be readily accessible to the following audiences:

- Anybody learning how to program for the first time.
- Students who intend to pursue studies in fields other than Computer Science and only require an introductory course in programming.
- Students who intend to pursue studies in Computer Science and require a sound foundation in the basics of object-oriented programming (OOP).
- Programmers with background from other languages wanting to migrate to Java.

Prerequisites

The book assumes basic knowledge in the use of the following:

- Basic computer equipment, i.e. computer with keyboard, mouse and screen.
- A normal graphical user interface with windows, buttons and menus.

- A command-line window, to execute commands in the operating system, for example to start a program.
- The file system, to create, delete and find files.
- A text editor, to write text files, for example *emacs* or *vi* on Unix, or *Notepad* on Windows.
- The operating system, to install new programs.
- A web browser, to search on the Internet for programming resources.

Book themes

The book emphasises the following themes:

- **OBP and its application.** The book is structured around OBP and shows its application in different contexts. The book requires no previous experience of Java programming, and explains concepts from the ground up. It uses the classes from the Java standard library and includes numerous examples of the development of user-defined classes.
- **Concepts before syntax.** The book emphasises concepts and shows how these are implemented by the language features in Java. Java syntax is illustrated through examples of typical usage of the language constructs, in which the elements of the syntax are clearly identified.
- **Fundamental data modelling.** Both *data modelling* and *programming* are necessary in order to solve problems on the computer. Modelling of abstractions and data structures is thoroughly explained and illustrated with diagrams.
- **Development of algorithms.** The book encourages algorithm development, and uses pseudocode to show the progression from problem analysis to implementation of the solution.
- **Example-driven exposition.** The book uses appropriate examples to explain and apply concepts. Each program example is complete and shows the output, or a screenshot, from the program, so that one can easily reproduce and compare the results. The reader is made aware of the common pitfalls in programming, and practical usage is emphasized through examples.
- **Use of UML (Unified Modelling Language).** We illustrate important programming concepts using easy-to-understand diagrams based on UML. Appendix H provides a short introduction to the notation. The book does not require any prior exposure to UML, and its use is applied only where it intuitively makes sense.
- **Focus on problem solving techniques.** The book uses a few well-chosen case studies to illustrate programming concepts. This approach ensures that the reader becomes familiar with the problem, and the book can focus on problem-solving techniques. Testing program behaviour is emphasised using assertions.

Book features

The source code for all the program examples in the book is available on the book's web site, and can be downloaded and experimented with. All examples are complete and can be compiled and run immediately. They have been tested thoroughly on several platforms.

Each chapter contains the following sections:

- **Learning objectives.** The objectives listed at the beginning of each chapter clearly outline the concepts and topics covered by the chapter.
- **Review questions.** Ample review questions test the topics covered in each chapter. Annotated answers to all review questions are provided in Appendix A.
- **Programming exercises.** The programming exercises vary in scale and level of difficulty. They help to develop programming skills.

In addition, the book offers the following:

- **Best practices callouts.** These callouts help to promote and facilitate good programming practices.
- **Appropriate cross-references.** The book provides appropriate cross-references that link related concepts.
- **An extensive index.** A comprehensive index aids in locating definitions, concepts and topics in the book.

Practical use of Java

We have paid special attention to the presentation and practical use of the Java programming language. The book uses:

- **Platform-independent programming language.** Java encourages platform-independent programming, and so does this book. Specific platform-dependent details are provided only where necessary.
- **Programming tool-independent exposition.** The book uses Java 6.0 and the standard tools provided by Java Development Kit 1.6 (JDK 1.6). Details about compiling and running Java programs using the standard command line tools *javac* and *java* are given in Appendix G. If it is desirable, other programming tools or IDEs (Integrated Development Environments) can be used. However, we feel that it is necessary to avoid idiosyncrasies of a full-blown IDE at the early stages when learning programming.
- **Use of the Java standard library.** Methods from classes in the Java standard library, which are used in the programming examples, are fully documented where they are used in the book. In addition, we recommend that the reader should have access to the documentation for the Java standard library, either online or installed locally.
- **Creating dialogue between the program and the user.** In the examples we do not use customised classes for interaction between the program and the user. However, the book offers two classes that can be used for this purpose: a class (`Console`) that can be used to read values from the terminal window, and a class (`GUIDialog`) for creating simple graphical user interfaces (GUI) for reading values via dialog boxes (see Appendix E). The `Console` class encapsulates the use of the `java.util.Scanner` class, while the `GUIDialog` class uses the `javax.swing.JOptionPane` class. Both classes offer methods for reading integers, floating-point numbers and strings.
- **Emphasising the Java Advantage.** The book uses what the Java language has to offer to an introductory course in programming. For example, assertions are introduced early in the book and used for verifying the behaviour of programs. The `Scanner` class is used to read input from the terminal window, and the `printf()`

method is used to format values. Other Java 2 features in the book include the enhanced for loop and enumerated types.

Topics in introductory programming courses

We have organized the material as follows:

- Part 1: Structured programming
- Part 2: Object-based programming (OBP)
- Part 3: Program building blocks

Structured programming (i.e. control structures) and OBP (i.e. objects only and no inheritance) form the core of the book. Program building blocks constitute a first look at simple sorting and searching algorithms for arrays, reading and writing text files, and creating simple GUI dialog boxes. This approach lays the foundation for a follow-up course to introduce more advanced topics in OOP (classes and interfaces using inheritance).

The reader can choose either a linear or a non-linear route through the book, depending on their choice of topics. Some suggestions as to how the book can be used to tailor different types of introductory programming courses (both in size and topic sequence) can be found in the diagram opposite. Topics up to and including OBP ought to be covered in all courses: these topics are shown in shaded boxes in the diagram. The extent of the course can be varied by selecting the remaining topics to be included. Solid arrows show optimal coverage of the material, and dashed arrows show the earliest point at which additional topics can be introduced to form appropriate course variants.

The initial chapter provides a brief overview of programming, and structured programming concepts are covered in the two following chapters. Objects are introduced next, allowing meaningful communication between objects as early as possible. We cover OBP in detail, dealing with the use of predefined classes and objects, followed by user-defined classes and communication between objects.

Searching and sorting ought to be in any programmer's skill set, and the book covers a few of the classical algorithms. A program must be able to exchange data with its surroundings. For this purpose, we provide coverage of the storage of data in text files and the design of of simple GUI dialog boxes.

Appendices provide annotated answers to review questions, useful references (keywords, operators, primitive data types, character codes, formatting code) and succinct introductions to supplementary topics (Console I/O and simple GUI dialog design, number representation, JDK tools, UML).

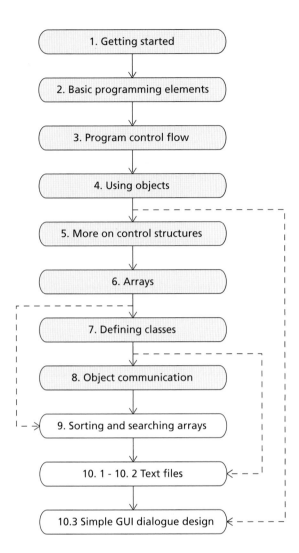

Conventions used in the source code

Names in Java source code

All class and interface names begin with an uppercase letter. Names of packages, variables and methods begin with a lowercase letter. Constants are always specified with uppercase letters in their names. In addition, all method names in the text end with () to distinguish them from other names.

Code-line references in the text

Code lines in examples or code snippets in the text often end with a comment, where a number in parenthesis, (), is specified after the comment characters //:

```
System.out.println("Important business"); // (4)
```

The number is used in the text to refer to the corresponding line in the code. For example, (4) in this text refers to the code line above that has the corresponding number.

The book's web site

We have created a web site for the book at http://www.ii.uib.no/~khalid/jact/.

The book's web site offers the following resources:

- Errata
- Source code for all the examples in the book
- Links to other useful resources: articles/tutorials on programming, web browsers, Java tools, and more.

In addition, the following resources for lecturers can be found here:

- Lecture notes
- Source code for all the examples in the lecture notes
- Links providing suggestions for projects and weekly assignments

Feedback

We appreciate getting feedback. Questions, comments, suggestions and corrections can be sent to: jact@ii.uib.no.

The authors

In 1997 the Department of Informatics, University of Bergen (UoB), switched to Java in its introductory course in programming. Mughal and Rasmussen were responsible for developing a new format for this course. In autumn 2004 the Norwegian Quality Reform in Higher Education led to further changes in the curriculum. Mughal was one of the main architects behind the revision of the programming courses at the Department of Informatics, UoB.

The three authors have collaborated on an introductory textbook for programming in Java, written in Norwegian, *Java som første programmingsspråk /Java as First Programming Language, Third Edition*, Cappelen Akademisk Forlag, ISBN 82-02-24554-0, Sept. 2006, http://www.ii.uib.no/~khalid/jfps3u/. This book, *Java Actually*, is heavily based on the Norwegian textbook.

Mughal and Rasmussen are also co-authors of a book on the first exam in certification for the Java technology, *A Programmer's Guide to Java Certification: A Comprehensive Primer, Second Edition*, Addison-Wesley, ISBN 0201728281, Aug. 2003, http://www.ii.uib.no/~khalid/pgjc2e/.

The three authors have been involved in developing web-based variants of the programming courses offered by the Department of Informatics, UoB. These web-based courses are offered every spring (see http://nettkurs.ii.uib.no/jafu/). Mughal and Hamre have run a series of seminars on object orientation at the Department of Informatics, UoB. The authors also collaborate on research in application of object-oriented technology.

Principal author – Khalid Azim Mughal

Khalid A. Mughal is an Associate Professor at the Department of Informatics, UoB. He has developed and given courses for students and the IT industry on programming in Java and Java-related technologies. In 1999, on the basis of the introductory course on programming in Java, he was awarded the Best Lecturer prize at the Faculty of Mathematics and Natural Sciences, UoB. His teaching experience spans programming languages, object-oriented software development, web application development, e-learning, data bases and compiler techniques.

His current work involves applying object-oriented technology in the development of learning content management systems, and building software security into applications.

He has spent over three years at the Department of Computer Science, Cornell University, both as a Visiting Fellow and as a Visiting Scientist. He is a member of the ACM.

Co-author – Torill Hamre

Torill Hamre is a Research Leader at the Nansen Environmental and Remote Sensing Center in Bergen. The Nansen Center is affiliated to the University of Bergen, where she is an Adjunct Associate Professor at the Department of Informatics.

Her main research is in marine information technologies. She develops object-oriented solutions for marine information systems. She has also given courses in object-oriented software development, both at the University and to the IT industry.

Co-author – Rolf W. Rasmussen

Rolf W. Rasmussen is a System Developer at *vizrt* in Bergen, a company that provides solutions for the television broadcasting industry worldwide. He works on control and information systems, video processing, typography and real-time graphics visualization. Over the years he has worked both academically and professionally with numerous programming languages, including Java. He has contributed to the development of GCJ (GNU's implementation of Java), which is a part of the GNU Compiler Collection, where he has worked on the clean room implementation of graphics libraries for Java.

Acknowledgements

First we would like to thank the following people at Thomson Learning: Gaynor Redvers-Mutton, Laura Priest, and Fiona Freel. Without Gaynor's conviction that we could pull this off, we are not sure whether we would have embarked on this venture. Thank you also for catering to our whims and for all the support during the writing process.

We are impressed with the results that FrameMaker guru Steve Rickaby of WordMongers Ltd. managed to conjure forth when it came to the design of the book. He fielded our questions with dexterity, and was ever obliging. Many thanks, Steve!

We are also very much indebted to the four anonymous technical reviewers who gave us encouraging and invaluable feedback on the initial draft of some of the book chapters.

We are fortunate to have Marit Seljeflot Mughal as our personal expert on language washing for our writing. Your efforts have saved us, not only from language bloopers, but also from errors in our Java code. Thank you for reading countless chapter drafts, and providing invaluable advice on improvements to the manuscript.

We would also like to thank the Department of Informatics, UoB, for providing an environment conducive to writing this book, and testing the course material on which the book is based.

Without family support, this book simply would not have seen the light of day. Many thanks for being patient, both when the dinner got cold and when family plans changed in favour of working on the book. We will try to get our priorities right, but no promises.

Bergen, 23 October, 2006.

Khalid A. Mughal
Torill Hamre
Rolf W. Rasmussen

CHAPTER 1

Getting started

LEARNING OBJECTIVES

By the end of this chapter you will understand the following:

- **The main activities involved in creating and maintaining programs.**

- **What source code is, and how we create it.**

- **What the basic components of a Java program are.**

- **How to compile the Java source code into an executable program.**

- **How to run a compiled Java program.**

INTRODUCTION

This chapter illustrates some important programming concepts by way of an example. We will look at how to write, build and run programs. Later chapters will provide a more thorough explanation of the concepts introduced here.

1.1 Programming

A *program* is a set of instructions that can be executed on a computer to accomplish a specific task. Modern computers execute sequences of instructions quickly, accurately and reliably. Most people who use computers today are *end users*, i.e. they do not write their own programs. They mainly use off-the-shelf programs (*software*) for many purposes: word processors to write documents, drawing programs to make illustrations and spreadsheets to perform calculations.

The task of writing new programs is called *programming*. We write programs using the language constructs of a programming language. The program in this form is called *source code* and is stored in *text files*. The source code contains human readable descriptions of the tasks the computer should perform, and usually needs to be translated before it can be executed on the computer.

FIGURE 1.1   Main activities in writing programs

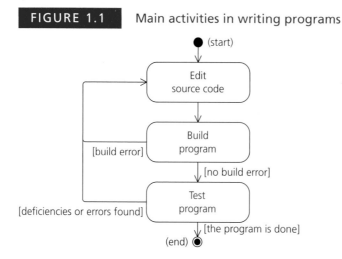

Figure 1.1 shows the main activities involved in creating programs. First we write the source code in text files, commonly called *source code files*. The source code describes exactly what tasks the computer should perform. Then we build an executable program from these source code files. At this point we need to correct any errors in the source code that prevent the program from being built. After building the program, we usually need to test it to make sure that it actually behaves the way we intended. If we detect any deficiencies or errors in the program, we need to go back and improve the source code.

Many other activities are involved when writing large programs, but the activities described in this chapter will be sufficient to get you started with programming.

There are many programming languages, but in this book we focus on the popular programming language, Java. Many of the concepts and programming techniques shown in this book are also applicable to other programming languages. The Java *compiler* is the program we use to build new programs from files containing Java source code.

Let's jump right in and take a quick look at some source code. Program 1.1 is the source code for a small program that calculates and reports the number of characters in a particular proverb. We will dissect this source code line by line later in the chapter, but for now it is sufficient to keep in mind that source code like this is stored in text files and is used to build executable programs. Before we examine the contents of Program 1.1 any further, we will look at how to enter the source code, build Java programs and run Java programs.

PROGRAM 1.1   The source code for a simple Java program

```
// (1) This source code file is called SimpleProgram.java
public class SimpleProgram {
    // Print a proverb, and the number of characters in the proverb.
    public static void main(String[] args) {                    // (2)
```

```
    System.out.println("A proverb:");                           // (3)

    String proverb = "Practice makes perfect!";                 // (4)
    System.out.println(proverb);                                // (5)

    int characterCount = proverb.length();                      // (6)
    System.out.println("The proverb has " + characterCount + " characters.");
  }
}
```

1.2 Editing source code

The source code files contain only characters that constitute the actual text of the source code, and no text formatting information. Word processors such as Microsoft Word are not suited for writing source code, because their primary function is creating formatted documents. Many text editors for editing source code exist (e.g. JEdit), but any application (e.g. Microsoft Notepad) that can edit and save plain text can be used.

BEST PRACTICES

Choose a good editor and spend a few hours learning its features. In the long run, this effort will pay off handsomely in terms of productivity.

Source code file naming rules

To build an executable program, the compiler requires the source code files to be named according to specific rules. A Java source code file usually contains a language construct called a *class*. The name of this class is important when naming source code files. When saving the source code of a Java program, you need to make sure that:

- The name of the source code file is the same as the name of the class it contains, followed by the extension ".java".
- Use of lower and uppercase letters is the same as in the class name.

According to these rules, the source code file for Program 1.1 must be named "SimpleProgram.java", as it contains a class named "SimpleProgram".

If a source code file contains more than one class, only one class is designated as the *primary class*. The primary class is declared with the keyword public, and the source code file is named after this class.

The desktop environment of some operating systems hides the extension at the end of the file name by default. The compiler will refuse to compile source code files whose names do not have the correct file extension. A common mistake is to store the source code file as either "*<name>*`.java.doc`" or "*<name>*`.java.txt`". Such file names will not be accepted by the compiler, even if the operating system shows them as simply "*<name>*`.java`". Microsoft Windows also provides alternative *short names* for files, e.g. "`MainCl~1.java`". Such file names are also not accepted by the compiler.

1.3 Development tools for Java

There are several ways to compile and run programs, depending on the development tools you are using. The following sections show how to compile and run programs using the standard software development tools for Java.

Sun Microsystems provides a package of tools called the Java Development Kit (JDK). This package contains the basic tools needed to compile and run programs written in Java. Appendix G provides more information about this development kit.

This book will show how to compile and run programs in a *terminal window*. Most operating systems have some sort of a terminal window with a command line where you can enter commands you want to run. Read through the documentation for your operating system if you need information on how to run commands from the command line in a terminal window.

1.4 Compiling Java programs

The syntax for running the Java compiler from the command line is:

```
> javac SimpleProgram.java
```

The `javac` compiler reads the source code from the specified Java source code file, and translates each class in the source code into a compiled form known as *Java byte code* (see Figure 1.2). The compiler creates files named "*<name>*`.class`" that contain the byte code for each class. Section 1.8 on page 11 explains byte code.

The compiler may detect errors in the source code when translating it to byte code. The compiler will report any errors and terminate the compilation. The errors must be corrected in the source code and the compiler run again to compile the program. With a little practice, you will be able to interpret the most common errors reported by the compiler, and identify the cause of the errors in the source code.

FIGURE 1.2   Compiling source code

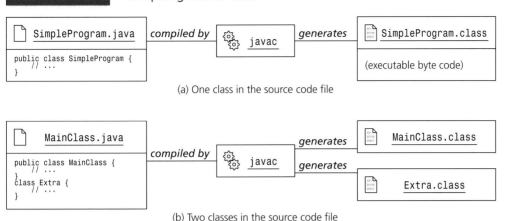

(a) One class in the source code file

(b) Two classes in the source code file

1.5 Running Java programs

The command for running a compiled Java program is "java". This command should not be confused with the command "javac" used to compile the source code.

The syntax for running a Java program from the command line is:

```
> java -ea SimpleProgram
```

The java command starts the *Java virtual machine* (see Section 1.8 on page 11) that provides the runtime environment for executing the byte code of a Java program. The virtual machine starts the execution in the main() method of the class specified on the command line. More information on the java command is provided in Appendix G.

FIGURE 1.3   Terminal window showing program execution

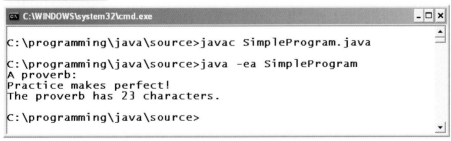

The output from running the SimpleProgram example is shown in Figure 1.3. The length of a string includes all characters between the double quotes, including any spaces.

The `java` command requires that the exact name of the class containing the `main()` method is specified. Here are some guidelines in case there are problems running the `java` command:

- Specify the exact class name, without any ".class" or ".java" extensions.
- Check the use of upper and lowercase letters in the class name.
- Make sure that the source code has been compiled, so that there is a ".class" file for each class in the program.

1.6 The components of a program

This section introduces terminology that we will use in the next section to identify the language constructs used in the source code of Program 1.1. Later chapters will elaborate on the concepts mentioned here.

Operations

When creating a new program, we break down the given problem into smaller tasks that can be accomplished by performing one or more operations. Each operation is realised by a sequence of actions that describe in detail what the computer should do. These actions are written in the chosen programming language.

Programming with objects

The operations that need to be performed to complete a task often involve several types of objects. To start thinking in terms of objects and operations, let's consider the operations needed to make an omelette:

1. Open the refrigerator
2. Take out an egg carton
3. Open the egg carton
4. Take out two eggs
5. Close the egg carton
6. Place the egg carton back in the refrigerator
7. Close the refrigerator
8. Turn on the stove
9. ...

In this context we can consider the refrigerator, the egg carton, the eggs and the stove to be different types of objects. The operations that are performed are inherently connected to these objects. The type of an object determines the operations that can be performed on it. For example, it is possible to open an egg carton, but it is not possible to open a frying pan.

Object-based programming

Object-based programming (OBP) involves describing tasks in terms of operations that are executed on objects. What the objects represent depends on what the program is trying to accomplish. A program to keep track of library loans, for example, might use objects to represent tangible items such as books, journals, audio tapes, etc., and also objects to represent non-tangible concepts such as the lending date and personal information about library users.

Programs usually have more than one object of the same type. Back in the kitchen we have several objects representing bottles of milk. Each bottle can be handled independently, but they all have certain common properties, e.g. they can be uncapped and drunk from. Objects that share a set of common properties can be considered to belong to the same *class* of objects. Every egg object is a concrete *instance* of a particular Egg class, just as every milk bottle is a concrete instance of a particular MilkBottle class. This distinction is illustrated in Figure 1.4.

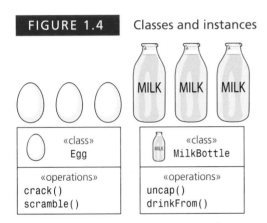

FIGURE 1.4   Classes and instances

A class is defined by describing the properties specific to the objects of the class, and the operations that can be performed on these objects. A program can consist of user-defined classes as well as classes from other sources. The Java language comes bundled with a large collection of ready-to-use classes called the *Java standard library*. These classes contain program code that can readily be used for solving a wide range of programming problems.

1.7   The Java programming language

Classes and methods

The language constructs of the Java programming language have a prescribed structure. We call this structure the *syntax* of the language. A *class declaration* is a language construct to define classes. Operations in a class are defined by *method declarations* containing sequences of *statements* describing the actions that need to be performed.

Figure 1.5 on page 8 shows the language constructs used in the source code of Program 1.1. The program has a class declaration that specifies a class called SimpleProgram, and this class has a method called main.

Comments and indentation

The first line of source code in Program 1.1 is:

```
// (1) This source code file is called SimpleProgram.java
```

This is a source code comment, and is ignored by the compiler. We write comments in the source code to aid programmers in understanding the inner workings of the program. Everything following the characters // on a line of source code is a comment.

When this book wants to draw attention to specific lines of code from the code examples, the code line have a comment of the form // (n), and the text refers to the lines using markers such as (n), where n is an integer.

FIGURE 1.5   Class and method declarations

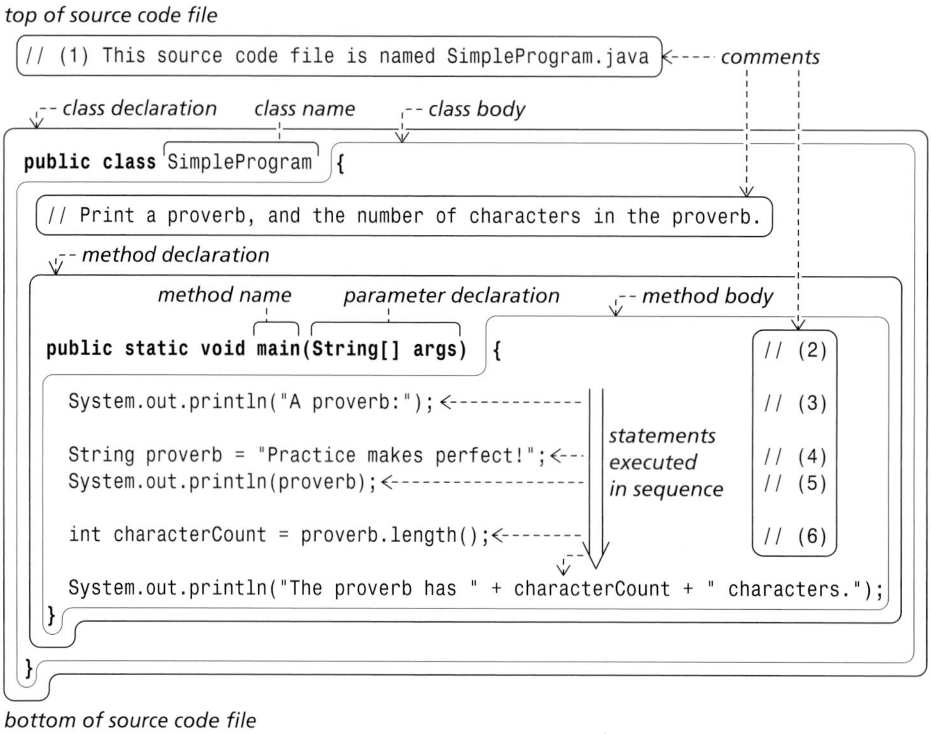

top of source code file

```
// (1) This source code file is named SimpleProgram.java  <---- comments

  -- class declaration    class name    -- class body

public class SimpleProgram {

  // Print a proverb, and the number of characters in the proverb.
  -- method declaration

       method name      parameter declaration    -- method body

  public static void main(String[] args) {                    // (2)

    System.out.println("A proverb:"); <------------           // (3)
                                                  statements
    String proverb = "Practice makes perfect!";<--  executed  // (4)
    System.out.println(proverb); <-----------------  in sequence  // (5)

    int characterCount = proverb.length();<--------           // (6)

    System.out.println("The proverb has " + characterCount + " characters.");
  }

}
```

bottom of source code file

The compiler completely ignores all comments, as well as some special characters such as spaces and end-of-line characters. As far as the compiler is concerned, the main() method declaration starting at (2) could just as well have been written like this:

```
public static void main(String[]args){System.out.println("A proverb:");
String proverb="Practice makes perfect!";System.out.println(proverb);int
characterCount=proverb.length();System.out.println("The proverb has "+
characterCount+" characters.");}
```

The layout of the source code has no bearing on program execution. It is a common practice to write one statement per line, and use indentation from the left margin to show the nesting of the language constructs. This book uses two spaces for each indentation step to conserve the available page width.

Program entry point

Line (2) of Program 1.1 is the start of a method declaration that defines a method called main:

```
  public static void main(String[] args) {                                    // (2)
```

The method being defined here has the *parameter declaration* String[] args, as shown in Figure 1.5. A parameter declaration specifies the information a method is given when it is executed. In this particular program we are not interested in giving any information to the method, so we will just ignore the parameter declaration for now.

Throughout this book we follow the convention of writing "()" at the end of names to indicate that the names refer to methods. This does not necessarily mean that the methods do not have any parameters.

For a Java program to be executable, it must define exactly one main() method that is declared with public static void main(String[] args) { ... }, which is the method where program execution will start. The statements within the method body obviously vary from program to program, reflecting the task each program is trying to accomplish. The significance of using a particular method declaration to designate the *entry point* where execution of the program starts becomes clear when writing programs that have more than one method declaration.

Each line in the main() method body in Program 1.1 is a separate statement. When the program starts to run, the statements in the main() method are executed one by one, starting with the first statement. Figure 1.6 on page 10 shows the statements annotated with the language constructs they use.

Method calls

The first statement that is executed when the program starts is (3):

```
System.out.println("A proverb:");                                    // (3)
```

This statement *calls* the method `println` in the object known as `System.out`. The method `println()` in this object is responsible for printing a line of text. The statement calling the `println()` method passes it the sequence of characters to be printed. Such a sequence of characters is called a *string*. The statement at (3) passes the string `"A proverb:"` as a parameter to the `println()` method. Figure 1.3 on page 5 shows a *terminal window* where Program 1.1 has been compiled and run. As we can see, the strings given in the `println()` method calls are printed to the terminal window.

FIGURE 1.6   Syntax of statements in Program 1.1

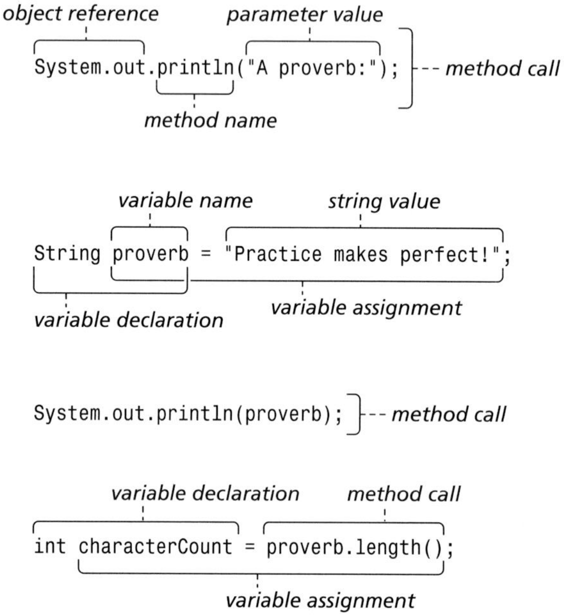

object reference   *parameter value*

```
System.out.println("A proverb:");  --- method call
```

method name

variable name   *string value*

```
String proverb = "Practice makes perfect!";
```

variable declaration   *variable assignment*

```
System.out.println(proverb);  --- method call
```

variable declaration   *method call*

```
int characterCount = proverb.length();
```

variable assignment

Variables

Variables are named locations in the computer's internal storage (memory) where values can be held during program execution. Methods often use variables to hold intermediate results. The `main()` method of Program 1.1 uses two such variables (`proverb` and `characterCount`) to store values it subsequently uses in later statements. Numeric values are very common, but as we will see later, there are other *types* of values. When we *assign* a value to a variable, we store the value in the variable so that the value can later be used by referring to the variable.

The statement at (4) declares a variable called `proverb`, and assigns the string `"Practice makes perfect!"` to it:

```
String proverb = "Practice makes perfect!";                          // (4)
```

The program can now refer to this text string using the name `proverb`. The statement at (5) prints the string referred by the variable `proverb` to the terminal window:

```
System.out.println(proverb);                              // (5)
```

A string of text is an object in Java, and statement (6) calls the method `length()` on the string object to find out how many characters there are in the string:

```
int characterCount = proverb.length();                   // (6)
```

The character count returned by the `length()` method is stored in the variable `characterCount` that is declared in the same line of code. The class of the `proverb` string objects is `String`, which is one of the many classes provided by the Java standard library. Later chapters will explore many classes from this library, including the `String` class.

When a method is called, as in statement (3), the body of the called method will be executed before program execution continues past the method call statement. Figure 1.7 shows the method calls that are executed when Program 1.1 is run. The *flow of execution* in the program can be traced by reading the method calls in Figure 1.7 from top to bottom.

FIGURE 1.7 Sequence of method calls during program execution

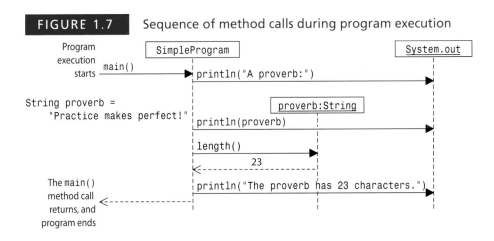

1.8 The Java Virtual Machine

The Java programming language provides a rich set of language constructs that allow us to express program behaviour in a way that is natural for humans. On the other hand, Java byte code is a small set of basic instructions suited for execution by machines. The Java language is considered a *high-level language*, while Java byte code is considered a *low-level language*.

During execution, the byte code is interpreted by a virtual machine (the *Java Virtual Machine, JVM*). Rather than being a physical machine, the virtual machine is a program that interprets byte code instructions, in the same way that a central processing unit (CPU) in a computer would execute machine code instructions.

Figure 1.8 shows how a few lines of Java source code are translated to an executable form. The Java compiler translates the source code to Java byte code. The byte code can now be interpreted by a Java Virtual Machine installed on any computer. We call this *platform independence*, since it is not limited to a particular type of computer. Some virtual machines interpret the byte code directly, while others recompile it to a third form called *machine code* during execution. Machine code is at an even lower level than byte code, and will always be created specifically for the instruction set of the CPU in the computer. This means that machine code can only be executed on the specific type of computer for which it has been compiled. The machine code shown in Figure 1.8 is specific to the x86-processor series.

Some programming languages do not have an intermediate byte code representation, and lock the program to a specific platform as soon as the source code is compiled. Such programming languages allow the programmer to obtain speed improvements by programming directly at the machine code level, but this also increases the risk of programming errors. Most Java programmers will never need to examine the byte code or the machine code representation of programs.

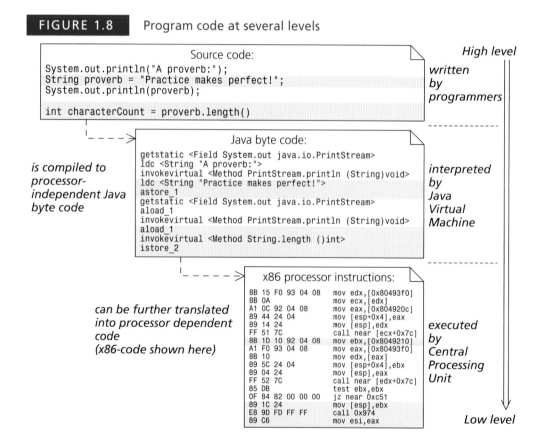

FIGURE 1.8   Program code at several levels

1.9 Review questions

1. How many comments does Program 1.1 have?

2. A computer has a _____ that executes low-level platform-specific instructions, and makes the computer work.

3. _____ is a high-level description of the tasks the computer should perform, which are written in a high-level _____ and stored in text files.

4. Which of these components are software?

    a A compiler.
    b A keyboard.
    c A virtual machine.
    d The result of compiled source code.
    e A CPU.

5. We specify the set of common properties we want a group of objects to share by defining a _____.

6. All Java programs have a _____ called _____, where the execution of the program starts.

7. Which statement best describes Object-Based Programming (OBP)?

    a Making an omelette.
    b Defining classes of objects that have common properties and operations that can be performed on these objects.
    c Compiling source code to Java byte code.
    d Translating programs to processor-dependent code.

8. Program 1.1 has a class called _____ and a method named _____.

9. The command _____ can be executed on the command line to compile a source code file called `TestProgram.java`.

10. The command _____ can be executed on the command line to run a Java program consisting of a primary class called `TestProgram`.

11. In which form is program code usually written and edited?

    a Source code.
    b Processor-independent byte codes.
    c Processor-dependent instructions.

12. Which of these file names are valid for a Java source code file that defines a primary class called `Dog`?

    a `Cat.java`
    b `Dog.jav`

c `Dog.java`

d `Dog.java.doc`

e `DOG.JAVA`

1.10 Programming exercises

1. Use a text editor to write a file called `SimpleProgram.java` containing the source code from Program 1.1.

2. Compile the source code you wrote in the previous exercise. Fix any errors that the compiler finds in the source code.

3. Run the program that was compiled in the previous exercise.

4. Write a program that prints out the number of characters in your surname. Use the source code from Program 1.1 as a base for your own program.

5. Llanfairpwllgwyngyllgogerychwyrndrobwllllantysiliogogogoch is the name of a village in Wales. Taumatawhakatangihangakoauauotamateapokaiwhenuakitanatahu is the name of a hill in New Zealand. Write a program to calculate the number of characters the hill in New Zealand has in its name compared to that of the village in Wales. The result should be printed out like this, where ? is replaced by the answer:

```
The hill has ? characters more than the village.
```

PART ONE

Structured Programming

Basic programming elements

INTRODUCTION

This chapter describes some basic programming elements that we need to master in order to write computer programs. Many of these elements are also found in other programming languages, and understanding them is therefore also useful for learning languages other than Java. However, this chapter focuses on basic programming elements provided in Java, and on demonstrating their use in simple, but functioning, programs.

2.1 Printing to the terminal window

The `print()` and `println()` methods

Programs can calculate values and print them directly to the terminal window. For example, the method call shown in Figure 2.1 prints the sum of the integers 9 and 7. Each of the integers is called a *literal*, and 9+7 is an *expression*. A literal is a value written directly in the source code. There are many types of expressions, one of the simplest being the addition of two integers. An expression always evaluates to a value.

FIGURE 2.1 Printing the sum of two integers to the terminal window

```
                    literals
                    ¦ ¦
                    ↓ ↓
System.out.println(9+7);
└─────────┘       ↑   └─┘
standard out      ¦   expression
                  ¦
       print and terminate the line
```

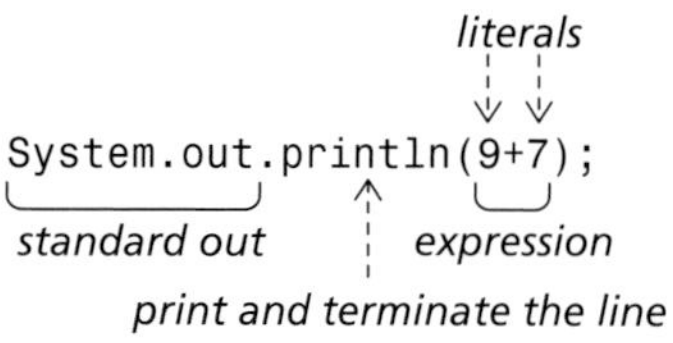

PROGRAM 2.1   Printing strings and numerical values to the terminal window

```java
// Printing text strings and numerical values to the terminal window.
public class SimplePrint {
    public static void main(String[] args) {            // (1)
        System.out.println("The value of 9 + 7 is ");   // (2)
        System.out.println(9+7);                        // (3)
        System.out.print("The value of 9 + 7 is ");     // (4)
        System.out.println(9+7);                        // (5)
    }
}
```

Program output:

```
The value of 9 + 7 is
16
The value of 9 + 7 is 16
```

Program 2.1 prints strings and numerical values to the terminal window at (2) to (5) using the `System.out` object. This object is called *standard out*, and is by default connected to the terminal window. The `System.out` object offers a `println()` method for printing a string and terminating the line. Terminating the current line results in the cursor in the terminal window moving to the beginning of the next line. There is also a `print()` method that does *not* move the cursor to the next line in the terminal window after printing on the current line. Thus, the code at (4) and (5) prints:

```
The value of 9 + 7 is 16
```

The following commands will compile and run the program, respectively:

```
> javac SimplePrint.java
> java -ea SimplePrint
```

The JVM will start the execution of the main() method, which must be declared exactly as shown at (1) in Program 2.1. The syntax is fully described in later chapters, but for now we will use the following source code as a template for our programs:

```
// Comment explaining the purpose of the program.
public class PrimaryClass {
   public static void main(String[] args) {

      // Code to solve the problem at hand...

   }
}
```

Creating program output using strings

A sequence of characters enclosed in double quotes (") is called a *string literal*, or just a *string*. We can see examples of strings at (2) and (4) in Program 2.1. The operator + can be used to *concatenate* strings and string representations of other values. Concatenation means that the contents of two strings are appended and the result is assigned to a new string. For example, concatenating the strings "High" and "Five" produces a new string "HighFive". Some more examples of string concatenation are provided below. Prudent use of the concatenation operator + and the print methods can aid in formatting results before they are printed.

Details of strings can be found in Section 4.2 on page 81. Here we will only use the string operator + to create the program output we want to print to the terminal window.

The two print statements below illustrate how we can use the + operator to create strings that can be printed by calling the println() method:

```
System.out.println("Multiple strings can be printed" + " on the same line");
System.out.println(
   "We can also print a number together with this string, e.g. " + 2006);
```

We get the following output from these statements:

```
Multiple strings can be printed on the same line
We can also print a number together with this string, e.g. 2006
```

In the first print statement, we join the two strings "Multiple strings can be printed" and " on the same line" using the + operator, and the resulting string "Multiple strings can be printed on the same line" is printed by the println() method.

In the second print statement, we join the string "We can also print a number together with this string, e.g. " and the string representation of the value 2006, i.e. "2006", and the resulting string "We can also print a number together with this string, e.g. 2006" is printed by the println() method. The value 2006 is converted to its representation "2006" by the + operator.

Using the + operator on numerical values, such as in the statement:

```
System.out.println(9+7);
```

causes the two values to be added. In this case the result will be the value 16, which is sent to the println() method as a parameter. This method call will print the given value, converted to a string, i.e. "16", to the terminal window.

The + operator can be used several times in a statement. This is commonly done, for example, to print a combination of text and numerical values to the terminal window in the same method call.

Thus, we can replace the statements at (4) and (5) in Program 2.1 with the following:

```
System.out.println("The value of 9+7 is " + (9 + 7));
```

Note the mandatory use of the parentheses around the expression 9 + 7. We want the result of the arithmetic addition, i.e. 16, to be joined with the explanatory text. Without the parentheses, the output would be:

```
The value of 9+7 is 97
```

The string "The value of 9+7 is " is first concatenated with the string representation of the value 9, then the result is concatenated with the string representation of the value 7.

2.2 Local variables

Programs can evaluate expressions and print results to the terminal window immediately. However, we often want to store values in computer memory, to retrieve them for use during program execution.

Programming languages offer *variables* for this purpose. A variable designates a location in memory where a value of a certain *data type* can be stored. A variable has a *name* that can be used to access the memory location. A data type (or just *type*) is defined by a set of valid values and a set of operations that can be performed on those values.

In this section we will look at variables defined inside methods. Such variables are called *local variables*.

Declaring variables

Figure 2.2 shows how we can declare a variable.

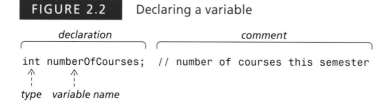

FIGURE 2.2   Declaring a variable

The declaration starts with a *keyword*, int, that specifies that the variable can only store integer values. The keyword is followed by the variable's name. A semicolon (;) terminates the declaration. The rest of the line is a comment explaining the purpose of the variable. The comment starts with the character sequence "//". It is not a part of the declaration.

If we need several variables of the same type, we can write them in the same declaration, separated by a comma (,). For example, two integer variables are declared by the following declaration:

```
int numberOfCourses, numberOfStudents; // number of courses and number of
                                       // students this semester
```

This declaration is equivalent to writing multiple declarations, one declaration per variable:

```
int numberOfCourses;  // number of courses this semester
int numberOfStudents; // number of students this semester
```

Some examples in this chapter leave out such comments, because the purpose of the variable is obvious from its name.

BEST PRACTICES

Documenting the source code with comments is very important, as it aids in understanding the program. Writing a short comment for each variable makes the purpose of the variable evident.

Assigning variables

After declaring a variable, we can *assign* a value to it. The first time we assign a value to a variable, we are *initializing* it. Later in the program we can change the value of the variable by assigning a new value. The old value is then overwritten by the new value.

In Java, we use the assignment operator = for this purpose. For example, the following statement assigns the value 2 to the integer variable numberOfCourses:

```
numberOfCourses = 2;
```

Whatever value the variable had before the assignment is overwritten.

FIGURE 2.3   Declaring and initializing a variable

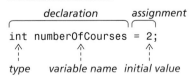

Program 2.2 uses two integer variables, numberOfCourses and numberOfStudents. After declaring and initializing the numberOfCourses variable, we print its value at (1). We can also initialize a variable as part of the declaration, as shown in Figure 2.3 and at (2) in

Program 2.2. If we want to update the value in a variable, we simply assign a new value, using the assignment operator =, as shown at (3).

A local variable must always be initialized before it is used. If we try to remove the line:

```
numberOfCourses = 2;
```

from Program 2.2, the compiler will report an error at (1), because the value of the variable numberOfCourses is not known. The compiler will not generate a class file, and we cannot run the program.

PROGRAM 2.2   A simple program with local variables

```
// Using local variables to hold numerical values.
public class LocalVariables {
  public static void main(String[] args) {
    int numberOfCourses = 2;
    System.out.println("Number of courses this semester is " +
                       numberOfCourses);                      // (1)

    int numberOfStudents = 37;                                // (2)
    System.out.println("The course Java-101 has " +
                       numberOfStudents + " students");

    numberOfStudents = 23;                                    // (3)
    System.out.println("The course Java-102 has " +
                       numberOfStudents + " students");
  }
}
```

Program output:

```
Number of courses this semester is 2
The course Java-101 has 37 students
The course Java-102 has 23 students
```

BEST PRACTICES

Declare local variables where they are first assigned a value. This initializes the variable properly. The source code is easier to understand, and the risk of using or modifying variables incorrectly is reduced.

Logical errors

Program 2.3 uses two local variables, which are both assigned integer values several times during program execution. It is important that if the value of a variable changes, calculations that depend on its value are also repeated, otherwise the program will report incorrect results. This is the case at (11) in Program 2.3, where we have intentionally skipped the calculation of the area variable after changing the value in the breadth variable at (10). The last printout is thus:

```
The area of a rectangle with length 6 and breadth 5 is 24
```

We have a *logical error* in our program, which does not behave as expected. The program reports the value that the area variable had before the value of the breadth variable was changed. The area must be recalculated with the new breadth in order to report the results correctly.

Figure 2.4 on page 24 shows how the values of the local variables change as the different assignment statements are executed from (1) to (10) in Program 2.3. The coloured background marks the value being changed by the corresponding statement (*i*).

PROGRAM 2.3 Assigning new values to local variables

```
// Calculating and printing the area of a rectangle.
public class Assignment {
  public static void main(String[] args) {
    int length = 5;                                              // (1)
    int breadth = 4;                                            // (2)
    int area = length * breadth;                                // (3)
    System.out.println("The area of a rectangle with length "
                      + length + " and breadth " + breadth
                      + " is " +  area);
    length = 2;                                                  // (4)
    breadth = length;                                           // (5)
    area = length * breadth;                                    // (6)
    System.out.println("The area of a rectangle with length "
                      + length + " and breadth " + breadth
                      + " is " +  area);
    length = 6;                                                  // (7)
    breadth = 4;                                                // (8)
    area = length * breadth;                                    // (9)
    breadth = 5;                                                // (10)
    System.out.println("The area of a rectangle with length "
                      + length + " and breadth " + breadth
                      + " is " +  area);                        // (11)
  }
}
```

Program output:

```
The area of a rectangle with length 5 and breadth 4 is 20
The area of a rectangle with length 2 and breadth 2 is 4
The area of a rectangle with length 6 and breadth 5 is 24
```

Literals and constants

A literal is written directly in the program. Literals can also be used to define mathematical constants (e.g. *pi*), a factor in an expression (e.g. the interest rate) or a size denoting some maximum capacity (e.g. the number of seats in a cinema hall). However, if the same literal is used in several places in a program, it is a good idea to define it as a constant.

A *constant* is a variable that cannot change its value after initialization. In Java, a constant is defined like this:

```
final double INTEREST_RATE = 3.5;
```

FIGURE 2.4	Assigning values to local variables (Program 2.3)

	length	breadth	area
After (1)	5		
After (2)	5	4	
After (3)	5	4	20
After (4)	2	4	20
After (5)	2	2	20
After (6)	2	2	4
After (7)	6	2	4
After (8)	6	4	4
After (9)	6	4	24
After (10)	6	5	24

We prefix the declaration with the keyword `final`, which indicates that the variable's value cannot be changed. If we try to assign a new value to such a variable, the compiler will report an error and the compilation will be terminated.

If the value of a constant needs to be changed, for example if the interest rate changes, we need only make the change in the declaration and compile the program. Names of constants are usually written with uppercase letters. This allows us to easily distinguish constants from variables, which may change value many times after initialization. Using uppercase letters for constants makes them easier to identify in the source code.

Choosing names

When choosing names for variables we need to remember two things: rules for what Java accepts as valid names, and conventions for variable names. The following example illustrates these rules:

```
// Rules for variable names
int agent007;        // Names can contain letters and digits
                     // but cannot start with a digit.
int 1001nights;      // This declaration will not compile!
```

```
                          // A digit CANNOT be the first character in a name.

   int my_lucky_number; // Underscore (_) is allowed.
   int _number_drawn;    // Underscore can be the first character in the name.
   int numberOfMinutes; // Java distinguishes between lower and upper-case
   int numberofminutes; // letters, so these are two different variables.
                          // However, both names are valid in Java.

   int int;              // This declaration will not compile!
                          // Keywords like int CANNOT be used as variable names.

   // Conventions for variable names
   int size              // Use lower-case letters.
       numberOfHours,    // Use lower-case letters, except for the first
       itemPrize,        // letter of each consecutive word.
       discountedItemPrize;

   final int DAYS_IN_WEEK = 7,   // Constants are always in upper-case letters,
            HOURS_IN_WEEK = 168;// and underscore is used to separate words.

   int sportscarWithFourCylinders; // Avoid more than 15-20 characters in a name.
```

Table B.1 on page 321 lists all keywords in Java. These keywords cannot be used as ordinary names. It is a good idea to avoid long names. Long names can be tiresome to type, and it is easy to make a mistake. Long names also make the source more difficult to read.

2.3 Numerical data types

Many programming languages provide *primitive data types* for numerical values. The primitive data types define the range of valid values and provide a set of *operators* to perform calculations on these values. A value of a primitive type is not an object, and therefore it is not possible to call any methods on a value of a primitive data type.

Java provides six different data types for integers (i.e. whole numbers) and floating-point numbers (i.e. decimal numbers). In this section, we will look at two of the most common primitive data types: int and double. In addition, Java provides the data type char for values that are single characters.

Primitive data type int

The primitive data type int in Java can hold values ranging from -2^{31} to $+2^{31}-1$, i.e. from -2147483648 to +2147483647. The language provides the common arithmetic operators (+, -, *, /) for calculations involving int values.

Integer values are commonly used for counting purposes, for example to keep track of the number of students enrolled in a course or the number of points scored in a game. Integer variables are also used to hold values that must be whole numbers, such as the number of characters in a string, and the number of books ordered from an online bookstore.

Primitive data type `double`

The data type `double` in Java can hold values ranging from approximately -1.7×10^{308} to $+1.7 \times 10^{308}$ (that is 170000000… followed by three hundred more zeros), with fifteen significant figures. This provides sufficient range and accuracy for floating-point values in most programming problems. The usual arithmetic operators (+, -, *, /) are provided for calculations involving `double` values.

Floating-point values can be used for fractional numbers. For example, when calculating the total cost of an order from an online bookstore, the current balance of a customer's bank account or the distance between two points when planning a hiking trip.

2.4 Arithmetic expressions and operators

The most common arithmetic operators for numerical values – multiplication, division, addition and subtraction – are available in all common programming languages. Figure 2.5 illustrates how some arithmetic expressions are constructed by using *operators* and one or more *operands*. An operator defines an arithmetic operation. Each operator accepts one or more operands as arguments, i.e. the values of the operands are used in the calculation for the chosen operation.

FIGURE 2.5   Operators and operands in arithmetic expressions

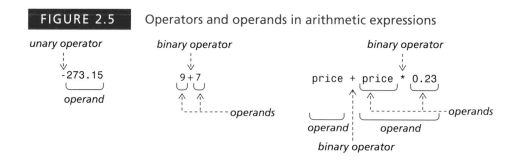

Arithmetic expression evaluation rules

The operators for multiplication (*), division (/), addition (+), subtraction (-) and modulus (%) all requires two operands. They are therefore termed *binary operators*.

You might be unfamiliar with the modulus operator (%). It calculates the remainder after division is performed. Here are some examples:

- `16 % 4` evaluates to 0
- `15 % 2` evaluates to 1
- `15 % 4` evaluates to 3

The modulus operator is useful to calculate, for example, the number of players without an opponent in a tennis tournament. If fifteen players have signed on, and they are to play single matches simultaneously, there will be `15 % 2`, i.e. one player, without an opponent.

For a tournament with double matches, on the other hand, there would be 15 % 4, i.e. three players left who would not be able to play a doubles match.

There are two *unary operators*, + (unary plus) and - (unary minus), which only accept one operand. This operand must also be an arithmetic expression that evaluates to a numerical value. The simplest forms of arithmetic expression are a literal, a variable or a constant.

The following expressions are all valid in Java:

- 4 + 16, which evaluates to the integer value 20
- 12 / 3, which evaluates to the integer value 4
- 12.0 / 3.0, which evaluates to the floating-point value 4.0
- -16.50 / -2.0, which evaluates to the floating-point value 8.25

With the exception of the addition operator +, the operators above are only defined for numerical values. The + operator can also be used to concatenate strings, as we have already seen.

Conversion between primitive data types

If the operands of a binary operator are of the same type, the result is also of the same type as the operands. If we combine numerical values of different types using a binary operator, the two values will be converted to a common type before the operation is performed. This is called *type conversion*. In some cases the rules of the Java programming language ensure that the proper conversion is implicitly carried out (*implicit conversion*), while in other cases we have explicitly to specify the conversion in the source code (*explicit conversion*).

Implicit conversions

Since the range of values for the data type double is broader than that of the data type int, we say that double is a *broader data type* than int. Vice versa, we say that int is a *narrower data type* than double.

If we use both integers and floating-point values in an expression, Java automatically converts the integer value to a floating-point value before the expression is evaluated. For example, the integer value 4 in the expression 4 + 12.6 will be converted to the floating-point value 4.0 before the addition is carried out. In arithmetic expressions with binary operators, Java automatically *promotes* operand values to the broader type before evaluation is performed.

Similarly, Java will automatically perform type conversion if we assign a value of a narrow data type to a variable of a broader data type. For example, when assigning an integer value to a floating-point variable, as in (1):

```
int numberOfFullHours = 10;
double numberOfHours = numberOfFullHours; // (1)
```

Java automatically performs an implicit conversion, converting the integer value 10 to the floating-point value 10.0 (of type double) before the assignment is performed.

Explicit conversions

If we assign a numerical value of a broad data type to a variable of a narrower data type, we risk loss of information. This can happen, for example, if we assign a floating-point value to an integer variable. If the floating-point value has a decimal part, this cannot be stored in the integer variable. To avoid accidental loss of information, Java demands that we explicitly specify that this type of conversion is to be performed, as shown below:

```
double numberOfHours = 40.65;
int numberOfFullHours = (int) numberOfHours; // (1) Value 40 is assigned.
```

The floating-point value is *truncated*. We specify explicit type conversion, or *casting*, by the notation (*typename*), where *typename* is the type *to* which we want to convert. If we leave out (int) from the assignment statement in (1) above, the compiler will reject it. Hence explicit conversion is required in cases where we would otherwise risk losing precision, such as when truncating a decimal value to the nearest integer. Explicit casts inform the compiler that we are aware of the potential loss of precision, and that this is acceptable in our program.

Precedence and associativity rules

Evaluation of the *operands* of an arithmetic operator in Java is always performed from left to right. How the *operators* are applied is determined by operator *precedence*, which specifies the mutual ranking between different operators. If two operators with *different precedence* are next to each other in an expression, the operator with the highest precedence is applied first. For example, the expression 4 + 5 * 2 will be interpreted as 4 + (5 * 2) during compilation. This expression will be evaluated to 4 + 10, and finally to 14, because the * operator has higher precedence than the + operator. The parentheses are used to indicate the sequence in which the compiler associates operands to operators when interpreting the expression.

We can change the order in which operators are applied by using parentheses. The parentheses in the expression below force the addition operator to be applied first, resulting in the value 18:

```
(4 + 5) * 2
```

Table 2.1 shows the precedence of the arithmetic operators in Java.

TABLE 2.1	Precedence of arithmetic operators	
Precedence level	Type operator	Operator
high	unary	+, -
	binary	*, /, %
low	binary	+, -

Associativity rules are used to determine which operator will be evaluated first if there are two consecutive operators with the *same precedence* in an expression. *Left associativity* means that *operands are grouped from left to right*. For example, the expression:

```
1 + 2 - 3
```

will be interpreted as ((1 + 2) - 3), since the binary operators + and - are both left-associative. *Right-associativity* means the operands are *grouped from right to left*. For example, the expression - - 4 will be interpreted as (- (- 4)), which evaluates to 4, because the unary operator - is right-associative.

Unary operators have higher precedence than binary operators. Multiplication, division and modulus are on the same level of the precedence hierarchy, and all have higher precedence than addition and subtraction. Consequently, the expression 5 * - 6 / 2 is evaluated as follows:

```
= 5 * (- 6) / 2
= (5 * -6) / 2
= -30 / 2
= -15
```

BEST PRACTICES

Use additional parentheses in arithmetic expressions to make the evaluation order explicit, and include extra spaces to make the expression easier to read.

Integer and floating-point division

Most arithmetic operators in Java behave as one would expect them to do from basic knowledge of arithmetic or from using a pocket calculator. One exception is the division operator / when both the numerator and denominator are integer expressions. *Integer division* always results in an integer value. If we try to calculate the expression 30 / 4 in a Java program, the result will be 7, and not 7.5 as a pocket calculator would have computed. However, if one of the operands of the division operator / is a floating-point value, a *floating-point division* is performed.

Program 2.4 illustrates arithmetic operators. It also shows what happens if we try to divide by zero. Note the difference between integer and floating-point division. If we divide the numerator by the floating-point value 0.0, we get the value *Infinity* or *NaN* (*Not a Number*), depending on whether the numerator is zero or not. Integer division by 0 always results in a runtime error, called an *exception*, no matter what value the numerator has. In this case, the Java Virtual Machine will print a message about the cause of the error and terminate the program.

Program 2.4 illustrates the use of the division and the modulus operators. It is instructive to try these operators on other values.

PROGRAM 2.4   Testing the division and modulus operators

```java
// Experimenting with the division operator.
public class Division {
  public static void main(String[] args) {
    System.out.println("Integer division and modulus:");
    System.out.println(" 3/2 = " + (3/2));
    System.out.println(" 4/4 = " + (4/4));
    System.out.println(" 3%2 = " + (3%2));

    System.out.println("Floating-point division and modulus:");
    System.out.println(" 3.0/2.0 = " + (3.0/2.0));
    System.out.println(" 3.0/4.0 = " + (3.0/4.0));
    System.out.println(" 3.0%2.0 = " + (3.0%2.0));

    System.out.println("Division by zero:");
    System.out.println(" 2.0/0.0 = " + (2.0/0.0));
    System.out.println(" 0.0/0.0 = " + (0.0/0.0));
    System.out.println(" 2.0/0 = " + (2.0/0));
    System.out.println(" 2/0 = " + (2/0));
  }
}
```

Program output:

```
Integer division and modulus:
 3/2 = 1
 4/4 = 1
 3%2 = 1
Floating-point division and modulus:
 3.0/2.0 = 1.5
 3.0/4.0 = 0.75
 3.0%2.0 = 1.0
Division by zero:
 2.0/0.0 = Infinity
 0.0/0.0 = NaN
 2.0/0 = Infinity
Exception in thread "main" java.lang.ArithmeticException: / by zero
  at Division.main(Division.java:18)
```

2.5 Formatted output

Program output printed to the terminal window can be formatted using the `printf()` method of the `System.out` object:

```
printf(String format, Object... args)
```

The parameter `format` specifies how formatting will be done. This is a *format string* containing *format specifications* that determine how each subsequent value in the parameter `args` will be formatted and printed. The parameter declaration `Object... args` means that the method accepts zero or more parameters.

The following calls to the `printf()` method:

```
System.out.printf("Player\Game        %6d%6d%6d%n", 1, 2, 3);
System.out.printf("%-20s%6d%6d%6d%n", "F. Reshmann", 320, 160, 235);
System.out.printf("%-20s%6d%6d%6d%n", "A. King", 1250, 1875, 2500);
```

will generate this tabular printout of game results:

```
Player\Game              1     2     3
F. Reshmann            320   160   235
A. King               1250  1875  2500
```

The format specifications used here are explained below when we write a short program to print a formatted bill for a computer store (see Program 2.5).

Format string

A format string can contain both *fixed text* and *format specifications*. The fixed text is printed exactly as specified in the format string. The format specifications control how the values of the subsequent parameters are formatted and printed.

Formatting of floating-point values is *localised*. This means that the formatting is customised to a *locale*. A locale defines, among other things, the character used as the decimal point in a country or a region. Comma (,) is used as decimal point in Norway and Denmark, while in many other countries, such as the United Kingdom and the USA, the dot (.) is used to separate the integer and decimal part of a floating-point value. We will primarily use the dot (.) as decimal point in this book.

Sample format specifications

Table 2.2 shows some common format specifications in Java. See also Appendix C. All values are converted to their string representation and formatted by the `printf()` method before being printed to the terminal window.

Printing with fixed field widths

Before diving further into formatted printing, let's look at an example. Program 2.5 on page 33 prints a simple bill using the `printf()` method.

At the top of the bill, the company name is printed at (1) with a format string that contains only fixed text. Date and time of day is printed on the same line, with leading zeros at (2). A heading is then printed at (3) by means of the format specification `"%-24s"` for the left-justified column `Item`, `"%8s"` for the right-justified columns `Price` and `Sum`, and `"%6s"` for the right-justified column `Count`.

TABLE 2.2 Format specifications in Java

Parameter value	Format specification	Example value	String printed	Comment
Integer	`"%d"`	125	`"125"`	Occupies as many character places as needed.
	`"%6d"`	125	`"   125"`	Occupies six character places and is right-justified. The printed string is padded with spaces to the left.
	`"%02d"`	3	`"03"`	Occupies two character places and is padded with leading zeros.
Floating point value	`"%f"`	16.746	`"16.746000"`	Occupies as many character places as needed, but always includes six decimal places.
	`"%.2f"`	16.746	`"16.75"`	Occupies as many character places as needed, but includes only two decimal places.
	`"%8.2f"`	16.7466	`"   16.75"`	Occupies eight character places, including the decimal point, and uses two decimal places.
String	`"%s"`	`"Hi!"`	`"Hi!"`	Occupies as many character places as are needed.
	`"%12s"`	`"Hi Dude!"`	`"    Hi Dude!"`	Occupies twelve character places and is right-justified.
	`"%-12s"`	`"Hi Dude!"`	`"Hi Dude!    "`	Occupies twelve character places and is left-justified.
Linefeed	`"%n"`	(none)	(none)	Moves the cursor to the next line in the terminal window.

Underneath the heading, the items purchased are printed at (4)–(5), (6)–(7) and (8)–(9) using the same field widths as the column headings. The item name is printed with the format string `"%-24s"`, resulting in a twenty-four character wide string, left justified. The item price and the total cost for each type of item are printed as floating-point values using the format specification `"%8.2f"`, and the number of items is printed as an integer using the format specification `"%6d"`. The strings are left-justified, while all numbers are right-justified. The character 's' is the *conversion code* for strings, while floating-point and integer values are printed using codes 'f' and 'i' respectively.

At (10) the total cost of all items is printed using the format specification "%8.2f". To position this value correctly under the column Sum, we print the string "Total:" using the format "%40s". The width of forty characters is found by adding the width of the first three columns of the bill and the spaces between them.

PROGRAM 2.5   Printing a simple bill for computer goods

```
// Using the printf() method to prepare a nicely formatted bill.
public class SmallBill {
  public static void main(String[] args) {
    System.out.printf("Easy Data Ltd.          ");           // (1)
    System.out.printf("%02d/%02d/%04d, %02d:%02d:%02d%n%n",   // (2)
                  20, 3, 2006, 19, 6, 9);
    System.out.printf("%-24s %8s %6s %8s%n",                  // (3)
                  "Item", "Price", "Count", "Sum");

    int count =2;
    double price = 132.25, sum = count*price, total = sum;
    System.out.printf("%-24s %8.2f %6d %8.2f%n",              // (4)
                  "Ultraflash, USB 2.0, 1GB", price, count, sum); // (5)

    count =1;
    price = 355.0; sum = count*price; total = total + sum;
    System.out.printf("%-24s %8.2f %6d %8.2f%n",              // (6)
                  "Mega HD, 300GB", price, count, sum);       // (7)

    count = 3;
    price = 8.33; sum = count*price; total = total + sum;
    System.out.printf("%-24s %8.2f %6d %8.2f%n",              // (8)
                  "USB 2.0 cable, 2m", price, count, sum);    // (9)

    System.out.printf("%40s %8.2f%n", "Total:", total);       // (10)
  }
}
```

Program output:

```
Easy Data Ltd.          20/03/2006, 19:06:09

Item                      Price  Count       Sum
Ultraflash, USB 2.0, 1GB  132.25      2    264.50
Mega HD, 300GB            355.00      1    355.00
USB 2.0 cable, 2m           8.33      3     24.99
                                 Total:    644.49
```

2.6 Reading numbers from the keyboard

The Scanner class

This book uses the class Scanner from the Java standard library to read numbers and strings from the keyboard. This class offers two methods, nextInt() and nextDouble(), for reading integer and floating-point values respectively.

Figure 2.6 shows the method calls involved in reading an integer in Program 2.6. First we have to tell the Java compiler that we want to use the Scanner class from the Java standard library in our program. This is done by the import statement at (1). In (2) we create a Scanner object and connect it to the keyboard through the System.in object, which is called the *standard in*. The program then prints a prompt at (3) to let the user know what type of value is required. Reading from the keyboard is done at (4) by calling the nextInt() method in the Scanner class. The value read is assigned to a variable of the correct type (in this case, int). At (5) the program echoes the number read, so that we can check whether reading from the keyboard was successful.

FIGURE 2.6   Reading from the keyboard

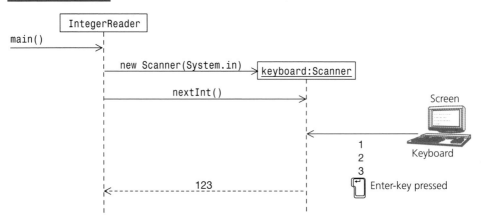

PROGRAM 2.6   Reading an integer from the keyboard

```
// Reading an integer from the keyboard using the Scanner class.
import java.util.Scanner;                                        // (1)
public class IntegerReader {
  public static void main(String[] args) {
    Scanner keyboard = new Scanner(System.in);                  // (2)

    System.out.print("Enter an integer: ");                     // (3)
    int numberRead = keyboard.nextInt();                        // (4)

    System.out.printf("You entered the number %d%n", numberRead); // (5)
  }
```

```
}
```

Program output:

```
Enter an integer: 123
You enterd the number 123
```

Reading integers

Values read from the keyboard can be stored in the program and used in computations. Program 2.7 shows how we can let a user enter the length and breadth of a rectangle at the keyboard to calculate the area of the rectangle.

At (1) and (3) the program prompts the user to enter a value. Reading the value is done at (2) and (4), and in both cases an integer value is read by calling the nextInt() method. When the area has been calculated at (5), its value is printed at (6). Note that the program uses the print() method, rather than the println() method, to display the explanatory text in the terminal window, allowing the user to enter a value on the same line as the prompt text.

PROGRAM 2.7 Reading multiple integers from the keyboard

```java
// Calculating the area of rectangle whose sides are input from the keyboard.
import java.util.Scanner;
public class IntegerArea {
  public static void main(String[] args) {
    Scanner keyboard = new Scanner(System.in);

    System.out.print("Enter the rectangle length [integer]: ");    // (1)
    int length = keyboard.nextInt();                                // (2)
    System.out.print("Enter the rectangle breadth [integer]: ");   // (3)
    int breadth = keyboard.nextInt();                               // (4)

    int area = length * breadth;                                     // (5)
    System.out.printf("A rectangle of length %d cm and breadth" +
                " %d cm has area %d sq. cm.%n",
                length, breadth, area);                             // (6)
  }
}
```

Program output:

```
Enter the rectangle length [integer]: 6
Enter the rectangle breadth [integer]: 4
A rectangle of length 6 cm and breadth 4 cm has area 24 sq. cm.
```

Reading floating-point numbers

To make the calculation of the area more flexible, we can modify the program to read floating-point values. The source code using floating-point variables and values is shown in Program 2.8. All variables are now of type `double`, and the program calls the `nextDouble()` method at (2) and (4) to read floating-point values. The program will also read any integer value entered at the keyboard as a floating-point value.

PROGRAM 2.8 Reading floating-point values from the keyboard

```java
// Calculating the area of rectangle whose sides are input from the keyboard.
import java.util.Scanner;
public class FloatingPointArea {
  public static void main(String[] args) {
    Scanner keyboard = new Scanner(System.in);

    System.out.print("Enter the rectangle length [decimal number]: ");// (1)
    double length = keyboard.nextDouble();                            // (2)
    System.out.print("Enter the rectangle breadth " +
                     "[decimal number]: ");                           // (3)
    double breadth = keyboard.nextDouble();                          // (4)

    double area = length * breadth;                                  // (5)
    System.out.printf(
      "A rectangle of length %.2f cm and breadth %.2f cm" +
      " has area %.2f sq. cm.%n",
      length, breadth, area);                                       // (6)
  }
}
```

Program output:

```
Enter the rectangle length [decimal number]: 15.5
Enter the rectangle breadth [decimal number]: 4.25
A rectangle of length 15.50 cm and breadth 4.25 cm has area 65.88 sq. cm.
```

Error handling

When entering numbers at the keyboard in Program 2.7 or Program 2.8, a user might unintentionally enter an invalid value. For example, typing a floating-point value when running Program 2.7 will result in the program terminating with the following error message:

```
Enter the rectangle length [integer]: 6.5
Exception in thread "main" java.util.InputMismatchException
at java.util.Scanner.throwFor(Unknown Source)
at java.util.Scanner.next(Unknown Source)
at java.util.Scanner.nextInt(Unknown Source)
at java.util.Scanner.nextInt(Unknown Source)

at IntegerArea.main(IntegerArea.java:7)
```

This type of error is called an *exception* and is explained in *Basic exception handling* on page 278.

The Scanner class will take the localisation into consideration when reading values. For example, if the localisation is for the UK, a dot (.) must be used as the decimal point. Should a user accidentally use a comma (,) as the decimal point, the nextDouble() method will print an error message similar to the one above and the execution will be aborted.

For both integer and floating-point values, the syntax of the input value determines whether it is accepted. The Scanner class has no way of catching values that are meaningless to the program. For example, a user can enter a negative value for length and/or breadth in Program 2.7 and Program 2.8. Since the program does not check the values, the area will still be computed. Input validation is the responsibility of the calling method, in this case the main() method. The Scanner class is meant to be flexible, and therefore only offers *syntactic validation* of input data.

Reading multiple values per line

Using the Scanner class, we can also read multiple values from the same line in the terminal window, as illustrated by Program 2.9. After the user has entered two integers, the call to the nextInt() method at (1) assigns the first value to the variable number1, and the call to the same method at (2) assigns the second value to the variable number2. The program then adds the two input values and prints the result to the terminal window at (3).

PROGRAM 2.9   Reading multiple values from the same line

```
// Reading multiple values from the same line on the keybouard.
import java.util.Scanner;
public class ReadingMultipleValues {
  public static void main(String[] args) {
    Scanner keyboard = new Scanner(System.in);

    System.out.print("Enter two numbers [integer integer]: ");
    int number1 = keyboard.nextInt();                          // (1)
    int number2 = keyboard.nextInt();                          // (2)
```

```
      int sum = number1 + number2;
      System.out.printf("The sum of integers %d and %d is %d%n",
                      number1, number2, sum);                              // (3)
   }
}
```

Program output:

```
Enter two numbers [integer integer]: 23 347
The sum of integers 23 and 347 is 370
```

Skipping the rest of the line when reading values from the keyboard

The previous example showed how to use the Scanner class to read multiple values from
the same line. If we instead want to read only *one* value per line, the program can read the
first value that is entered, then call the nextLine() method in the Scanner class to skip the
rest of the current line.

Program 2.10 calls the nextDouble() method at (1) to read the first value that is entered
on the current line. The nextLine() method is called at (2) to skip any input remaining in
the current line. Even if the user enters two or more values on the line, only the first value
will be read by the program, and the rest skipped.

| PROGRAM 2.10 | Skipping the rest of the current line when reading

```
// Calculating the area of rectangle whose sides are input from the keyboard.
import java.util.Scanner;
public class FloatingPointArea2 {
  public static void main(String[] args) {
    Scanner keyboard = new Scanner(System.in);

    System.out.println("Area calculation - one value per line");
    System.out.print("Enter the rectangle length [decimal number]: ");
    double length = keyboard.nextDouble(); // (1)
    keyboard.nextLine();                     // (2) Empty the rest of the line.
    System.out.print("Enter the rectangle breadth [decimal number]: ");
    double breadth = keyboard.nextDouble();

    double area = length * breadth;
    System.out.printf(
      "A rectangle of length %.2f cm and breadth %.2f cm " +
      "has area %.2f sq. cm.%n",
      length, breadth, area);
  }
}
```

Program output:

```
Area calculation - one value per line
Enter the rectangle length [decimal number]: 15.5 3.9
Enter the rectangle breadth [decimal number]: 4.25
A rectangle of length 15.50 cm and breadth 4.25 cm has area 65.88 sq. cm.
```

Program 2.8 does not use the nextLine() method. When running that program, the user can enter both numbers on the same line, as illustrated below:

```
Enter the rectangle length [decimal number]: 15.5 4.25
Enter the rectangle breadth [decimal number]: A rectangle of length 15.50 cm
and breadth 4.25 cm has area 65.88 sq. cm.
```

The program will read the second floating-point value on the first line of input, and assign it to the variable breadth. The second prompt and the result of the calculation are then printed on the same line in the terminal window. The program reports the correct answer, but the printout is a bit confusing. If we want our program to read multiple values, but only one value per line, the nextLine() method can be used, as illustrated in Program 2.10. We empty the current line by calling nextLine() method before reading the next value.

2.7 Review questions

1. What is printed to the terminal window by the method calls below?

    ```
    System.out.println("10+10 is " + 20);
    System.out.println("10+10 is " + 10 + 10);
    System.out.println(10 + 10 + 20);
    ```

2. What is a variable? What is a local variable?

3. Write the declaration for an integer variable called numberOfPoints, and initialize it to the value 35. What do we call a value that is written directly in the source code?

4. What is a constant? Modify the declaration from Question 2.3 to declare a constant.

5. Which of the following variable names are valid in Java? Which variables have meaningful names? Justify your answer.

    a minimum-Price

    b minimumPrice

    c XYZ

    d xCoordinate

    e y2k

    f isDone

    g numberOfDaysInALeapYear

    h JDK_1_6_0

6. What is a data type? What is a primitive data type?

7. Fill in the blanks.

   a An arithmetic expression can consist of _____ and operands.

   b Multiplication (*) requires ___ operands, and is thus a _____ operator.

   c The operator - in the expression -4 is a _____ operator, while the operator - in the expression 5 - 4 is a _____ operator.

8. The operands in an expression in Java are always evaluated from _____ to _____.

   If two operators with different _____ are next to each other in an expression, the operator with the _____ will be evaluated first.

9. If two operators with the same precedence are next to each other in an expression, _____ rules are used to determine which operator will be evaluated first.

   The operator - (unary minus) is left-associative and groups from _____ to _____, while the operator - (subtraction) is right-associative and groups from _____ to _____.

10. Evaluate the following expressions. Explain in what order the operators are evaluated in each case.

    a `3 + 2 - 1`

    b `2 + 6 * 7`

    c `- 5 + 7 - - 6`

    d `2 + 4 / 5`

    e `5 * 2 - - 3 * 4`

    f `10 / 0`

    g `2 + 4.0 / 5`

    h `10 / 0.0`

    i `4.0 / 0.0`

    j `2 * 4 % 2`

11. Use the `System.out.printf()` method to print the following values:

    a A six-digit integer, including the sign, e.g. `123456` as `+123456`.

    b The floating-point value `123456789.3837` in scientific notation, i.e. as `1.234567e+08`.

    c The string `"We are 100% motivated to learn Java!"`.

    d The number `1024` as a right-justified eight-digit integer, i.e. as `00001024`.

2.8 Programming exercises

1. Write a program that converts the temperature in degrees Celsius to degrees Fahrenheit. In this version of the program, do the conversion for a particular temperature in degrees Celsius, say 25.5°C. Use the following formula for doing the conversion:

   $fahrenheit = (9.0 \times celsius)/5.0 + 32.0$

2. Extend the program in Exercise 2.1 to also calculate the corresponding temperature in degrees Kelvin. The following formula calculates the temperature in degrees Kelvin:

$$kelvin = celsius + 273.16$$

3. Extend the program in Exercise 2.2 to read the temperature value from the keyboard. Print a suitable prompt to the terminal window before reading the value, so that the user knows what type of value is expected.

4. Write a program that calculates the volume v of a cube with dimensions l, b and h, all floating-point values, using the following formula:

$$v = l \times b \times h$$

Print a suitable prompt to the terminal window before reading values from the keyboard using the Scanner class.

5. Write a program that calculates the area a and circumference c of a circle:

$$a = p \times r^2$$

$$c = 2 \times p \times r$$

where p is a mathematical constant, and r is the radius of the circle. The square of the radius can be calculated by multiplying r with itself. Assume a value of 3.1415927 for p, which should be defined as a constant in your program.

Print a suitable prompt to the terminal window before reading a value for the radius from the keyboard.

6. A company pays its salesmen based on commissions on their sales. For example, a salesman that has sold products for 5000 GBP receives a payment of 200 GBP plus 9% of 5000 GBP, i.e. 650 GBP.

The price of the different products are:

- Product A: 239.99 GBP.
- Product B: 129.75 GBP.
- Product C: 99.95 GBP.
- Product D: 350.89 GBP.

Write a program that reads the number of sales for each product in the current week by a salesman, and calculates the salary based on these sales. The program should print a formatted salary slip, including the number of units sold and the unit price of each product sold. The user dialogue and program output could look like this:

```
Salesman's salary calculation

Enter units sold of Product A [integer]: 25
Enter units sold of Product B [integer]: 2
Enter units sold of Product C [integer]: 12
Enter units sold of Product D [integer]: 4
```

```
Enter provision rate in percent [decimal value]: 9.0

Salary slip

Product A:  20 units x 239.99 GBP =  4799.80 GBP
Product B:   2 units x 129.75 GBP =   259.50 GBP
Product C:  12 units x  99.95 GBP =  1199.40 GBP
Product D:   4 units x 350.89 GBP =  1403.56 GBP
                                    --------------
                      Total sales =  7662.26 GBP

Fixed part of salary             =   200.00 GBP
Provision (9% of sales)          =   689.03 GBP
                                    --------------
                      Total salary =   889.03 GBP
```

7. Your company provides IT consultancy services to the public sector, and the financial department in each country wants a program to print invoices for their national customers. Write a program that allows an accountant to specify the regular hours worked, the hourly rate, the number of hours worked overtime and the percentage increase in hourly rate for the overtime. Here is an example of a dialogue between the program and the user:

```
Invoice preparation for IT ConsultPro Inc.
Your national currency is GBP

Enter the client name [string]: Orange County
Enter the regular working hours [decimal number]: 120.0
Enter the hourly rate [decimal number]: 60.0
Enter the number of hours worked overtime [decimal number]: 40.0
Enter the percentage increase in hourly rate [decimal number]: 25.0
```

Based on this information, the program should print a formatted invoice:

```
IT ConsultPro Inc. - Invoice for Orange County

Regular working hours  : 120 hours a 60 GBP:  7200 GBP
Overtime work          :  40 hours a 75 GBP:  3000 GBP
-----------------------------------------------------------
                                 Total : 10200 GBP
```

The national currency used should be defined as a constant in the program.

The name of the client company can be read by the following code:

```
Scanner keyboard = new Scanner(System.in);
String clientName = keyboard.nextLine();
```

Any input on the current line will be read as one string and assigned to the client-Name variable. This code allows text with multiple words to be read as one string, for example "Orange County".

8. Your multinational company has just started offering IT consultancy to governmental organisations in the European Union, and must provide invoices in Euros (€). Modify the program in Exercise 2.7 to allow the national currency to be used, as well as the exchange rate between the national currency and the Euro.

9. Extend the program in Exercise 2.5 to read the units measurement for the radius, e.g. cm, m or km, as a string. You can use the nextLine() method for this purpose, as explained in Exercise 2.7.

    Run the program to calculate the circumference of the Earth at equator, when the equatorial radius is 6378.135 km.

10. Write a program that calculates how much an amount deposited in a bank account at $r\%$ annual interest has grown to after one, two and three years. The general formula for computing the amount including interest after n years is:

$$K_n = K_0 \times (1 + r / 100)^n$$

when K_0 is the principle amount. The user dialogue and output from the program could look like this:

```
Calculation of deposits with interests

Enter the initial amount deposited [decimal value]: 10000.00
Enter the interest rate [decimal value]: 4.5
Enter the currency used [string]: USD

Amount with interest after 1 year :   10450.00 USD
Amount with interest after 2 years:   10920.25 USD
Amount with interest after 3 years:   11411.66 USD
```

Program control flow

INTRODUCTION

Until now we have written programs where the statements are executed sequentially, i.e. one at a time in the order in which they are written in the source code. This is not very flexible, as we would like to control the order in which statements are executed, allowing us to express more complex logic in our programs.

This chapter introduces selection statements and loops for controlling the flow of execution. Selection statements enable us to define multiple actions, where the selection of an action to be executed is dependent on a condition being satisfied. Loops enable us to execute the same statements repeatedly, dependent on a condition being satisfied.

Conditions controlling the execution flow are specified as Boolean expressions, which are constructed using relational and logical operators. Such expressions are also used to define assertions, which allow us to check program properties during execution.

3.1 Boolean expressions

Boolean primitive data type

The primitive data type `boolean` in Java defines two *Boolean values*, represented by the literals `true` and `false`. As with other primitive data types, we can declare variables of the type `boolean` and assign Boolean values to them:

```
boolean itemIsOnSale = true;
```

By testing the value in the Boolean variable `itemIsOnSale`, we can determine whether to give a discount on an item or not. As we shall see, Boolean values facilitate decision making over the actions that should be executed during program execution.

Relational operators

A *relational operator* enables us to compare values. Table 3.1 gives an overview of the relational operators found in Java. The following expression in Java is a *Boolean expression*:

```
numHours >= 37.5
```

It evaluates to `true` if the value of the variable `numHours` is greater than or equal to `37.5`, otherwise it evaluates to `false`.

Since a Boolean expression evaluates to a Boolean value, we can assign its value to a Boolean variable:

```
boolean workedOvertime = numHours >= 37.5;
```

Since relational operators have *higher* precedence than the assignment operator `=`, the statement is executed as one would expect: first the Boolean expression and then the assignment.

The operands of a relational operator can be any arithmetic expression:

```
heads + tails == tosses
```

Since arithmetic operators have *higher* precedence than relational operators, the Boolean expression executes as follows:

```
((heads + tails) == tosses) // test for equality
```

I.e. we compare the sum of two variables on the left-hand side with the value of variable on the right-hand side. The `==` operator compares for equality, i.e. if both operands have the same value. Note that this operator is written as `==`, with no space in between. It is a common mistake to mix the equality operator with the assignment operator (`=`):

```
((heads + tails) = tosses) // ERROR!
```

In this case, the compiler reports an error:

```
Exception in thread "main" java.lang.Error: Unresolved compilation problem:
The left-hand side of an assignment must be a variable
at TestBooleanError.main(TestBooleanError.java:8)
```

TABLE 3.1	Relational operators in Java
Operator	Meaning
==	Equal to
!=	Not equal to
<	Less than
>	Greater than
<=	Less than or equal to
>=	Greater than or equal to

Understanding relational operators

We can calculate a series of Boolean expressions and print their values. We can also print what we expect the values to be. Program 3.1 shows a program that does this comparison.

PROGRAM 3.1 Calculating Boolean expressions with relational operators

```java
// Testing relational operators in boolean expressions.
public class TestRelationalOperators {
  public static void main(String[] args) {
    // Tests for integers.
    System.out.printf("Expression          Expected    Calculated%n");
    System.out.printf("%-20s%-12s%-12s%n", "3 == 3", true, (3 == 3));
    System.out.printf("%-20s%-12s%-12s%n", "3 != 3", false, (3 != 3));
    System.out.printf("%-20s%-12s%-12s%n", "7 > 4", true, (7 > 4));
    System.out.printf("%-20s%-12s%-12s%n", "7 < 4", false, (7 < 4));
    System.out.printf("%-20s%-12s%-12s%n", "6 <= 6", true, (6 <= 6));
    System.out.printf("%-20s%-12s%-12s%n", "6 >= 6", true, (6 >= 6));
  }
}
```

Program output:

```
Expression          Expected    Calculated
3 == 3              true        true
3 != 3              false       false
7 > 4               true        true
7 < 4               false       false
6 <= 6              true        true
6 >= 6              true        true
```

The printout from the program allows us to compare the calculated and expected values for the Boolean expressions. The print methods of the System.out object are useful for printing results to test that our program behaves as expected.

Logical operators

We can combine Boolean expressions by means of *logical operators*, creating new Boolean expressions:

```
boolean payBonus = workedOvertime || salesAboveAverage;
```

The expression above will be evaluated to true if the employee has worked overtime or sold more than the average sales during the week, or if both conditions are satisfied. Table 3.2 shows the logical operators defined in Java.

TABLE 3.2	Logical operators in Java
Operator	Meaning
!	Negation, results in inverting the truth value of the operand, i.e. !true evaluates to false, and !false evaluates to true.
&&	Conditional And, evaluates to true if both operands have the value true, and false otherwise.
||	Conditional Or, evaluates to true if one or both operands have the value true, and false otherwise.

BEST PRACTICES

Avoid using Boolean variables that must be negated to serve as conditions in selection state-ments and loops. An expression such as payBonus is easier to understand than !noBonusPaid.

Precedence for logical operators

The *precedence of the logical operators* is as follows: the negation operator ! has higher precedence than the conditional And operator &&, which in turn has higher precedence than the conditional Or operator ||. Given three Boolean variables b1, b2 and b3, the following expression:

```
b1 || !b2 && b3
```

will be interpreted as:

```
(b1 || ((!b2) && b3))
```

The *associativity rules for logical operators* are as follows: The negation operator ! associates from right to left. The conditional And operator && and the conditional Or operator || both associate from left to right.

As a consequence of the evaluation rules, the variable b2 above will be associated with the negation operator !, and the expression (!b2) forms one of the operands to the conditional And operator &&. Because of the precedence rules, the conditional And operator && is applied before the conditional Or operator ||.

We can quickly verify this by writing a short program containing the following statements:

```
boolean b1 = false, b2 = false, b3 = true;
System.out.printf("b1 || !b2 && b3 evaluates to %s%n", b1 || !b2 && b3);
System.out.printf("(b1 || ((!b2) && b3)) to %s%n", (b1 || ((!b2) && b3)));
```

and checking that the same Boolean value is printed by each printf() method call.

The logical operators have *lower precedence* than the relational operators. Thus, in the expression

```
weekday >= 6 || weekday == 3
```

the simple Boolean expression (weekday >= 6) is evaluated first, followed by the evaluation of the second simple expression (weekday == 3), and finally the logical operator || is applied to the resulting Boolean values of the two expressions. Assuming that the variable weekday represents the number of a weekday (1 for Monday, 2 for Tuesday, and so on), this test will return the value true for the weekdays Wednesday, Saturday and Sunday, and false otherwise.

The source code below allows us to verify that this holds:

```
int weekday = 4;
System.out.printf("Weekday number is %d%n", weekday);
System.out.printf("Wednesday, Saturday or Sunday: %s%n",
    weekday >= 6 || weekday == 3);
```

The printout from these lines will be:

```
Weekday number is 4
Wednesday, Saturday or Sunday: false
```

Combining the tests of precedence shown in this subsection into a workable program is left as an exercise.

Short-circuit evaluation

The operands in a Boolean expression are normally evaluated from left to right. However, the evaluation of a Boolean expression involving the logical operators will end as soon as the value of the expression can be determined. This is called *short-circuit evaluation*. For example, the expression:

```
(4 == 3) && (3 < 4)
```

will first evaluate to:

```
false && (3 < 4)
```

As the conditional And operator && will always return `false` if one of its operands has the value `false`, the final value of the expression can be determined without having to evaluate the second operand. Similarly, the Boolean expression:

```
(4 > 3) || (5 < 4)
```

first evaluates to (`true` || (5 < 4). Thereafter, the evaluation stops, because the final value of the Boolean expression must be `true`, regardless of the value of the second operand to the conditional Or operator ||.

De Morgan's laws

In some cases, complicated expressions can be simplified by means of De Morgan's laws:

1 `!(b1 && b2)` is equivalent to (`!b1 || !b2`)

2 `!(b1 || b2)` is equivalent to (`!b1 && !b2`)

when `b1` and `b2` both are Boolean expressions.

If we, for example, want to determine whether an integer value t falls inside a given interval with lower limit a and upper limit b, we can write this as `t >= a && t <= b`, or as `!(t < a || t > b)`, using De Morgan's second law. Both of these expressions will be evaluated to the same Boolean value for all values of a, b and t. Thus, we can choose the form we find easier to understand.

For example, whether a purchase is neither cheap nor good can be formulated as (`!cheap || !good`) or as `!(cheap && good)`. According to De Morgans first law, these two Boolean expressions are equivalent.

Using Boolean expressions to control flow of execution

We often want to perform different actions depending on whether a given condition is satisfied. This condition can be formulated as a Boolean expression, and its value can then be used to determine which actions should be executed.

Let's look at how we can calculate the salary for an employee, given the number of hours the employee has worked during the week. Many employees will receive a fixed salary as long as they work the normal number of hours during a week, with additional payment for any overtime. We need a statement that allows us to specify a condition that will determine any overtime, and a corresponding action to compute the additional salary. This type of statement is called a *selection statement*.

Other types of problems require that certain actions be executed repeatedly. For example, to compute the salary for *all* employees in a company, we need repeatedly to execute the actions for calculating the salary of an employee. This type of problem can be solved by a *loop* statement, allowing us to repeat actions a certain number of times based on the value of a condition.

Selection and repetition statements allow us to control which actions are performed by the program. These statements therefore determine the *control flow* of the program. Figure 3.1a shows the control flow determined by a selection statement called the `if` statement. This statement executes an action, the *if body*, if the given condition is satisfied. Figure 3.1b illustrates the control flow determined by a type of loop called the *pre-test loop*, where the condition is tested before the *loop body* is executed. While the `if` statement only allows its body to be executed at most once, the pre-test loop allows the loop body to be executed multiple times as long as the *loop condition* is satisfied.

FIGURE 3.1 Control flow in selection statements and loops

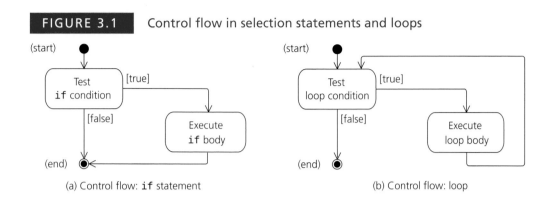

(a) Control flow: `if` statement   (b) Control flow: loop

3.2 | Control flow: selection statements

Simple selection statement: `if`

A *simple selection statement* performs an action if a given condition is satisfied. The condition is written as a Boolean expression, as illustrated in Figure 3.2. If the Boolean expression evaluates to `true`, i.e. the condition is satisfied, the action in the *if body* is executed. On the other hand, if the expression evaluates to `false`, the action in the *if body* is skipped, and the execution continues after the `if` statement.

FIGURE 3.2 Simple selection statement

keyword
    boolean expression

```
if (numHours > 37.5)
    salary = salary + (numHours - 37.5) * 30.0;   if body
```

Note that in Figure 3.2 we have used indentation to indicate which statement constitutes the if body. This is a useful programming practice, but has no impact on how the compiler translates the `if` statement. The compiler will treat the first statement after the Boolean expression as the `if` body, regardless of how the source code is formatted. Consistent indentation, however, makes the source code easy to read.

Program 3.2 uses the simple selection statement to calculate the weekly salary for an employee. A person working thirty-seven and a half hours (or less) receives a basic salary of 750 USD. If they work overtime, they receive an additional 30 USD per hour for the extra time worked.

At (1), the variable salary is initialized to the basic salary. The condition to determine whether there is any overtime, numHours > 37.5, is evaluated at (2). If the condition is satisfied, salary for overtime is calculated and added at (3). Finally, at (4), the weekly salary is printed to the terminal window.

PROGRAM 3.2   Calculating salary using a simple selection statement

```
// Calculating weekly salary, version 1.
import java.util.Scanner;
public class Salary1 {
  public static void main(String[] args) {
    final double NORMAL_WORKWEEK = 37.5;

    // Read the number of hours worked this week.
    Scanner keyboard = new Scanner(System.in);
    System.out.print("Enter the number of hours worked [decimal number]: ");
    double numHours = keyboard.nextDouble();

    // Calculate the weekly salary and print it to the terminal window.
    double salary = 750.0;                          // (1) weekly salary
    if (numHours > NORMAL_WORKWEEK)                            // (2)
      salary = salary + (numHours - NORMAL_WORKWEEK) * 30.0;   // (3)
    System.out.printf("Salary for %.1f hours is %.2f USD%n",
                      numHours, salary);                      // (4)

  }
}
```

Program output:

```
Enter the number of hours worked [decimal number]: 39.5
Salary for 39.5 hours is 810.00 USD
```

Blocks of statements: { ... }

A sequence of statements can be enclosed in curly brackets, {}, to specify a *block of statements*. Such a block is called a *compound statement*, and can be used anywhere that a single statement can be used.

The use of such a block is illustrated in Figure 3.3, where the if body is specified as a block, allowing us to execute more than one action when the if condition is satisfied. If we had left out the block notation, only the first statement after the Boolean expression, i.e.

```
double overtime = numHours - NORMAL_WORKWEEK;
```

would constitute the if body. However, the compiler will report an error in the next statement, as the overtime variable is not accessible outside the if body.

FIGURE 3.3 A block of statements

```
                              block starts
                                  ⌄
    if (numHours > NORMAL_WORKWEEK) {
      ┌─────────────────────────────────────────────────┐
      │ double overtime = numHours - NORMAL_WORKWEEK;    │ if body
      │ salary = salary + overtime * 30.0;               │
      └─────────────────────────────────────────────────┘
    }
    ^
block ends
```

Local variables in a block

We can define new variables inside a block, as shown in Figure 3.3. Such local variables can only be accessed inside the block.

The part of the program where such a variable can be accessed is called its *scope*. The scope of a variable defined within a block is from its declaration in the block to the end of the block. When a variable is no longer accessible, we say that it is *out of scope*. The compiler will produce an error message if we try to access local variables outside their scope. This is the case for the local variable overtime at (1) in Program 3.3, if we were to remove the comment designator // at the beginning of the line.

PROGRAM 3.3 Variables defined inside a block

```java
// Calculating weekly salary, version 1b.
import java.util.Scanner;
public class Salary1b {
  public static void main(String[] args) {
    final double NORMAL_WORKWEEK = 37.5;

    // Read the number of hours worked this week.
    Scanner keyboard = new Scanner(System.in);
    System.out.print("Enter the number of hours worked [decimal number]: ");
    double numHours = keyboard.nextDouble();

    // Calculate the weekly salary and print it to the terminal window.
    double salary = 750.0;                        // (1) weekly salary
    if (numHours > NORMAL_WORKWEEK) {             // if body is a block
      double overtime = numHours - NORMAL_WORKWEEK; // local variable
      salary = salary + overtime * 30.0;
    }
    System.out.printf("Salary for %.1f hours is %.2f USD%n",
                      numHours, salary);
//  System.out.printf("Number of hours overtime: %.1f%n", overtime); // (1)
  }
}
```

Program output:

```
Enter the number of hours worked [decimal number]: 39.5
Salary for 39.5 hours is 810.00 USD
```

Selection statement with two choices: `if-else`

We often need to choose between two alternative actions, where the program will execute one alternative if a given condition is satisfied, and the other if the condition is not satisfied. Java offers an `if-else` statement for this purpose. Figure 3.4 shows an example of this type of selection statement.

FIGURE 3.4 A selection statement with two alternatives

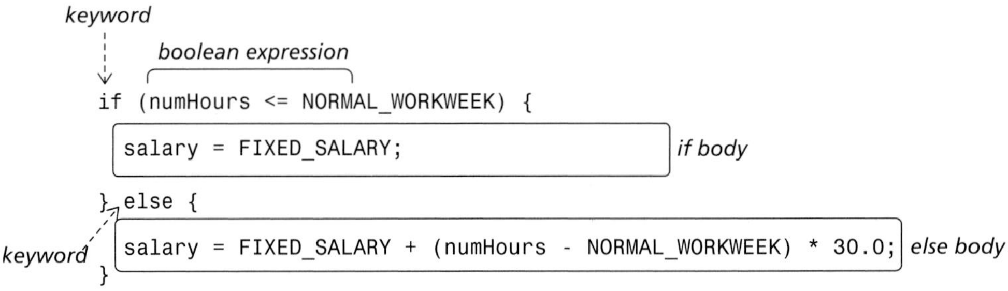

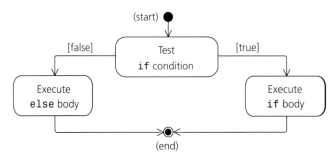

The first part of an `if-else` statement is the same as a simple `if` statement. The *if body* is executed if the Boolean expression evaluates to `true`, and the *else body* is executed otherwise. The keyword `else` starts the *else body*.

Figure 3.5 illustrates the execution of an `if-else` statement. Depending on the value of the Boolean expression, one of the two alternative actions is executed.

FIGURE 3.5 Executing a selection statement with two alternatives

Program 3.4 solves the same problem as Program 3.2, but using an `if-else` statement, where the *if body* calculates the basic salary for an employee who has not worked overtime, while the *else body* calculates the basic salary plus overtime compensation, for an employee who has worked overtime.

The condition for payment of basic salary, i.e. that the employee has worked 37.5 hours or less, is defined at (1). If this condition is satisfied, the variable salary is assigned the basic payment at (2). The keyword else at (3) marks the start of the alternative action, that calculates the weekly salary for an employee who has worked overtime, as shown at (4).

PROGRAM 3.4   Selecting alternative actions

```java
// Calculating weekly salary, version 2.
import java.util.Scanner;
public class Salary2 {
  public static void main(String[] args) {
    final double NORMAL_WORKWEEK = 37.5;
    final double FIXED_SALARY = 750.0;

    // Read the number of hours worked this week.
    Scanner keyboard = new Scanner(System.in);
    System.out.print("Enter the number of hours worked [decimal number]: ");
    double numHours = keyboard.nextDouble();

    //  Calculate the weekly salary and print it to the terminal window.
    double salary = 0.0;                          // weekly salary
    if (numHours <= NORMAL_WORKWEEK) {            // (1)
      salary = FIXED_SALARY;                      // (2) if body
    } else {                                      // (3)
      salary = FIXED_SALARY +
              (numHours - NORMAL_WORKWEEK) * 30.0;       // (4) else body
    }
    System.out.printf("Salary for %.1f hours is %.2f USD%n",
                      numHours, salary);
  }
}
```

Running Program 3.3 with the same input as Program 3.1 yields:

```
Enter the number of hours worked [decimal number]: 39.5
Salary for 39.5 hours is 810.00 USD
```

Program output for an employee who has worked overtime:

```
Enter the number of hours worked [decimal number]: 42.5
Salary for 42.5 hours is 900.00 USD
```

Nested selection statements

In Program 3.5 the selection statement at (1) has a new selection statement at (5) nested in its *else body*. If is only executed if the employee has worked overtime. Note that Program 3.5 gives the same result as Program 3.6 when run with the same input.

Calculating payment with a nested selection statement

```
// Calculating weekly salary, version 3.
import java.util.Scanner;
public class Salary3 {
  public static void main(String[] args) {
    final double NORMAL_WORKWEEK = 37.5;
    final double FIXED_SALARY = 750.0;

    // Read the number of hours worked this week.
    Scanner keyboard = new Scanner(System.in);
    System.out.print("Enter the number of hours worked [decimal number]: ");
    double numHours = keyboard.nextDouble();

    // Calculate the weekly salary and print it to the terminal window.
    double salary = 0.0;
    if (numHours <= NORMAL_WORKWEEK) {          // (1) if statement
      salary = FIXED_SALARY;                    // (2) if body
    } else {                                    // (3) else body
      salary = FIXED_SALARY + (numHours - NORMAL_WORKWEEK) * 30.0; // (4)
      if (numHours > 42.0) {                    // (5) nested if statement
        salary = salary + 100.0;                // (6)
      }
    }                                           // (7)
    System.out.printf("Salary for %.1f hours is %.2f USD%n",
                      numHours, salary);

  }
}
```

Program output for Program 3.2:

```
Enter the number of hours worked [decimal number]: 35.5
Salary for 35.5 hours is 750.00 USD
```

Program output for Program 3.4:

```
Enter the number of hours worked [decimal number]: 39.5
Salary for 39.5 hours is 810.00 USD
```

Program output for Program 3.5:

```
Enter the number of hours worked [decimal number]: 42.5
Salary for 42.5 hours is 1000.00 USD
```

When nesting selection statements, we must be careful to ensure that the program logic is correct. Using block statements may be necessary explicitly to specify which actions are to be executed when selection statements are nested. In the following code, the *else part* is associated with the if part at (2):

```
if (condition1)                 // (1)
    if (condition1)             // (2)
```

```
        System.out.println("nested if");
    else                          // Associated with (2)
        System.out.println("else body");
```

In the following code, the else part is associated with the if part at (1):

```
  if (condition1) {              // (1)
    if (condition1)              // (2)
      System.out.println("nested if");
  } else                         // Associated with (1)
    System.out.println("else body");
```

Note that the *else body* is always attached to the *nearest unattached* if part.

BEST PRACTICES

Always enclose both the if body and the else body of an if-else statement in a block, even if they just contain a single statement. This makes the program easier to understand, and reduces the chance for errors should the if statement be modified.

Chaining *if-else* statements

The *else body* in an if-else statement can be another if-else statement, as shown in Figure 3.6. Here, the second if-else statement will be executed as *one* statement if the first Boolean expression, numHours <= 37.5, evaluates to false. If this is the case, the second Boolean expression, numHours <= 42.0, will be evaluated, and one of the alternative actions of the second selection statement will be executed.

FIGURE 3.6   Chaining **if-else** statements

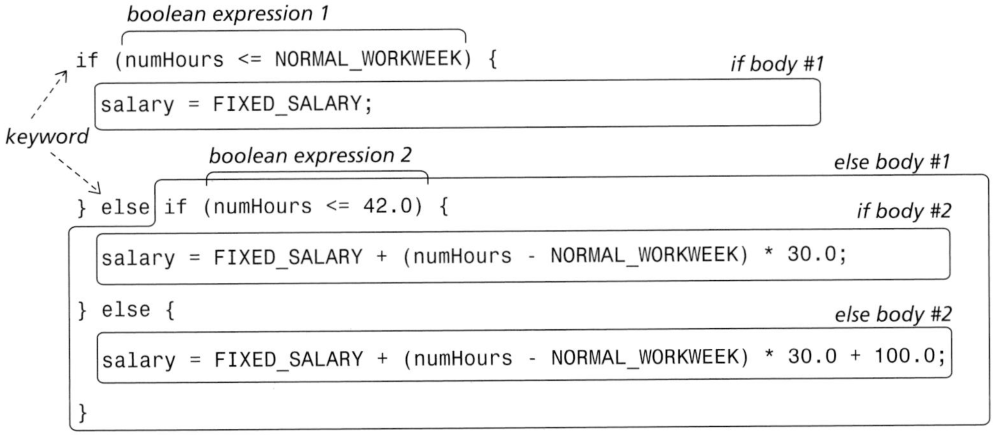

Figure 3.7 shows the execution of chained if-else statements. We can repeatedly extend the chain by replacing the last else body with another if-else statement.

FIGURE 3.7   Execution of chained **if-else** statements

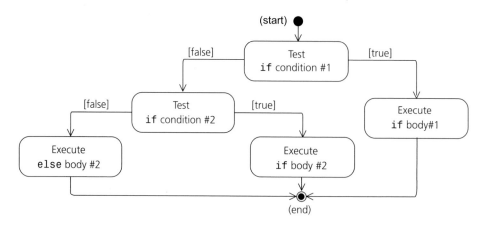

Program 3.6 uses a chain of if-else statements to extends the salary calculation from the previous examples, by allocating an additional payment of 100 USD for employees who have worked more than forty-two hours a week.

First, the Boolean expression (numHours <= 37.5) at (1) is evaluated. If this condition is satisfied, the statement at (2) is executed. On the other hand, if this condition is not satisfied, the Boolean expression (numHours <= 42.0) at (3) is evaluated. If this condition evaluates to true, the statement at (4) is executed. Otherwise, the statement at (5), in the last else body, is executed.

PROGRAM 3.6   Calculating salary with a chain of **if-else** statements

```java
// Calculating weekly salary, version 4.
import java.util.Scanner;
public class Salary4 {
  public static void main(String[] args) {
    final double NORMAL_WORKWEEK = 37.5;
    final double FIXED_SALARY = 750.0;

    // Read the number of hours worked this week.
    Scanner keyboard = new Scanner(System.in);
    System.out.print("Enter the number of hours worked [decimal number]: ");
    double numHours = keyboard.nextDouble();

    // Calculate the weekly salary and print it to the terminal window.
    double salary = 0.0;
    if (numHours <= NORMAL_WORKWEEK) {                              // (1)
      salary = FIXED_SALARY;                                       // (2)
    } else if (numHours <= 42.0) {                                 // (3)
      salary = FIXED_SALARY + (numHours - NORMAL_WORKWEEK) * 30.0; // (4)
    } else {
      salary = FIXED_SALARY +
              (numHours - NORMAL_WORKWEEK) * 30.0 + 100.0;         // (5)
```

```
      }
      System.out.printf("Salary for %.1f hours is %.2f USD%n",
                         numHours, salary);
   }
}
```

Testing alternative 1:

```
Enter the number of hours worked [decimal number]: 35.5
Salary for 35.5 hours is 750.00 USD
```

Testing alternative 2:

```
Enter the number of hours worked [decimal number]: 39.5
Salary for 39.5 hours is 810.00 USD
```

Testing alternative 3:

```
Enter the number of hours worked [decimal number]: 42.5
Salary for 42.5 hours is 1000.00 USD
```

3.3 Control flow: loops

A loop statement can be used to execute an action repeatedly. The action is specified in the *loop body*. The action can consist of zero or more statements. Each execution of the loop body is called an *iteration*.

The loop executes the loop body for as long as a given loop condition is satisfied. The condition is specified as a Boolean expression.

Loop test before loop body: `while`

In a while statement the loop condition is tested *before* the loop body is executed. That is why this kind of loop called a *pre-test loop*. Figure 3.8 illustrates the syntax of while loop.

FIGURE 3.8 Example of a **while** loop

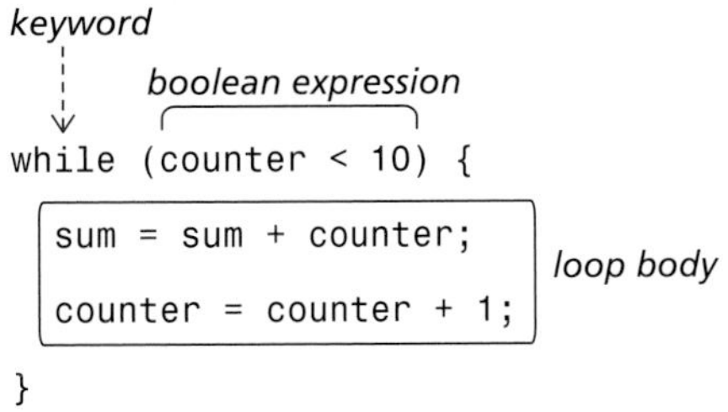

```
keyword
   │        boolean expression
   ↓    ┌──────────────┐
while (counter < 10) {
   ┌─────────────────────┐
   │ sum = sum + counter;│  loop body
   │ counter = counter + 1;│
   └─────────────────────┘
}
```

Figure 3.9 shows how a while loop is executed. First the loop condition, which is a Boolean expression, is evaluated. If the expression evaluates to true, the loop body is executed. After each iteration, the loop condition is tested. The execution of the loop body repeats until the loop condition evaluates to `false`. If the condition is not satisfied when control enters the loop for the first time, the loop body is skipped altogether.

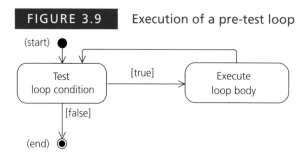

FIGURE 3.9   Execution of a pre-test loop

Loop test after loop body: `do-while`

A `do-while` loop evaluates the loop condition *after* the loop body has been executed. That is why it is often called a *post-test loop*. The syntax of this loop is illustrated in Figure 3.10. Since this is a post-test loop, the loop body of a `do-while` loop is executed *at least once*, as is evident from Figure 3.11.

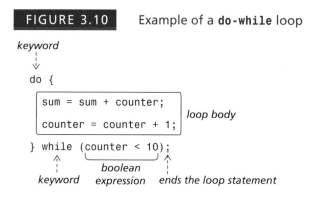

FIGURE 3.10   Example of a **do-while** loop

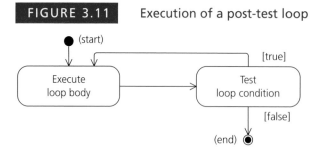

FIGURE 3.11   Execution of a post-test loop

Infinite loops

The execution of a loop body must at some point affect the loop condition such that it evaluates to `false`, otherwise the loop will never terminate. A loop that never terminates is called an *infinite loop*. Should an infinite loop occur in a program, the program will need to be terminated explicitly. On most platforms pressing the key combination *Ctrl-C* terminates program execution and thus the infinite loop.

Some examples of infinite loops are given in Section 5.5 on page 110.

Using loops to implement user dialogue

Loops are often used to implement dialogue between the user and the program, in which the program repeatedly asks the user to enter values. The number of values that will be entered is either read first, or a specific value, called the *sentinel value*, is used to mark the end of input. This allows the user to control the number of loop iterations. Figure 3.8 and Figure 3.10 are both examples in which the user enters a value controlling the number of iterations of the loop, while Exercise 3.5 on page 69 shows an example that uses a sentinel value to control the loop.

Program 3.7 calculates the sum of integers entered by the user. Again, we use the `Scanner` class to read the user input. A `Scanner` object is created, and connected to the keyboard with the following statement:

```
Scanner keyboard = new Scanner(System.in);
```

At (1) in Program 3.7 the number of values to add is then read from the keyboard. The program uses this value to control the execution of the loop at (2). Each new number is added to the accumulated sum of the numbers read so far. The reading of numbers is done by the `while` loop at (2), where the condition (`numberCounter < totalNumbers`) controls the execution of this loop. If the condition evaluates to `true`, the loop body is executed, reading the next number to add, updating the sum so far, and incrementing the counter for the number of values read so far. After each iteration, the condition is tested again. The testing of the loop condition and execution of the loop body is repeated until the condition evaluates to `false`. The loop is guaranteed to terminate, as the value of the number counter increases after each iteration, and will eventually become equal to the total numbers of values to read. After the loop terminates, the sum of the numbers read is printed to the terminal window at (4).

PROGRAM 3.7   Adding a sequence of integers using loops

```
// Adding a series of integers read from the keyboard.
import java.util.Scanner;
public class IntegerAddition {
  public static void main(String[] args) {

    Scanner keyboard = new Scanner(System.in);
    System.out.print("Enter the number of integers to add [integer]: ");
    int totalNumbers = keyboard.nextInt();    // (1) No. of integers to add
    keyboard.nextLine();                      // Skip rest of input
```

```
    int numberCounter = 0;                          // Numbers read so far
    int sum = 0;                                     // Sum of numbers so far

    while (numberCounter < totalNumbers) {                        // (2)
      System.out.print("Enter the next number [integer]: ");
      int nextInteger = keyboard.nextInt();   // Read the next number
      keyboard.nextLine();
      sum = sum + nextInteger;
      numberCounter = numberCounter + 1;
    }                                                            // (3)

    System.out.printf("The sum of %d integers is %d%n",
                      numberCounter, sum);                       // (4)
  }
}
```

Program output:

```
Enter the number of integers to add [integer]: 4
Enter the next number [integer]: 12
Enter the next number [integer]: 34
Enter the next number [integer]: 4
Enter the next number [integer]: -2
The sum of 4 integers is 48
```

Choosing the right loop

Which form of the loop to choose depends on the problem. A rule of the thumb is that, if the loop body needs to be executed at least once, a do-while loop is preferred. A while loop is the best choice if the loop body should not be executed for some input cases. Both forms can often be used to provide a solution, and choosing between the two forms becomes more a matter of taste.

Some problems lend themselves more naturally to one form of loop than the other. For example, in Program 3.7 we could have use a do-while loop to ensure that the user did not enter a negative value for the number of values to read:

```
    int totalNumbers = keyboard.nextInt();                       // (1)
    keyboard.nextLine();        // skip rest of input line

    while (totalNumbers < 0) {     // read again until a valid count is given
      totalNumbers = keyboard.nextInt();
      keyboard.nextLine();
    }

    int numberCounter = 0;                          // Numbers read so far
    int sum = 0;                                     // Sum of numbers so far
```

Nested loops

A loop body can contain another loop as one of its statements. We then have *nested loops*: an *outer loop* and an *inner loop*. Program 3.8 prints a multiplication table from 1 to 10 using two nested while loops. We note that in the program, for each iteration of the outer loop, the inner loop executes 10 iterations.

PROGRAM 3.8   Nested loops

```
// Printing a multiplication table using nested loops.
public class NestedLoops {
  public static void main(String[] args) {
    int number = 1, limit = 10;
    while (number <= limit) {              // Outer loop
      int times = 1;
      while (times <= limit) {             // Inner loop
        int product = number * times;
        System.out.println(number + " x " + times + " = " + product);
        times = times + 1;
      }
      number = number + 1;
    }
  }
}
```

Partial program output:

```
1 x 1 = 1

1 x 2 = 2

1 x 3 = 3

...

1 x 10 = 10

2 x 1 = 2

2 x 2 = 4

2 x 3 = 6

...

10 x 8 = 80

10 x 9 = 90

10 x 10 = 100
```

3.4 Assertions

Making assertions

We can make sure that a program satisfies a certain assumption about its properties at a given point in its source code by defining an *assertion*. The assert statement allows us to specify an assertion about the program's behaviour as a Boolean expression. This expression is evaluated during program execution. If the expression evaluates to false, an error message is generated and execution is aborted. If the expression evaluates to true, execution continues after the assert statement. We can, for example, check that the variable width holds a positive value by formulating the following assertion:

```
assert width > 0.0;
```

This assertion will lead to program termination if the variable width does not hold a positive value when the assert statement is executed.

To provide more information about the cause of assertion failure, explanatory text can be specified after the Boolean expression:

```
assert width > 0.0 : "The width of the rectangle must be > 0.0";
```

If the variable width holds a non-positive value when the assert statement is executed, the program will terminate with an error message similar to the following:

```
> javac FloatingPointArea3.java
> java -ea FloatingPointArea3
Enter the rectangle length [decimal number]: 12.5
Enter the rectangle width [decimal number]: -2.5
Exception in thread "main" java.lang.AssertionError:
    The width of the rectangle must be > 0.0
        at FloatingPointArea3.main(FloatingPointArea3.java:16)
```

The printout gives information about where the assertion is defined (the main() method in the FloatingPointArea3 class), the name of the source code file (FloatingPoint-Area3.java) and the line number in this file (16). Note that the flag "-ea" must be specified on the command line when the program is run. This option turns on the validation of assertions in the program during execution (see Appendix G).

Assertions as a testing technique

Program 3.9 uses assert statements at (1) and (2) to *validate user input* before the values are used in calculations. The area is only calculated if both the length and the width are positive values.

The assertions at (1) and (2) in Program 3.9 can be combined as follows:

```
assert width > 0.0 && length > 0.0;
```

We can also specify an explanatory text to be printed if the assertion fails:

```
assert width > 0.0 && length > 0.0 : "Rectangle width and length must be > 0.0";
```

In previous code examples we have only controlled the value of variables. However, the Boolean expression in an assertion can be more complicated, but it must not have *side-effects*, meaning that its execution must not, for example, change the value of variables in the program. If it did, the execution of the program would depend on the assertions, and that would be inappropriate, as assert statements are only executed if the program is run with the "-ea" option.

Assertions provide a useful testing technique that can help us detect errors early, and well before a program is delivered to the user. Assertions can be turned on when running the program for test purposes, and turned off when the program is shipped to the user. Should problems occur after delivery, the assertions can be turned on again by means of the "-ea" flag, enabling problems to be detected when running in the user environment.

3

PROGRAM 3.9 Using assertions to validate user input and computed results

```
// Using assertions to verify user input and calculated values.
import java.util.Scanner;
public class FloatingPointArea3 {
  public static void main(String[] args) {
    Scanner keyboard = new Scanner(System.in);

    // Read rectangle dimensions
    System.out.print("Enter the rectangle length [decimal number]: ");
    double length = keyboard.nextDouble();
    keyboard.nextLine();
    System.out.print("Enter the rectangle width [decimal number]: ");
    double width = keyboard.nextDouble();

    // Validate user input
    assert length > 0.0 : "The length of the rectangle must be > 0.0";// (1)
    assert width > 0.0 : "The width of the rectangle must be > 0.0";  // (2)

    double area = length * width; // Calculate area of the rectangle

    // Print the correct answer
    System.out.printf(
      "A rectangle of length %.2f cm. and width %.2f cm. has" +
      " area %.2f sq. cm.%n",
```

```
        length, width, area);
    }
}
```

3.5 Review questions

1. A Boolean expression can only evaluate to one of two values, _____ or _____. The value of such an expression can be assigned to a _____ variable.

2. Name the two types of operators that can be used in Boolean expressions.

3. Which of the following assignments are allowed in Java, when the variables test1, test2 and test3 all are of data type boolean? Compute the value of all valid expressions.

   a test1 = 2 < 3;

   b test1 = 2 + 3 < 1 - - 5;

   c test1 = "true";

   d test2 = false;

4. What is the value of the expression b1 && !b2 || !b1 == b3, when the Boolean variables b1, b2 and b3 have the values true, false and true, respectively?

5. Selection and loop statements offer two mechanisms for controlling the _____. Such statements enable us to _____ alternative actions, or to _____ an action a _____ or _____ number of times.

6. What is the value of the variable test at (1) to (4)? Are all assignments valid in Java?

```
boolean test;
int numMen = 12;
int numWomen = 7;
test = numMen < numWomen;        // (1)
test = numMen = numWomen;        // (2)
test = numMen * numWomen >= 90;  // (3)
test = 2 * numWomen < numMen;    // (4)
```

7. The Java operators __ (negation), __ (conditional And), and __ (conditional Or) expect operands of type _____.

8. To what values are the following Boolean expressions evaluated, when the value of the Boolean variables b1, b2 and b3, are true, false and true, respectively?

a b3 || 3 * 0.5 < 2 + 3 * -1

b 4 + 1 == 8 - 3 && b

c 5 < 4 || !b2

d b1 && !b2 || b3

e (b2|| 2 < 3) && (!b3 || b1)

f ! ((b1 && b3) || (b2 != b1))

9. Use De Morgan's laws to simplify the following Boolean expressions, when b1 and b2 are Boolean variables:

   a !(b1 || b2)

   b !(b1 == b2 && b2)

   c !(!b2 || b1 == true)

   d (!b1 == b2 || b2)

   e (!(b1 == b2) || !(b2 == b1))

10. Write a selection statement that prints a message explaining whether the integer variable numPoints contains a value that is an even or an odd number. (Even numbers can be divided by two without a remainder).

11. A repetition statement is often called a _____. The condition for repeating the _____ is specified as a _____ expression.

12. Explain the difference between the while and do-while loops.

13. An assert statement specifies a _____ expression, and (optionally) a _____. The _____ is printed to the terminal window if the expression evaluates to _____, and the execution is _____.

14. Which of these statements are true?

    a Assertions are always executed when the program is run.

    b If the Boolean expression in the assert statement evaluates to true at runtime, the execution aborts.

    c If the Boolean expression in the assert statement evaluates to false at runtime, the execution aborts.

3.6 Programming exercises

1. Write a program that reads the duration of a time interval in seconds, and then prints the corresponding number of hours, minutes and seconds to the terminal window. For example, if the user enters the number 3603, the program should output:

   ```
   3603 seconds = 1 hour, 0 minutes and 3 seconds
   ```

   Ensure that the program prints the time units grammatically, i.e. 0 hours, 1 hour, 2 hours, etc. Tip: Use a selection statement to determine whether the time units should be written in singular or plural form.

Use assertions to check that the values for each time unit are within expected limits.

2. Write a program that determines whether a user-supplied value is inside or outside an interval. For example, the value 6 is inside the interval from 2 to 8, while the value 8 is outside the interval ranging from 1 to 5 (cf. figure below).

Write a program that:

1. Reads the lower and upper limits of an integer interval.

2. Reads a value.

3. Reports back if the value is inside or outside the given interval.

The program output should look this:

```
Enter the lower limit of interval [integer]: 2
Enter the upper limit of interval [integer]: 8
The value 6 lies within the interval [2, 8].
```

Print an appropriate report if the input value lies outside the interval.

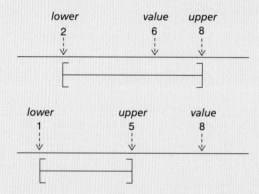

3. Write a program that determines in which quadrant of a Cartesian coordinate system a given point (x, y) lies. For example, if x has the value 2 and y has the value 3, the program should print:

```
The point (x=2,y=3) is placed in the upper, right quadrant.
```

If x has the value -3 and y has the value -1, the program should print:

```
The point (x=-3,y=-1) is placed in the lower, left quadrant.
```

Let the program read an x- and a y-coordinate, and report the quadrant in which the point (x, y) lies.

4. Write a program that reads n integers from the keyboard and calculates their sum, using a do-while loop. Your program shall have the same functionality as Program 3.7.

5. Write a program that reads a sequence of positive integers from the keyboard and prints their average. Use a negative integer as a sentinel value. If the user enters the following sequence:

        23
        42
        53
        3
        54
        82
        37
        43
        29
        44
        -1

    the program should output as follows:
    ```
    The sum of the integers is 410.
    The average of the 10 numbers is 41.
    ```

6. Assume that the user also wants to calculate the average value of negative numbers, and that the numbers may be floating-point values. Modify the program in Exercise 3.5 so that it accepts a user-supplied sequence of values, and prints the average of these values. The number of values in the sequence is read first, followed by the specified number of values:

        7
        -3.25
        -4.44
        2.14
        3.66
        3.78
        3.67
        -4.33

    The program should print a report similar to the one in Exercise 3.5:
    ```
    The sum of the values is 1.01
    The average of the 7 numbers is 0.14
    ```

    Print an explanatory text before asking the user for the number of values to read. You may assume that the user will always enter at least one value.

7. Write a program that assigns the grades A–F based on the number of points a student has scored in an exam. The intervals for the grades are: A for 91–100 points, B for 81–90 points, C for 61–80 points, D for 31–60 points and E for 15–30 points.

    If a student gets less than 15 points, the grade F is assigned.

    The program should read the student ID and number of points, where the ID is an even integer between 2 and 200, and permissible values for points are from 0.0 to 100.0.

Output from the program may look like this:

```
Enter the student id [integer]: 20
Enter the number of points [decimal number]: 87.5
Student with id 20 gets grade B
```

Output from the program when the student ID is valid, but the number of points is not, should be in the form:

```
Input student id [integer]: 24
Input number of points [decimal number]: 102.3
Exception in thread "main" java.lang.AssertionError:
Invalid number of points for the exam: 102.3
Allowed values range from 0.0 to 100.0
        at Grade.main(Grade.java:26)
```

8. Write a program that calculates the volume of different solids:

   1 Cube: $v = length \times length \times length$

   2 Cylinder: $v = p \times r^2 \times height$

   3 Sphere: $v = 4 / 3 \times p \times r^3$

   where *length* is the length of each side of the cube, *height* is the height of the cylinder, *r* is the radius on the cylinder base or of the sphere, and *p* is a mathematical constant. Use the constant Math.PI as the value for *p*.

   Use the Scanner class to create a user dialogue where the user can select the type of solid.

   Sample output from the program:

   ```
   Calculation of volume for solid objects

   Enter 1 for cube, 2 for cylinder or 3 for sphere: 2
   Enter the radius of cylinder [decimal value]: 2.5
   Enter the height of cylinder [decimal value]: 1.5
   Enter the unit for radius and height [text]: cm

   The volume of a cylinder with radius 2.50 cm and height 1.50 cm
   is 9.62 cubic cm.
   ```

9. Extend the program in Exercise 3.7 to ask the user whether another volume should be calculated or whether the program should terminate.

10. Write a program that calculates how much the amount deposited in a bank account has grown at the annual interest rate of *r*% after *n* years. The general formula for computing the amount, including interest, after *n* years is:

$$K_n = K_0 \times (1 + r / 100)^n$$

when K_0 is the principle amount.

Sample user dialogue and output from the program:

```
Calculation of Compound Interest

Enter the initial amount deposited [decimal value]: 10000.00
Enter the interest rate [decimal value]: 4.5
Enter the number of years [integer]: 10
Enter the currency used [string]: GBP


Amount with interest after 10 years:   15529.69 GBP
```

Write assertions to verify both the input data and the computed amount.

11. Modify the program in Exercise 3.10 to calculate how much an amount has grown in n years for an interval of interest rates from r_{min}% to r_{max}%. Let the user provide the minimum and maximum interest rates, and calculate the amount obtained after n years for each 0.5% increment in the interest rate inside this interval.

Sample user dialogue and output from the program:

```
Calculation of deposits with interests for min - max rates

Enter the initial amount deposited [decimal value]: 10000.00
Enter the minimum interest rate [decimal value]: 4.5
Enter the maximum interest rate [decimal value]: 8.25
Enter the number of years [integer]: 5
Enter the currency used [string]: GBP


Amounts will be printed with 0.5% increment in interest rates.
Amount with interest after 5 years with rate 4.5%:  12461.82 GBP
Amount with interest after 5 years with rate 5.0%:  12762.82 GBP
...
Amount with interest after 5 years with rate 7.5%:  14356.29 GBP
Amount with interest after 5 years with rate 8.0%:  14693.28 GBP
```

Write assertion statements to verify your assumptions about input data and the computed amount.

PART TWO

Object-based Programming

CHAPTER 4

Using objects

LEARNING OBJECTIVES

By the end of this chapter you will understand the following:

- **The relationship between a class and its objects.**
- **Representing the properties and behaviour of an object with fields and instance methods respectively.**
- **Creating objects using the new operator.**
- **Manipulating objects by reference variables.**
- **Calling methods on objects and accessing fields in objects.**
- **Representing characters in the computer.**
- **Using methods from the String class to create and manipulate strings.**
- **Distinguishing between reference equality and value equality for objects.**
- **Using primitive values as objects.**

INTRODUCTION

In this chapter we will create objects from pre-defined classes, and manage them using references. Strings are used frequently in programming, and Java offers extensive support for handling such objects. We also discuss how primitive values can be used as objects.

4.1 Introduction to the object model

In any field, we need to master the terminology to understand the subject matter. This is also true for programming. The goal in this section is to introduce some important concepts without going into too much detail. The details will be filled in as we build our conceptual apparatus.

Abstractions, classes and objects

We use abstractions to handle the diversity that surrounds us in everyday life. An *abstraction* represents the relevant properties of an object required to solve the problem at hand, so that we can distinguish it from other types of objects. Both a Volvo S40 and a Toyota Avensis will be perceived as vehicles. Our ability to create an abstraction of what we perceive as a vehicle helps us with this task. The colour or the model is not relevant, the deciding factor is that it can be driven.

When we write programs that process information about abstractions from reality, it is helpful to represent the *properties* and *behaviour* of these abstractions in the computer. In Java, abstractions can be represented by classes. A *class* describes objects of a particular type – what information they can contain and what they can do, i.e. it specifies the properties and behaviour of these objects.

We will illustrate the relationship between a class and the objects it represents by specifying a simple class for music CDs. Such a CD has certain properties: a title and a number of music tracks. (Let's presume that the name of the artist or the title of the tracks is not important in the present context.) For a CD it should be possible to determine its title and how many tracks there are on it. An abstraction that we use in the computer need not be an exact model of a CD in real life. In our abstraction of a CD, we will change the title and number of tracks on the CD, but this is not usually the case with a real CD. To keep the example simple, we are also not concerned about other behaviours of a CD, for example being able to read the names of all the tracks on the CD.

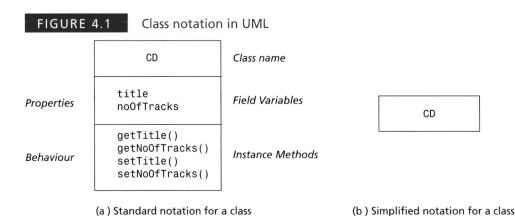

FIGURE 4.1   Class notation in UML

(a) Standard notation for a class   (b) Simplified notation for a class

A *class declaration* contains a number of *declarations* that define the properties and behaviour of its objects. Figure 4.1 shows the class CD in UML notation (Appendix H). The corresponding class in Java is shown in Figure 4.2. A class declaration begins with the keyword class followed by the name of the class. Declarations in a class are always enclosed in curly brackets, {}.

FIGURE 4.2   Class declaration in Java

Class name
↓

```
class CD {
```

```
// Declaration of field variables                          Properties
String title;
int    noOfTracks;
————————————————————————————————————————————
// Declaration of instance methods                         Behaviour
String getTitle()        { return title; }
int    getNoOfTracks() { return noOfTracks; }
void   setTitle(String newTitle)  { title = newTitle; }
void   setNoOfTracks(int nTracks) { noOfTracks = nTracks; }
```

```
}
```

The properties of the objects of a class are specified with the help of *field variables* (also just called *fields*). The declaration of the class CD has two field variables, title and noOfTracks, which store information about the title and number of tracks on a CD respectively. The behaviour of the objects is specified by *instance methods*. The class CD has four such methods, with the names getTitle, getNoOfTracks, setTitle and setNoOfTracks. These methods are used to look up and change information about the title and the number of tracks on a CD. A method contains operations that exhibit the desired behaviour in an object when the method is executed.

Objects, reference values and reference variables

A class is a "blueprint" for creating objects that have properties and behaviour defined by the class. In the literature, the term *instance* is often used as a synonym for an object. There is only one CD class, but we can create several CD objects. When we create an object from a class, we get a *reference value* for the newly-created object. Each object of a class is unique (i.e. has a unique identity indicated by the reference value), even though all the objects of the class represent the same properties and behaviour.

A *reference variable* (often shortened to just *reference*) is a variable that can store a *reference value* of an object. References are analogous to variables of primitive data types that store values of primitive data types, and store reference values of objects. A reference thus *refers to* the object identified by the reference value stored in the reference. We manipulate an object via a reference that holds the reference value of the object.

A *reference variable declaration* is used to declare a reference variable. It specifies the *name* of the reference and its *reference type*. A class is a reference type. References can only refer to objects that have this type, i.e. that are objects of the specified class. The following declaration will result in memory being allocated for the reference favouriteAlbum that can store the reference value of a CD object:

```
CD favouriteAlbum;
```

4

The **new** operator

No object is created as a result of declaring a reference. The following expression statement is responsible for creating an object of the class CD:

```
new CD();
```

This language construct consists of two parts: the operator new and a *constructor call*, CD(). The operator new creates an object of class CD, whose name is specified in the constructor call, and returns the reference value of the new object. The constructor call also specifies *a list of parameter values* (empty in the constructor call above) that can be used to initialize the field variables in the new object that was created from the declared class.

Often we combine the declaration of a reference and the creation of an object whose reference value is assigned to the reference, as shown in Figure 4.3.

FIGURE 4.3   Object creation

Reference declaration   *Constructor call*

Reference type → CD favouriteAlbum = new CD();

Reference variable Operator │ Parameter list
Class name

Figure 4.4a shows the result of executing the declaration statement above in UML notation, with explicit specification of a reference to the newly-created object. We see that the fields title and noOfTracks have the values null and 0 respectively. This will always be the case for each CD object we create using the new operator, because of the way we have defined the CD class.

The notation in Figure 4.4a might seem cumbersome. In that case, we can use alternative notations shown in Figure 4.4b and Figure 4.4c. In UML, objects are typically designated with both the reference name and the class name, in the following format: *referenceName: className*.

Using objects

After an object has been created, a reference that refers to the object can be used to send messages to the object. Messages take the form of a *method call* in Java (see Figure 4.5a).

A method call to an object specifies:

- the reference to the receiving object
- the name of the method that is to be executed
- any other information (in a parameter list) that the method needs to execute its statements (see Method calls and actual parameter expressions in Chapter 7).

Note the dot (.) between the reference and the method name. The class of the referred object must define the method that is called. In Figure 4.5a, the method call will result in the method setTitle() in the class CD being executed. From Figure 4.2 we see that this method assigns the value it receives in its parameter list to the field title, i.e. the field `title` in the object referred by the reference `favouriteAlbum` will be assigned the reference value of the `String` object `"Java Jam Hits"`.

FIGURE 4.4   Object notation in UML

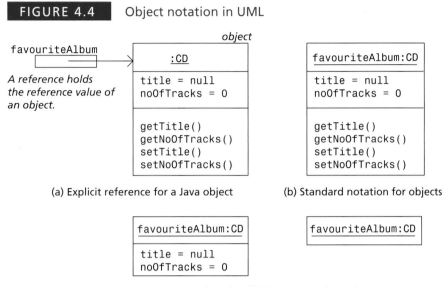

(a) Explicit reference for a Java object

(b) Standard notation for objects

(c) Other simplified notations for objects

We can use the dot-notation, together with a reference, to access the field variables in an object. An example is shown in Figure 4.5b. The code line in Figure 4.5b will give the same result as the method call in Figure 4.5a. If a computation is required to set the value of a field variable, it is generally a good idea to call an instance method in the object, rather than repeating the code for the computation whenever the field value is set. This helps to ensure that the field is updated properly and consistently.

FIGURE 4.5   Dot notation

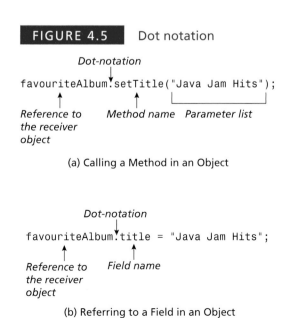

(a) Calling a Method in an Object

(b) Referring to a Field in an Object

Object state

Each object has its own copy of field variables. The fields of different objects of class CD can therefore have different values, as shown in Figure 4.6. The values of the fields in an object at any given time constitute the *state* of the object. The behaviour of an object is given by the instance methods. Coding of a method, i.e. the code that constitutes a method declaration, is called a *method implementation*, and objects of the same class share method implementations (see Method execution and the return statement in Chapter 7).

Program 4.1 declares a class CDSampler that uses objects of the class CD. It is a useful exercise to identify the concepts we have introduced so far in this chapter by examining this code. Information that the program prints corresponds to the state of the CD objects illustrated in Figure 4.6.

FIGURE 4.6   Object state

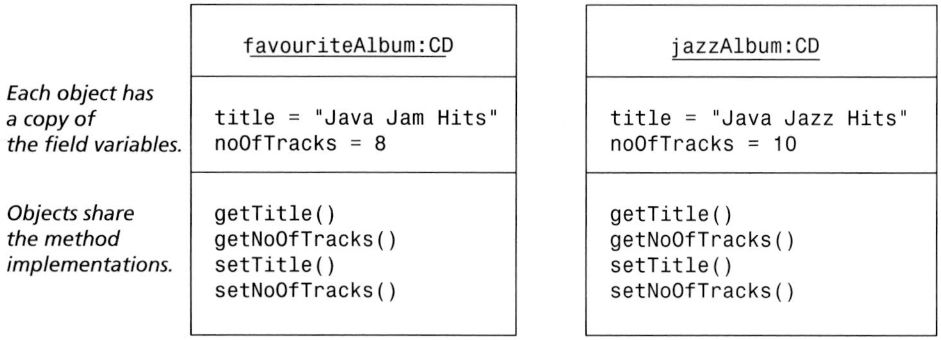

	favouriteAlbum:CD
Each object has a copy of the field variables.	title = "Java Jam Hits" noOfTracks = 8
Objects share the method implementations.	getTitle() getNoOfTracks() setTitle() setNoOfTracks()

	jazzAlbum:CD
	title = "Java Jazz Hits" noOfTracks = 10
	getTitle() getNoOfTracks() setTitle() setNoOfTracks()

PROGRAM 4.1   Objects

```java
// Using CD-objects
public class CDSampler {
    public static void main(String[] args) {
        // Create 2 CDs.
        CD favouriteAlbum = new CD();
        CD jazzAlbum = new CD();

        // Set state of the CDs.
        favouriteAlbum.setTitle("Java Jam Hits");
        favouriteAlbum.setNoOfTracks(8);
        jazzAlbum.setTitle("Java Jazz Hits");
        jazzAlbum.setNoOfTracks(10);

        // Print state of the CDs.
        System.out.println("Title of favourite album: " +
                            favouriteAlbum.getTitle());
        System.out.println("Number of tracks on favourite album: " +
                            favouriteAlbum.getNoOfTracks());
```

```
         System.out.println("Title of jazz album: " + jazzAlbum.getTitle());
         System.out.println("Number of tracks on jazz album: " +
                            jazzAlbum.getNoOfTracks());
    }
}
```

Program output:

```
Title of favourite album: Java Jam Hits
Number of tracks on favourite album: 8
Title of jazz album: Java Jazz Hits
Number of tracks on jazz album: 10
```

BEST PRACTICES

A class declaration should only declare properties and behaviour that are relevant for the problem at hand.

4.2 Strings

Text is a common medium for representing information. Text consists of *characters*. In programming languages, text is usually *a sequence of characters*, and is called a *text string*, or just *string*. Java provides a primitive data type, char, and a pre-defined class, String, that can be used to handle characters and strings respectively.

Characters and strings

In the computer each character is represented by an integer value called the *code number*. This is true for all characters, including letters, digits and other special characters. Java uses a standard called *Unicode* to represent characters. This standard assigns a unique code number for each character.

The primitive data type char represents the code number of each character as a 16-bit integer value, so that it is possible to represent 65 536 (2^{16}) different characters in the data type. This is large enough to represent the characters found in most of the languages in the world. The Unicode values (i.e. the code numbers in the Unicode standard) are usually specified as hexadecimal numbers. For example, the letter 'a' has the Unicode value \u0061, the digit '0' has the Unicode value \u0030, and the character '€' has the Unicode value \u20ac. The prefix \u indicates that the value is a code number for a character in the Unicode standard.

Character literals

To write a character as a char value in a Java program, we enclose the character or its Unicode value in single quotes ('). For example, the letter a can be written as 'a' or

'\u0061'. This notation defines a character literal that is the code number of a particular character. Without the single quotes, the character a alone will be interpreted as a one-letter name in the program. Some examples of character literals are given in Table 4.1.

As we can see from Table 4.1, we must precede a single quote (') by a back slash (\), and both the characters (\') must be enclosed in single quotes ('\'') to specify the character literal for a single quote. The backslash character (\) is used to "escape" the special meaning of a character. Some special characters, like those that do not have a visible representation but have a special meaning (for example, newline with the Unicode value \u000a), have predefined literals. For example, the newline literal is '\n'.

TABLE 4.1 Characters, Unicode representation and character literals

Character	Decimal value	Unicode value	Character literal
0 (zero)	48	\u0030	'0'
a	97	\u0061	'a'
A	65	\u0041	'A'
?	63	\u003f	'?'
single quote: '	39	\u0027	'\''
double quote: "	34	\u0022	'\"'
backslash: \	92	\u005c	'\\'
newline	10	\u000a	'\n'
tab	9	\u0009	'\t'
space	32	\u0020	' '

Character variables and arithmetic expressions

A character literal has the data type char. We can declare variables that can store characters, meaning that the code numbers these variables store are interpreted as characters:

```
char newline = '\n', tab = '\u0009';
char char1, char2, char3, char4;
char1 = char4 = 'a'; char2 = char3 = 'b';
```

Since a character is represented by an integer value, a character can be an integer operand in an arithmetic expression:

```
int sumCodeNumbers = char1 + char2 + char3 + char4;   // 97+98+98+97 => 390
int number = '5' - '0';                                // 53 - 48 => 5
```

The code numbers of lowercase letters (a to z), uppercase letters (A to Z) and digits (0 to 9) are numbered consecutively in the Unicode standard, with lowercase letters from

\u0061 (a) to \u007a (z), uppercase letters from \u0041 (A) to \u005a (Z), and the digits from \u0030 (0) to \u0039 (9) (Appendix D). We can compare characters, and it is the code numbers that are actually compared:

```
boolean test1 = char1 == char4; // true
boolean test2 = char1 > char2;  // false,
                                // since 'a' (\u0061) < 'b' (\u0062)
```

String literals

Analogous to character literals, we can define string literals by enclosing a sequence of characters in double quotes ("). In contrast to character literals that are integer values, string literals are objects of the class String. For example, the string literal "abba" is a String object. This object stores the characters 'a', 'b', 'b' and 'a' as a sequence. Other examples of string literals are given in Table 4.2. The table also shows the result of printing string literals, for example by calling the System.out.println() method. Note that any double quotes (") that actually occur in a string must be escaped with a backslash (\), and that string literals cannot span more than one line in the source code.

TABLE 4.2   String literals

String literal	Printout
`"Welcome to Forevereverland"`	`Welcome to Forevereverland`
`""`	The empty string has no visible representation.
`"!"`	`!`
`"\"Move it!\", said the teacher."`	`"Move it!", said the teacher.`
`"A string cannot` `span more than one line."`	Compile time error.
`"Wrap a long string\n with a newline literal."`	`Wrap a long string` `with a newline literal.`

String concatenation

As with other reference variables, we can declare variables of class String that can refer to string literals.

```
String firstName = "Leif", lastName = "Eriksen";
```

The character sequence in a String object cannot be modified, i.e. a String object is *immutable*. Calling methods in the String class that seemingly modify the string in a String object actually result in a new String object with the modified string. We will see several examples of string immutability later in this section.

A useful operation on strings is to join two strings, referred to as *string concatenation*. A new string is created, whose contents are the characters from the first string followed by the characters from the second string. The binary operator +, which also performs arithmetic addition, is used for concatenating two strings:

```
String fullName = firstName + " " + lastName; // "Leif Eriksen"
```

If one of the operands of the + operator is a string and the other is not, the other operand is automatically converted to its string representation before the concatenation is performed. The concatenation operator is left-associative, i.e. the concatenation is performed from left to right resulting in a new String object with the final string. The operator returns the reference value of the new String object. After execution of the statement above, the reference fullName will refer to a String object containing the string "Leif Eriksen".

Program 4.2 illustrates string concatenation. After execution of the statement at (1), the reference course will refer to the string "Introductory course in programming". Note the result of the concatenation in the statements at (2) and (3). In (2), the string literals "C" and "S" are concatenated with the int variable courseNumber, resulting in the string "CS100", as the value 100 in the variable courseNumber is converted to the string "100" before concatenation. In (3), the character literals 'C' (int value 67) and 'S' (int value 83) are added before addition to the int variable courseNumber (int value 100), resulting in the int value 250. This value is converted to a string and concatenated with the String variable course.

PROGRAM 4.2   String concatenation

```
// Illustrating string concatenation
public class StringConcatenation {
  public static void main(String[] args) {
    String course = "programming";
    course = "Introductory course in " + course;                    // (1)
    System.out.println("course: " + course);
    int courseNumber = 100;
    String course1 = "C" + "S" + courseNumber + ": " + course; // (2)
    String course2 = 'C' + 'S' + courseNumber + ": " + course; // (3)
    System.out.println("course1: " + course1);
    System.out.println("course2: " + course2);
    System.out.println((int)'C');
    System.out.println((int)'S');
  }
}
```

Program output:

```
course: Introductory course in programming
course1: CS100: Introductory course in programming
course2: 250: Introductory course in programming
```

Creating string objects

Earlier in this section we saw how a variable can be assigned a string literal. Specification of a string literal in the program implies creation of a String object that contains the string, and the reference value of this object can be assigned to a String reference variable:

```
String star = "madonna";
```

If several reference variables are subsequently assigned the same string literal, they are aliases: they will refer to the same String object as the string literal (see Figure 4.7):

```
String singer = "madonna"; // The reference singer refers to the same
                           // String-object as the reference star.
```

Another way of creating String objects is by using the new operator together with a String constructor call:

```
String newSinger = new String("madonna");  // (1)
String artist    = new String(newSinger);  // (2)
```

Use of the new operator implies creation of a new String object. In (1) a new String object is created based on the string literal "madonna", and in (2) a new String object is created based on the String object referred to by the reference newSinger. The reference variables star, newSinger and artist refer to three different String objects that have the same state (see Figure 4.7).

4

| FIGURE 4.7 | String creation |

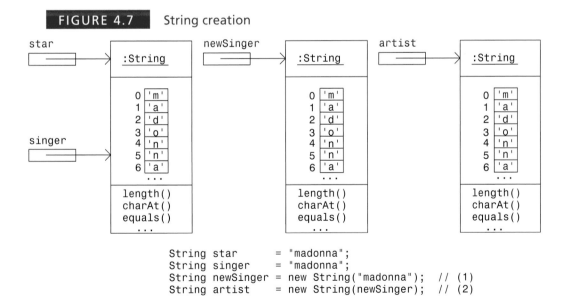

```
String star      = "madonna";
String singer    = "madonna";
String newSinger = new String("madonna");  // (1)
String artist    = new String(newSinger);  // (2)
```

String comparison

Comparison of strings is based on *lexicographical order*, i.e. characters in corresponding positions in the two strings are compared based on their Unicode values. Entries in a telephone directory or words in a dictionary are listed according to lexicographical order. Based on lexicographical order, the string "abba" is *less* than the string "aha", since the

Unicode value of second character, 'b', in string "abba" is less than the Unicode value of the second character, 'h', in the string "aha".

The method compareTo() in the String class can be used to compare strings. We call this method on one string and send the second string as a parameter in the method call. The return value from the call to the method indicates the result of the comparison, as explained in Table 4.3 on page 87. In the program, the return value can be used to determine further action:

```
int result1 = star.compareTo(singer);     // == 0
int result2 = star.compareTo(newSinger);  // == 0

String group1 = "abba", group2 = "aha";
int result3 = group2.compareTo(group1);   // > 0
int result4 = group.compareTo(group2);    // < 0
if (result4 < 0) { // true in this case.
   System.out.println(group1 + " is smaller!"); // Prints: abba is smaller!
}
```

In Table 4.3 we see that the methods compareTo() and equals() require a parameter of class Object. Such a parameter makes it possible to send any object as parameter to the method. The compiler will accept this, but during execution a runtime error can occur if the object passed is not of the right data type for the comparison.

Equivalence between two strings means that both String objects have the same state, i.e. the strings in the two objects have identical character sequences. This is called *value equality*. If we only want to compare two strings for value equality, we can use the equals() method rather than the compareTo() method:

```
boolean flagA = star.equals(singer);      // true
boolean flagB = star.equals(newSinger);   // true
```

The equality operator == cannot be used for comparing objects for value equality. This operator compares two *references* to determine whether they are aliases. This is called *reference equality*:

```
boolean flag1 = (star == singer)      // true
boolean flag2 = (star == newSinger)   // false
```

Converting primitive values to strings

It is often necessary to convert primitive values to their string representations. The static method valueOf() in the String class will convert a primitive value to a String object that contains the string representation of its value.

```
String numberStr = String.valueOf(3.14);   // "3.14"
String boolStr   = String.valueOf(true);   // "true"
```

If a string is a string representation of a primitive value and we wish to convert it to its corresponding primitive value, it is convenient to use a suitable parse*Type*() method from the wrapper classes (see *Primitive values as objects* on page 92).

If a string contains the string representation of several primitive values, we can use the java.util.Scanner class to read the string and convert the characters to primitive values:

TABLE 4.3   Selected methods from the **String** class

java.lang.String	
int compareTo(Object s2)	Compares two strings. For example, given the code line: int result = s1.compareTo(s2); where s1 and s2 are strings, we can conclude the following, depending on the value of the result variable: If result < 0, string s1 is less than string s2. If result == 0, string s1 is equal to string s2. If result > 0, string s1 is greater than string s2.
boolean equals(Object s2)	Compares two strings for equality, i.e. whether the respective strings have identical sequences of characters, and returns true if that is the case. Otherwise the method returns false.
int length()	Returns the number of characters in the string, i.e. the *length* of the string.
static String valueOf(T t)	Depending on the type T, returns a string representation of the value in t. For example, type T can be boolean, char, double, float, int or long.
char charAt(int index)	Returns the character at the index in the string. The first character is at *index* 0. Invalid index values will result in an IndexOutOfBoundsException.

int indexOf(int charValue)
int indexOf(String subString)
int indexOf(int charValue,
            int startIndex)
int indexOf(String subString,
            int startIndex)
	Returns the index of the charValue or index of the start of the substring in the string, otherwise returns -1. Argument startIndex can be used to start the search from a particular index, otherwise the search starts at index 0.

String substring(
    int startIndex,
    int endIndex)
	Returns a new string consisting of the sequence of characters from startIndex to (endIndex-1). The returned string has length (endIndex-startIndex). Invalid index values will result in an IndexOutOfBoundsException.

String toLowerCase() String toUpperCase()	Returns a new string in which all characters that are letters in the original string are converted to either lowercase or uppercase, respectively.
String trim()	Returns a new string where invisible characters at the start and end of the original string are deleted. These invisible characters can be, for example, space, tab or newline.

4

```
Scanner input   = new Scanner("101 25.0 2006");      // (1)
int     code    = input.nextInt();                   // 101
double salesTax = input.nextDouble();                // 25.0
long    year    = input.nextLong();                  // 2006L
```

Note that the string representation of a floating number is according to the rules of the *locale* for a country. For example, in Norway the decimal character is a comma (,) and not a period (.).

Other useful methods for strings

Table 4.3 on page 87 shows a selection of methods from the String class. The class has many useful methods for creating new String objects, for comparing strings, searching for characters in strings and converting String objects.

If the character index passed to any of the methods in the String class is not a valid index in the interval [0, *n*-1], where *n* is the length of the string, an IndexOutOfBoundsException is thrown. Exceptions signal a runtime error, and are discussed in Chapter 10. Program 4.3 illustrates some of the methods. The statement in (1) is commented out, as a String object can obviously not be compared with an Integer object.

PROGRAM 4.3   Use of miscellaneous **String** methods

```
// Illustrating misc. String methods
public class MiscStringMethods {
  public static void main(String[] args) {
    String group1 = "abba", group2 = "aha";
    int result3 = group2.compareTo(group1);           // > 0
//  int result4 = group2.compareTo(new Integer(10)); // (1) Error!
    if (result3 > 0) // True in this case.
      // "aha" is greater lexicographically.
      System.out.println(group2 + " is greater lexicographically!");
    if (group1.length() > group2.length())            // 4 > 3
      // "abba" is greater in length.
      System.out.println(group1 + " is greater in length!");

    String star = "madonna";
    int strLength = star.length();                    // 7
    System.out.println(star.charAt(strLength-4));     // o (index: 3,
                                                      //    i.e. 4th. char)
    System.out.println(star.indexOf('n'));            // 4
    System.out.println(star.substring(0,3));          // "mad"
  }
}
```

Program output:

```
aha is greater lexicographically!
abba is greater in length!
o
4
mad
```

BEST PRACTICES

Remember that `String` objects are immutable. Operations that seemingly modify a `String` object actually return a new `String` object. Consider using the `StringBuilder` class if string content is modified frequently.

4.3 Manipulating references

A reference value identifies an object in the computer's memory. A Java object can only be referenced by its reference value. When the reference value is stored in a reference variable, we can use the reference variable to manipulate the object.

Reference types and variables

The primitive data types define which values are legal and which operations can be performed on these values. Analogous to a primitive data type, a class defines a data type called a *reference type*. Later in the book we will meet other kinds of reference types.

Assignment to reference variables

Just as an `int` variable can only store values of the `int` data type, a reference variable of a specific reference type can only store reference values of objects of that reference type. Analogous to changing the value in an `int` variable, we can change the reference value stored in a reference variable. In this way, a reference variable can refer to different objects of the same reference type at different times.

Aliases: one object, several references

The same reference value can be assigned to several reference variables. Assignment never copies any object, only the reference value. When a reference value is assigned to several reference variables, these variables are called *aliases* for the object identified by the reference value stored in them. An object can be manipulated by any of its aliases. Figure 4.7 showed that the reference variables `star` and `singer` are aliases for the same `String` object.

The null literal

The literal null is a special reference value that can be assigned to any reference variable. The reference value null indicates that the reference variable does not refer to any object. After assignment of null to a reference, the object previously referred to by the reference will no longer be available via this reference. Program 4.4 shows that a runtime error (NullPointerException) can occur if we use a reference that has the value null.

Comparing objects

In the subsection *String comparison* on page 85 we distinguished between value equality and reference equality for String objects. We can now generalize the discussion about strings to other objects. What does it mean if we say that two cars are equal, or two beers are equal? To compare objects for value equality, the class must provide its own implementation of the equals() method. This method has a special position in Java, and is used for comparing two objects for value equality.

The equals() method must check that it is meaningful to compare the two objects for value equality. For example, there is no obvious reason to compare a car with a beer for value equality, or for that matter, compare a String object with a CD object. As we have seen, the class String implements its own equals() methods for comparing two strings for value equality.

The equality operator == can be used to determine whether two references are aliases, i.e. the operator only compares the reference values stored in the references. See *Aliases: one object, several references* on page 89 for examples of reference equality.

Program 4.4 shows an example of how we can swap reference values in reference variables. Figure 4.8 illustrates the process. To swap values, we need to use an extra reference variable. Note that assignment copies reference values, not objects. The figure also shows which aliases are created as the program executes.

The output from Program 4.4 shows that a reference variable (groupName) with the value null has the string representation "null". During execution the program terminates at (6) with the message that an NullPointerException has occurred. The cause of the error is that we are using the reference groupName, which has the value null, to call the method length() on a non-existent String object.

BEST PRACTICES

Make sure that a reference variable refers to an object before the reference is used. Any alias of the object can be used to manipulate the object.

PROGRAM 4.4   Swapping reference values

```
// Illustrating aliases
public class ReferenceValueSwapping {
  public static void main(String[] args) {
```

```
        String group1 = "abba", group2 = "aha", groupName;      // (1)
        groupName = group1;                                      // (2)
        group1 = group2;                                         // (3)
        group2 = groupName;                                      // (4)
        groupName = null;                                        // (5)
        System.out.println("group1 refers to: " + group1);
        System.out.println("group2 refers to: " + group2);
        System.out.println("groupName refers to: " + groupName);
        System.out.println(groupName.length());                  // (6)
    }
}
```

Program output:

```
group1 refers to: aha
group2 refers to: abba
groupName refers to: null
Exception in thread "main" java.lang.NullPointerException
    at ReferenceSwapping.main(ReferenceSwapping.java:12)
```

FIGURE 4.8   Aliases

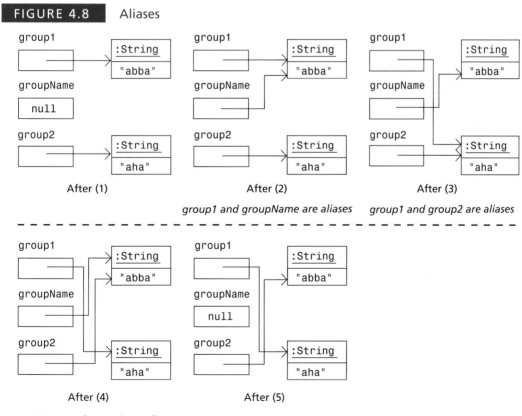

After (1)

group1 and groupName are aliases   *group1 and group2 are aliases*

After (4)   After (5)

groupName and group2 are aliases

4.4 Primitive values as objects

In Java, primitive values are not objects. Java offers *wrapper* classes so that values of primitive data types such as `int` and `double` can be treated as objects. Table 4.4 shows the wrapper classes that can be used to encapsulate primitive values. There is a wrapper class for each primitive data type, and their names make the correspondence between the primitive data types and the wrapper classes clear. Note that the wrapper class for `int` values is called `Integer`.

TABLE 4.4   Wrapper classes for primitive values

Primitive data type	Corresponding wrapper class
boolean	Boolean
char	Character
byte	Byte
short	Short
int	Integer
long	Long
float	Float
double	Double

Auto-boxing

Auto-boxing is the process of automatic conversion from a primitive value to a corresponding wrapper object. Converting from primitive values to objects of the corresponding wrapper class is simple: we specify the primitive value where we want to use the corresponding wrapper object:

```
Integer iRef = 10; // (1) Auto-boxing, 10 is encapsulated in an Integer object.
```

The right-hand side of the assignment operator can be any `int` expression. Its value will be evaluated and automatically encapsulated in an `Integer` object, whose reference value will be assigned to the reference variable on the left-hand side of the declaration.

Auto-unboxing

Auto-unboxing is the process of automatic conversion from a wrapper object to the corresponding primitive value. This process reverses the encapsulating process. We specify the reference to the wrapper object where we want to use the primitive value encapsulated in the wrapper object:

```
int j = iRef;      // (2) Auto-unboxing, j gets the value 10.
```

The right-hand side of the assignment operator can be any expression that evaluates to a reference value of an `Integer` object. The `int` value encapsulated in the `Integer` object will be assigned to the variable on the left-hand side.

Auto-boxing and unboxing work similarly for the other primitive types.

Explicit boxing and unboxing

We can also do explicit conversion between primitive data values and wrapper objects. Wrapper classes have constructors that take a primitive value for encapsulation, and methods to read the value in the wrapper object.

```
Integer iRef = new Integer(10);    // (1) Explicit boxing
int j = iRef.intValue();           // (2) Explicit unboxing
```

The method `intValue()` in the class `Integer` returns the value in the wrapper object as an `int` value. Program 4.5 shows examples of boxing and unboxing.

PROGRAM 4.5   Conversion between a primitive value and an object

```
// Conversions: wrapper <--> primitive value
public class PrimitiveValueWrapper {
  public static void main(String[] args) {
    // A primitive value.
    int valueIn = 2006;

    // Two ways of creating an object from a primitive value:
    Integer valueObject;
    valueObject = new Integer(valueIn);
    valueObject = valueIn;              // Simple variant

    // Two ways of creating a primitive value from an object:
    int valueOut;
    valueOut = valueObject.intValue();
    valueOut = valueObject;            // Simple variant
    assert(valueIn == valueOut);       // Assert: same primitive value
    System.out.println("valueIn: " + valueIn + ", valueOut: " + valueOut);
  }
}
```

Program output:

```
valueIn: 2006, valueOut: 2006
```

Useful methods in the wrapper classes

A selection of methods from the `Integer` class is shown in Table 4.5. The other numerical wrapper classes offer similar methods. Note that wrapper objects are immutable, i.e. we cannot change the primitive value in an wrapper object, only read it.

TABLE 4.5   Selected methods from the **Integer** class

java.lang.Integer	
int intValue()	Returns the value in the wrapper object as an int.
String toString()	Conversion from wrapper object to string. Returns a string representation of the primitive value in the wrapper object.
static String toString(int i)	Conversion from wrapper object to string. Returns a string representation of the int value passed as argument.
static int parseInt(String s)	Conversion from string to primitive value. Interprets a string as an int value. This method accepts strings containing digits and the minus operator (-) only. It throws a NumberFormatException (see Chapter 10) if the string does not represent an int value.

Figure 4.9 shows conversions between an int value, a string and an Integer object. Program 4.6 tests the transitions in Figure 4.9. Case A shows conversion of a string to an Integer object that is further converted to a primitive value, and this value is finally converted back to a string. We have used methods from Table 4.5. During execution of the program, the assertion at (1) tests that the final string is equivalent to the original string. Case B shows the conversion of a string that represents a floating-point number to a primitive value first, followed by a conversion to a wrapper object, and then back to a string. During execution of the program, the assertion at (2) tests that the final string is equivalent to the original string.

PROGRAM 4.6   Conversions between strings, primitive values and wrappers

```
// Conversions: string --> wrapper --> primitive
public class PrimitiveValueRepresentation {
  public static void main(String[] args) {
    String string1, string2;

    // Case A: string --> wrapper --> primitive --> string
    string1 = "2005";
    Integer iWrapper = new Integer(string1);
    int iPrimitive = iWrapper;
    string2 = Integer.toString(iPrimitive);
    assert(string1.equals(string2));  // (1)

    // Case B: string --> primitive --> wrapper --> string
    string1 = "12.5";
    double dPrimitive = Double.parseDouble(string1);
    Double dWrapper = dPrimitive;
    string2 = dWrapper.toString();
    assert(string1.equals(string2));  // (2)
```

```
    }
}
```

FIGURE 4.9   Conversions between strings, primitive values and wrappers

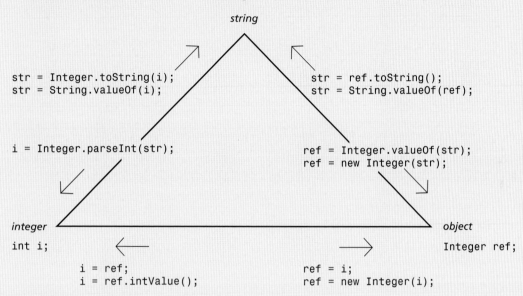

```
                              String str;

                                string
str = Integer.toString(i);                    str = ref.toString();
str = String.valueOf(i);                      str = String.valueOf(ref);



i = Integer.parseInt(str);                    ref = Integer.valueOf(str);
                                              ref = new Integer(str);


integer                                                      object
int i;                                                       Integer ref;
        i = ref;                    ref = i;
        i = ref.intValue();         ref = new Integer(i);
```

4.5 Review questions

1.   A class specifies the _____ and _____ of objects that can be created from the class.

2.   Instance variables represent _____, and instance methods represent the _____ of objects that can be created from a class.

3.   Which statements are true?

     a An object is created from a class.

     b A class creates an object.

     c A reference stores the reference value of an object.

     d A reference stores the reference value of a class.

     e Two objects can be aliases.

     f References that refer to the same object are aliases.

     g References ref1 and ref2 are aliases if (ref1 == ref2) is true.

4.   The following code line will create an object of class CD referred to by the reference myCD. True or false?

```
CD myCD;
```

5. Given the class CD, rewrite the following code lines so that there are no compile time errors.

```
CD cd1 = CD;
CD cd2 = CD();
CD cd3 = new CD;
CD cd4 = new;
new CD cd5;
```

6. How many objects of the class CD exist after the execution of the following statements?

```
CD cd1 = new CD();
Cd cd2 = cd1;
```

7. Given a reference to an object, what notation can we use to call a method or access a field in an object?

8. Given the reference myCD, that refers to a CD object, which expressions are valid?

    a myCD.getTitle()
    b CD.getTitle()
    c myCD.getTitle
    d myCD.title
    e CD.title

9. What is the difference between 'z' and "z"?

10. Assume that we have two references, str1 and str2, that refer to String objects. If (str1 == str2) is true, then str1.equals(str2) is always true. But the converse is not always true. Explain why.

11. What will the following statements print?

```
System.out.println(2000 + 2);      // (1)
System.out.println(2000 + '2');    // (2)

System.out.println(2000 + "2");    // (3)
```

12. Given the following code, which statements will read the double value correctly?

```
Scanner source = new Scanner("3.14");
```

    a double pi = source.getDouble();
    b double pi = source.nextDouble();
    c double pi = source.readDouble();
    d double pi = source.parseDouble();

13. Given the following declarations, which statements will not compile?

```
int iVal;
double dVal;
Integer iRef;
Double dRef;
```

a iRef = 12;

b iVal = iRef;

c dVal = iRef;

d dVal = 12;

e dVal = 12.5;

f dRef = 12;

g dRef = 6 * 2.0;

4.6 Programming exercises

1. Write a program that prints the following pattern:

```
" " " " "
    "
    "
    "
  " "
```

2. Write a program that asks the user for relevant information (indicated by the upper-case words below) in order to print the following horoscope for the user:

```
Expect bad news, NAME.
Your manager, MANAGER, is not happy with WHATEVERYOUDO,
and is planning to move you to the DEPARTMENTNAME department.
Your salary will be reduced by PERCENT%.
But your manager also has a surprise coming: SURPRISE.
```

3. Write a program that reads a line of text from the keyboard, and prints an acronym formed from the first letter of each word.

Example:

```
Enter a line of text: Just another valuable artifact
JAVA
```

4. Write a program that reads a line of text from the keyboard, and prints it back after replacing each occurrence of any four-letter word in the text with the word "x***", where x is the first character in the four-letter word.

Example:

```
Enter a line of text: I love Java very much
I l*** J*** v*** m***
```

5. Write a program that reads a string from the keyboard in which substrings are separated by the character literal '|'. The program should print the substrings in a suitable format. For example, given the string "DOT-COM|IT Place 1|5020|Bergen", the program prints:

```
DOT-COM
IT Place 1
5020
Bergen
```

More on control structures

INTRODUCTION

Loops can be used to execute actions repeatedly. The for(;;) statement allows great flexibility in writing loops, and counter-controlled loops in particular. We discuss how the continue and the break statements change the control flow in a loop, but also caution on their use. These two statements are considered harmful if they are not used with care, as they foster what is colloquially known as *spaghetti code*, i.e. code with many control flow paths that is difficult to comprehend. We also discuss common pitfalls when writing loops, such as unintentional infinite loops and one-off errors.

The simple if statement and the if-else statement limit the number of selections. We discuss the switch statement, which allows multiple selections to be specified. We give examples of different scenarios of control flow through the switch statement. In particular, we discuss how the break statement affects the control flow in a switch statement. While the break statement is best avoided in loops, it allows us to control the program execution in a switch statement.

5.1 The extended assignment operators

A very common operation is computing the new value for a variable based on its old value, as in the following assignment:

```
x = x + (y);                           // (1)
```

The variable x occurs as an operand for a binary operator (in this case +) on the right-hand side of the assignment operator (=), where (y) is any valid expression, and the result of the binary operation is assigned to the variable x. In such a case, we can use the *extended assignment operator*:

```
x += (y);                              // (2)
```

The assignment statement (2) is equivalent to assignment statement (1), where += is an extended assignment operator. Note that there is no space between the + operator and the = operator.

Java provides a number of such extended assignment operators that combine arithmetic operations with assignment. Program 5.1 illustrates the use of such operators.

PROGRAM 5.1   Using extended assignment operators

```java
// Illustrating use of extended assignment operators
public class ExtendedAssignmentOperators {

  public static void main(String[] args) {
    int i = 5, j = 10;
    double x = 5.0, y = 10.5, z = 10.0;
    i += j;                // i = i + (j)
    x -= y + 30.5;         // x = x - (y + 30.5)
    j *= i + 20;           // j = j * (i + 20)
    y /= 5.0;              // y = y / (5.0)
    z %= 3.0;              // z = z % (3.0)
    System.out.println("i : " + i);
    System.out.println("x : " + x);
    System.out.println("j : " + j);
    System.out.println("y : " + y);
    System.out.println("z : " + z);
  }
}
```

Program output:

```
i : 15
x : -36.0
j : 350
y : 2.1
z : 1.0
```

5.2 The increment and decrement operators

Very often we need to increment the value in a variable by 1. Both the following assignments can be used for this purpose:

```
x = x + 1;            // (1)
x += 1;               // (2)
```

To increment by 1, we can also use the *increment operator*:

```
x++;                  // (3) The value in x is incremented by 1.
```

The statement in (3) achieves the same result as the statements in (1) and (2): the value in x is incremented by 1.

We can use the *decrement operator* to decrement the value in a variable by 1:

```
x--;                  // (4) The value in x is decremented by 1.
```

The increment and decrement operators come in two flavours, as *pre* (++x and --x) and as *post* (x++ and x--) *operators*, i.e. as prefix and postfix to the operand. It does not matter which form we use in the examples above but, as Program 5.2 shows, one should be careful when expressions such as x++ and x-- are used as operands in other expressions.

In Program 5.2 the value of the variable i is incremented by 1 in (1) and (2), but the value that is assigned to the variable j is different. The reason for this difference is that the pre-increment operator ++ in the expression (++i) adds one to the value of i, and returns the *new* value as the value of the expression (++i). On the other hand, the post-increment operator ++ in the expression (i++) returns the *current* value of i as the value of the expression (i++), but it also increments the value of i by 1.

The side-effect of both pre- and post-increment operators is to increment the value in its operand by 1. The pre- and post-decrement operators behave analogously, but decrement the value of the operand by 1. If we are only interested in the side-effect of these operators, as in (3) and (4) above, then it is irrelevant whether we use the pre- or the post-form.

5

PROGRAM 5.2 Using increment and decrement operators

```java
// Illustrating use of increment and decrement operators
public class IncrAndDecrOperators {

  public static void main(String[] args) {
    int i = 10, j;
    j = i++; // (1) Postfix: j gets the value 10, and i gets the value 11
    System.out.println("j : " + j + " and i: " + i);
    i = 10;
    j = ++i; // (2) Prefix: j gets the value 11, and i gets the value 11
    System.out.println("j : " + j + " and i: " + i);
  }
}
```

Program output:

```
j : 10 and i: 11
j : 11 and i: 11
```

5.3 Counter-controlled loops

The while statement is suitable for implementing *conditional loops* in which the number of times the loop should iterate is not known. However, there are situations in which the number of iterations is known beforehand. Such loops are called *counter-controlled loops*, as we use a counter to repeat the loop an exact number of times. In Java, the for(;;) statement is specifically designed to implement counter-controlled loops.

Figure 5.1a illustrates the syntax of the for(;;) loop. The loop consists of a *loop header* and a *loop body*. Inside the loop header we specify the three parts: *initialization, loop condition* and *updating*. In Figure 5.1a, the loop body comprises a *statement block*, but it can also be a single statement without the block notation, {}.

The initialization part declares a loop variable (i) and assigns a *start value* (1) to it. The loop variable i acts as the counter for the number of times the loop is executed. As can be expected, the initialization is only executed once, to declare and initialize the loop variable. The value of the loop variable i is compared to a *final value* (5) in the loop condition (i <= 5). If the condition is true, the loop body is executed, otherwise the loop terminates and execution continues after the for(;;) loop statement. Immediately after the execution of the loop body, the loop variable is incremented in the updating part (i++) to keep track of the number of iterations executed so far. After updating the loop variable, the loop condition is always tested.

Updating the loop variable means that at some point the loop condition will become false. As long as the loop condition is true, the loop body is executed one more time. The execution of the for(;;) loop is illustrated in Figure 5.2.

FIGURE 5.1

The `for(;;)` loop syntax

1: Initialisation 2: loop condition 4: Updating

loop header

```
for ( int i = 1; i <= 5; i++ ) {
```

3: loop body

```
System.out.println(i + "\t\t" + (i*i));
```

```
}
```

(a) `for(;;)` Loop Syntax

1: Initialisation

```
int i = 1;
```

2: loop condition

```
while ( i <= 5 ) {
```

3: loop body

```
System.out.println(i + "\t\t" + (i*i));
```

4: Updating

```
i++;
```

```
}
```

(b) Equivalent `while` Loop

FIGURE 5.2
Executing the `for(;;)` loop

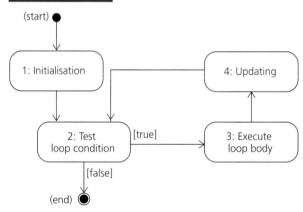

The `for(;;)` loop in Figure 5.1a is executed five times, printing the squares of the numbers from 1 to 5 in the terminal window:

```
1        1
2        4
3        9
4        16
5        25
```

After five iterations, the loop variable i has the value 6, and the loop condition evaluates to false. The loop thus terminates after the desired number of iterations.

The `for(;;)` loop in Figure 5.1a is shown in Figure 5.1b coded as a `while` loop. Note that in Figure 5.1b the initialization is executed only once before the `while` statement. The updating of the loop variable is always done *after* the execution of the loop body. The loop body is skipped entirely if the loop condition is `false` at the start of the loop. That is the reason why the `for(;;)` loop is a *pretest loop*.

If the loop condition is not formulated properly, we can risk it never becoming `false` and the loop never terminating (called *infinite loop*). Care must be taken not to change the value of the loop variable in the loop body, as this might result in the loop not iterating the correct number of times.

Program 5.3 uses a `for(;;)` loop to spell out a phone number in words. The telephone number is read as a string from the keyboard at (1). Each character in the string (`input-PhoneString`) represents a digit in the phone number.

A `for(;;)` statement at (2) is used to iterate over the input string `inputPhoneString`. The loop body is executed for values from 0 to n-1, where n is the length of the input string. The loop condition (`i < inputPhoneString.length()`) ensures that the loop terminates when the value in the loop variable `i` is equal to the value returned by the method call `inputPhoneString.length()`, i.e. n.

For each iteration of the loop, an `if` statement translates one character to the corresponding word. The words are concatenated into a string (`outputPhoneString`) as the input string is processed, and the resulting string is printed out after the loop terminates. Note that the variable `outputPhoneString` will refer to a new `String` object after each concatenation operation.

PROGRAM 5.3   Use of the `for(;;)` statement

```java
import java.util.Scanner;
// Program spells out a telephone number: if statement version
public class Telephone {
  public static void main(String[] args) {
    System.out.print("Enter the telephone number (as 55584152): ");
    Scanner keyboard = new Scanner(System.in);
    String inputPhoneString = keyboard.next(); // (1)
    String outputPhoneString = "";
    for (int i = 0; i < inputPhoneString.length(); i++) { // (2)
      char aChar = inputPhoneString.charAt(i);
      if (aChar == '1') {
        outputPhoneString += "one ";
      } else if (aChar == '2') {
        outputPhoneString += "two ";
      } else if (aChar == '3') {
        outputPhoneString += "three ";
      } else if (aChar == '4') {
        outputPhoneString += "four ";
      } else if (aChar == '5') {
        outputPhoneString += "five ";
      } else if (aChar == '6') {
        outputPhoneString += "six ";
      } else if (aChar == '7') {
        outputPhoneString += "seven ";
```

```
    } else if (aChar == '8') {
      outputPhoneString += "eight ";
    } else if (aChar == '9') {
      outputPhoneString += "nine ";
    } else if (aChar == '0') {
      outputPhoneString += "zero ";
    } else {
      System.out.println(aChar + " is not a digit!");
    }
  }
  System.out.println(outputPhoneString);
  }
}
```

Program output:

```
Enter the telephone number (as 55584152): 55584152
five five five eight four one five two
```

Local variables in the for(;;) loop

We have described a simple form of the for(;;) statement for counter-controlled loops, in which a loop variable is first declared and initialized, and subsequently updated, so that the loop condition eventually becomes false, resulting in the loop being terminated. The initialization in Figure 5.1a contains a *declaration* for the variable i. A variable that is declared in the initialization part of the loop header or in the loop body can only be used in the for(;;) loop, as they are local variables and therefore not accessible outside the loop. The code below shows that the local variables j and m are not accessible outside the for(;;) loop:

```
for (int j = 1; j <= 5; j++) {
  int m = 20;
  System.out.println(j + "\t" + (j*m));
}
System.out.println("j has the value: " + j); // Compile time error!
System.out.println("m has the value: " + m); // Compile time error!
```

If we need to access the values of the variables j and m outside the loop, we can declare them before the loop, as shown at (1) in the code below. Note that the initialization part of the loop header at (2) is now an assignment to initialize the variable j to the start value. The type declaration is omitted, as the loop variable is already declared outside the loop. Note also that the value of the loop variable j is 6 (and not 5) after the termination of the loop.

```
int j, m;                                    // (1)
for (j = 1; j <= 5; j++) {                    // (2)
  m = 20;
  System.out.println(j + "\t" + (j*m));
}
System.out.println("j has the value: " + j); // Prints "6"
System.out.println("m has the value: " + m); // Prints "20"
```

Other increments in `for(;;)` loops

We are not limited to increments of 1 in the updating part of the for(;;) loop. We can specify other increments using extended assignment operators. The code at (2) in Program 5.4 will only print the squares of odd numbers from 1 to 5. The loop variable i is initialized to the start value 1, and incremented by 2 after each iteration of the loop. The loop terminates when the value of the loop variable i is 7. Care must be taken not only to initialize and increment the loop variable correctly, but also to ensure that the loop condition is formulated correctly.

Counting backwards with `for(;;)` loops

We can also write for(;;) loops that count backwards. The code at (3) in Program 5.4 illustrates how to write such a loop. The start value (10) is greater than the final value (0), so that the loop condition (i > 0) becomes false when the loop variable i gets the value 0. We use the decrement operator -- to decrease the value of the loop variable i by 1 after each iteration of the loop.

Nested `for(;;)` loops

The loop body can also be a for(;;) loop, as it is a statement. We then have *nested* for(;;) loops. The code at (4) in Program 5.4 uses two nested for(;;) loops to print the multiplication tables from 1 to 5. The outer loop runs from 1 to 5, and the inner loop runs from 1 to 10. This means that for each iteration of the outer loop, the inner loop is executed ten times, resulting in the inner loop being executed altogether fifty times (5 × 10). This also means that the value of the loop variable in the inner loop changes more frequently than the value of the loop variable in the outer loop.

| PROGRAM 5.4 | Several examples using the `for(;;)` statement |

```
// Illustrating various uses of the for(;;) loop
public class ForExamples {
  public static void main(String[] args) {

    // (1) Simple for loop
    // Print the square of numbers from 1 to 5.
    System.out.println("Square of numbers from 1 to 5");
    for (int i = 1; i <= 5; i++) {
      System.out.println(i + "\t\t" + (i*i));
    }

    // (2) Increment by other than 1
    // Print the square of odd numbers from 1 to 5.
    System.out.println("Square of odd numbers from 1 to 5");
    for (int i = 1; i <= 5; i += 2) {
      System.out.println(i + "\t\t" + (i*i));
    }

    // (3) "Backwards" for loop
    // Print the square of numbers from 5 to 1.
```

```
System.out.println("Square of numbers from 5 to 1");
for (int i = 5; i > 0; i--) {
  System.out.println(i + "\t\t" + (i * i));
}

// (4) Nested for loops
// Print the multiplication tables from 1 to 5.
for (int i = 1; i <= 5; i++) {
  System.out.println("Multiplication table for " + i);
  for (int j = 1; j <= 10 ; j++) {
    System.out.printf("%2d x %2d = %2d%n", i, j, (i*j));
  }
}
}
}
```

Program output:

```
Square of numbers from 1 to 5
1    1
2    4
3    9
4    16
5    25
Square of odd numbers from 1 to 5
1    1
3    9
5    25
Square of numbers from 5 to 1
5    25
4    16
3    9
2    4
1    1
Multiplication table for 1
 1 x  1 =  1
...
Multiplication table for 2
 2 x  1 =  2
...
Multiplication table for 3
 3 x  1 =  3
...
Multiplication table for 4
 4 x  1 =  4
...
Multiplication table for 5
 5 x  1 =  5
...
```

5

5.4 Changing control flow in loops

The break and the continue statements in Java have special significance when they are executed in any loop (while, do-while and for loops). These statements change the normal execution of a loop that we have discussed so far.

The **break** statement

Execution of the break statement in a loop body results in the rest of the loop body being skipped and the loop terminated: execution continues after the loop. Program 5.5 demonstrates the execution of a break statement in the body of the for(;;) loop at (1). When the value of the loop variable i becomes 4, the break statement at (3) in the if statement at (2) is executed. The remaining statement (4) in the loop body is skipped and the loop terminated, and execution continues at (5), after the loop.

A loop terminates when the loop condition becomes false. Using a break statement in a loop introduces another exit from the loop, and can make the program *unstructured*, i.e. difficult to understand, with all the problems that can entail. The code below shows a simple technique that can be used to ensure that exit is always from one place in the loop: through the testing of the loop condition. It introduces a flag variable (done) that is initialized to false (1) and always tested *first* in the loop condition (2), effectively making sure that the loop is not executed if the flag variable is false. An if-else statement (3) is used to set the flag variable and to control which statements are executed in each iteration of the loop body.

```
boolean done = false;                                    // (1)
for (int i = 1; !done && i <= 5; i++) {                   // (2)
   if (i == 4) {                                          // (3)
      System.out.println("Terminates the loop when i is equal to " + i);
      done = true;
   } else
      System.out.println(i + "\t\t" + (i * i));
}
```

The **continue** statement

Execution of the continue statement in a loop body results in the rest of the loop body being skipped. What happens next depends on the loop statement. In a while-loop execution will continue with the testing of the loop condition, but in a for(;;) loop execution will continue with the updating of the loop variable.

Program 5.5 demonstrates the execution of a continue statement in the body of the for(;;) loop at (6). When the value of the loop variable i becomes 3, the continue statement at (8) in the if statement at (7) is executed. The remaining statement (9) in the loop body is skipped, and execution continues normally with updating of the loop variable at (6).

PROGRAM 5.5   Using **break** and **continue** statements in a **for(;;)** loop

```java
// Illustrating use of break and continue statements
public class BreakAndContinue {
  public static void main(String[] args) {

    // for loop with a break statement.
    System.out.println("Square of numbers from 1 to 5");
    for (int i = 1; i <= 5; i++) {                          // (1)
      if (i == 4) {                                         // (2)
        System.out.println("Terminates the loop when i is equal to " + i);
        break;                                              // (3)
      }
      // Never executed when i == 4, as the loop terminates.
      System.out.println(i + "\t\t" + (i * i));             // (4)
    }

    // for loop with a continue statement.
    System.out.println("Square of numbers from 1 to 5");    // (5)
    for (int i = 1; i <= 5; i++) {                          // (6)
      if (i == 3) {                                         // (7)
        System.out.println("Skips rest of the loop body" +
                           " when i is equal to " + i);
        continue;                                           // (8)
      }
      // Skipped when i == 3, otherwise executed.
      System.out.println(i + "\t\t" + (i * i));             // (9)
    }
  }
}
```

Program output:

```
Square of numbers from 1 to 5
1    1
2    4
3    9
Terminates the loop when i is equal to 4
Square of numbers from 1 to 5
1    1
2    4
Skips rest of the loop body when i is equal to 3
4    16
5    25
```

5.5 Common pitfalls in loops

Infinite loop: `for(;;)`

Initialization and updating can be omitted in a for(;;) loop. The for(;;) loop then executes like a while loop, as only the loop condition is specified in the loop header. However, the loop condition can also be omitted, but this can have major consequences for the execution of the loop. Omitting the loop condition in a for(;;) loop means that the test to execute the loop body is always true, effectively creating an infinite loop:

```
for (;;) {  // Always true
    System.out.println("Stop! I want to get off!");
}
```

A break statement can seem to offer a solution for terminating a loop that omits the loop condition, but as we have shown in the previous section, the program logic can be expressed effectively without the break statement, by formulating an appropriate loop condition for the loop.

One-off errors

A common type of programming error is a *one-off error*, i.e. the loop body is executed either one more or one less time than the correct number of iterations. Say we wish to add all the even numbers up to and including 10. In the code below we have a one-off error: the loop executes one less time than required. The start value of the variable counter is 2 and it is incremented by 2, therefore the value in the variable counter is always an even number. When the variable counter reaches 10, the loop condition (counter < 10) becomes false, and the loop terminates without adding the value 10. Changing the loop condition to (counter <= 10) remedies the situation.

```
int result = 0;
for (int counter = 2; counter < 10; counter += 2) {
    result += counter;
}
```

Errors in initialization

The loop variable is often not initialized correctly. In the code below, the variable result is initialized to 0. Its value does not change after the execution of the loop body. The loop condition remains true in the do-while loop. Most probably the variable should have been initialized to 1.

```
result = 0;
do {
  result *= 2;            // Always 0
} while (result < 100); // Infinite loop
```

Errors in the loop condition

It is important to make sure that the loop condition is formulated correctly. In the code below, since the start value is one and the variable counter is incremented by 2, the final value of counter is never 100, so that the loop can terminate. The loop condition (counter <= 100) would at least terminate the loop.

```
result = 0;
for (int counter = 1; counter != 100; counter += 2) {
  result += counter;
} // Infinite loop!
```

Optimizing loops

A loop body can be executed repeatedly. To a large extent, program execution time is dependent on how many times the statements in a loop body are executed. If we can make loop execution more effective, we can improve the execution time of the program. One source for such *optimisations* is computations in the loop that do not change value during execution, i.e. they have a constant value. Such computations are called *loop invariants*. By moving such computations out of the loop, we can reduce the execution time of the program.

```
double pi = 3.14;
for (double r = 0.0; r < 100.0; r++) {
  System.out.println("Radius: " + r +
                 ", Circumference: " + (2.0 * pi * r));
  // (2.0 * pi) does not change in the loop, and can be moved out of the loop
}
```

In the code above, the expression 2.0 * pi is calculated during each iteration, even though its value does not change during the execution of the loop. The expression 2.0 * pi is thus a loop invariant. We can move its computation out of the loop, so that we compute it just once and store it in a new variable (factor), as shown below. This variable can be used in the loop instead of the loop invariant.

```
double pi = 3.14;
double factor = 2.0 * pi;
for (double r = 0.0; r < 100.0; r++) {
  System.out.println("Radius: " + r + ", Circumference: " + (factor * r));
}
```

5.6 Multiple-selection statements

An if statement allows a single action to be selected and an if-else statement allows one of two actions to be selected, based on the value of a boolean expression. The switch statement allows one of many actions to be selected, based on the value of an expression. Figure 5.3 illustrates the form of a switch statement. The switch header specifies the switch expression, which in Figure 5.3 is the variable adviceNumber. The switch block specifies a list of case labels. Figure 5.3 shows three case labels. Each case label has a unique value and a corresponding action. Each action can be a sequence of statements. In Figure 5.3 the values of the three case labels are 1, 2 and 3.

During execution, the value of the switch expression is compared to the value of each case label in turn. If the value of the switch expression is equal to the value of a case label, the corresponding action is executed. If the value of the adviceNumber variable is 2 in Figure 5.3, the action corresponding to the case label with the value 2 is executed. The action in this case is a sequence of statements comprising a call to the method println() and a break statement. The call prints the string "See no evil!" in the terminal window, and the break statement transfers program control to *after* the switch statement. A break statement in a switch statement always skips the rest of the switch statement, terminating the execution of the switch statement.

FIGURE 5.3   Multiple selection statement: **switch**

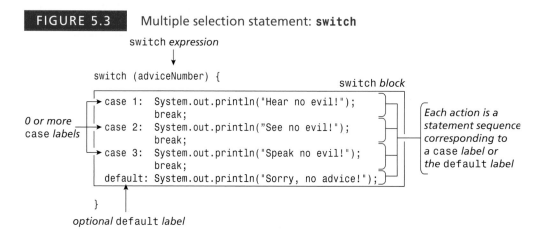

The **default** label

Figure 5.4 illustrates the execution of a switch statement. If no case label has the same value as the switch expression, the action corresponding to the default label is executed. The default label is optional in a switch statement. If no case label value is found and no default label is specified, the switch statement is skipped. If the value of the adviceNumber variable is 4 in Figure 5.3, the action corresponding to the default label is executed. This action is a call to the method println() to print the string "Sorry, no advice!". As this is the last statement in the switch block, program execution continues after the switch statement.

The default label and any other case labels can be specified in any order in a switch statement. The convention is to specify the case labels in increasing order of their values, and to specify the default label last.

BEST PRACTICES

In a switch statement, the convention is to specify the case labels in increasing order of their values, and to specify the default label last. Always include the default label, as it can help to catch errors in the program.

FIGURE 5.4   Executing **switch** statement

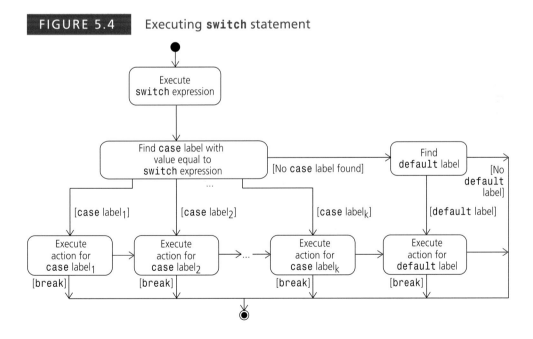

The **case** label values

The value of a case label is a *constant expression* that the compiler can evaluate. The values for the case labels must also be unique. The type of the value must be integer, including char, but not long. Boolean and floating-point values are also not permitted for case labels, and neither are string literals. In a later chapter we will see how constant values defined by enumerated types can be used as case label values (see *Enumerated types* on page 192).

The type of the case label value must be compatible with the type of the switch expression for their values to be compared for *equality*. This is in contrast to an if statement, in which the condition is an arbitrary boolean expression.

Program 5.6 is a new version of Program 5.3 to spell out a phone number, in which a switch statement is used instead of an if statement. The type of the case label values is char. Each case label translates a digit. The corresponding action ends with a break statement to terminate the switch statement after a digit is processed.

Variables declared in a switch block cannot be used outside the block. If you need to access a local variable outside the block, the variable must be declared before the switch statement. In Program 5.6, the variable outputPhoneString is an example of such a variable.

PROGRAM 5.6   Using a **switch** statement

```java
import java.util.Scanner;
// Program spells out a telephone number: switch statement version
public class TelephoneII {
  public static void main(String[] args) {
    System.out.print("Enter the telephone number (as 55584152): ");
    Scanner keyboard = new Scanner(System.in);
    String inputPhoneString = keyboard.next();
    String outputPhoneString = "";
    for (int i = 0; i < inputPhoneString.length(); i++) {
      char aChar = inputPhoneString.charAt(i);
      switch (aChar) {
        case '1':
          outputPhoneString += "one ";
          break;
        case '2':
          outputPhoneString += "two ";
          break;
        case '3':
          outputPhoneString += "three ";
          break;
        case '4':
          outputPhoneString += "four ";
          break;
        case '5':
          outputPhoneString += "five ";
          break;
        case '6':
          outputPhoneString += "six ";
          break;
        case '7':
          outputPhoneString += "seven ";
```

```
        break;
      case '8':
        outputPhoneString += "eight ";
        break;
      case '9':
        outputPhoneString += "nine ";
        break;
      case '0':
        outputPhoneString += "zero ";
        break;
      default:
        System.out.println(aChar + " is not a digit!");
    } // end switch
  } // end for
  System.out.println(outputPhoneString);
  }
}
```

Program output:

```
Enter the telephone number (as 55584152): 55584152
five five five eight four one five two
```

Falling through case labels

We need not use the block notation, [], to enclose the sequence of statements for an action corresponding to a case label. Enclosing these statements in a block does *not* affect the control flow in a switch statement. However, the execution of a break statement as part of an action has a profound effect on the control flow in a switch statement: as we have seen, it terminates the switch statement. If a break statement is not the last statement that is executed for an action, execution can continue with the next action that is specified. In other words, unless a statement transfers control elsewhere, control will "fall through" to subsequent statements, regardless of whether they have a label or not. Note also that a break statement is not part of the syntax for a switch statement.

```
final int YES = 1;
final int NO = 0;
int whatToDo;
...
switch(whatToDo) {
  case YES:
    System.out.print("Falling ");
  case NO:
    System.out.print("through. ");
  default:
    System.out.println("Come on down.");
}
```

In the code above, if the value of the variable whatToDo is 1, the following is printed:

```
Falling through. Come on down.
```

If the value of the variable whatToDo is 0, the following is printed:

```
through. Come on down.
```

For any other integer value in the variable whatToDo, only the string "Come on down." is printed.

A consequence of falling through case labels is that several case labels can share the same action. Program 5.7 illustrates this special case. The program prints the season depending on the month of the year. Since it is winter during December, January and February (at least in some parts of the World), case labels with corresponding month numbers 12, 1 and 2 have the same action: print the string "It's winter.".

PROGRAM 5.7 Common action for case labels in a **switch** statement

```
import java.util.Scanner;
public class Seasons {
  public static void main(String[] args) {
    System.out.print("Enter a month number [1-12]: ");
    Scanner keyboard = new Scanner(System.in);
    int monthNumber = keyboard.nextInt();
    switch (monthNumber) {
      case 12: case 1: case 2:// Common action for several case labels
        System.out.println("It's winter!");
        break;
      case 3: case 4: case 5:
        System.out.println("It's spring!");
        break;
      case 6: case 7: case 8:
        System.out.println("It's summer!");
        break;
      case 9: case 10: case 11:
        System.out.println("It's autumn!");
        break;
      default:
        System.out.println(monthNumber + " is not a valid month number!");
    } // end switch
  }
}
```

Program output:

```
Enter a month number [1-12]: 4
It's spring!
```

Judicious use of the `break` statement to terminate the actions for a `case` label helps to prevent unintentional fall through in a `switch` statement.

5.7 Review questions

1. What are the four statements in Java that we can use to increment the value in an integer variable i by 1?

2. What will the following code print?

   ```
   int counter = 4;
   System.out.println(counter++);
   System.out.println(++counter);
   System.out.println(counter--);
   System.out.println(--counter);
   System.out.println(counter);
   ```

3. If the number of iterations is known in advance, would you choose a `for(;;)` loop or a `while` loop?

4. Which part (initialization, loop condition, updating) in the `for(;;)` loop header can be omitted?

5. Which statements are true about the `for(;;)` loop? Assume that the loop body does not execute any statement that transfers control out of the loop.

   a Initialization is done once.

   b Loop condition is tested at least once.

   c Loop body is executed at least once.

   d If the loop body is executed, the updating and the loop condition are always executed.

6. Rewrite the following code using a `for(;;)` loop. How many times is the loop body executed?

   ```
   int i = 10, sum = 0;
   while (i >= 5) {
      sum += i;
      i -= 2;
   }
   ```

7. What is the value of the variable i after the execution of the `for(;;)` loop? How many times does the loop body execute?

   ```
   a int i;
      for (i = 0; i < 10; i += 2)
   ```

```
       System.out.println(i);
```

b
```
for (int i = 0; i < 10; i += 3)
       System.out.println(i);
```

8. Which `for(;;)` loops can be used to print the string `"Move it!"` three times in the terminal window?

   a
```
for (int i = 1; i <= 3; i++);
       System.out.println("Move it!");
```

   b
```
for (int i = 1; i <= 3; i++)
       System.out.println("Move it!");
```

9. Which statements are true about nested `for(;;)` loops?

   a The outer loop completes all its iterations for every iteration of the inner loop.

   b The inner loop completes all its iterations for every iteration of the outer loop.

   c The total number of times the inner loop executes is the product of the number of times each outer loop is executed.

   d The total number of times the inner loop executes is the sum of the number of times each outer loop is executed.

10. Which statements are true about the `switch` statement?

    a A `default` label must always be included in a `switch` statement.

    b Boolean values and floating-point values cannot be specified as `case` labels.

    c A string literal can be specified as a `case` label.

    d A `break` statement is part of the `switch` statement.

11. Rewrite the following code using a `switch` statement:

```
if (i == 10 || i == 20)
   System.out.println("10 or 20");
else if (i == 15)
   System.out.println("15");
else
   System.out.println("Not valid");
```

12. Which `switch` statements will not compile? If so, explain why not. Assume the following declarations:

```
int result = 100, finalValue = 12;
char letter = 'k';
boolean flag = false;
String msg = "";
```

   a
```
switch(result) {
   case 100:
      msg = "Falling ";
   case 200:
      msg += "through";
```

```
    }

b  switch(letter) {
     case 'O': case 'o':
       System.out.println("O");
       break;
     case 'K': case 'k':
       System.out.println("K");
       break;
   }

c  switch(finalValue) {
     default:
       System.out.println("Not ok");
       break;
     case 100:
       System.out.println("Ok");
   }

d  switch(flag) {
     case true:
       System.out.println("It's true.");
       break;
     case false:
       System.out.println("It's false.");
       break;
     default:
       assert false: "Can never happen.";
   }

e  switch(finalValue % 2) {
     case 1:
       System.out.println("Odd");
       break;
     case 0:
       System.out.println("Even");
       break;
     default:
       assert false: "Can never happen.";
   }

f  switch(finalValue / 2.0) {
     case 5:
       System.out.println("Accepted");
       break;
     default:
       System.out.println("Rejected");
   }

g  switch(result > 0) {
     case 5: case 10:
       System.out.println("Too low");
```

```
        break;
    case 30: case 5:
        System.out.println("Too high");
}
```

5.8 Programming exercises

1. Write a program that prints the even numbers from 1 to 100. Use a `for(;;)` loop.

2. Write a program that prints the even numbers from 1 to 100 backwards. Use a `for(;;)` loop that counts backwards.

3. Write a program that asks the user for a string and then prints how many times the first character occurs in the string. Use a `for(;;)` loop to solve the problem.

    Example:

    ```
    Enter a string: hahaha
    The letter 'h' occurs 3 times.
    ```

4. Write a program that reads a sentence (i.e. a line of input) from the keyboard and reports the number of lowercase and uppercase letters in the input.

    Example:

    ```
    Enter your sentence: BIG MOUTH, small feet.
    Number of lowercase characters: 9
    Number of uppercase characters: 8
    Number of lowercase characters is greater than the number of
    uppercase characters.
    ```

5. A *palindrome* is a string that has identical character sequence regardless of whether you read it backwards or forwards. For example, "aha", "abba" and "00700" are all palindromes according to this definition. The string can have several words, and you can choose to ignore the spaces between the words if you wish. For example, "roma amor" is a palindrome. Write a program that reports whether a line of input read from the keyboard is a palindrome. Use a `for(;;)` loop for this purpose.

6. Write a program that reads two values from the keyboard. The numbers represent an interval on the Celsius temperature scale. The program prints the values in the corresponding interval on the Fahrenheit temperature scale. Use the following formula, where fTemp and cTemp represent the temperature in degrees Fahrenheit and Celsius, respectively:

    ```
    fTemp = (9.0/5.0) * cTemp + 32.0;
    ```

    Example:

    ```
    Enter the interval for degrees Celsius: 10.0 100.00
    Celsius      Fahrenheit
      10.0          50.0
      11.0          51.8
    ```

```
    . . .              . . .
    99.0              210.2
   100.0              212.0
```

7. Write a program that computes the *factorial* of an integer, i.e. $n! = n \times (n-1)! = 1 \times 2 \times 3 \times 4 \times \ldots \times (n-1) \times n$, where $n > 0$. What is the largest value of n that your program works correctly for?

8. Embed the `switch` statement from Figure 5.3 in a loop to give advice to the user. The program reads the advice number from the keyboard.

9. Rewrite the `switch` statement in Program 5.7, using an `if` statement.

10. Write a program that gives change in notes and coins. UN currency comprises UN dollars (UND) and cents. This fictitious currency has notes for the following denominations: 1000 UND, 500 UND, 200 UND, 100 UND, and 50 UND. There are coins for 20 UND, 10 UND, 5 UND, 1 UND, and 50 cents (100 cents equals 1 UND).

An amount that is less than 25 cents is rounded down to 0 cents. An amount greater than or equal to 25 cents, but less than 75 cents, is rounded to 50 cents. Lastly, an amount greater than 75 cents, but less than 1 UND, is rounded up to 1 UND.

The program always tries to give change such that notes and coins delivered always have the highest possible denomination. For example, 5732.60 UND give the following change:

```
Number of 1000 UND notes: 1
Number of 500 UND notes: 1
Number of 200 UND notes: 1
Number of 20 UND coins: 1
Number of 10 UND coins: 1
Number of 1 UND coins: 2
Number of 50 cents coins: 1
```

5

Arrays

INTRODUCTION

We often need to organize values so that they can be processed as a group, a unit or a collection. Such an organisation of values is called a *data structure*. An array is a simple form of data structure. For example, we can create an array to store the number of text messages sent each day of the week from a mobile phone. This array would collectively represent the weekly figures for the number of text messages sent from a mobile phone. Such an array would hold seven integers, one for each day of the week, indicating the number of text messages sent on a particular day. How would one find in such an array, for example, the number of messages sent on Wednesday for a given week? Or the total of text messages sent during the week? To answer such questions, we first have to look at the properties of arrays.

Finally in this chapter we discuss pseudo-random numbers. As an example we simulate the throwing of two dice, and storing the frequency of each throw value in an array.

6.1 Arrays as data structures

An *array* is a fixed-length sequence of elements in which all elements have the same type. An array is thus a data structure that has a fixed *length*, indicating the number of values that can be stored in the array. Each *array element* can store a value. The type of the elements is called the *(array) element type*. Since an array is a sequence, it means that the elements are numbered. Their position in the array is given by a position number, called the *index*. Positions in an array are always numbered from 0 upwards. The lowest index, 0, indicates the position of the first element, and if the length of the array is *n*, the last element in the array has index *n-1*. Figure 6.1 illustrates an array.

FIGURE 6.1   An array

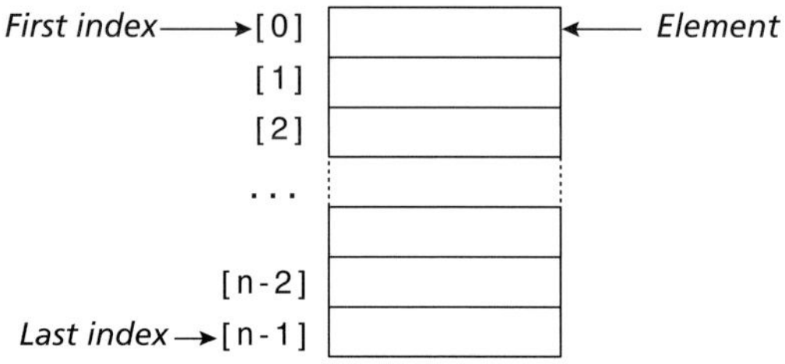

First index ⟶ [0] ⟵ Element
[1]
[2]
. . .
[n-2]
Last index ⟶ [n-1]

An array of length n

In our example of an array for recoding the number of text messages sent from a mobile phone for each day of the week, the array length is 7 as there are seven days in a week, and the element type is int, as we want to store an integer representing the number of text messages sent from a mobile phone. If we decide that index 0 indicates the element with the text messages sent on the first day of the week (for example Monday), then index 2 indicates the element with the number of text messages sent on Wednesday.

An array with integers that represent the number of text messages sent for each day of the week is an example of an array with values of a primitive data type, in this case int. We can create arrays of integers, floating-point numbers, characters and Boolean values. The element type in each case is a specific primitive data type.

We can also create *arrays of objects*. Elements in such an array are thus references to objects, and the element type is a reference type (for example, a specific class). Note that the array does not actually contain the objects, only references to objects. Arrays are themselves objects in Java, and since array elements can be references to objects, we can create *arrays of arrays*, i.e. arrays in which the elements are references to other arrays.

In the rest of the chapter we look at how arrays can be *declared, created, initialized* and *used* in Java.

6

6.2 Creating and using arrays

Declaring array reference variables

An *array reference variable* is a reference that can only refer to objects that are arrays. In a reference declaration we have to specify the reference type. For arrays, the reference type is specified using brackets, [], and is called the *array type*. For example, we can declare the following array reference variable noOfTextMessages that can refer to an array of integers:

```
int[] noOfTextMessages;
```

Note that without the brackets, the name noOfTextMessages would be declared as a variable of type int, and not a variable of an array type.

The declaration above does *not* create any array. It only declares that the reference noOfTextMessages can refer to an array. The array type is int[], and the element type is int. No array length is specified either. The declaration says that the reference noOfTextMessages can refer to an arbitrary array as long as its element type is int, regardless of the length of the array.

Creating arrays

We used the new operator, together with a constructor call, to create objects from classes. We also use the new operator to create an array, but we must specify the element type and the desired array length:

```
noOfTextMessages = new int[7]; // An array to store 7 int values.
```

The expression on the right-hand side creates an array that can store seven int values. The array length can be any expression that evaluates to a non-negative integer value. The length of the array cannot be changed after the array has been created. After the execution of this declaration statement, the reference noOfTextMessages will refer to the array and can be used to manipulate the array (see Figure 6.2b).

Default initialization

The array creation expression in the previous section says nothing about which seven int values are stored in the array, so all elements in the array will be assigned a value of 0. The rule is that when an array is created as shown, the elements are automatically initialized to the *default value* for the element type. The default value for the int type is 0 (see Figure 6.2b). Table 6.1 shows the default values for the primitive and reference types. If we create an array of boolean values, i.e. boolean[], all the elements will be assigned the value false.

6

FIGURE 6.2 Declaration, creation and default initialization of arrays

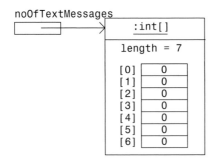

Array reference declaration   *Array creation*

int[] noOfTextMessages = new int[7];

Array type   *Array name*   *Operator*   *Array length*

Element type

(a) Array reference declaration and creation

noOfTextMessages

:int[]
length = 7
[0] 0
[1] 0
[2] 0
[3] 0
[4] 0
[5] 0
[6] 0

noOfTextMessages:int[]
length = 7
[0] 0
[1] 0
[2] 13
[3] 0
[4] 0
[5] 0
[6] 17

After executing:
noOfTextMessages = new int[7];

After executing:
noOfTextMessages[2] = 13;
noOfTextMessages[6] = noOfTextMessages[2] + 4;

(b) Notation showing explicit array reference

(c) More compact notation for an array

TABLE 6.1   Default values for types

Type	Default value
boolean	false
char	'\u0000'
Integer (int, long)	0
Floating-point (double)	+0.0d
All reference types	null

Arrays of objects

In the same way as creating arrays of primitive types, we can create arrays of objects. The following declaration statement combines the declaration of the array reference variable and the creation of the array:

```
String[] cdTrackNames = new String[4]; // An array of 4 String references.
```

After execution of the above statement, the reference cdTrackNames will refer to an array of length four, whose elements can refer to String objects (see Figure 6.3a). The elements are implicitly initialized to the default value for reference types, i.e. the value null (see Table 6.1). The array type is String[], and the element type is String.

FIGURE 6.3   Array of objects

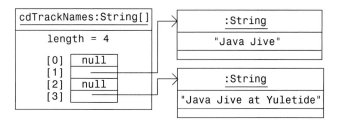

After executing:
```
String[] cdTrackNames = new String[4];
```

After executing:
```
cdTrackNames[1] = "Java Jive";
cdTrackNames[3] = cdTrackNames[1] + " at Yuletide";
```

(a) Creating an array of `Strings`   (b) Initialising an array of `Strings`

The `length` field

Each array has a field called `length` whose value is the array length. The value is set when the array is created, and cannot be changed. The value of this field can be accessed using the dot notation:

```
System.out.println(noOfTextMessages.length); // Prints 7.
System.out.println(cdTrackNames.length);     // Prints 4.
```

As opposed to the method `length()` in the `String` class, the name `length` is a field in every array.

Accessing an array element

To access an element in an array we need to specify both the array reference and the index of the element in the array. We can access the value in the element that holds the number of text messages sent on Wednesday using the expression `noOfTextMessages[2]`. Similarly, the expression `noOfTextMessages[6]` indicates the number of text messages sent on Sunday. The index is always specified between brackets.

We can change the element values using the assignment operator:

```
noOfTextMessages[2] = 13; // Index 2 for Wednesday.
```

After execution of this assignment statement, the number of text messages sent on Wednesday is now thirteen. If the number of text messages sent on Sunday is four more than the number sent on Wednesday, we can update the number of text messages sent on Sunday as follows:

```
noOfTextMessages[6] = noOfTextMessages[2] + 4; // Index 6 for Sunday.
```

Figure 6.2c illustrates the array after execution of these two statements. The expression `noOfTextMessages[2]` behaves exactly like a variable. As the expression specifies an array reference and an index, we call it an *indexed variable*.

We can imagine the array referenced by the array reference `noOfTextMessages` as consisting of seven integer variables. One might be tempted to declare seven different integer variables to maintain the seven values indicating the number of text messages sent each day of

6

the week, but that is not a good idea. What if we need to maintain several thousand elements in an array?

We can access elements in an array of objects similarly. The expression `cdTrackNames[1]` indicates the element with index 1 in an array of `String` objects. Each such indexed variable is like any other reference, and has either the value `null`, or refers to an object of the element type. The following statements show examples of accessing elements of an array of `String` objects:

```
cdTrackNames[1] = "Java Jive";
cdTrackNames[3] = cdTrackNames[1] + " at Yuletide"; // "Java Jive at Yuletide"
```

Figure 6.3b illustrates the array after execution of these two assignment statements.

Array bounds

So far we have used an integer literal as an index, but in fact the index can be any arbitrary expression that evaluates to an `int` value. The index value must be in the range of valid index values for an array, i.e. the index value must be greater than or equal to 0 and less than the array length (0 ≤ index value < array length). At runtime, the index value is always checked before accessing the array. An invalid index results in an out-of-bounds error: the program is terminated after reporting an exception of type `ArrayIndexOutOf-BoundsException`. See the output from Program 6.1.

Array aliases

As arrays are objects, we can create aliases to arrays:

```
int[] messageCounters = noOfTextMessages;
String[] trackTitles = cdTrackNames;
```

The references `noOfTextMessages` and `messageCounters` are aliases to the same array. The same applies to the references `cdTrackNames` and `trackTitles`. Any alias to an array can be used to manipulate the array. Therefore the expressions `noOfTextMessages[2]` and `messageCounters[2]` both refer to the same element in the array, i.e. the number of text messages sent on Wednesday.

Note that array variables are references, and assigning one reference to another does *not* copy the elements of one array to another. In Section 6.7 we will see how we can copy element values from one array to another.

Alternate notation for array declaration

There is an alternate notation for declaring array references in which the brackets are placed after the array reference variable:

```
int noOfTextMessages[]; // Alternate notation for array reference declaration
```

Both forms declare the reference `noOfTextMessages` to have the type `int[]`, i.e. an array of `int` values. The difference between the two forms becomes apparent when a list of variables are specified in the declaration:

```
int[] arrayA, arrayB, arrayC;      // (1)
```

```
int arrayA[], arrayB[], arrayC[]; // (2)
int arrayA[], arrayB, arrayC[];   // (3)
```

(1) and (2) are equivalent: all three references have the type int[]. In (3) only references arrayA and arrayC have the type int[], whereas the variable arrayB is of type int. The standard convention is the form in (1), which we follow in this book.

BEST PRACTICES

The prevailing practice is to declare array reference variables using the following notation:

```
int[] arrayRefName;
```

6.3 Initializing arrays

We saw that when we create an array using the new operator and specifying the array length, the elements of the array are initialized to the default value for the element type. If we wish to store other values in the elements when we create the array, we must explicitly specify the values. This is called (*explicit*) *array initialization*. Figure 6.4 shows two language constructs that initialize an array when it is created. These constructs are practical when we wish to create small-size arrays with specific values.

FIGURE 6.4   Array creation with initialization

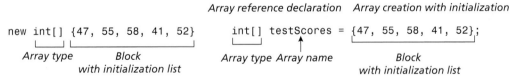

(a) Creating an anonymous array   (b) Array declaration, creation and initialization

The form in Figure 6.4a is an expression that creates an *anonymous array* of the specified array type, that is, one initialized with the values specified within the block. The length of the array is implicitly given by the number of values in the block. The values in the block all have the same element type (int), and these values are stored in the array with the first value at index 0, the second value at index 1 and so on. This form is called an "anonymous array" because it does not require the reference value of the array be assigned to an array variable. A typical use for an anonymous array is when we need to create a small array "on the fly", for example, as an actual parameter in a method call.

Like any other reference value, the reference value returned by the array creation expression can be assigned to an array variable:

```
int[] testScores; // (1) Only declaration, no array creation.
// Array creation, explicit initialization and assignment
```

```
    testScores = new int[] {47, 55, 58, 41, 52};        // (2) 5 initial values
```

Of course we can combine the declaration (1) and the assignment (2) as before:

```
    // Array declaration, creation, explicit initialization and assignment
    int[] testScores = new int[] {47, 55, 58, 41, 52}; // (3) 5 initial values
```

In (3) the array type (int[]) is repeated on both sides of the assignment. This is superfluous. In this particular case, (3) can be simplified to the form shown in Figure 6.4b:

```
    int[] testScores = {47, 55, 58, 41, 52};            // (4) Simplified form
```

The new operator and the array type are omitted on the right-hand side in (4). The form in Figure 6.4b can only be used when we *declare* an array variable, whereas the form in Figure 6.4a can be used anywhere an array reference is allowed. For example, the form in Figure 6.4b cannot be used in an assignment statement (compare with (2) above):

```
    testScores = {47, 55, 58, 41, 52}; // (5) Compile time error!
```

Below we give some more examples of array initialization for different kinds of arrays:

```
    // (1) An integer array with 8 elements
    int[] intArray = {1, 3, 49, 55, 58, 41, 52, 3146};
    // (2) A boolean array with 4 elements
    boolean[] booleanArray = new boolean[] {true, false, false, true};
    // (3) A character array with 4 characters
    char[] charArray = {'J', 'a', 'v', 'a'};
    // (4) An array with 4 floating-point values
    double fpArray = new double[] {25.0, 3.14, 1.5, 0.75};
    // (5) An array with 4 strings
    String[] pets = {"crocodiles", "elephants", "crocophants", "elediles"};
    // (6) An array with 3 strings,
    //     but only 2 elements are initialized with non-null values.
    pets = new String[] {"cat", null, "dog"};
```

Note the use of the null value in the initialization list in (6). Element pets[1] does not refer to an object. It's a common programming error to use such a reference to refer to an object.

Program 6.1 demonstrates array declaration, creation, initialization and assignment discussed so far. The assertions in the program show the assumptions we can make about arrays.

PROGRAM 6.1 Array declaration, creation, initialization and assignment

```
// Array initialisation
public class ArrayInitialisation {
  public static void main(String[] args) {

    final int NO_OF_TESTS = 5;

    // Array declaration:
    int[] testScores;  // (1) Only declaration, no array creation
```

```
    // Array creation, default initialisation and assignment:
    testScores = new int[NO_OF_TESTS];        // (2) Array length specified
    assert(testScores != null);
    assert(testScores.length == NO_OF_TESTS);
    assert(testScores[0] == 0);                       // First value
    assert(testScores[NO_OF_TESTS - 1] == 0); // Last value
    // and the other elements are also initialised to the default value 0.

    // Combined (1) and (2).
    // Array declration, creation, default initialisation and assignment:
    int[] testScoresII = new int[NO_OF_TESTS];

    // Array declaration:
    int[] testScoresIII;  // (3) Only declaration, no array creation
    // Array creation, explicit initialisation and assignment:
    testScoresIII = new int[] {47, 55, 58, 41, 52}; // (4) Anonymous array
    assert(testScoresIII.length == NO_OF_TESTS);
    assert(testScoresIII[0] == 47);                    // First value
    assert(testScoresIII[NO_OF_TESTS -1] == 52); // Last value
    // and the other elements are also explicitly initialised accordingly.

    // Combined (3) and (4)
    // Array declaration, creation, explicit initialisation
    // and assignment:
    int[] testScoresIV = new int[] {47, 55, 58, 41, 52};
    int[] testScoresV = {47, 55, 58, 41, 52}; // Simplified form
//  testScoresV = {47, 55, 58, 41, 52};       // Compile time error!

    System.out.println(testScoresV[NO_OF_TESTS]); // Out-of-bounds error
  }
}
```

Program output:

```
Exception in thread "main" java.lang.ArrayIndexOutOfBoundsException: 5
at ArrayInitialization.main(ArrayInitialization.java:37)
```

BEST PRACTICES

Array elements are initialized to the default value of their type if no explicit initialization is specified when the array is created. As the default type of a reference type is null, elements of an array of objects must explicitly be initialized before use to avoid a NullPointerException.

6.4 Iterating over an array

A common task in programming is accessing elements in an array successively to perform the same operation on each element of the array. For example, to calculate the total number of text messages sent during the week in our example, we would have to add each element of the array that represents the number of text messages sent each day. Accessing elements of an array successively is called *iteration* over the array.

To iterate over an array with *n* elements, we start with the first element at index 0, continue successively with the elements at index 1, 2 and so on until the last element at index *n-1* has been processed.

It should not come as a surprise that a counter-controlled for(;;) loop is convenient for iterating over arrays. Each iteration of the loop accesses a new element of the array. The index, represented by the loop variable, is initialized to 0 in the initialization part of the for(;;) loop. After each iteration the index is incremented by 1 in the update part of the for(;;) loop. But what should the loop test be? As long as the index is *less* than *n*, not all the elements have been accessed. The loop body accesses the current element using the current value of the index:

```
// Code pattern for iterating over an array.
for (int index = 0; index < array.length; index++) {
  // ... current element given by array[index] ...
}
```

The code pattern above guarantees that the loop will iterate through all the elements of the array successively: the index value will always be valid, and using it to access the designated element in the array will not result in an out-of-bounds error.

Program 6.2 illustrates the use of arrays by looking at four simple problems related to the array noOfTextMessages.

Comparing all values in an array with a given value

Problem (1) in Program 6.2 deals with finding how many days have a number of text messages equal to or greater than a specified lower bound. The lower bound is read from the keyboard. We use a counter (noOfDays) to count the number of days that satisfy this criterion. During each iteration of the loop we compare whether the current day (given by the loop variable index) has a number of text messages (given by noOfTextMessages[index]) equal to or greater than the lower bound. If this is the case, we increment the counter.

Finding the lowest value in an array

Problem (2) in Program 6.2 deals with finding the lowest number of text messages sent during the week. We use a variable (lowestNoOfTextMessages) to keep track of the lowest number of text messages sent on a day as we iterate over the array. We initialize the variable lowestNoOfTextMessages with the value of the first day of the week (noOfTextMessages[0]). Assuming that the first day has the lowest number of text messages sent during the week, we begin the loop iteration with an index of 1. In this case we cannot use a value that is lower than any of the values in the array, because the lowest value has to be one of the values in the array. Alternatively, we can use a value that is greater than any of the values in the array, for example Integer.MAX_VALUE, and begin the loop iteration with an index of 0.

During each iteration of the loop we test whether the number of text messages for the current day (given by noOfTextMessages[index]) is less than the current lower bound (given by the variable lowestNoOfTextMessages). If this is the case, then the current day has the lowest number of text messages so far, and we must update the variable lowest-NoOfTextMessages to reflect the new lower bound.

Finding the highest value in an array

Problem (3) in Program 6.2 deals with finding the highest number of text messages sent during the week, and the days on which that number of messages were sent. We first find the highest number of text messages sent during the week, similar to problem (2). To find the days with the highest number of text messages, we iterate over the array again, printing the name of the day if the number of text messages sent on this day equals the maximum number of text messages sent on a specific day during the week.

Adding the values in an array

Problem (4) in Program 6.2 deals with finding the total number of messages sent during the week. We use a counter (totalNoOfTextMessages) to accumulate the value for each day. After each iteration of the loop, the variable totalNoOfTextMessages has the current total.

PROGRAM 6.2   Iterating over an array

```java
import java.util.Scanner;
public class ArrayIteration1 {

    public static void main(String[] args) {
        // Array with the names of week days
        String[] daysOfTheWeek = {"Monday", "Tuesday", "Wednesday",
                          "Thursday", "Friday", "Saturday", "Sunday"};
        // Array with the no. of text messages sent during a day.
        int[] noOfTextMessages = new int[7];

        // Explicit initialisation
        noOfTextMessages[0] = 20;                          // Monday
        noOfTextMessages[1] = 12;                          // Tuesday
        noOfTextMessages[2] = 13;                          // Wednesday
        noOfTextMessages[3] = noOfTextMessages[1];         // Thursday
        noOfTextMessages[4] = 10;                          // Friday
        noOfTextMessages[5] = noOfTextMessages[0];         // Saturday
        noOfTextMessages[6] = noOfTextMessages[2] + 4;     // Sunday

        // Setup to read from the terminal window.
```

```java
Scanner keyboard = new Scanner(System.in);

// Problem (1) Find how many days have their number of text messages
// equal to or greater than a specified lower bound.
System.out.print("Enter the lower bound for " +
                 "the no. of text messages: ");
int lowerBound = keyboard.nextInt();
int noOfDays = 0;
for (int index = 0; index < noOfTextMessages.length; index++) {
  if (noOfTextMessages[index] >= lowerBound) {
    noOfDays++;
  }
}
System.out.println("No. of days with more than " + lowerBound +
                   " text messages: " + noOfDays);

// Problem (2) Find the lowest number of messages sent during the week.
int lowestNoOfTextMessages = noOfTextMessages[0];
for (int index = 1; index < noOfTextMessages.length; index++) {
  if (lowestNoOfTextMessages > noOfTextMessages[index]) {
    lowestNoOfTextMessages = noOfTextMessages[index];
  }
}
System.out.println("Lowest no. of text messages: " +
                   lowestNoOfTextMessages);

// Problem (3) Find the highest no. of text messages sent during
// the week and the days on which that number of messages were sent.
// Find the highest no. of text messages sent during a day.
int highestNoOfTextMessages = 0;
for (int index = 0; index < noOfTextMessages.length; index++) {
  if (highestNoOfTextMessages < noOfTextMessages[index]) {
    highestNoOfTextMessages = noOfTextMessages[index];
  }
}
System.out.println("Highest no. of text messages: " +
                   highestNoOfTextMessages);
// Print all days with the highest no.of text messages sent.
System.out.println("Days with the highest no. of text messages:");
for (int index = 0; index < noOfTextMessages.length; index++) {
  if (highestNoOfTextMessages == noOfTextMessages[index]) {
    System.out.println(daysOfTheWeek[index]);
  }
}

// Problem (4) Find the total number of messages sent during the week.
int totalNoOfTextMessages = 0;
for (int index = 0; index < noOfTextMessages.length; index++) {
  totalNoOfTextMessages += noOfTextMessages[index];
}
```

```
        System.out.println("Total no. of text messages: " +
                            totalNoOfTextMessages);
    }
}
```

Program output:

```
Enter the lower bound for the no. of text messages: 13
No. of days with more than 13 text messages: 4
Lowest no. of text messages: 10
Highest no. of text messages: 20
Days with the highest no. of text messages:
Monday
Saturday
Total no. of text messages: 104
```

Iterating over an array of objects

Program 6.3 illustrates iteration over an array of String objects. The program prints all the track titles that contain the word "Java". In each iteration of the loop (1) the current track name is given by the reference cdTrackNames[trackNumber], where trackNumber is the current index in the array cdTrackNames. For each track name, we call the method indexOf() from the String class with the literal "Java" as argument. If the return value is not -1, this means that the word "Java" occurs in the current track name and the track name can be printed.

PROGRAM 6.3   Iterating over an array of strings

```
// Array iteration
public class ArrayIteration2 {
  public static void main(String[] args) {
    String[] cdTrackNames = {
      "The Ballad of the Loop Variable",
      "Do the Java Jive",
      "My Loop will go on",
      null
    };
    cdTrackNames[3] = cdTrackNames[1] + " at Yuletide";

    // Print all track names with the word "Java" in them.
    for (int trackNumber = 0;                                 // (1)
         trackNumber < cdTrackNames.length;
         trackNumber++) {
      if(cdTrackNames[trackNumber].indexOf("Java") != -1) {
        System.out.println(cdTrackNames[trackNumber]);
      }
    }
  }
}
```

6

Program output:

```
Do the Java Jive
Do the Java Jive at Yuletide
```

6.5 Multidimensional arrays

Arrays we have seen so far are called *simple* or *one-dimensional arrays*, and only *one index* is required to identify elements in the array. We used a simple array to record the number of text messages sent from a mobile phone for each day of the week. What if we need to keep the same statistics for several mobile phones? We could use many simple arrays, one for each mobile phone, and have different array names to distinguish between them. This solution would not be viable if we needed to maintain statistics for many mobile phones. Using many different array names for the simple arrays would soon become unwieldy. We would like a way to maintain several simple arrays as values in a data structure. *Multidimensional arrays* provide the answer.

In this section we look closely at how we can declare, create, initialize and use multidimensional arrays.

Creation and initialization of multidimensional arrays

We want to maintain the weekly data about text messages sent from several mobile phones. Figure 6.5a shows the data for three mobile phones for a whole week. The telephones are identified by a phone index, and the day of the week by a day index. The phone with an index value of 2 and the day with an index value of 0 has the value 18. These two indices are necessary to access the number of text messages sent by a particular phone on a particular day. The tabular form in Figure 6.5a can be implemented by a two-dimensional array, requiring two indices to identify an element.

Multidimensional arrays can be implemented in Java by creating arrays of arrays. The declaration statement in Figure 6.5b declares an array reference (`weeklyData`) and creates a two-dimensional array that has three rows and seven columns.

The number of indices indicates the *dimension* of the array. The indices are interpreted from left to right, where the first index indicates the row and the second indicates the column. The number of indices on both sides of the assignment operator in the declaration statement must be the same. After the execution of the declaration statement, all the twenty-one elements of the two-dimensional array have the default value for the int type (0).

FIGURE 6.5 A two-dimensional array

No. of mobile phones is 3. No. of days is 7.

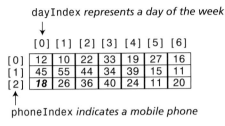

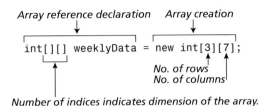

(a) Illustrated as rows and columns   (b) Creating arrays of arrays

We want to store the data from Figure 6.5a in the two-dimensional array weeklyData. After its creation as shown in Figure 6.5b, we can assign values to the elements individually:

```
// Initialization of 1st mobile phone
weeklyData[0][0] = 12; weeklyData[0][1] = 10; weeklyData[0][2] = 22;
weeklyData[0][3] = 33; weeklyData[0][4] = 19; weeklyData[0][5] = 27;
weeklyData[0][6] = 16;
// Initialization of 2nd mobile phone
weeklyData[1][0] = 45; weeklyData[1][1] = 55; weeklyData[1][2] = 44;
weeklyData[1][3] = 34; weeklyData[1][4] = 39; weeklyData[1][5] = 15;
weeklyData[1][6] = 11;
// Initialization of 3rd mobile phone
weeklyData[2][0] = 18; weeklyData[2][1] = 26; weeklyData[2][2] = 36;
weeklyData[2][3] = 40; weeklyData[2][4] = 24; weeklyData[2][5] = 11;
weeklyData[2][6] = 20;
```

It is important to note that the expressions weeklyData[2][0] and weeklyData[0][2] indicate different elements in the array. The expression weeklyData[2][0] indicates the third mobile phone on Monday, while the expression weeklyData[0][2] indicates the first mobile phone on Wednesday. It is important to understand what the indices represent, and be consistent in their usage.

Generalising what we have said about simple arrays, we can also declare, create and initialize the two-dimensional array weeklyData with the following declaration statement:

```
int[][] weeklyData = { // Declaration, creation and initialization.
  {12, 10, 22, 33, 19, 27, 16},  // 1st mobile phone
  {45, 55, 44, 34, 39, 15, 11},  // 2nd mobile phone
  {18, 26, 36, 40, 24, 11, 20}   // 3rd mobile phone
};
```

6

In the declaration statement above, we see that the array reference declaration is the same as in Figure 6.5b. We have used the block notation to initialize the two-dimensional array. The outer block encloses a list of inner blocks, in which each inner block specifies the weekly data for one mobile phone, and the number of values in each block corresponds to the number of days in a week. The initialization makes it clear that each element in the outer block is a simple array.

Conceptually we can think of a two-dimensional array as the tabular form shown in Figure 6.5a. However, the actual data structure created is shown in Figure 6.6. The reference `weeklyData` actually refers to a simple array of length 3, in which each element corresponds to a row in the tabular form shown in Figure 6.5a. Each element is thus in turn a simple array that has a length of 7, in which each element holds an `int` value indicating the number of text messages sent. All multidimensional arrays are constructed from several simple arrays, as shown in Figure 6.6. Not surprisingly, such data structures are called *arrays of arrays*.

| FIGURE 6.6 | Array of arrays: explicit structure |

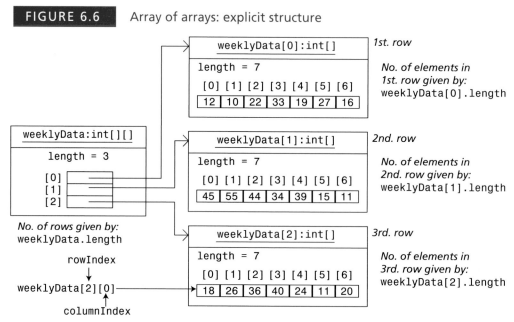

Array of arrays, weeklyData, has type `int[][]`, i.e. an array of arrays of `int`.
Each row, `weeklyData[rowIndex]`, has type `int[]`, i.e. an array of `int`.
Each element in each row, `weeklyData[rowIndex][columnIndex]`, has type `int`.

The expression `weeklyData[2][0]` indicates a particular element in the structure shown in Figure 6.6, in which the first index represents a particular mobile phone and the second index represents a particular weekday. The expression `weeklyData[2]` therefore refers to a simple array that stores the data for the third mobile phone. The expression `weekly-Data[2].length` indicates the number of elements in this simple array, namely 7.

The declaration:

```
int[][] weeklyData; // Declaration only
```

declares that the reference `weeklyData` can refer to any two-dimensional array of `int` values (i.e. has the type `int[][]`). Each row, `weeklyData[rowIndex]`, is a simple array of `int` values (i.e. has the type `int[]`), and each element, `weeklyData[rowIndex][columnIndex]`, is an integer (i.e. has the type `int`).

Program 6.4 uses the two-dimensional array `weeklyData` to accomplish some typical tasks that involve iterating over a multi-dimensional array.

Printing a two-dimensional array in tabular form

Problem (1) in Program 6.4 prints the array data in tabular form, using two nested `for(;;)` loops. The outer loop iterates over the phone indices, and the inner loop iterates over the simple array for each mobile phone that is identified by the phone index, printing the weekly data for each mobile phone in turn. The values are aligned in columns using the format specification `"%4d"`.

Iterating over a specific row in a two-dimensional array

Problem (2) in Program 6.4 calculates the total number of text messages sent from the mobile phone indicated by index 1. This result is computed by iterating over the row `weeklyData[1]`, and adding each value given by the expression `weeklyData[1][dayIndex]`, 0 `<= dayIndex < weeklyData[1].length`.

Iterating over a specific column in a two-dimensional array

Problem (3) in Program 6.4 calculates the total number of text messages sent from all mobile phones on Wednesday (day index 2). This result is computed by adding the values in the column indicated by the day index 2. Each value in this column is given by the expression `weeklyData[phoneIndex][2]`, 0 `<= phoneIndex < weeklyData.length`.

Iterating over all the columns in a two-dimensional array

Problem (4) in Program 6.4 finds days on which the total number of text messages sent from all mobile phones is greater than 100. We have to add the values for all the telephones for each day (analogous to Problem (3)), and see if the sum is greater than 100.

6

We have used two nested `for(;;)` loops for this. The inner loop adds the values in each column (i.e. adds the values for all telephones for each day), and if the count is greater than 100, we print the day index. The outer `for(;;)` loop makes sure that all the columns (i.e. all the days of the week) are handled, using the expression `weeklyData[0].length` for the number of days in the week for all telephones. As all the rows have the same length (i.e. the same number of days in a week), we could use the length of any row in the loop condition of the outer loop.

```java
// Multi-dimensional Array Iteration using for(;;) loop
public class MultidimesionalArrayIteration {

  public static void main(String[] args) {

    int[][] weeklyData = { // Declaration, creation and initialisation.
        {12, 10, 22, 33, 19, 27, 16},  // 1st mobile phone
        {45, 55, 44, 34, 39, 15, 11},  // 2nd mobile phone
        {18, 26, 36, 40, 24, 11, 20}   // 3rd mobile phone
      };

    // Problem (1) Print the data in tabular form
    for (int phoneIndex = 0;
         phoneIndex < weeklyData.length;
         phoneIndex++) {
      System.out.print("Phone index " + phoneIndex + ": ");
      for (int dayIndex = 0;
           dayIndex < weeklyData[phoneIndex].length;
           dayIndex++) {
        System.out.printf("%4d", weeklyData[phoneIndex][dayIndex]);
      }
      System.out.println();
    }

    // Problem (2) Find the total number of text messages sent from
    // the mobile phone indicated by index 1
    int sumWeek = 0;
    for (int dayIndex = 0; dayIndex < weeklyData[1].length; dayIndex++) {
      sumWeek += weeklyData[1][dayIndex];
    }
    System.out.println(
      "Total no. of text messages sent from the mobile phone given" +
      " by index 1: " + sumWeek);

    // Problem (3) Find the total number of text messages sent from all
    // mobile phones on Wednesday (day index 2)
    int sumMessages = 0;
    for (int phoneIndex = 0;
         phoneIndex < weeklyData.length;
         phoneIndex++) {
      sumMessages += weeklyData[phoneIndex][2];
    }
    System.out.println(
      "Total no. of text messages sent from all mobile phones on" +
      " Wednesday: " + sumMessages);

    // Problem (4) Find which days the total no. of text messages sent
```

```
    // from all mobile phones is greater than 100.
    for (int dayIndex = 0; dayIndex < weeklyData[0].length; dayIndex++) {
      int sumDays = 0;
      for (int phoneIndex = 0;
           phoneIndex < weeklyData.length;
           phoneIndex++) {
        sumDays += weeklyData[phoneIndex][dayIndex];
      }
      if (sumDays > 100) {
        System.out.println("The day with index " + dayIndex +
                           " has over 100 text messages registered.");
      }
    }
  }
}
```

Program output:

```
Phone index 0:    12  10  22  33  19  27  16
Phone index 1:    45  55  44  34  39  15  11
Phone index 2:    18  26  36  40  24  11  20
Total no. of text messages sent from the mobile phone given by index 1: 243
Total no. of text messages sent from all mobile phones on Wednesday: 102
The day with index 2 has over 100 text messages registered.
The day with index 3 has over 100 text messages registered.
```

Ragged arrays

Each row in a two-dimensional array is a simple array, but these inner simple arrays need not have the same length. The length of the rows can vary. Such arrays are called *ragged arrays*.

Suppose we want to create an overview of rainfall measurements at weather stations across a country. Each row of an array can represent a region and each column can represent the measurement of rainfall at a weather station in the region. It is not certain that each region has the same number of weather stations. The code below shows how an array of arrays can be constructed to model the rainfall statistics.

```
// Create a two-dimensional array with the required no. of rows for
// the regions with weather stations.
double[][] rainfallData = new double[3][]; // (1)
// (2) Create a simple array for each region with required no. of stations.
rainfallData[0] = new double[2]; // Two weather stations
rainfallData[1] = new double[1]; // One weather station
rainfallData[2] = new double[4]; // Four weather stations
```

Note that in (1) we specify the length of the first dimension from the left that represents the number of regions. Since each element in the two-dimensional array rainfallData is a simple array, each row can be created individually, as in (2). After execution of the code above, all the seven elements are initialized to the default value for the type double, 0.0. We can now assign other values to the elements.

As an alternative, we can also use the block notation in a declaration statement to create and initialize the elements of the two-dimensional array to specific values. This approach is illustrated by Program 6.5. In iterating over a ragged array, we make sure that the inner loop uses the correct length for each row. The loop at (2) explicitly refers to the row length by the expression rainfallData[regionIndex].length.

Note that we cannot change the number of rows in a multi-dimensional array, but we can replace the rows with other arrays. For example, if we want to replace the rainfall measurements for a region, we can create a new simple array and replace the old one with:

```
rainfallData[regionIndex] = new double[] {25.5, 12.75, 9.5};
```

PROGRAM 6.5   Ragged arrays

```
// Using ragged arrays
public class RaggedArrays {

  public static void main(String[] args) {

    // (1) Create and initialise the two-dimensional array
    // with rainfall data
    double[][] rainfallData = {
      {56.6, 30.2},            // Two weather stations
      {20.5},                  // One weather station
      {15.8, 7.0, 45.8, 0.6} // Four weather stations
    };

    // Print rainfall data.
    for (int regionIndex = 0;
         regionIndex < rainfallData.length;
         regionIndex++) {
      System.out.printf("Rainfall for region%2d: ", regionIndex);
      for (int stationIndex = 0;                                     //(2)
           stationIndex < rainfallData[regionIndex].length;
           stationIndex++) {
        System.out.printf("%10.2f",
                          rainfallData[regionIndex][stationIndex]);
      }
      System.out.println();
    }
  }
}
```

Program output:

```
Rainfall for region 0:     56.60     30.20
Rainfall for region 1:     20.50
Rainfall for region 2:     15.80      7.00     45.80      0.60
```

Arrays with more than two dimensions

We give an example of a three-dimensional array here, but arrays of any number of dimensions can be created in a similar fashion. However, arrays of dimension 4 and higher become more difficult to visualise.

Imagine we use containers to transport bicycles. These containers can be stacked in a rectangular grid in a ship's hold. The length and breadth of this grid measures 10 containers by 20 containers respectively. We can stack containers 15 high. The following three-dimensional array can be used to keep track of the number of bicycles in each container in the ship's hold:

```
int[][][] bicycles = int [10][20][15]; // [l][b][h]
```

The three indices identify a particular container stacked in the ship's hold. The reference `bicycles[l]` refers to a particular two-dimensional array (`int[][]`), and the reference `bicycles[l][b]` refers to a particular one-dimensional array (`int[]`). The value of `bicycles[l][b][h]` is the number of bicycles in a particular container. We could also construct this three-dimensional array piecemeal as we did with the construction of a ragged array. This approach is left to the reader as an exercise.

BEST PRACTICES

When iterating over a multi-dimensional array, use the length of *each* row explicitly, to avoid the `ArrayIndexOutOfBoundsException` in the case of a ragged array

E.g. `twoDimArray[i].length`.

6.6 More on iteration: enhanced for loop

We often want to iterate over a collection of elements, such as an array, modifying the elements. Earlier we used a `for(;;)` loop for this purpose, for example to read the values in the array `noOfTextMessages` for Problem (1) in Program 6.2:

```
// Problem (1) Find how many days have a number of text messages
// equal to or greater than a specified lower bound.
...
for (int index = 0; index < noOfTextMessages.length; index++) {
  if (noOfTextMessages[index] >= lowerBound)
    noOfDays++;
}
```

The *enhanced* `for` loop is tailored to successively reading all the values in a *collection*. In each iteration of this loop the current element can be accessed. Figure 6.7 shows the `for(;;)` loop above rewritten using the enhanced `for` loop statement.

6

FIGURE 6.7   Enhanced **for** loop

element declaration   *collection*

```
for (int element : noOfTextMessages)
{
    if (element >= lowerBound)
        noOfDays++;
}
```

loop body

In this book we will use the notation for(:) for the enhanced for loop, in contrast to the notation for(;;) for the counter-controlled for loop. The body of the for(:) loop is executed for *each* value in the collection (referenced by the variable in the element declaration). In Figure 6.7, the collection is an array.

The type of the element variable is the element type of the collection. In Figure 6.7 the array type is int[] and the element variable is declared as having the type int, which is the element type. The for(:) loop iterates over the specified collection, and for each iteration of the loop, the element variable is assigned a new value from the collection. The element variable is declared in the header of the for(:) loop, and can only be used in the loop body. In other words, the element variable is a local variable in the for(:) loop. However, changing its value in the loop body does *not* change any value in the collection. With the for(:) loop we also avoid out-of-bounds errors.

Here are cases where the for(;;) loop is preferable to the for(:) loop:

- Requiring the index to access particular element(s) or change element value(s).
- Iteration over more than one collection simultaneously.
- Iteration needs to be in increments other than one.
- The direction of the iteration is in reverse order.

Iterating over multidimensional arrays with the **for(:)** loop

Enhanced for loops can also be nested, for example to iterate over a multidimensional array. Problem (1) from Program 6.4 uses two nested for(;;) loops:

```java
// Problem (1) Print the data in table form
for (int phoneIndex = 0;
     phoneIndex < weeklyData.length;
     phoneIndex++) {
  System.out.print("Phone index " + phoneIndex + ": ");
  for (int dayIndex = 0;
       dayIndex < weeklyData[phoneIndex].length;
       dayIndex++) {
    System.out.printf("%4d", weeklyData[phoneIndex][dayIndex]);
  }
  System.out.println();
}
```

We can simplify this code by using two nested for(:) loops:

```
// Problem (1) Print the data in table form
int rowIndex = 0;
for (int[] mobilephoneData : weeklyData) {
  System.out.print("Phone index " + (rowIndex++) + ": ");
  for (int noOfTextMessagesPerDay : mobilephoneData) {
    System.out.printf("%4d", noOfTextMessagesPerDay);
  }
  System.out.println();
}
```

This iterates over a two-dimensional array (int[][]) referenced by the array variable weeklyData. Each element in this two-dimensional array has the type int[], i.e. it is a simple array of int. This type is specified for the element variable mobilephoneData in the outer for(:) loop. The inner for(:) loop iterates over a simple array of int values (int[]). In the inner for(:) loop, the element variable noOfTextMessagesPerDay indicates an int value in a simple array given by the reference mobilephoneData that is declared in the outer for(:) loop.

To keep track of which mobile phone we are dealing with, we use an extra int variable rowIndex, which is incremented explicitly as the outer for(:) loop iterates through the mobile phones.

BEST PRACTICES

Use the for(:) loop to iterate over an array if the element index is *not* required in the loop body, otherwise use the for(;;) loop.

6.7 More miscellaneous operations on arrays

Copying arrays

We have already noted that assigning one array reference to another array reference does not copy the elements from one array to the other. We must do the copying *element-wise*, i.e. we must copy the value of the element at a given index to the corresponding element in the other array at the same index. Problems (1) and (2) in Program 6.6 illustrate copying arrays.

Copying arrays of primitive values

Problem (1) in Program 6.6 illustrates copying primitive values from one array to another. The two arrays have the same length. We use a for(;;) loop to copy the int value in each element from one array to the corresponding element in the other array. In each iteration of the loop, the loop variable i indicates the corresponding elements in the two arrays. After the completion of the loop, corresponding elements in the two arrays have the same int value.

Copying arrays of objects

Problem (2) in Program 6.6 illustrates copying one array of objects to another. The operation is analogous to Problem (1). The elements of an array of objects are references, and hold reference values that identify objects. In each iteration of the loop, the reference value in an element of one array is assigned to the corresponding element in the other array. After the completion of the loop, corresponding elements in the two arrays are *aliases* to the same object. In other words, the two arrays share their objects. This kind of copying is called *reference value copying*.

Comparing arrays

If we want to find out whether two arrays are equal, i.e. have the same values in the corresponding elements, we cannot do that by comparing the array references using the == operator. As we know, comparison with the == operator only determines whether the two references are aliases. We have to do the comparison *element-wise*. Problem (3) and (4) in Program 6.6 illustrate comparison of arrays.

Comparing arrays of primitive values

Problem (3) in Program 6.6 uses a for(;;) loop to compare the values in the corresponding elements of the two int arrays. A guard variable (equalValues) terminates the loop as soon as the values in any two corresponding elements are not equal. Program output shows that the int arrays intValuesI and intValuesII are equal, which is not surprising, because we copied int values from the array intValuesI to the array intValuesII in Problem (1).

Comparing arrays of objects

Problem (4) in Program 6.6 illustrates comparison of arrays of objects. Problem (2) demonstrated reference value copying for arrays of objects. To compare such arrays, we compare the elements for *reference value* equality (or inequality) using the == (or !=) operator. This problem is essentially the same as Problem (3). Program output correctly shows that the String arrays refValuesII and refValuesIII are not equal, as the corresponding elements are not aliases.

PROGRAM 6.6   Copying and comparing arrays

```
// Misc. Array Operations
public class MiscArrayOperations {
  public static void main(String[] args) {
    // Problem (1) Copying an array of primitive values
    int[] intValuesI = {1, 3, 1949};              // Copy from this array
    int[] intValuesII = new int[intValuesI.length];// to this array.
    for (int i = 0; i < intValuesI.length; i++) {
      intValuesII[i] = intValuesI[i];
    }

    // Problem (2) Copying an array of objects (Reference value copying)
    String[] refValuesI = {"1.", "March", "1949"}; // Copy from this array
    String[] refValuesII = new String[refValuesI.length];// to this array.
    for (int i = 0; i < intValuesI.length; i++) {
```

```
      refValuesII[i] = refValuesI[i];
  }

  // Problem (3) Comparing arrays of primitive values
  boolean equalValues = true;
  for (int i = 0; equalValues && i < intValuesI.length; i++)
    if (intValuesI[i] != intValuesII[i]) {
      equalValues = false;
    }
  String notStr = "not ";
  if (equalValues) {
    notStr ="";
  }
  System.out.println("Arrays intValuesI and intValuesII are " + notStr +
                    "equal");

  // Problem (4) Comparing arrays of objects for reference value equality
  String[] refValuesIII = {"1949", "March", "1."};
  boolean equalRefValues = true;
  for (int i = 0; equalRefValues && i < refValuesIII.length; i++) {
    if (refValuesIII[i] != refValuesII[i]) {
      equalRefValues = false;
    }
  }
  notStr = "not ";
  if (equalRefValues) {
    notStr ="";
  }
  System.out.println("Arrays refValuesIII and refValuesII are " +
                    notStr + "equal");
  }
}
```

Program output:

```
Arrays intValuesI and intValuesII are equal
Arrays refValuesIII and refValuesII are not equal
```

Working with partially-filled arrays

Creating an array requires information about the length of the array. However, it is not always known in advance how many items will be stored in the array. For example, when reading data from the terminal window or a file, we may have no clue beforehand how many items will be read. One solution is to overestimate the length of the array. However, if the array is not filled completely, i.e. it is partially-filled, we have to keep track of how many items are actually stored in the array. Processing of data in the array must ensure that only elements with valid data are processed. The field length in the array cannot be used for this purpose. One solution is to associate an integer variable with the array. This variable acts as a counter and keeps track of how many valid items are in the array at any given time.

Program 6.7 illustrates how to process data in a partially-filled array. The program reads a sentence entered by the user. Each word in the sentence is stored as a String object in an array of strings. A word in our context is any sequence of characters delimited by whitespace. We stipulate that the maximum number of words in a sentence is fifty.

We use an index counter (wordIndex) to keep track of where the last word read from the terminal window was stored in the array. The loop condition at (1) ensures that the end-of-line string ("EOL") has not been read and there is still room in the array.

The loop at (2) prints the words in the sentence, but does so in reverse. The index i has the initial value wordCount-1 and is decremented after each iteration until its value is less than 0. The associated counter wordCount helps to keep track of how many elements have valid data in the array.

PROGRAM 6.7   Working with partially-filled arrays

```java
import java.util.Scanner;

public class PartiallyFilledArrays {
  public static void main(String[] args) {

    // Setup to read from the terminal window
    Scanner keyboard = new Scanner(System.in);

    // Create the array to hold maximum 50 words
    String[] sentence = new String[50];

    System.out.print("Enter a sentence (terminate with \"EOL\"): ");

    int wordIndex = -1;
    String word = keyboard.next(); // Read the first word.
    while (!word.equals("EOL") && wordIndex < sentence.length) { // (1)
      wordIndex++;                      // Index is incremented before storing
      sentence[wordIndex] = word;
      word = keyboard.next();        // Read the next word.
    }
    int wordCount = wordIndex + 1;
    System.out.println("No. of words: " + wordCount);

    // Print the words in reverse.
    for (int i = wordCount - 1; i >= 0; i--) {                       // (2)
      System.out.printf("%s ", sentence[i]);
    }
    System.out.println();
  }
}
```

Program output:

```
Enter a sentence (terminate with "EOL"): Don't worry, be happy. EOL
No. of words: 4
happy. be worry, Don't
```

6.8 Pseudo-random number generator

In computer games and simulations we often need to generate a sequence of random numbers. For a dice game it is necessary to simulate rolling the dice, i.e. generating a dice roll value between one and six. Ideally, the probability of a given value is the same (one sixth) for each value on a die. The numbers generated this way are called *random numbers*. To generate random numbers with the help of a program is not possible, as a program can only compute values, not pick them randomly. To guarantee equal probability for all cases is very difficult, so we have to settle for *pseudo-random numbers*, i.e. a sequence of numbers that closely approximates a sequence of random numbers. A lot of research has gone into finding mathematical formulae that compute good approximations to random numbers. We will look at what Java provides in this area.

The Random class

The java.util.Random class implements pseudo-random generators for many primitive data types (boolean, byte, int, long, float, double), but we will concentrate on a pseudo-random generator for int values.

First we need to create an object of the class Random:

```
Random generator = new Random();
```

We can then call the method nextInt() repeatedly on this object:

```
int number = generator.nextInt();
```

Each call to the method will return a random integer in the interval $[-2^{31}, 2^{31}-1]$, which is the range of the data type int.

Determining the range

We often are interested in generating random numbers in a particular range. For example, the following code will return a random number in the interval [0, 10]:

```
number = generator.nextInt(11);      // Random integer in [0, 10]
```

If the parameter value is *n*, the integer returned is in the interval [0, *n*-1]. By supplying a new value to the nextInt() method, we can change the upper bound of the original interval.

If we want to shift the interval, we can add (or subtract) an *offset* from the value returned by the nextInt() method. In the code below, values generated in the original interval [0,

6

10] will now lie in the interval [2, 12], i.e. the offset 2 maps the interval [0, 10] onto the interval [2, 12]:

```
number = 2 + generator.nextInt(11);   // Random integer in [2, 12]
```

If we want the values in the interval to have a *distance* greater than 1, we can multiply the value generated by a distance value:

```
number = 2 + 3*generator.nextInt(5); // Random integer in {2, 5, 8, 11, 14}
```

With a distance value of 3, the expression 3*generator.nextInt(5) always returns a value in the set {0, 3, 6, 9, 12}, while an offset of 2 ensures that the variable number is assigned a value from the set {2, 5, 8, 11, 14}.

Simulating a dice roll

Program 6.8 illustrates how we can roll two dice:

```
int result = (1 + generator.nextInt(6)) + // 1st. die
             (1 + generator.nextInt(6));   // 2nd. die
```

The program rolls the two dice a certain number of times, as read from the keyboard. It counts the number of times each value between 2 and 12 occurs as the sum of a two-dice roll. The frequencies are stored in an array, and are printed at the end. Note that we ignore the first two elements of the array frequency, as the values 0 and 1 cannot occur as a roll value for a roll of two dice.

PROGRAM 6.8   Frequency of dice roll values using two dice

```
import java.util.Random;
import java.util.Scanner;
// Simulates dice roll using a pseudo-random number generator, and
// computes the frequency of two dice values [2,12] and their probability
public class TwoDiceRollFrequency {
  public static void main(String[] args) {

    // Array for counting the frequency of two-dice values.
    int[] frequency = new int[13]; // Ignore frequency[0] and frequency[1].
    Scanner keyboard = new Scanner(System.in);
    System.out.print("Enter the number of times to roll the two dice: ");
    int noOfThrows = keyboard.nextInt();

    Random generator = new Random();   // Pseudo-random number generator

    for (int i = 1; i <= noOfThrows; i++) {
      // Roll two dice.
      int result = (1 + generator.nextInt(6)) + // 1st. die
                   (1 + generator.nextInt(6));   // 2nd. die
      // Increment the frequency of the value for two dice.
      frequency[result]++;
    }
```

```
    for (int i = 2; i < frequency.length; i++) {
      System.out.printf("Sum of two dice values: %2d, " +
        "no. of times: %4d, probability: %.2f%n",
          i, frequency[i], ((double)frequency[i]/noOfThrows));
    }
  }
}
```

Program output:

```
Enter the number of times to roll the two dice: 4000
Sum of two dice values:  2, no. of times:   88, probability: 0.02
Sum of two dice values:  3, no. of times:  224, probability: 0.06
Sum of two dice values:  4, no. of times:  327, probability: 0.08
Sum of two dice values:  5, no. of times:  432, probability: 0.11
Sum of two dice values:  6, no. of times:  598, probability: 0.15
Sum of two dice values:  7, no. of times:  663, probability: 0.17
Sum of two dice values:  8, no. of times:  573, probability: 0.14
Sum of two dice values:  9, no. of times:  460, probability: 0.12
Sum of two dice values: 10, no. of times:  298, probability: 0.07
Sum of two dice values: 11, no. of times:  220, probability: 0.06
Sum of two dice values: 12, no. of times:  117, probability: 0.03
```

Generating the same sequence of pseudo-random numbers

The way in which we have used the pseudo-random number generator up to now cannot guarantee the same sequence of pseudo-random numbers each time the program is run. This is because the pseudo-random number generator is based on the time of the system clock. This is obviously different each time the program is run. If we want to generate the same sequence of pseudo-random numbers each time the program is run, we can specify a *seed* in the call to the Random constructor:

```
Random persistentGenerator = new Random(31);
```

In the declaration above, the seed is the prime number thirty-one. The seed is usually a prime number (i.e. a number that is only divisible by itself or one), as such numbers are highly suitable for implementing good pseudo-random number generators.

6

6.9 Review questions

1. Given that the reference row refers to a simple array, how would we find the number of elements in the array?

2. Name the three different ways in which the bracket notation [] is used.

3. Which lines of code create a simple array of integers referenced by the array called age?

   a `int[] age;`

   b `int[] age = int[100];`

   c `int age = new int[10];`

   d `int[] age = new int(10);`

   e `int[] age = new int[];`

   f `int[] age = new int[10];`

4. Which of the following statements about arrays are true?

   a All arrays have a method with the name length().

   b All arrays have a public field with the name length.

   c Given that the reference arrayRef refers to an array, the first element in the array is accessed by arrayRef[1].

   d When an array is created with new *type*[*n*], all elements of the array are initialized with the default value of *type*.

5. Which code will create and initialize an array for CDs?

   a `CD[] cdCollection = { new CD(), new CD(), new CD() };`

   b `CD[] cdCollection;`
      `cdCollection = { new CD(), new CD(), new CD() };`

   c `CD[] cdCollection = new CD[3];`
      `cdCollection = { new CD(), new CD(), new CD() };`

   d `CD[] cdCollection = new CD[3];`
      `cdCollection[0] = new CD();`
      `cdCollection[1] = new CD();`
      `cdCollection[2] = new CD();`

   e `CD[] cdCollection = new CD[10];`
      `cdCollection = new CD[] { new CD(), new CD(), new CD() };`

   f `CD[] cdCollection = new CD[] { new CD(), new CD() };`

6. Which of the following statements about arrays are true?

   a Index out of bounds is checked at compile time.

b Index out of bounds is checked at runtime.

c The index value can be any expression that evaluates to an integer value.

d Index value must satisfy the relation $0 \le$ *index-value* < *array-length*.

7. Given the following declaration, what is the type of twoDimArrayName, twoDimArray-Name[1] and twoDimArrayName[1][2]?

```
String[][] twoDimArrayName = String[5][4];
```

8. Which code will create and initialize an *array of arrays* with CDs, where each row is a shelf of CDs?

```
a CD[][] cdShelves = {
       { new CD() },
       { new CD(), new CD() },
       { new CD(), new CD(), new CD() }
   };
```

```
b CD[][] cdShelves;
   cdShelves = {
       { new CD() },
       { new CD(), new CD() },
       { new CD(), new CD(), new CD() }
   };
```

```
c CD[][] cdShelves = new CD[3][2];
   cdShelves = {
       { new CD(), new CD() },
       { new CD(), new CD() },
       { new CD(), new CD() }
   };
```

```
d CD[][] cdShelves = new CD[3][2];
   cdShelves[0][0] = new CD(); cdShelves[0][1] = new CD();
   cdShelves[1][0] = new CD(); cdShelves[1][1] = new CD();
   cdShelves[2][0] = new CD(); cdShelves[2][1] = new CD();
```

```
e CD[][] cdShelves  = new CD[][] {
       { new CD() },
       { new CD(), new CD() },
       { new CD(), new CD(), new CD() }
   };
```

```
f CD[][] cdShelves  = new CD[][] {
       null, null, null
   };
   cdShelves[0] = new CD[] { new CD() };
   cdShelves[1] = new CD[] { new CD(), new CD() };
   cdShelves[2] = new CD[] { };
```

```
g CD[][] cdShelves = {
       { new CD() },
       { new CD(); new CD(); new CD() },
```

```
      { new CD(); new CD() }
   };
```

9. Which statements are true for a for(:) loop? Assume that the loop body does not execute statements that terminate the loop.

   a The element variable cannot be declared outside the loop.
   b The collection can be empty.
   c The loop body is executed at least once.
   d Assignment to the element variable will change the values in the collection.

10. Which for(:) loops are valid? Assume that we have the following declaration:

    ```
    String[] strArray = new String[5];
    ```

    a
    ```
    String str;
    for (str : strArray) {
       System.out.println(str);
    }
    ```

    b
    ```
    for (String str : strArray) {
       System.out.println(str);
    }
    ```

    c
    ```
    for (String str : strArray) {
       str = "^_^";
       System.out.println(str);
    }
    ```

    d
    ```
    str i = 0;
    for (String str : strArray) {
      System.out.println(i++ + ": " + str);
    }
    ```

11. What is printed by the following program:

    ```
    class ArrayPrint_PE1 {
       public static void main(String[] args) {
          int[] elements = new int[4];
          for (int i = 0; i < elements.length; i++)
             elements[i] = i + 1;
          for (int value : elements)
             System.out.printf("%2d", value);
       }
    }
    ```

    a 1 2 4 6

    b 0 1 2 3

    c 1 3 6 10

    d 1 2 3 4

12. What is printed by the following program:

```
class ArrayPrint_PE2 {
    public static void main(String[] args) {
        int[] elements = new int[4];
        int i = 0;
        for (int value : elements) {
            value = i + 1;
            i++;
        }
        for (int value : elements)
            System.out.printf("%2d", value);
    }
}
```

a 1 2 4 6

b 0 1 2 3

c 0 0 0 0

d 1 2 3 4

13. In a street there are two hotels with three floors each. Each floor in a hotel has four rooms. Which declaration creates a multidimensional array exactly large enough to store information about the number of guests in each room on each floor in each hotel?

a `int[][][] noOfGuests = new int[2][3][4];`

b `int[][][] noOfGuests = new int[4][3][2];`

c `int[][][] noOfGuests = new int[2][][];`
  `noOfGuests[0] = new int[3][4]; noOfGuests[1] = new int[3][4];`

d `int[][][] noOfGuests = new int[2][][];`
  `noOfGuests[0] = noOfGuests[1] = new int[3][4];`

14. What is printed by the following program:

```
class Length_PE3 {
    public static void main(String[] args) {
        String[] slogan = {"Java", "Jive"};
        int noOfChar = 0;
        for(int i = 0; i < slogan.length(); i++)
            noOfChar += slogan[i].length;
        System.out.println(noOfChar);
    }
}
```

a 8

b 0

c The program will not compile.

15. Which statements are true about pseudo-random numbers? Assume the following declarations:

```
Random generator = new Random();
int number;
```

a The variable number contains a value from the interval [0, 5], inclusive, after the assignment:

```
number = generator.nextInt(5);
```

b The variable number contains a value from the interval [-5, 0], inclusive, after the assignment:

```
number = -5 + generator.nextInt(6);
```

c The variable number contains a value from the interval [-5, 5], inclusive, after the assignment:

```
number = -5 + generator.nextInt(10);
```

d The variable number contains a value from the set {0, 2, 4, 6, 8} after the assignment:

```
number = 2 * generator.nextInt(5);
```

e The variable number contains a value from the set {3, 5, 7, 9, 11} after the assignment:

```
number = 3 + 2 * generator.nextInt(5);
```

6.10 Programming exercises

1. Write a program that reads a sequence of integers from the terminal window and prints a frequency report showing how many times the integers 0, 1, ..., 9 occur in the sequence. Assume that the sequence is terminated by a negative integer. For example, if the user enters the following sequence:

```
8
0
2
8
8
9
5
9
-3
```

The program prints the following frequency report:

```
0 occurs 1 time
2 occurs 1 time
5 occurs 1 time
8 occurs 3 times
9 occurs 2 times
```

Tip: create an array of ten integers in which each element is a counter for its index value.

2. Extend the program from Exercise 6.1 so that a histogram is printed in which the columns are horizontal. A column corresponds to the number of occurrences of each integer.

Example:

```
0: *
1: ***
2: *
3:
4: **
5: *
6: ****
7:
8: ***
9: **
```

3. Modify the program from Exercise 6.2 so that the histogram is printed with vertical columns.

Example:

```
                    *
    *               *      *
    *        *      *      *   *
  *   *      *   *  *      *   *
  ==0==1==2==3==4==5==6==7==8==9==
```

4. Write a program that reads a list of ten integers from the terminal window and stores them in an array. The program should print the position of the smallest number in the array.

If the position of the smallest number is other than 0, the program should swap the number in position 0 with the smallest value. After swapping, the smallest number is now in position 0 and the number that was previously in position 0 is now where the smallest number was. Finally the program should print the values in the array.

5. Modify Program 6.3 so that it uses the for(:) loop.

6. Modify Program 6.4 so that the values for the two-dimensional array weeklyData are read from the terminal window.

7. Modify Program 6.4 so that it calculates the total number of text messages sent each day, and the total number of text messages sent from each mobile phone:

```
Day no.          0    1    2    3    4    5    6    Sum(phone):
Phone index 0:  12   10   22   33   19   27   16   139
Phone index 1:  45   55   44   34   39   15   11   243
Phone index 2:  18   26   36   40   24   11   20   175
Sum(day):       75   91  102  107   82   53   47
```

8. Write a program to play the game of *Craps*. The game is played by rolling two dice, where the sum of the rolled values of the two dice determines the course of the game. The program simulates the game by enforcing the following rules:

- If the sum of the roll values is 7 or 11 at the first roll, the player has won. The sum of the roll values is called a *natural*.
- If the sum of the roll values is 2 (*snakes eyes*), 3 (*cross eyes*) or 12 (*box cars*) at the first roll, the player has lost.
- If the sum of the roll values is 4, 5, 6, 8, 9 or 10 at the first roll, the sum of the roll values establishes a *point* and the player can roll the dice again. The player continues to roll the dice until the sum of the roll values is either 7 or equal to the point. A sum of the roll values equal to 7 means the player has lost, while a sum of the roll values equal to the point means the player has won.

9. Write a program to play the game of *Mastermind*. The aim of the game is to guess a secret code which is a finite sequence of digits, usually four. The program generates the code and gives feedback to the player after each guess based on the following rules:

- Number of *bulls* in the guess, i.e. number of digits that are correctly identified in the code and are in the correct position.
- Number of *cows* in the guess, i.e. number of digits that are correctly identified in the code, but are not in the correct position.

Example (the code is 9464):

```
Guess no. 1: 4444
No. of bulls: 2
No. of cows: 0
Guess no. 2: 4675
No. of bulls: 0
No. of cows: 2
Guess no. 3: 3494
No. of bulls: 2
No. of cows: 1
...
```

10. Write a program to grade a multiple-choice quiz. The correct answers for the quiz are:

```
1. A    6. C
2. D    7. B
3. B    8. A
4. C    9. D
5. D    10. A
```

Pass marks are seven out of ten.

The program stores the correct answers in an array. The candidate's answers are read from the terminal window and are stored in another array. Let the character 'X' represent a question not answered by the candidate.

The program calculates and prints the following results:

- Whether the candidate passed the quiz or not.
- The total number of questions answered correctly by the candidate.
- The total number of questions answered incorrectly by the candidate.
- The total number of questions not answered by the candidate.
- A list of all the questions, showing what the candidate answered and what the correct answer was.

Example:

```
Enter in the answers: A D C C D C X B D A
The candidate PASSED
No. of questions answered correctly: 7
No. of questions answered incorrectly: 2
No. of questions not answered: 1
Question    Candidate Ans. Correct Ans.
1.          A              A
2.          D              D
3.          C              B
...
```

Defining classes

INTRODUCTION

Chapter 4 introduced the object model that is the foundation for object-oriented programming, in which programs are composed of objects that collaborate to provide the required functionality. An object belongs to a class that defines the common properties and behaviour of a particular type of objects. When writing programs, defining and understanding problem-specific classes is essential. In this chapter we focus on how to define and use our own classes, called user-defined classes, as apposed to the predefined classes found in the Java standard library. We also introduce a special kind of class that can be used to define finite sets of symbolic constants, called enumerated types.

7.1 Class members

A *class declaration* defines the properties and the behaviour of the objects of the class. We will discuss the purpose of the different declarations that can be specified in a class declaration. We will also look at how these declarations are used inside the class and by other classes. These declarations are called *member declarations*.

Figure 7.1 gives an overview of the different *members* that can be declared in a class. *Field variables* represent properties and *instance methods* define the behaviour of the *objects* of the class. The term *instance* means an object of a class. Field variables and instance methods are collectively called *instance members*, and belong to the objects of the class.

In Java, a class can also define the properties and behaviour that belong to the class (see Figure 7.1). *Static variables* represent properties, and *static methods* define the behaviour of the class. Static variables and static methods are collectively called *static members*, and belong to the *class*, *not* to the objects of the class. Static members are discussed in Section 7.4.

Member declarations in a class can be declared in any order. It's common practice to group instance and static members separately, and further organise them according to fields and methods, as shown in Figure 7.1.

FIGURE 7.1   Overview of members in a class declaration

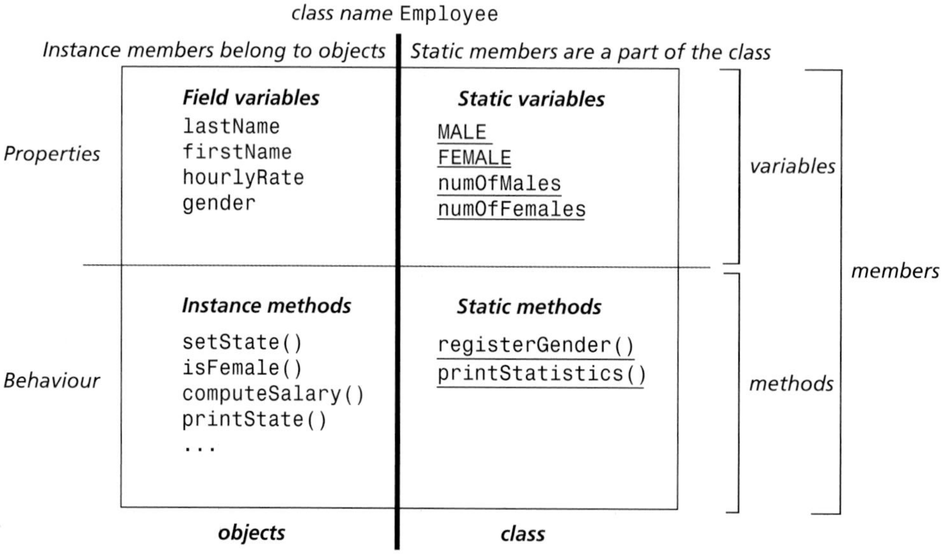

In addition to the members mentioned above, a class can also declare *constructors*. Constructors resemble methods, but the primary use of a constructor is to set the state of an object when the object is created. Section 7.5 discusses constructors.

We will use a class for employees in a company as a running example, and fill in the details of the class declaration in subsequent sections. You may find it useful to refer to

Figure 7.1 as we discuss the various members, to help identify to which group a member belongs.

7.2 Defining object properties using field variables

Field declarations

As we have noted, field variables in a class declaration define the properties of objects that can be created from the class. Each object gets its own copy of the field variables. A *field declaration* specifies both the *field type* and the *field name*, just like in the declaration of local variables. The code below defines four field variables for the class EmployeeV1:

```
class EmployeeV1 {            // Assume that no constructors are declared.
  // Field variables
  String  firstName;
  String  lastName;
  double  hourlyRate;
  boolean gender;            // false means male, true means female
  // ...
}
```

The field declarations above show that a field can be either a variable, such as the field name hourlyRate, that can store a value of a primitive type, for example the primitive type double, or it can be a reference variable, such as the field name firstName, that can store a reference value of an object, for example that of the String class. Objects that are created from the class will have a field for each of the field declarations in the class declaration.

Initializing fields

We create objects from a class using the new operator, which requires a constructor call:

```
EmployeeV1 anEmployee = new EmployeeV1();
```

The new operator creates a new object of the EmployeeV1 class in memory. This object will have room for all the fields declared in the class EmployeeV1. In the current version of the class, all objects created this way will have their fields initialized to *default values*, as shown in Figure 7.2a.

The *state* of an object comprises all values in the field variables of the object at any given time. The state can change over time, as the field values change. In the case of the EmployeeV1 class, the *initial state* of an object is thus the default values of the field variables (Figure 7.2a).

7

FIGURE 7.2 Field initialization (no constructors defined)

```
anEmployee:EmployeeV1

lastName    = null
firstName   = null
hourlyRate  = 0.0
gender      = false
```

```
employeeA:EmployeeV2

lastName    = "Joe"
firstName   = "Jones"
hourlyRate  = 15.50
gender      = false
```

(a) Field initialization with default values   (b) Field initialization with initial values

It is possible to assign an initial value to the variable in a variable declaration. The same can be done for field variables. The class EmployeeV2 specifies an initial value for all its field variables:

```
class EmployeeV2 {                    // Assume that no constructors are declared.
    // Field variables with initial values
    String  firstName  = "Joe";
    String  lastName   = "Jones";
    double  hourlyRate = 15.50;
    boolean gender     = false;  // false means male, true means female
    // ...
}
```

We can create an object of the class EmployeeV2 using the new operator:

```
EmployeeV2 employeeA = new EmployeeV2();
```

Execution of the expression new EmployeeV2() will always return an object with the initial state shown in Figure 7.2b, assuming that the class does not define any constructors that initialize the fields. Section 7.5 explains how the initial state can be customised by using constructors.

BEST PRACTICES

Always initialize the fields of a newly-created object in a constructor, so that the object gets a valid initial state.

7.3 Defining behaviour using instance methods

Method declaration and formal parameters

In Chapter 3 we saw that a method declaration comprises a method header and a method body. Figure 7.3 shows the declaration of the method computeSalary() in the class EmployeeV3. The method header declares the *return type*, the *method name* and the *parameter list*.

The return type of the method `computeSalary()` is the primitive type `double`, which means that the method returns a floating-point number when the method is called. If a method is not supposed to return a value, the keyword `void` should be specified instead of the return type. For example, see the method `setState()` in class `EmployeeV3` shown in Program 7.1. A non-void method must specify a return type.

The name of the method reflects what it does. The parameter list of the method indicates what information the method needs to do its job. The parameter list declares *formal parameters* for the method, in which each parameter is specified as a variable declaration with the parameter name and the parameter type. The method `computeSalary()` has a formal parameter `numOfHours` with the primitive type `double`. The type of a formal parameter can also be a reference type, for example a class or an array. The parameter list is always enclosed in parentheses, `()`, even if the method has no parameters. The method and the parameter list constitute the *signature* of the method. The signature determines which method declaration is chosen for execution by a method call. The method `compute-Salary()` has the following signature:

```
computeSalary(double)
```

FIGURE 7.3   Method declaration

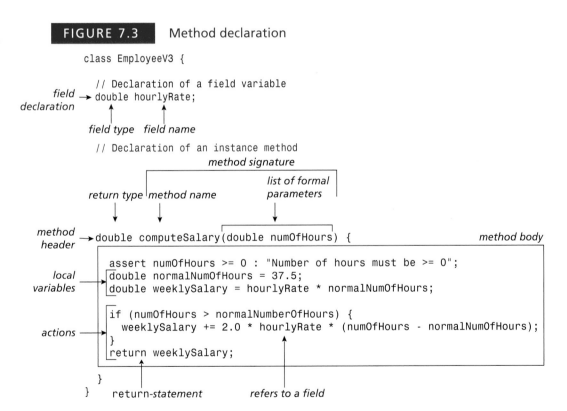

The method body comprises variable declarations and actions. Variable declarations in the method body define the local variables needed to hold values during the execution of the method. Such variables are accessible only in the method body, and are not accessible outside the method in which they are declared. Formal parameters are also local variables. Several methods can have the same names for their local variables, but these are only accessible within the method in which they are declared. The method `computeSalary()` has the following local variables: `normalNumOfHours`, `numOfHours`, `weeklySalary`.

The method body implements the actions. For example, the `if` statement in the body of the method `computeSalary()` is used to determine whether the employee that the object represents should receive any compensation for overtime. There are several statements, such as assignments, control flow statements and method calls, that can be used when implementing the behaviour of objects.

Local variables and statements can be defined in any order, but the rule is that a local variable must be declared before it can be used in the method body. It is a good idea to declare a local variable at the same time as when first assigning a value to it. This aids in making the purpose of the program clear.

PROGRAM 7.1   Declaration of instance methods

```
class EmployeeV3 {                    // Assume that no constructors are declared.
   // Field variables
   String firstName;
   String lastName;
   double hourlyRate;
   boolean gender;                    // false means male, true means female

   // Instance methods

   // Assign values to the field variables of an employee.
   void setState(String fName, String lName,
                 double hRate, boolean genderValue) {
      firstName = fName;
      lastName = lName;
      hourlyRate = hRate;
      gender = genderValue;
   }

   // Determines whether an employee is female.
   boolean isFemale() { return gender; }

   // Computes the salary of an employee, based on the number of hours
   // worked during the week.
   double computeSalary(double numOfHours) {
      assert numOfHours >= 0 : "Number of hours must be >= 0";
      double normalNumOfHours = 37.5;
      double weeklySalary = hourlyRate * normalNumOfHours;
      if (numOfHours > normalNumOfHours) {
         weeklySalary += 2.0 * hourlyRate * (numOfHours - normalNumOfHours);
      }
      return weeklySalary;
   }

   // Prints the values in the field variables of an employee.
```

```
  void printState() {
    System.out.print("First name: " + firstName);
    System.out.print("\tLast name: " + lastName);
    System.out.printf("\tHourly rate: %.2f", hourlyRate);
    if (isFemale()) {
      System.out.println("\tGender: Female");
    } else {
      System.out.println("\tGender: Male");
    }
  }
}
```

Method calls and actual parameter expressions

A method call is used to execute a method body. Figure 7.4 shows an example. A call specifies the object whose method is called (given by the reference manager in this case), the name of the method and any information the method needs to execute its actions. These are referred to as *actual parameters*, or *arguments*. An actual parameter is an *expression*, in contrast to a formal parameter specified in the method declaration, which is always a *variable*. The *signature of a method call* consists of the method name and the type of the actual parameter expressions. In Figure 7.4, for example, the method call has the following signature:

```
setState(String, String, double, boolean)        // (1) Call signature
```

The compiler checks that a method exists that corresponds to the method call. It requires the signature of the method call to be compatible with the signature of the method declaration. This compatibility implies that the value of the first actual parameter can be assigned to the first formal parameter, the value of the second actual parameter can be assigned to the second formal parameter and so on. In Figure 7.4 the declaration of the method setState() has the following signature:

```
setState(String, String, double, boolean)        // (2) Method signature
```

We can therefore see that the signature of the call to the method setState() at (1) corresponds to the signature of the method declaration at (2). For all formal parameters, the value of the actual parameter type is actually assigned to the corresponding formal parameter variable, as shown in Figure 7.4 on page 168.

Finally, here are some examples of method calls that result in compile time errors. The following method calls to the method setState():

```
manager.setState(name, hourlyRate*2.0, "Jones", false); // (3) Method call
manager.setState(name, "Jones", hourlyRate*2.0);        // (4) Method call
```

have the following signatures respectively:

```
setState(String, double, String, boolean)  // (5) Call signature
setState(String, String, double)           // (6) Call signature
```

We can see that the call signatures at (5) and (6) do not correspond to the method signature in (2) above. The call signature at (5) results in a compile time error, because of the second parameter in the call, as a value of type `double` cannot be assigned to a `String` reference in the method signature. In the call signature at (6), the number of actual parameters is not correct – it should be four.

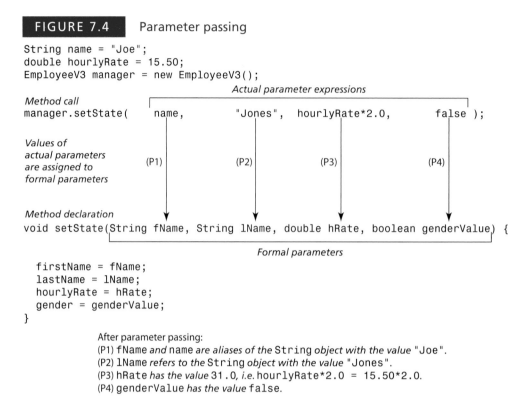

FIGURE 7.4   Parameter passing

After parameter passing:
(P1) `fName` and `name` *are aliases of the* `String` *object with the value* `"Joe"`.
(P2) `lName` *refers to the* `String` *object with the value* `"Jones"`.
(P3) `hRate` *has the value* `31.0`*, i.e.* `hourlyRate*2.0` `=` `15.50*2.0`.
(P4) `genderValue` *has the value* `false`.

Parameter passing: call-by-value

An actual parameter expression is evaluated and its value is assigned to the corresponding formal parameter variable. All actual expressions are evaluated before the call to the method is executed. In the call to the `setState()` method in Figure 7.4, all actual parameters are simple expressions that evaluate to the following values: a reference value of a `String` object with the value `"Joe"`, a reference value of a `String` object with the value `"Jones"`, the floating-point value `31.0` (`hourlyRate*2.0` `=` `15.5*2.0`), and the Boolean value `false`.

Before the method is executed, values of the actual parameter expressions are assigned to the corresponding formal parameter variables. Parameter passing in Figure 7.4 is equivalent to the following assignments:

```
String fName = name;            // (P1) reference value of "Joe"
String lName = "Jones";         // (P2) reference value of "Jones"
double hRate = 31.0;            // (P3) primitive value 31.0
boolean genderValue = false;    // (P4) primitive value false
```

At (P1) and (P2) in Figure 7.4, the actual parameter values are *reference values*, so these reference values are passed before execution of the method `setState()` starts. The assignment at (P1) implies that references `fname` and `name` are aliases to the same `String` object with the value `"Joe"` at the start of execution of the method `setState()`. Analogously, the reference `lName` at (P2) refers to the `String` object with the value `"Jones"` at the start of the execution in the method `setState()`. Note that no objects are copied, only reference values. (P3) and (P4) show the passing of primitive values, `double` and `boolean` respectively. This way of passing parameters in which only values are passed is called *call-by-value*.

Program 7.2 illustrates the execution of the method call in Figure 7.4. The program prints the state of the `EmployeeV3` object referred to by the `manager` reference before and after the call to the `setState()` method. The program output confirms that the state of the `EmployeeV3` object created in (1) was updated with the values of the actual parameter expressions in the method call at (2).

The remainder of Program 7.2 is explained in *Consequences of call-by-value* on page 170.

PROGRAM 7.2   Parameter passing: call-by-value

```
// Illustrating parameter passing
public class Client3A {
  public static void main(String[] args) {

    String name = "Joe";
    double hourlyRate = 15.50;
    EmployeeV3 manager = new EmployeeV3();                      // (1)
    System.out.println("Manager state before call to setState() method");
    manager.printState();
    manager.setState(name, "Jones", hourlyRate*2.0, false);  // (2)
    System.out.println("Manager state after call to setState() method");
    manager.printState();
    System.out.println();

    System.out.printf("Manager hourly rate before adjusting: %.2f%n",
                      manager.hourlyRate);                     // (3)
    adjustHourlyRate(manager.hourlyRate);    // (4) LOGICAL ERROR!
    System.out.printf("Manager hourly rate after adjusting: %.2f%n",
                      manager.hourlyRate);
    System.out.println();

    EmployeeV3 director = new EmployeeV3();                     // (5)
    System.out.println("Director state before call to copyState() method");
    director.printState();
    copyState(manager, director);                              // (6)
    assert (manager.lastName.equals(director.lastName) &&
            manager.firstName.equals(director.firstName) &&
            manager.hourlyRate == director.hourlyRate &&
            manager.gender == director.gender) :
            "Manager and director have different states after copying.";
    System.out.println("Director state after call to copyState() method:");
    director.printState();
```

```
        System.out.println("Manager state after call to copyState() method:");
        manager.printState();
        System.out.println();
    }

    // Method that tries to adjust the hourly rate.
    static void adjustHourlyRate(double hourlyRate) {          // (7)
        hourlyRate = 1.5 * hourlyRate;                         // (8)
        System.out.printf("Adjusted hourlyRate: %.2f%n", hourlyRate);
    }

    // Method that copies the state of one employee over to another employee.
    static void copyState(EmployeeV3 fromEmployee,
                          EmployeeV3 toEmployee) {              // (9)

        toEmployee.setState(fromEmployee.firstName,            // (10)
                            fromEmployee.lastName,
                            fromEmployee.hourlyRate,
                            fromEmployee.gender);

        toEmployee = fromEmployee = null;                      // (11)
    }
}
```

Program output:

```
Manager state before call to setState() method
First name: null  Last name: null Hourly rate: 0.00 Gender: Male
Manager state after call to setState() method
First name: Joe Last name: Jones  Hourly rate: 31.00  Gender: Male

Manager hourly rate before adjusting: 31.00
Adjusted hourlyRate: 46.50
Manager hourly rate after adjusting: 31.00

Director state before call to copyState() method
First name: null  Last name: null Hourly rate: 0.00 Gender: Male
Director state after call to copyState() method:
First name: Joe Last name: Jones  Hourly rate: 31.00  Gender: Male
Manager state after call to copyState() method:
First name: Joe Last name: Jones  Hourly rate: 31.00  Gender: Male
```

Consequences of call-by-value

Inside the method body a formal parameter is used like any other local variable in the method, so that changing its value in the method has no effect on the value of the corresponding actual parameter in the method call.

The class `Client3A` defines a static method `adjustHourlyRate()` at (7) in Program 7.2. This method changes the value of the formal parameter `hourlyRate`:

```
hourlyRate = 1.5 * hourlyRate;                                    // (8)
```

The method `adjustHourlyRate()` is called at (4) in the hope of adjusting the hourly rate of an employee. Output from the program shows that changing the value of the formal parameter `hourlyRate` in the method has no effect on the value of the variable `manager.hourlyRate`, which is the corresponding actual parameter. A simple solution for getting the adjusted value from the method `adjustHourlyRate()` is to modify the method so that it returns the adjusted value:

```
static double adjustHourlyRate(double hourlyRate) {              // (7)
  hourlyRate = 1.5 * hourlyRate;                                 // (8)
  System.out.printf("Adjusted hourly rate: %.2f%n", hourlyRate);
  return hourlyRate;
}
```

The value returned by the method call can then be assigned explicitly:

```
manager.hourlyRate = adjustHourlyRate(manager.hourlyRate);
```

Reference values as actual parameter values

The state of an object whose reference value is passed to a formal parameter variable can be changed in the method, and the changes will be apparent after return from the method call. Such a state change is illustrated by the method `copyState()` in Program 7.2.

The class `Client3A` defines the static method `copyState()` at (9), which copies the state of one employee to another employee. The method is called at (6):

```
copyState(manager, director);                                   // (6)
```

After the call we see from the output that the state of the `Employee3V` object referred to by the reference `director` has the same state as the `Employee3V` object referred to by the reference `manager`. Only the reference values of the two objects are passed in the method call. The state of the employee object referred to by the reference `director` is changed via the formal parameter reference `toEmployee`. These changes are apparent after return from the method call, as confirmed by the program output. At (11) the values of both the formal variables are set to `null`, but this has no effect on the variables that make up the actual parameter expressions. These variables, `manager` and `director`, still refer to their respective objects after return from the method.

Arrays as actual parameter values

Passing arrays as parameter values does not differ from what we have seen earlier for other objects that occur in actual parameter expressions. If the actual parameter evaluates to a reference value of an array, for example, then this reference value is passed. Program 7.3 illustrates the use of arrays as actual parameters.

Four arrays are created with information about three employees at (1) in Program 7.3. The same index in all the four arrays gives information about the same employee. This information is used to create an array of three employees in (2), (3) and (4). In addition,

7

an array contains the number of hours each employee has worked in a week, at (5). Finally, the salaries of all the employees in the array `employeeArray` are computed by a call to the static method `computeSalaries()`.

Because we use the `[]` notation to declare an array, we use the same notation to declare an array reference as a formal parameter. An example of such a declaration is shown at (7) in Program 7.3:

```
static void computeSalaries(EmployeeV3[] employeeArray,
                            double[] hoursArray) {...}
```

The references `employeeArray` and `hoursArray` refer to arrays of type `Employee3V[]` and `double[]`, respectively. Without the `[]` notation, these references would not be array references. (6) shows a call to this method:

```
computeSalaries(employeeArray, hoursArray);
```

Again parameter passing is equivalent to the following assignments in which the reference values of the arrays are passed:

```
EmployeeV3[] employees = employeeArray;    // Reference value of array
double[]     hours     = hoursArray;       // Reference value of array
```

We don't use the `[]` notation for array variables when these are passed as actual parameters in a method call. Instead, the reference value of the array is passed just like the reference value of any other object, as shown in the assignments above. Note that the signature of the method is:

```
computeSalaries(EmployeeV3[], double[])    // Method signature
```

and the signature of the method call corresponds to the method signature. Note also that there is no requirement on the length of the array in the method call, which is implicitly given by the `length` field of the array. However, the call must have the right *array type*.

If an *array element* occurs in an actual parameter expression, the value of the element is used in the evaluation of the expression and the expression value is passed, as one would expect. If the actual parameter is an array element of a primitive type, for example `hourlyRateArray[2]`, whose type is `double`, the primitive value is passed. If the actual parameter is an array element of a reference type, for example `lastNameArray[1]`, whose type is `String`, the reference value of the element object is passed. (4) in Program 7.3 shows a call to the method `setState()`, in which the actual parameter expressions are array elements. Note that the types of the actual parameters at (4) are in agreement with the type list (`String, String, double, boolean`) in the signature of the `setState()` method.

PROGRAM 7.3 Arrays as actual parameters

```
// Passing arrays
public class Client3B {

  public static void main(String[] args) {
    // (1) Associated arrays with information about employees:
    String[] firstNameArray = { "Tom", "Dick", "Linda" };
```

```
   String[] lastNameArray = { "Tanner", "Dickens", "Larsen" };
   double[] hourlyRateArray = { 30.00, 25.50, 15.00 };
   boolean[] genderArray = { false, false, true };

   // (2) Array with employees:
   EmployeeV3[] employeeArray = new EmployeeV3[3];

   // (3) Create all employees:
   for (int i = 0; i < employeeArray.length; i++) {
     employeeArray[i] = new EmployeeV3();
     employeeArray[i].setState(firstNameArray[i], lastNameArray[i],
                       hourlyRateArray[i], genderArray[i]);   // (4)
   }

   // (5) Array with hours worked by each employee:
   double[] hoursArray = { 50.5, 32.8, 66.0 };

   // (6) Compute the salary for all employees:
   computeSalaries(employeeArray, hoursArray);
 }

 // (7) Compute the salary for all employees:
 static void computeSalaries(EmployeeV3[] employees,
                       double[] hours) {
   for (int i = 0; i < employees.length; i++) {
     System.out.printf("Salary for %s %s: %.2f%n",
                   employees[i].firstName,
                   employees[i].lastName,
                   employees[i].computeSalary(hours[i]));
   }
 }
}
```

Program output:

```
Salary for Tom Tanner: 1905.00
Salary for Dick Dickens: 956.25
Salary for Linda Larsen: 1417.50
```

The current object: **this**

When we call an instance method of an object, we say that the method is *invoked* on the object. The object whose method is invoked becomes the *current object*. Inside the method, the current object can be referred to by the keyword this, i.e. the keyword this is a reference. We can think of the this reference as an implicit actual parameter that is passed to an instance method each time it is invoked. For example, in the method call:

```
manager.setState(name, "Jones", hourlyRate*2.0, false);   // (2)
```

the reference value held in the reference manager will be available in the this reference inside the method setState() when the method is executed. So the method setState() in Program 7.1 could be declared as follows using the this reference:

```
void setState(String fName, String lName,
              double hRate, boolean genderValue) {
  this.firstName  = fName;
  this.lastName   = lName;
  this.hourlyRate = hRate;
  this.gender     = genderValue;
}
```

The reference this can be used exactly like any other reference in the method, except that its value cannot be changed, i.e. it is a final reference. For example, we can refer to the field firstName in the current object by using the expression this.firstName, as shown above in the declaration of the method.

If a local variable has the same name as a field variable, the local variable will *shadow* the field variable, as shown in this declaration of the same method:

```
void setState(String firstName, String lastName,
              double hRate, boolean genderValue) {
  firstName  = firstName;  // (1)
  lastName   = lastName;   // (2)
  hourlyRate = hRate;
  gender     = genderValue;
}
```

The first two formal parameters have the same names as the field variables firstName and lastName. Formal parameters are local variables, and inside the method these two names refer to the formal parameters. At (1) and (2) above, values of the formal parameters are assigned back to the formal parameters. We can use the this reference to distinguish the field variable from the local variable when they have the same name:

```
void setState(String firstName, String lastName,
              double hRate, boolean genderValue) {
  this.firstName  = firstName;  // (1')
  this.lastName   = lastName;   // (2')
  this.hourlyRate = hRate;
  this.gender     = genderValue;
}
```

Method execution and the **return** statement

When we invoke a method on an object, the method can in turn invoke other methods, either on the current object or on other objects. Figure 7.5 illustrates invocation of the method setState() in which we have introduced two local variables (i and s) and two calls to the method printState():

```
void setState(String firstName, String lastName,
              double hRate, boolean genderValue) {
```

```
    // Some superfluous local variables
    int i;
    String s;

    this.printState();                  // Print state before
    this.firstName  = firstName;
    this.lastName   = lastName;
    this.hourlyRate = hRate;
    this.gender     = genderValue;
    this.printState();                  // Print state after
  }
```

The call to the method setState() is not complete when the executions of the two calls to the method printState() has completed. The current object is an object of class EmployeeV3, and its state will be printed twice. Note that execution continues in the method setState() after return from the calls to the method printState(). The execution of the calls to the method printState() is embedded in the call to the method setState().

A local variable is not initialized to a default value during method execution. If we try to use a local variable before it has been assigned a value, the compiler will report an error.

BEST PRACTICES

Always initialize local variables when they are declared.

We can see from Figure 7.5 on page 176 that control returns from the method setState() only after the last statement in the method has been executed. This need not always be the case: the return statement can be used to end execution of a method wherever appropriate.

The return statement comes in two forms. The first form of the statement consists of the keyword return only:

```
    return;       // Method execution stops, and control returns.
```

This form can be used when the method does not return a value, for example in the method setState(). We could have included a return statement as the last statement, but that would be redundant, as the execution of the method will end anyway when there are no more statements left to execute in the method body.

7

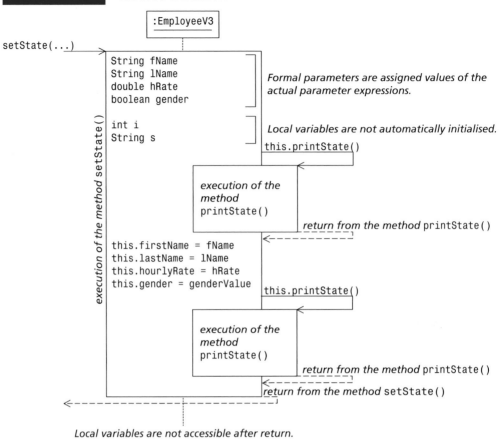

FIGURE 7.5   Method execution

Figure 7.5 Method execution

The second form of the return statement requires an expression in addition to the keyword return. The value of this expression is returned after the execution of the method stops at the return statement. The method must explicitly specify the *return type* in the method header, and the *return value* must be of this return type. The return statement is required for methods that return a value, and the compiler will insist upon it. The method computeSalary() below illustrates the use of the return statement:

```
double computeSalary(double numOfHours) {
    assert numOfHours >= 0 : "Number of hours must be >= 0";
    double normalNumberOfHours = 37.5;
    double weeklySalary = hourlyRate * normalNumberOfHours;
    if (numOfHours <= normalNumberOfHours) {
        return weeklySalary;                                    // (1)
    }
    return weeklySalary +
            2.0 * hourlyRate * (numOfHours - normalNumberOfHours);     // (2)
}
```

The execution of the method stops when either (1) or (2) is executed. The method will return the value of the expression in the return statement that was executed. In both (1)

and (2) the expression evaluates to a value of type double, which is the return type specified in the method header. A method can return only one value, either a value of a primitive type or a reference value of an object.

The method computeSalary() above has two exits, corresponding to the two return statements. Execution can be difficult to understand if a method has too many exits. We can rewrite the method computeSalary() so that it has only one exit and in which the variable weeklySalary always holds the correct salary, allowing for overtime:

```
double computeSalary(double numOfHours) {
   assert numOfHours >= 0 : "Number of hours must be >= 0";
   double normalNumberOfHours = 37.5;
   double weeklySalary = hourlyRate * normalNumberOfHours;
   if (numOfHours > normalNumberOfHours) {
      weeklySalary += 2.0 * hourlyRate * (numOfHours - normalNumberOfHours);
   }
   return weeklySalary;
}
```

BEST PRACTICES

Keeping the number of exits from a method to a minimum aids in understanding the program logic.

Passing information using arrays

Program 7.4 shows two ways of passing information between methods using arrays.

At (1a) the method main() calls the method fillStringArray() declared at (3a), passing an empty array of strings. The method fillStringArray() reads as many strings as the length of the array, and fills the array. After control returns from the method fillStringArray(), the actual parameter firstNameArray still refers to the same array whose reference value was passed, but which is now filled with string values. The method call and the method declaration are as follows:

```
fillStringArray(firstNameArray);                        // (1a) Call
...
static void fillStringArray(String[] strArray) { ... } // (3a) Declaration
```

At (2a) the method main() calls the method createStringArray() declared at (4a). The method createStringArray() first asks the user for the number of values to read. It then creates an array of strings of this size, and subsequently fills the array. The method createStringArray() returns the reference value of the array, which on return is assigned to the local reference variable lastNameArray. The array object created in the method createStringArray() continues to exist even after the method has finished executing, because the reference value of the array was stored in a local reference variable on return. The method call and the method declaration in this case are as follows:

```
String[] lastNameArray = createStringArray();// (2a) variable type String[]
```

```
...
static String[] createStringArray() { ... }  // (4a) return type String[]
```

Which approach is best depends on how much work the calling method wants the called method to do, i.e. more than just read the values and fill the array.

PROGRAM 7.4   Handling arrays

```
import java.util.Scanner;
public class ArrayMaker {

  public static void main(String[] args) {
    // (1) Read first names:
    String[] firstNameArray = new String[3];
    System.out.println("Read first names");
    fillStringArray(firstNameArray);                    // (1a)
    printStrArray(firstNameArray);

    // (2) Read last names:
    System.out.println("Read last names");
    String[] lastNameArray = createStringArray();       // (2a)
    printStrArray(lastNameArray);
  }

  // (3) Reference value of the array to be filled is passed
  //     as formal parameter:
  static void fillStringArray(String[] strArray) {      // (3a)
    Scanner keyboard = new Scanner(System.in);
    for (int i = 0; i < strArray.length; i++) {
      System.out.print("Next: ");
      strArray[i] = keyboard.nextLine();
    }
  }

  // (4) The method creates and fills an array of strings.
  //     The reference value of this array is returned by the method:
  static String[] createStringArray() {                 // (4a)
    Scanner keyboard = new Scanner(System.in);
    System.out.print("Enter the number of items to read: ");
    int size = keyboard.nextInt();
    String[] strArray = new String[size];
    keyboard.nextLine();                    // Clear any input first
    for (int i = 0; i < strArray.length; i++) {
      System.out.print("Next: ");
      strArray[i] = keyboard.nextLine();
    }
    return strArray;
  }

  // (5) Prints the strings in an array to the terminal window:
```

```
    static void printStrArray(String[] strArray) {
      for (String str : strArray) {
        System.out.println(str);
      }
    }
}
```

Program output:

```
Read first names
Next: Tom
Next: Dick
Next: Linda
Tom
Dick
Linda
Read last names
Enter the number of items to read: 3
Next: Tanner
Next: Dickens
Next: Larsen
Tanner
Dickens
Larsen
```

Automatic garbage collection

Objects that are no longer in use are taken care of by the JVM without the program having to do anything special. These objects are deleted from memory, and the memory freed can be used for new objects. It is always the JVM that decides *when* such a clean up should take place, for example when it starts to run out of free memory. This clean-up process is called *automatic garbage collection*.

Note that if a method creates an object and return its reference value, the reference value of the object can be used after the method returns. Such an object would therefore not be a candidate for garbage collection. If the reference value of an object is only stored in a local variable, the object will not be accessible after return from the method. Such an object can be garbage collected by the JVM.

7.4 Static members of a class

Static members specify properties and behaviour of the *class*, and are therefore not a part of any object created from the class.

The following simple example illustrates the use of static members. How can we keep track of the number of male and female employee objects that have been created? We can define two counters that are incremented, depending on whether a male or a female employee is created. If these counters are declared as instance variables in the class declaration, they will exist in every employee object we create from the class. Each object will have two counters, so which counters should we use to do the book keeping? One solution is to maintain the counters as static variables for the class only, and update the appropriate counter each time an employee object is created.

We use the keyword `static` in the declaration of static members to distinguish them from instance members. Program 7.5 shows declarations of static variables and methods at (1) and (2) respectively.

The class `EmployeeV4` in Program 7.5 declares the following two static variables (see under (1)):

```
static int numOfFemales;
static int numOfMales;
```

Static variables are *global variables* in the sense that there is only one occurrence of such variables and that is in the class, in contrast to instance variables that exist in each object created from the class.

Static variables are also useful for defining *global constants*. Once a value is assigned to such a variable its value cannot be changed. Such constants can be used inside the class and by other classes. If we decide that the Boolean value `true` indicates a female employee, then the Boolean value `false` indicates a male employee. Instead of using the Boolean values directly for this purpose, we can define and use constants with meaningful names (see (1) in Program 7.5):

```
static final boolean MALE = false;
static final boolean FEMALE = true;
```

The keyword `static` states that they can be considered as global variables, and the keyword `final` prevents the values assigned to these variables from being changed, i.e they are global constants. Section 7.6 on page 192 illustrates a more elegant solution for defining a fixed number of such constants.

The class `EmployeeV4` also declares two static methods: `registerGender()` and `printStatistics()` at (2). The method `registerGender()` increments the relevant counter depending on the value of its parameter, and the method `printStatistics()` prints the number of male and female employees registered at any given time. We will put these methods to use in the next subsection.

Figure 7.6 shows the UML diagram for the class `EmployeeV4` with all its members. Static members are underlined in the diagram to distinguish them from instance members.

7

PROGRAM 7.5 Static members

```
class EmployeeV4 { // Assume that no constructors are declared.

  // (1) Static variables:
  static final boolean MALE = false;
  static final boolean FEMALE = true;
  static final double NORMAL_WORKWEEK = 37.5;
  static int numOfFemales;
```

```
    static int numOfMales;

    // (2) Static methods:
    // Register an employee's gender by updating the relevant counter.
    static void registerGender (boolean gender) {
      if (gender == FEMALE) {
        ++numOfFemales;
      } else {
        ++numOfMales;
      }
    }
    // Print statistics about the number of males and females registered.
    static void printStatistics() {
      System.out.println("Number of females registered: " +
                         EmployeeV4.numOfFemales);                    // (3)
      System.out.println("Number of males registered: " +
                         EmployeeV4.numOfMales);                      // (4)
    }

    // Rest of the specification is the same as in class EmployeeV3
    // ...

}
// Accessing static members
public class Client4A {

  public static void main(String[] args) {
    // (5) Print information in class EmployeeV4 before any objects
    //     are created:
    System.out.println("Print information in class EmployeeV4:");
    System.out.println("Females registered: " +
                       EmployeeV4.numOfFemales);        // (6) class name
    System.out.println("Males registered: " +
                       EmployeeV4.numOfMales);           // (7) class name

    // (8) Create a male employee.
    EmployeeV4 coffeeboy = new EmployeeV4();
    coffeeboy.setState("Tim", "Turner", 30.00, EmployeeV4.MALE);
    coffeeboy.registerGender(EmployeeV4.MALE);          // (9) referanse
    System.out.println("Print information in class EmployeeV4:");
    coffeeboy.printStatistics();                        // (10) referanse

    // (11)  Create a female employee.
    EmployeeV4 receptionist = new EmployeeV4();
    receptionist.setState("Amy", "Archer", 20.50, EmployeeV4.FEMALE);
    EmployeeV4.registerGender(EmployeeV4.FEMALE);
    System.out.println("Print information in class EmployeeV4:");
    EmployeeV4.printStatistics();
  }
}
```

7

Program output:

```
Print information in class EmployeeV4:
Females registered: 0
Males registered: 0
Print information in class EmployeeV4:
Number of females registered: 0
Number of males registered: 1
Print information in class EmployeeV4:
Number of females registered: 1
Number of males registered: 1
```

FIGURE 7.6   UML diagram showing all members in a class

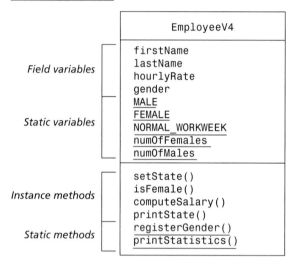

Accessing static members

A static member can be accessed using the notation *className.memberName*. At (3) and (4) in Program 7.5 the method `printStatistics()` refers to the static variables `numOfFe-males` and `numOfMales` using this notation: `EmployeeV4.numOfFemales` and `EmployeeV4.numOf-Males`.

We can use the member name to refer to static members in the same class inside any method, provided that the name is not shadowed by a local variable. The method `regis-terGender()` in Program 7.5 refers to the static variables `numOfFemales` and `numOfMales` in class `EmployeeV4`.

Inside an instance method, we can also use the `this` reference to refer to static members in the same class. The `this` reference refers to the current object, and an object has a refer-ence type (for example, its class), thus the notation `this.staticMember` uniquely identifies the member in the class.

In Program 7.1 on page 166 the method computeSalary() in the class EmployeeV3 declares a local variable normalNumOfHours that represents the normal number of working hours in a week (37.5). If other methods need this information, this value must be duplicated locally where it is needed. If the normal number of hours changes in the future, the value must be changed in all places in the code where it is used. This value is an obvious candidate for a global constant:

```
static final double NORMAL_WORKWEEK = 37.5;
```

Now it is only necessary to change the value in one place and recompile the code. Its name makes it obvious what the value represents. The method computeSalary() below uses the value of the global constant NORMAL_WORKWEEK. This new declaration of the method shows the three ways in which we can refer to a static member inside an instance method in the same class:

```
double computeSalary(double numOfHours) {
  assert numOfHours >= 0 : "Number of hours must be >= 0";
  double weeklySalary = hourlyRate * this.NORMAL_WORKWEEK;              // (1)
  if (numOfHours > EmployeeV4.NORMAL_WORKWEEK) {                        // (2)
    weeklySalary += 2.0 * hourlyRate * (numOfHours - NORMAL_WORKWEEK); // (3)
  }
  return weeklySalary;
}
```

Program 7.5 also shows how static members of a class can be accessed from other classes using the class name, as shown at (6) and (7). They can also be accessed using a reference of the class. The method main() in class Client4A calls the static methods registerGender() and printStatistics() in class EmployeeV4, using the reference coffeeboy at (9) and (10). We don't need to create an object of the class to refer to the static members of the class.

No this reference for static members

Static methods cannot refer to instance members by name, not even by using the this reference – static methods have no this reference. They are a part of the class, and not a part of the current object.

Initializing static variables

Static members of a class are initialized automatically before the class is used. If a static variable specifies an initial value, the static variable will be initialized with that value, otherwise it will be initialized with the default value of its data type specified in the declaration. Output from (6) and (7) in Program 7.5 correctly shows that the static variables EmployeeV4.numOfFemales and EmployeeV4.numOfMales are initialized to the default value 0.

7

The `main()` method and program arguments

A Java application must have a primary class that defines a method main and which has the method header:

```
public static void main(String[] args)
```

Execution always starts in the main() method of the class. In the examples we have seen so far, the program terminates when all the actions in the main() method have been executed.

The signature of the main() method above shows that it has an array of strings (String[]) as a formal parameter. *Program arguments* specified on the command line are stored in an array of strings. The reference value of this array is assigned to the formal parameter args before the execution of the main() method starts. In the program, the main() method can obtain these program arguments from the array using the formal parameter variable args. The strings in the array can be indexed the usual way, with the first string as args[0] and the last string as args[args.length-1]. If there are no program arguments, the parameter variable args will refer to an array of strings with zero elements, i.e. args.length is zero. Any attempt to index a value in this case will result in an ArrayIndexOutOfBoundsException, since the array has no elements.

Program 7.6 shows an example in which the program receives information about an employee from the command line in the form of program arguments. The command line specifies the following information:

> **java Client4B Mona Lisa 20.5 true**

The program arguments are specified after the class name. Program 7.6 checks at (1) that the array args has exactly four program arguments. If this is the case, the program arguments are printed at (2). The values in the args array are assigned to local variables at (3). At (4) and (5) the string values are converted to values of the correct type. An employee object is created and assigned these values at (6). Note that the values from the command line are passed as strings, and must be explicitly converted to other values if it is necessary in the program.

PROGRAM 7.6   Reading program arguments

```
// Using program arguments
public class Client4B {

    public static void main(String[] args) {
```

```
    // (1) Check that all information about an employee is given
    //      on the command line:
    if (args.length != 4) {
      return;
    }

  // (2) Print the array args:
    System.out.println("Program arguments:");
    for (String arg : args) {
      System.out.println(arg);
    }

    // (3) Assign information from the array args to local variables:
    String firstName = args[0];
    String lastName = args[1];
    double hourlyRate = Double.parseDouble(args[2]); // (4) Floating-point
    boolean gender;
    if (args[3].equals("true")) {                          // (5) Boolean value
      gender = EmployeeV4.FEMALE;
    } else {
      gender = EmployeeV4.MALE;
    }

    // (6) Create an employee, and print its state:
    EmployeeV4 decorator = new EmployeeV4();
    decorator.setState(firstName, lastName, hourlyRate, gender);
    System.out.println("Information about an employee:");
    decorator.printState();
    System.out.printf("Salary: %.2f%n", decorator.computeSalary(40.0));
  }
}
```

Program output:

```
> javac EmployeeV4.java Client4B.java
> java Client4B Mona Lisa 20.5 true
Program arguments:
Mona
Lisa
20.5
true
Information about an employee:
First name: Mona    Last name: Lisa    Hourly rate: 20.50    Gender: Female
Salary: 871.25
```

7.5 Initializing object state

Default constructors: implicit or explicit

Constructors have a special role in a class declaration. The use of the new operator, together with a constructor call, results in the execution of the constructor that corresponds to the constructor call. The main purpose of a constructor is to set the initial state of the current object, i.e. the object that has been created by the new operator.

If the class EmployeeV5 does not declare a constructor, the compiler will generate a constructor for the class equivalent to the following declaration:

```
EmployeeV5() { ... }     // (1)
```

Note the use of the class name and the absence of parameters in the constructor header. The actual contents of the constructor body are not important for this discussion, except to note that the constructor body has *no* actions to initialize the state of the current object.

The constructor declaration resembles a method declaration, but it is not a method. It is called the *default constructor* for the class EmployeeV5. Because it was generated by the compiler, it is called the *implicit default constructor*. If we create an object of this class:

```
EmployeeV5 cook = new EmployeeV5();    // (2)
```

the constructor call EmployeeV5() will result in the constructor at (1) being executed. This constructor has no effect on the state of the current object.

As we can see, the implicit default constructor is not always adequate, as it does *not* effect the state of the current object. The field variables will always be initialized to their default values (or to any initial value specified in the field declarations). Therefore a class will usually provide explicit constructors to set the initial state of an object. This ensures that the object is initialized properly before it is used.

A class can choose to declare an *explicit default constructor*. For example, the class Employee5V declares such a constructor at (3):

```
class EmployeeV5 {
  // Explicit default constructor
  EmployeeV5() {                            // (3) No parameters
    firstName  = "Joe";
    lastName   = "Jones";
    hourlyRate = 15.50;
    gender     = MALE;
  }
  // Rest of the specification is the same as in class EmployeeV4
}
```

Now the constructor call at (2) above will result in the explicit default constructor at (3) being executed. Each object created in this way will always have the same state, as shown in Figure 7.2b on page 164. A standard constructor is not adequate, however, for situations that require a more customised initial object state.

A constructor always has the same name as the class, so that the signature comprises the class name and type of the formal parameters. It is called in conjunction with the new operator to return the reference value of the object that has been created. A constructor cannot return a value. Apart from that, the constructor body can contain declarations and actions, similar to an instance method body. A constructor can use the this reference to refer to the current object, and all members in the class can be accessed in the constructor body.

Constructors with parameters

A class can declare constructors with formal parameters, to create objects with appropriate initial states. Constructors with parameters are called *non-default constructors*.

Program 7.7 shows the use of non-default constructors to initialize fields in objects created with the new operator. Declaration (2) and (3) create two objects of the class EmployeeV6. Parameter passing takes place in the same way as for method calls. The initial state of the objects referred to by the references operator1 and operator2 are shown in Figure 7.4a and Figure 7.4b respectively. In addition to initializing the state of the object with the values of the actual parameter expressions in the constructor call, the constructor in the class EmployeeV6 also calls the static method registerGender() to update the count of male and female employees.

If a class declares *any* constructor, the *implicit* default constructor cannot be applied. In Program 7.7, the declaration at (1) results in a compiler time error:

```
EmployeeV6 clerk = new EmployeeV6();    // (1) Compile time error!
```

The signature of the constructor call at (1) is not compatible with the signature of the non-default constructor:

```
EmployeeV6(String, String, double)      // Non-default constructor signature
```

The class EmployeeV6 must declare the default constructor *explicitly* to allow this constructor to be called.

BEST PRACTICES

Always declare an explicit default constructor.

FIGURE 7.7   Initializing of object state with non-default constructors

```
EmployeeV6 operator1 = new EmployeeV6("Tim", "Tanner", 20.60, EmployeeV6.MALE);   // (2)
EmployeeV6 operator2 = new EmployeeV6("Amy", "Archer", 18.50, EmployeeV6.FEMALE); // (3)
```

```
        operator1:EmployeeV6                          operator2:EmployeeV6
 ┌────────────────────────────┐            ┌────────────────────────────┐
 │ lastName   = "Tim"         │            │ lastName   = "Amy"         │
 │ firstName  = "Tanner"      │            │ firstName  = "Archer"      │
 │ hourlyRate = 20.60         │            │ hourlyRate = 18.50         │
 │ gender     = false         │            │ gender     = true          │
 └────────────────────────────┘            └────────────────────────────┘
            (a)                                         (b)
```

PROGRAM 7.7   Non-default constructors

```java
class EmployeeV6 {
  // Only non-default constructor
  EmployeeV6(String fName, String lName, double hRate, boolean gender) {
    this.firstName = fName;          // field access via this reference
    this.lastName = lName;
    this.hourlyrate = hRate;
    this.gender = gender;
    this.registerGender(gender);     // call to static method
  }
  // Rest of the specification is the same as in class EmployeeV4
  // ...
}
// Using constructors
public class Client6 {

  public static void main(String[] args) {

    // EmployeeV6 clerk = new EmployeeV6();     // (1) Compile time error!
                                               // No default constructor.
    // Print information in class EmployeeV6
    System.out.println("Print information in class EmployeeV6:");
    EmployeeV6.printStatistics();
    System.out.println();

    // Create an employee, and print its information
    EmployeeV6 operator1 = new EmployeeV6("Tim", "Turner", 30.00,
                                      EmployeeV6.MALE);          // (2)
    printEmployeeInfo(operator1, 40.0);
    System.out.println();

    // Create a new employee, and print its information
    EmployeeV6 operator2 = new EmployeeV6("Amy", "Archer", 20.50,
                                      EmployeeV6.FEMALE);        // (3)
    printEmployeeInfo(operator2, 50.0);
  }
```

```
    static void printEmployeeInfo(EmployeeV6 employee,
                                  double numOfHours) {
      System.out.println("Printing information about an employee:");
      employee.printState();
      System.out.printf("Salary: %.2f%n",
                        employee.computeSalary(numOfHours));
      System.out.println("Print information in class EmployeeV6:");
      EmployeeV6.printStatistics();
    }
  }
}
```

Program output:

```
Print information in class EmployeeV6:
Number of females registered: 0
Number of males registered: 0

Printing information about an employee:
First name: Tim Last name: Turner   Hourly rate: 30.00  Gender: Male
Salary: 1275.00
Print information in class EmployeeV6:
Number of females registered: 0
Number of males registered: 1

Printing information about an employee:
First name: Amy Last name: Archer   Hourly rate: 20.50  Gender: Female
Salary: 1281.25
Print information in class EmployeeV6:
Number of females registered: 1
Number of males registered: 1
```

Overloading constructors

If necessary a class can declare several constructors. Each constructor call will result in the execution of the constructor that has a signature compatible with the constructor call, analogous to method calls – see the subsection *Method calls and actual parameter expressions* on page 167.

Program 7.8 shows a class EmployeeV7 that declares three constructors. We say that the constructors are *overloaded*, i.e. they have the same class name, but their signatures differ because they have different formal parameter lists.

The class Client7 creates three objects of the EmployeeV7 class and prints pertinent information about them. The initial state of each object is dependent on which constructor was executed when the object was created. Creating the object at (4) results in the constructor at (1) being executed. Creating the object at (5) results in the constructor at (2) being executed. Finally, creating the object at (6) results in the constructor at (3) being executed.

Any initialization code in the constructor overrides initial values specified in the field declarations. Therefore it is a good idea always to initialize fields in one place: in the constructor.

PROGRAM 7.8 Constructor overloading

```
class EmployeeV7 {
    static final double STANDARD_HOURLY_RATE = 15.50;

    // Constructors
    EmployeeV7() {                                              // (1)
        firstName  = "Joe";
        lastName   = "Jones";
        hourlyRate = STANDARD_HOURLY_RATE;
        gender     = MALE;
        registerGender(MALE);
    }

    EmployeeV7(String fName, String lName, boolean gender) {    // (2)
        this.firstName  = fName;
        this.lastName   = lName;
        this.hourlyRate = STANDARD_HOURLY_RATE;
        this.gender     = gender;
        this.registerGender(gender);
    }

    EmployeeV7(String fName, String lName,
               double hRate, boolean gender) {                  // (3)
        this.firstName  = fName;
        this.lastName   = lName;
        this.hourlyRate = hRate;
        this.gender     = gender;
        this.registerGender(gender);
    }

    // The rest of the specification is the same as in class EmployeeV6
}
// Using overloaded constructors
public class Client7 {

    public static void main(String[] args) {

        // Print information in class EmployeeV7
        System.out.println("Printing information in class EmployeeV7:");
        EmployeeV7.printStatistics();
```

```
    // Create an employee, and print its information
    EmployeeV7 guard1 = new EmployeeV7();                            // (4)
    printEmployeeInfo(guard1, 50);

    // Create an employee, and print its information
    EmployeeV7 guard2 = new EmployeeV7("Tim", "Turner",
                                  EmployeeV7.MALE);                   // (5)
    printEmployeeInfo(guard2, 40);

    // Create a new employee, and print its information
    EmployeeV7 guard3 = new EmployeeV7("Amy", "Archer", 20.50,
                                  EmployeeV7.FEMALE);                 // (6)
    printEmployeeInfo(guard3, 35);

    // Print information in class EmployeeV7
    System.out.println("\nPrinting information in class EmployeeV7:");
    EmployeeV7.printStatistics();
  }

  static void printEmployeeInfo(EmployeeV7 employee, double numOfHours) {
    System.out.println();
    System.out.println("Printing information about an employee:");
    employee.printState();
    System.out.printf("Salary: %.2f%n",
                      employee.computeSalary(numOfHours));
  }
}
```

Program output:

```
Printing information in class EmployeeV7:
Number of females registered: 0
Number of males registered: 0

Printing information about an employee:
First name: Joe Last name: Jones    Hourly rate: 15.50  Gender: Male
Salary: 968.75

Printing information about an employee:
First name: Tim Last name: Turner   Hourly rate: 15.50  Gender: Male
Salary: 658.75

Printing information about an employee:
First name: Amy Last name: Archer   Hourly rate: 20.50  Gender: Female
Salary: 768.75

Printing information in class EmployeeV7:
Number of females registered: 1
```

7.6 Enumerated types

Simple form of enumerated types

An *enumerated type* (also called *enum* for short) defines a fixed number of enum constants. An enumerated constant is a unique name that refers to a particular object. Figure 7.8 shows the simple form of the enum type. The keyword enum indicates that the declaration is an enumerated type. The enum constants are specified in a list in the block that comprises the body of the enumerated type. Thus the enum type Weekday defines seven enum constants, one for each day of the week.

The set of objects for an enum type is confined to the objects listed by the declaration of the enum type. These objects are created automatically only once during program execution. It is not possible to create more objects of the enum type with the new operator. We can consider the enum constants as global constants that are declared static and final.

The enum type Weekday defines a reference type. Just as with other reference types, we can declare variables of the enum type, but these variables can only refer to objects that are designated by the enum constants:

```
Weekday lateOpeningDay = Weekday.THURSDAY;
```

FIGURE 7.8   Simple form of enumerated types

Enum type name

```
enum Weekday {                                          Enum constants

  MONDAY, TUESDAY, WEDNESDAY, THURSDAY, FRIDAY, SATURDAY, SUNDAY

}
```

Selected methods for enumerated types

Table 7.1 shows two methods that can be applied to all enumerated types. The method toString() returns the name of the enum constant. This method is applied implicitly to the parameters of the println() method in the following code examples:

```
System.out.println(lateOpeningDay);      // Prints THURSDAY.
System.out.println(Weekday.SUNDAY);      // Prints SUNDAY.
```

We can also compare constants in an enumerated type:

```
assert(lateOpeningDay != Weekday.SUNDAY);   // true
assert(lateOpeningDay == Weekday.THURSDAY); // true
```

Enum constants can also be used as case labels in a switch statement. Given that the variable day has the type Weekday, the switch statement below will determine whether it is a working day or falls on a weekend. Note that enum constants in case labels are not referred to by the name of the enum type, because it is implied by the type of the switch statement, which in this case is the type of the variable day, i.e. Weekday:

```
switch(day) {                              // (1)
  case SATURDAY: case SUNDAY:
    System.out.println("The day is " + day + ", it must be weekend.");
    break;
  default:
    System.out.println(day + " is a working day.");
}
```

If we need to iterate over all the constants of an enumerated type, we can first create an array with all the constants by calling the static method values(), and then use a for(:) loop to iterate over the array:

```
Weekday[] daysArray = Weekday.values();
for (Weekday day : daysArray) {
  // switch statement given at (1) above
}
```

Program 7.9 shows the execution of the code examples presented in this subsection.

TABLE 7.1 Selected method for all enumerated types

Methods for enumerated types	
`String toString()`	Returns the string representation of the current enum constant, i.e. the name of the current constant.
`static enumTypeName[] values()`	Returns an array with the enum constants that are declared in the enum type that has the *enumTypeName*. The order of the constants in the array is the same as the order in the enum declaration.

PROGRAM 7.9 Use of enumerated types

```
// An enum client
public class Weekdays {
  public static void main(String[] args) {

    Weekday lateOpeningDay = Weekday.THURSDAY;  // Reference of enum type

    // Method toString() applied implicitly
    System.out.println(lateOpeningDay);         // Prints THURSDAY.
    System.out.println(Weekday.SUNDAY);         // Prints SUNDAY.

    // Testing for equality
    assert(lateOpeningDay != Weekday.SUNDAY);   // true
```

```
      assert(lateOpeningDay == Weekday.THURSDAY); // true

      // Iterate over days of the week:
      System.out.println("Days of the week:");
      Weekday[] daysArray = Weekday.values();
      for (Weekday day : daysArray) {
        switch(day) {                                    // (1)
          case SATURDAY: case SUNDAY:
            System.out.println("The day is " + day +
                              ", it must be weekend.");
            break;
          default:
            System.out.println(day + " is a working day.");
        }
      }
    }
  }
}
```

Program output:

```
THURSDAY
SUNDAY
Days of the week:
MONDAY is a working day.
TUESDAY is a working day.
WEDNESDAY is a working day.
THURSDAY is a working day.
FRIDAY is a working day.
The day is SATURDAY, it must be weekend.
The day is SUNDAY, it must be weekend.
```

General form of enumerated types

The general form of the enumerated type declaration is shown in Figure 7.9. An enumerated type can declare constructors and other members, analogous to those in a class declaration. In this way, it is possible to define properties and behaviour of enum constants in an enumerated type.

Constructors cannot be called directly. A constructor is called *implicitly* when an object representing an enum constant is created automatically from the enum declaration during execution. Each constant name in the enum type MealTime is declared with an *actual* parameter list. The constructor which has the corresponding formal parameter list is executed. Specifying BREAKFAST(7, 30) in the enum constant list results in the constructor being called with 7 and 30 as values of the formal parameters tt and mm, representing hours and minutes, respectively.

FIGURE 7.9 The general form of enumerated types

Enum type name

```
enum MealTime {
```

Enum constants are always declared first
```
// Enum constants for meals.
BREAKFAST(7,30), LUNCH(12,15), DINNER(19,45);
```

Any constructors
```
// Constructor for a meal time.
MealTime(int tt, int mm) {
    servingTime = new Time(tt, mm);
}
```

Any other members
```
// Field for meal time.
private Time servingTime;

// Returns meal time.
Time getServingTime() {
    return this.servingTime;
}
```
```
}
```

The enumerated type MealTime in Figure 7.9 declares a field, servingTime, of reference type Time (see the listing in Program 7.9). Each object of the enumerated type MealTime will have this field, which will be initialized by the call to the constructor. The three objects, corresponding to each of the enum constants, will have states corresponding to the serving times for the different meals. The enumerated type MealTime also declares an instance method, getServingTime(), which returns the time for serving a meal. The enumerated type MealTime has only three objects that are referred to by the enum constants in the declaration. We can invoke the method getServingTime() on these objects in the usual way:

```
System.out.println(MealTime.BREAKFAST.getServingTime()); // Prints 07:30
```

The class MealService in Program 7.9 prints the times when the different meals are served.

PROGRAM 7.10 Serving meals

```
// Time is given as hours (0-23) and minutes (0-59).
class Time {

  // Fields for the time.
  int hours;
  int minutes;

  // Constructor
  Time(int hours, int minutes) {
    assert (0 <= hours && hours <= 23 &&
            0 <= minutes && minutes <= 59) :
            "Invalid hours and/or minutes";
    this.hours = hours;
```

```
      this.minutes = minutes;
    }

    // String representation of the time, TT:MM
    public String toString() {
      return String.format("%02d:%02d", hours, minutes);
    }
  }
  // Using enums
  public class MealService {
    public static void main(String[] args) {

      // (1) Create an array of meals:
      MealTime[] meals = MealTime.values();

      // (2) Print meal times:
      for (MealTime meal : meals) {
        System.out.println(meal + " is served at " + meal.getServingTime());
      }
    }
  }
```

Program output.

```
> javac MealTime.java Time.java MealService.java
> java -ea MealService
BREAKFAST is served at 07:30
LUNCH is served at 12:15
DINNER is served at 19:45
```

Declaring enumerated types inside a class

So far we have declared an enumerated type as a top-level declaration in its own separate source file. Other clients can access enum constants by using the class name and the constant name. An enumerated type can also be declared as a member in a class declaration. It makes sense to do this if the use of the enum constants is localised to a single class. The code below shows the declaration of the enumerated type Weekday as a member of the class Weekdays. Access to the enum constants is the same as it was before (see also Program 7.9):

```
  // Enum type as member in a class
  public class Weekdays {
    // Enum type as member in a class.
    enum Weekday {
      MONDAY, TUESDAY, WEDNESDAY, THURSDAY, FRIDAY, SATURDAY, SUNDAY
    }
    public static void main(String[] args) {
      // Same as before.
    }
  }
```

7.7 Review questions

1. Identify all the members and constructors in the declaration of the class Counter. Group them as shown in Figure 7.1.

```
class Counter {
    final static int MAX_VALUE = 100;
    static String description = "This class creates counters.";
    int value;

    Counter() { value = 1; }
    Counter(int initialValue) { value = initialValue; }

    int getCounter() { return value; }
    void setCounter(int newValue) { value = newValue; }
    void incrementCounter() { ++value; }
    void decrementCounter() { --value; }
    void resetCounter() { value = 0; }

    static String getDiscription() { return description; }

}
```

2. _____ belong to objects, while _____ belong to the class.

3. Values of all the field variables in an object comprise its _____.

4. What do we mean by the initial state of an object?

5. What is the default value for any reference variable?

6. In the class RectangleV2, which field variables are initialized with default values and which are initialized with an initial value when an object of the class is created?

```
class RectangleV2 {
    double length;
    double breadth;
    double area = length * breadth;

}
```

7. Which of the following statements are true?

   a Members in a class can be declared in any order.

   b A class must always provide an explicit default constructor.

   c The implicit default constructor is always executed when an object of the class is created using the new operator.

   d The explicit default constructor can have formal parameters.

8. In the class ClientA, identify the class names, local variables, method calls, formal parameters and actual parameters. The class Counter is defined in Exercise 7.1.

```
// Counting cars
```

```
public class ClientA {
  public static void main(String[] args) {
    int numOfCars = 10;
    Counter carCounter = new Counter(numOfCars);
    carCounter.incrementCounter();
    System.out.println(carCounter.getCounter());
  }

}
```

9. Given the class `Variables` and a reference `obj` that refers to an object of this class, what will be printed by the method call `obj.doIt(2)`.

```
class Variables {
  static String s = " is equal to ";

  double d = 20;

  int k = 10;

  void doIt(int d) {
    for (int k = 0; k < 2; k++) {
      System.out.println("k + d" + s + (k + d)); // (1)
    }
    System.out.println("k + d" + s + (k + d));    // (2)
    String s = " = ";
    System.out.println("k + d" + s + (k + d));    // (3)
  }

}
```

10. Which statements are true about methods?

   a The method signature comprises the return type, method name and type of the formal parameters.

   b Formal and actual parameters must be compatible with regard to type, number and order.

   c Parameter passing in Java entails that the values of the actual parameter expressions are assigned to the corresponding formal parameter variables.

   d A method always returns a value.

   e The return value must always be assigned to a variable.

11. Answer "yes" or "no" to the following questions:

   a Is it possible to declare several methods with the same name, but different parameter lists, in the same class?

   b If the actual parameter in a method call is a variable name, can the corresponding formal parameter variable have the same name?

   c Can a void method contain a return statement?

12. Determine whether you would use a void or a non-void method for the following tasks. If implementing a non-void method, which return type would you choose?

   a Determine whether a person has reached retirement age.

   b Give an explanation to the user of what the program does.

   c Find the largest of two numbers.

   d Read an int value entered by the user.

   e Assign an int value to a field variable.

   f Create an array of Counter objects for a client (see Question 7.1).

   g Create a two-dimensional array of strings.

   h Create statistics for the number of newspapers sold per day for a four-week period, given that the weekdays are numbered from 0 upwards (Monday has weekday number 0).

13. What will the following program print? The class Counter is declared in Question 7.1.

```
// Parameter passing
public class ParameterClient {
    public static void main(String[] args) {
        Counter counter = new Counter();
        int numOfTimes = 5;

        System.out.println("Before method call: " +
            "counter value is equal to " + counter.getCounter() +
            " and number of times is " + numOfTimes);
        updateCounter(counter, numOfTimes);
        System.out.println("After method call: " +
            "counter value is equal to " + counter.getCounter() +
            " and number of times is " + numOfTimes);
    }

    static void updateCounter(Counter counter, int numOfTimes) {
        for (; numOfTimes > 0; --numOfTimes) {
            counter.incrementCounter();
        }
    }
}
```

14. What will the following program print? The class Counter is declared in Question 7.1.

```
// More parameter passing
public class SwapClient {
    public static void main(String[] args) {
        int startvalue = 10;
        Counter counter1 = new Counter(startvalue);
        Counter counter2 = new Counter(startvalue * 2);
        System.out.println("Before swapping: " +
            "counter1 is " + counter1.getCounter() +
            " and counter2" + " is " + counter2.getCounter());
        swap(counter1, counter2);
```

```
        System.out.println("After swapping: " +
            "counter1 is " + counter1.getCounter() +
            " and counter2" + " is " + counter2.getCounter());
    }

    static void swap(Counter counter1, Counter counter2) {
        Counter t3 = counter1;
        counter1 = counter2;
        counter2 = t3;
    }

}
```

15. Given the following declarations, where the class `Counter` is declared as in Question 7.1:

```
Counter counterA = new Counter();
Counter[] counterArrayA = new Counter[5];
Counter[][] counterArrayB = new Counter[2][3];
```

and the following method declaration:

```
static void playingWithParameters(Counter counter, Counter[] array)
    { /* ... */ }
```

Which of these method calls are valid?

a `playingWithParameters(counterA, counterArrayA[]);`

b `playingWithParameters(counterA, counterArrayA);`

c `playingWithParameters(counterArrayA[2], counterArrayA);`

d `playingWithParameters(counterArrayA[3], counterArrayB[0]);`

e `playingWithParameters(counterArrayB[1][3], counterArrayA);`

f `playingWithParameters(counterArrayB[0][2], counterArrayB[1]);`

g `playingWithParameters(counterA, counterArrayB);`

16. Rewrite the class `Counter` declared in Question 7.1 using the `this` reference explicitly.

17. Which of these statements are valid, given the declaration of the class `Counter` from Question 7.1, and that `ref` refers to an object of this class?

a `System.out.println(ref.value);`

b `System.out.println(Counter.value);`

c `System.out.println(ref.MAX_VALUE);`

d `System.out.println(Counter.MAX_VALUE);`

e `System.out.println(ref.getCounter());`

```
f  System.out.println(Counter.getCounter());

g  System.out.println(ref.getDescription());

h  System.out.println(Counter.getDescription());
```

18. Which of the following statements are true about constructors?

   a A constructor is a method.

   b A constructor must specify a return type.

   c If a class declares more than one constructor, then these are overloaded.

   d Actions in a constructor can refer to all members of the class.

   e The this reference cannot be used in a constructor.

19. Given the following class:
```
// Being four-sided
public class FourSided {
    public static void main(String[] args) {
        Rectangle shape = new Rectangle();
        System.out.println(shape.length * shape.breadth);
    }
}
```

What will the program above print if we use the following declarations for the class Rectangle?

   a
```
class Rectangle {
    double length;
    double breadth;
}
```

   b
```
class Rectangle {
    double length = 20;
    double breadth = 30;
}
```

   c
```
class Rectangle {
    double length = 20;
    double breadth = 30;

    Rectangle() {
        length = 10;
        breadth = 5;
    }
}
```

20. Given the following variable declarations (1) and (2):
```
Counter counter1 = new Counter();   // (1)
Counter counter2 = new Counter(2);  // (2)
```

Determine whether the variable declarations (1) and (2) are valid if we use the following declarations of the class Counter:

a
```
class Counter {
    int value;
}
```

b
```
class Counter {
    int value;
    Counter() { value = 1; }
}
```

c
```
class Counter {
    int value;
    Counter(int startValue) { value = startValue; }
}
```

d
```
class Counter {
    int value;
    Counter() { value = 1; }
    Counter(int startValue) { value = startValue; }
}
```

21. Which lines of code in the declaration of the NewCounter class will result in a compile time error?
```
class NewCounter {
    static String description = "A new class that creates counters.";

    int value;

    NewCounter(int initialValue) {                      // A constructor
        System.out.println(value);                      // (1)
        System.out.println(this.value);                 // (2)
        System.out.println(NewCounter.value);           // (3)
        System.out.println(description);                // (4)
        System.out.println(this.description);           // (5)
        System.out.println(NewCounter.description);     // (6)
        value = initialValue;
    }

    void resetCounter() {                               // An instance method
        NewCounter t1 = new NewCounter(10);
        System.out.println(value);                      // (7)
        System.out.println(this.value);                 // (8)
        System.out.println(t1.value);                   // (9)
        System.out.println(NewCounter.value);           // (10)
        System.out.println(description);                // (11)
        System.out.println(this.description);           // (12)
        System.out.println(t1.description);             // (13)
        System.out.println(NewCounter.description);     // (14)
        value = 0;
```

```
        }

        static String getDescription() {              // A static method
            NewCounter t1 = new NewCounter(10);
            System.out.println(value);                 // (15)
            System.out.println(this.value);            // (16)
            System.out.println(t1.value);              // (17)
            System.out.println(NewCounter.value);      // (18)
            System.out.println(description);           // (19)
            System.out.println(this.description);      // (20)
            System.out.println(t1.description);        // (21)
            System.out.println(NewCounter.description); // (22)
            return description;
        }

    }
```

22. Which of the following statements are not true of enumerated types?

    a An enumerated type is a reference type defined with the keyword enum.

    b An enumerated type can be declared in its own separate source code file.

    c An enumerated type can declare constructors.

    d An enumerated type can declare members, as in a class declaration.

    e Enum constants must always be declared first in an enumerated type declaration.

    f We can use the new operator to create objects of an enumerated type.

23. Given the following declaration of an enumerated type:

    ```
    enum LightColour { RED, YELLOW, GREEN }
    ```

    and the following variable declaration:

    ```
    LightColour colour;
    ```

    Which of these statements will not compile?

    a `colour = GREEN;`

    b
    ```
    for (LightColour colour : LightColour) {
        System.out.println(colour);
    }
    ```

    c
    ```
    switch(colour)
        case LightColour.RED: System.out.println("STOP!"); break;
        case LightColour.GREEN: System.out.println("GO!"); break;
        case LightColour.YELLOW: System.out.println("CAREFUL!"); break;
        default: assert false: "UNKNOWN COLOUR!";
    }
    ```

    d `Boolean b = colour.equals(GREEN);`

    e `LightColour.GREEN = colour;`

7.8 Programming exercises

1. Modify the class Counter from Question 7.1 on page 197 so that it meets the following criteria:

   - It is possible to create a counter that counts within an interval. The interval is given by a lower and an upper limit. It should be possible to specify the initial value of the counter, which must be within the interval.
   - If no initial value is specified together with the interval, counting starts from the lower limit of the interval.
   - If no interval is specified, but the initial value *is* specified, counting starts with the initial value and continues upwards.
   - If neither the interval nor the initial value are specified, counting starts at 0 and continues upwards.
   - It should be possible to increment and decrement a counter.
   - It should be possible to get the current value of a counter, and to reset a counter to an initial value.
   - Where necessary, check that the counter has a valid value.

   Write a separate class to test the class Counter.

2. We will write a class called Forex that can be used for converting between two currencies. An object of the class stores the exchange rate between two currencies (for example, NOK 11.54 = GBP 1). The class offers two methods for converting between the two currencies. Choose suitable names for all members.

   Write a client that creates several Forex objects and tests conversion between different currencies.

3. Write a class Reverse that reads program arguments and prints them in reverse. In the printout the arguments should be separated by comma (,). Write a separate method that takes care of the printout.

   Example of program execution:

   ```
   > java Reverse To be or not to be
   be, to, not, or, be, To
   ```

4. Given the following skeleton of a class:
   ```
   class Rectangle {
       double length;
       double breadth;
       // ...
   }
   ```

   Modify the class Rectangle so that:

   - It is possible to create an object of the class Rectangle without specifying the dimensions, and the dimensions in this case should be initialized to the value 1.0.
   - It is possible to create a rectangle whose dimensions can be specified.

- The dimensions of a rectangle are never less than 0.0.

The class should offer methods for getting and setting the dimensions of a rectangle. The class should also offer methods to compute the area and the perimeter of a rectangle.

Write a client to test the class Rectangle.

5. In a program we will write a class to represent water bottles. The water bottles have the following properties:

- All bottles have a maximum capacity, measured in litres.
- All bottles contain a quantity of water at any given time, also measured in litres.

We can perform the following operations on the bottles:

- Fill a bottle completely from the tap.
- Empty a bottle.
- Pour water from one bottle to another bottle.

Write a class called Bottle that implements the properties described above. Let the constructor of the class allow the maximum capacity of a bottle to be specified. To begin with, let all new bottles be empty. Which instance variables should be declared in the class Bottle?

Implement the following methods:

a quantity(), which returns the amount of water in the current bottle at the moment.

b remaining(), which returns the amount of water that can be filled in the current bottle before it is full.

c fillFully(), which fills the current bottle completely.

d empty(), which empties the current bottle.

e pour(Bottle b), which pours water from the bottle b to the current bottle. The amount of water poured into the current bottle is limited either by the capacity of the current bottle or by the amount of water in bottle b.

Implement auxiliary methods where necessary.

6. Write a client that uses the Bottle class from Exercise 7.5. The client should be able to do the following:

a Create two Bottle objects: one two-litre bottle and one seven-litre bottle.

b Fill the seven-litre bottle completely.

c Pour water from the seven-litre bottle to the two-litre bottle.

d Empty the two-litre bottle.

e Print the amount of water in each bottle.

How many litres of water are left in the seven-litre bottle in the end?

7. Based on Exercise 7.5, write a client that creates two `Bottle` objects: one three-litre bottle and one five-litre bottle.

    Find a way of filling the five-litre bottle with only four litres of water, using only combinations of methods `fillFully()`, `empty()` and `pour()` on the two bottles.

8. In Program 7.5 on page 180 the class `EmployeeV4` defines the constants `EmployeeV4.MALE` and `EmployeeV4.FEMALE`. Write a separate source file with the declaration of an enumerated type called `Gender` that defines the enum constants `MALE` and `FEMALE`. Rewrite the classes `EmployeeV4` and `Client4A` to use this enumerated type.

CHAPTER 8

Object communication

LEARNING OBJECTIVES

By the end of this chapter, you will understand the following:

- **Eliminating source code duplication.**
- **Assigning suitable responsibilities and roles to objects.**
- **Making objects cooperate to perform tasks.**
- **Linking objects together so that they can find each other.**
- **How the compiler selects a method when there are several methods with the same name.**
- **Documenting source code to aid maintenance and further development.**

INTRODUCTION

This chapter shows how to create programs in which objects cooperate to solve problems. By writing classes that have well-defined responsibilities, we can build large but easy to understand programs.

8.1 Responsibilities and roles

All code in a Java program must be defined within classes. In a well-designed program, it is not arbitrary which class contains which piece of code. Each object in a program is given a specific role. The properties and behaviour that are defined in a class determine the responsibilities the class has and the roles the objects of this class will play during program execution.

Being able to identify the role that each object has during execution makes it easier to understand the program as a whole. Classes that combine related properties and behaviour are a lot easier to understand than classes in which the responsibilities have been spread in an arbitrary manner.

A naive solution to a given problem

We want to create a program that reads information about two employees from the terminal window, and prints a report stating which of them has the higher hourly rate. Using local variables, as shown in Program 8.1, provides a simple but naive solution. The program code fulfils the requirements of the stated problem, but, as we shall see, the code has some deficiencies that should be corrected.

PROGRAM 8.1 Naive employee information processing

```java
import java.util.Scanner;
public class UglyComparison {
  public static void main(String[] args) {
    Scanner input = new Scanner(System.in);
    String firstNameA, firstNameB, lastNameA, lastNameB;
    double hourlyRateA, hourlyRateB;

    System.out.printf("Input information about employee A:\n");
    System.out.printf("- First name: ");                            // (1)
    firstNameA = input.nextLine();
    System.out.printf("- Last name: ");
    lastNameA = input.nextLine();
    System.out.printf("- Hourly rate: ");
    hourlyRateA = input.nextDouble();
    input.nextLine(); // skip the rest of the line

    System.out.printf("Input information about employee B:\n");
    System.out.printf("- First name: ");                            // (2)
    firstNameB = input.nextLine();
    System.out.printf("- Last name: ");
    lastNameB = input.nextLine();
    System.out.printf("- Hourly rate: ");
    hourlyRateB = input.nextDouble();
    input.nextLine(); // skip the rest of the line

    if (hourlyRateA == hourlyRateB) {
      System.out.printf("Both earn $%.2f per hour.\n", hourlyRateA);
    } else if (hourlyRateA > hourlyRateB) {
      System.out.printf("%s %s has the higher hourly rate: $%.2f "
          + "per hour.\n", firstNameA, lastNameA, hourlyRateA);     // (3)
    } else {
      System.out.printf("%s %s has the higher hourly rate: $%.2f "
          + "per hour.\n", firstNameB, lastNameB, hourlyRateB);     // (4)
    }
```

```
      }
}
```

Program execution example:

```
Input information about employee A:
- First name: Gina
- Last name: Fillion
- Hourly rate: 31.65
Input information about employee B:
- First name: Edward
- Last name: Wolfram
- Hourly rate: 29.75
Gina Fillion has the higher hourly rate: $31.65 per hour.
```

It is apparent that Program 8.1 contains a lot of duplicated code. Code duplication is an indication that the source code should be restructured. In this example the code at (1) and (2) reads information about each of the employees in exactly the same manner, apart from storing the result in different variables. Imagine the code duplication if the program had to read information about a hundred employees from the terminal window. This type of code duplication can be difficult to maintain, since modifying the behaviour requires changing the code in several places.

Because the information is spread across various local variables, there is no simple way to keep track of which variables belong together. The programmer must keep track of the fact that hourlyRateA is associated with firstNameA and not firstNameB. Both lines (3) and (4) perform the same operation, except that (3) uses firstNameA, lastNameA and hourlyRateA, while (4) uses firstNameB, lastNameB and hourlyRateB. Only the programmer knows the connection between the first name, the last name and the hourly rate of an employee, and must therefore state these connections manually.

Combining properties and behaviour in classes

The next revision of the program uses a class that represents employees. The class EmployeeV7 in Program 7.8 on page 190 defines related properties and behaviour about an employee. This class can be used to simplify the code from Program 8.1, as shown in Program 8.2.

PROGRAM 8.2   Combining related properties and behaviour

```
import java.util.Scanner;

public class BetterComparison {
  public static void main(String[] args) {

    // Uses the class EmployeeV7 from Chapter 7.
    EmployeeV7 employeeA = new EmployeeV7();
    EmployeeV7 employeeB = new EmployeeV7();
```

8

```java
        System.out.printf("Input information about employee A:\n");   // (1)
        inputEmployeeInfo(employeeA);

        System.out.printf("Input information about employee B:\n");   // (2)
        inputEmployeeInfo(employeeB);

        if (employeeA.hourlyRate == employeeB.hourlyRate) {
          System.out.printf("Both earn $%.2f per hour.\n",
                            employeeA.hourlyRate);
        } else {
          EmployeeV7 higherPaid;
          if (employeeA.hourlyRate > employeeB.hourlyRate) {           // (3)
            higherPaid = employeeA;
          } else {
            higherPaid = employeeB;
          }

          System.out.printf("%s %s has the higher hourly rate: $%.2f "
                            + "per hour.\n",
                            higherPaid.firstName,                      // (4)
                            higherPaid.lastName,
                            higherPaid.hourlyRate);
        }
    }

    static void inputEmployeeInfo(EmployeeV7 anEmployee) {
      Scanner input = new Scanner(System.in);
      System.out.printf("- First name: ");
      anEmployee.firstName = input.nextLine();
      System.out.printf("- Surname: ");
      anEmployee.lastName = input.nextLine();
      System.out.printf("- Hourly rate: ");
      anEmployee.hourlyRate = input.nextDouble();
      input.nextLine(); // skip rest of the line
    }
}
```

Most of the duplicated code in Program 8.1 is eliminated in Program 8.2. Code for reading information about an employee has been moved to the helper method inputEmployeeInfo(). This helper method accepts a reference to an employee. The main() method calls the helper method twice instead of repeating the code for reading information about each employee.

Users of the new version of the program will not see any change in its behaviour compared to Program 8.1. Programmers, on the other hand, will now have less difficulty in understanding the source code. Since Program 8.2 now uses the EmployeeV7 class, it is easy to see that:

- The program reads information about exactly two employees.
- The same information is needed for both employees.
- The information read for both employees is the first name, the last name and the hourly rate.
- If one employee earns more than the other, the phrasing of the report that is printed is identical, regardless of which employee earns the most.

Using references as parameters

The main() method in Program 8.1 constructs two objects of class EmployeeV7 that are referred to by the reference variables employeeA and employeeB. Information is read into each of these objects by calling the inputEmployeeInfo() method at (1) and (2).

The inputEmployeeInfo() method accepts a reference value of an employee object. The method can use this reference value to change the state of the object by reading the first name, the last name and the hourly rate into the field variables of the object.

The first time that the inputEmployeeInfo() method is called, the parameter anEmployee refers to the same object as employeeA. The second time it is called, the parameter refers to the same object as employeeB. In other words: the same code in the inputEmployeeInfo() method can be used to change the state of any employee object simply by passing a reference to the object.

The inputEmployeeInfo() method does not return a value, but instead stores the information it reads from the terminal window in the employee object. Since the main() method has references to the employee objects, it can later retrieve this information from the objects. Figure 8.1 shows how the inputEmployeeInfo() method stores a first name in an EmployeeV7 object, and how the main() method later retrieves the same first name from the EmployeeV7 object.

FIGURE 8.1   Modifying the state of an object given as a parameter

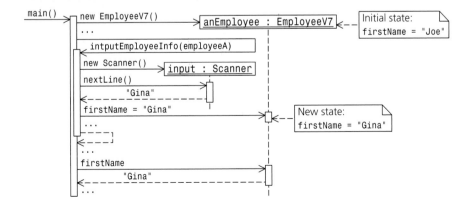

Passing reference values of objects as parameters is quite common in programming. Each time System.out.printf() is called, the first argument given to the method is a reference value to a String object. Unlike the inputEmployeeInfo() method, the printf() method does not modify the state of the object whose reference value is passed as an argument.

With the help of the inputEmployeeInfo() method we have now eliminated the duplicated code for reading employee information. The duplicated code for printing the report can also be eliminated by splitting the task into two parts:

a Select the object that should be processed: find the object that represents the employee with the higher hourly rate.

b Perform operations on the selected object: retrieve and report information from the employee object.

In the if statement at (3) in Program 8.2, the reference variable higherPaid is assigned the reference value of the EmployeeV7 object with the higher hourly rate. The code at (4) can then use this reference value to perform operations on the object. The printing done at (4) is executed in exactly the same manner, regardless of which object was selected at (3).

Advantages of good abstractions

The EmployeeV7 class is responsible for keeping track of the first name, the last name, the hourly rate and the gender of an employee. The comparison program only uses some of the functionality provided by the EmployeeV7 class. A simple extension to the program would for example be to print the weekly salary, assuming a 37.5 hour work week. To implement this, we need only insert this line after (4):

```
System.out.printf("The weekly salary for a 37.5 hour standard "
    + "work week is $%.2f", higherPaid.computeSalary(37.5));
```

Another advantage of placing the responsibility for specific operations on the actual objects is that different parts of a program can then take advantage of the operations.

Part of the challenge of creating a good program structure is deciding which responsibilities should be given to which class. Often there is no single obvious correct answer to how to distribute responsibilities. However, a rule of thumb is to try to minimize the amount of code and data duplication in the program. The design decisions that are made should be written down in the source code documentation. This will aid programmers who did not participate in the development process.

Rethinking responsibility

Having found an acceptable solution for the problem posed at the beginning of the chapter, let us re-examine the responsibilities of the EmployeeV7 class from Chapter 7. Each object of this class represents an employee and has fields to store pertinent information about an employee.

The EmployeeV7 class is also responsible for keeping track of the number of male and female employees. This particular functionality was used in Chapter 7 to illustrate *static members*. However, it is time to reconsider whether this is a suitable responsibility for an employee class. This type of gender statistics typically is stored in the employee register of a company. We should consider removing this functionality from the employee class.

Program 8.2 defines the method `inputEmployeeInfo()`, which obtains information about an employee from the user. It is worth considering whether this method should be moved out of the `BetterComparison` class. We would like to collect all operations that interact with the terminal window into a single class, which would make it easier to replace the terminal window with a different data input strategy. The employee class is no longer responsible for interacting with the terminal window, and should therefore no longer provide a `printState()` method.

8.2 Communication and cooperation

A program typically uses many objects to accomplish a task. Each object is given a specific role, and the objects cooperate to perform the whole task.

In Java an object interacts with another object, either by calling a method, or by manipulating a field variable of the other object. In Program 8.2 the methods of the `BetterComparison` class interact with the `Scanner` object by calling methods, and interact with the `EmployeeV7` objects by storing and retrieving values in their field variables. Since no `BetterComparison` object is created and the methods of the `BetterComparison` class are static, this interaction cannot be characterised as *cooperation between objects*. However, it illustrates that this cooperation is possible through method calls and access to field variables.

Dividing and assigning responsibility

The `BetterComparison` class in Program 8.2 contains both program logic (in the `main()` method) and code for user interaction (in the `inputEmployeeInfo()` method). The latter is likely to change over time, for example if we decide to develop a graphical user interface (GUI). We therefore want to give the responsibility of all user interaction in the program to a new object, thereby collecting all user interface code in one location in the program. The class declaration in Program 8.3 defines the behaviour of such an object. All code dealing with the terminal window is now collected in the class `TextUserInterface`. This class uses a new class `Employee` and the enumerated type `Gender`: these are defined in Program 8.4.

The new definition of the `Employee` class has more tightly focused responsibilities than earlier revisions of the class: it is responsible for storing information and calculating the weekly salary. Everything related to gender statistics has been removed, since we decided that this lies outside the responsibilities of an employee.

PROGRAM 8.3 Class responsible for communicating with the user

```java
import java.util.Scanner;

class TextUserInterface {
  Scanner input = new Scanner(System.in);
```

8

```java
String requestString(String wantedInfo) {
  System.out.printf("- %s: ", wantedInfo);
  return input.nextLine();
}

double requestDouble(String wantedInfo) {
  System.out.printf("- %s: ", wantedInfo);
  double value = input.nextDouble();
  input.nextLine(); // skip the rest of the line
  return value;
}

boolean requestYesNoAnswer(String wantedInfo) {
  String answer = requestString(wantedInfo + " (y/n)");
  return answer.equals("y");
}

Employee inputEmployee(String label, boolean inputGender) {
  System.out.printf("Input information about %s:\n", label);
  String firstName = requestString("First name");
  String lastName = requestString("Last name");
  double hourlyRate = requestDouble("Hourly rate");
  Gender gender = Gender.UNKNOWN;

  if (inputGender) {
    gender = requestGender();
  }

  return new Employee(firstName, lastName, hourlyRate, gender);
}

Gender requestGender() {
  if (requestYesNoAnswer("Is this a woman?")) {
    return Gender.FEMALE;
  }

  return Gender.MALE;
}

void reportSameHourlyRate(double hourlyRate) {
  System.out.printf("Both earn $%.2f per hour.\n", hourlyRate);
}

void reportHigherHourlyRate(Employee employee) {
  System.out.printf("%s %s has the higher hourly rate: $%.2f "
                    + "per hour.\n",
                    employee.firstName,
                    employee.lastName,
                    employee.hourlyRate);
}
```

```java
void reportIncomeDifference(Employee employee, Employee manager,
        double income_difference)
{
  System.out.printf("%s %s earns $%.2f less than the manager %s %s "
                  + "during a normal work week\n",
                  employee.firstName, employee.lastName,
                  income_difference,
                  manager.firstName, manager.lastName);
}

void reportPercentageWomen(int employeeCount, double percentageWomen) {
  System.out.printf("The company has %d employees, %.1f%% of which are "
                  + "women.\n", employeeCount, percentageWomen);
}
}
```

PROGRAM 8.4   Employee class with clear responsibilities

```java
// File: Employee.java
class Employee {
  static final double STANDARD_HOURLY_RATE = 15.50;
  static final double NORMAL_WORKWEEK = 37.5;
  static final double OVERTIME_COMPENSATION_PERCENTAGE = 200.0;
  static final double OVERTIME_COMPENSATION_FACTOR =
    OVERTIME_COMPENSATION_PERCENTAGE / 100.0;

  String firstName;
  String lastName;
  double hourlyRate;
  Gender gender;
  Employee boss;                                              // (1)

  Employee(String fName, String lName, double hRate, Gender gender) {
    this.firstName = fName;
    this.lastName = lName;
    this.hourlyRate = hRate;
    this.gender = gender;
  }

  double overtimeHourlyRate() {                               // (2)
    return hourlyRate * OVERTIME_COMPENSATION_FACTOR;
  }

  double overtimeHours(double hoursWorkedDuringAWeek) {       // (3)
    assert hoursWorkedDuringAWeek >= 0 : "Number of hours must be >= 0";
    double overtime = hoursWorkedDuringAWeek - NORMAL_WORKWEEK;
```

8

```
    if (overtime < 0) {
      return 0;
    }

    return overtime;
  }

  double computeSalary(double hoursWorkedDuringAWeek) {              // (4)
    return NORMAL_WORKWEEK * hourlyRate
      + overtimeHours(hoursWorkedDuringAWeek) * overtimeHourlyRate();
  }
}
// File: Gender.java
enum Gender { UNKNOWN, MALE, FEMALE }
```

Program 8.2 can now be rewritten to use the following three objects: one TextUserInter-face object that communicates with the user through the terminal window, supplying information to two employee objects. This rewrite results in the GoodComparison class shown in Program 8.5. Note that some of the methods in the TextUserInterface class are not used in Program 8.5. These methods will be used later in Program 8.6 and Program 8.7.

PROGRAM 8.5   Responsibilities and object communication

```
public class GoodComparison {
  public static void main(String[] args) {
    TextUserInterface ui = new TextUserInterface();              // (1)
    Employee employeeA = ui.inputEmployee("employee A", false);  // (2)
    Employee employeeB = ui.inputEmployee("employee B", false);  // (3)

    if (employeeA.hourlyRate > employeeB.hourlyRate) {
      ui.reportHighestHourlyRate(employeeA);
    } else if (employeeB.hourlyRate > employeeA.hourlyRate) {
      ui.reportHighestHourlyRate(employeeB);
    } else {
      ui.reportSameHourlyRate(employeeA.hourlyRate);
    }
  }
}
```

Clarifying the responsibilities of classes in the program

The TextUserInterface object created at (1) in Program 8.5 will be used for all commu-nication with the user. Each of the two calls to the readEmployeeInfo() method at (2) and (3) asks the TextUserInterface object to create an Employee object and set its state with the information that the user enters. The string argument passed for each method call is used as a prompt to indicate to the user what input is expected. The reference values that are returned from the method calls are stored in the variables `employeeA` and `employeeB`.

The method `reportHigherHourlyRate()` in the `TextUserInterface` object is called to report when one employee earns more than the other employee. Here there is a clear separation between the responsibility of the `main()` method of the `GoodComparison` class, the `TextUserInterface` class, and the `Employee` class:

- The `main()` method in the `GoodComparison` class knows how to determine which employee is paid more, but knows nothing about obtaining information about employees or how to report the difference in salary to the user.
- The `TextUserInterface` class knows how to obtain information about an employee from the user, and how to report the difference in salary to the user, but knows nothing about determining which employee is paid more.
- The responsibility of the `Employee` class is to store information about employees and compute salaries, but not to determine which employee earns more, nor read from or print information to the terminal window.

With the help of the user interface abstraction, the `main()` method has now been freed from communicating with the user directly: instead it simply delegates this work to an `TextUserInterface` object. Changing the way the `TextUserInterface` class communicates with the user would affect neither the `GoodComparison` class nor the `Employee` class as long as the `TextUserInterface` object still fulfils its role in the program.

Communication between objects at runtime

All communication between objects in the program is done through method calls, and information flows from one object to another through parameters, return values and field access. Methods and fields are accessed using object references. The big question now becomes how to obtain reference values that point to the object with which we want to work. Up to now all the reference values we have needed have been available in local variables that are available only within the current method call. Section 8.3 shows how to keep reference values available even after the method call has ended.

Running the programs `UglyComparison`, `BetterComparison` and `GoodComparison` will give exactly the same results. One could ask what has actually been achieved by restructuring the program, given that its behaviour has remained unchanged. The answer is that the last revision of the program is easier to understand, maintain, and develop further. The benefits may not seem like much for small programs, but this type of restructuring is essential to prevent large programs from becoming complex and unwieldy. The process of restructuring source code without changing its behaviour is called *refactoring*.

One of the benefits of refactoring the `UglyComparison` program into the `GoodComparison` program is that we now also have the classes `TextUserInterface` and `Employee`, which can be used without modification in other programs. This is a result of giving the classes clear responsibilities.

Assigning the responsibility for calculating salaries

The task of calculating the weekly salary has now been split across three methods, where each method has been given a clearly defined sub-task:

- The method `overtimeHourlyRate()` at (2) calculates the compensation for each hour exceeding the normal weekly working hours.
- The method `overtimeHours()` at (3) calculates the number of hours overtime an employee has worked during a week.
- The method `computeSalary()` at (4) still calculates the weekly salary, but has now been greatly simplified by delegating much of the work to the other two methods.

In addition to being used for calculating the weekly salary, the new methods can be useful for other tasks as well. This versatility indicates that the responsibility has been sensibly split across the methods. For example, to denote a rule that an employee can only work 200 hours of overtime during a year, one could write:

```
accumulatedOvertimeThisYear += overtimeHours(hoursThisWeek);
boolean overtimeLimitExceeded = accumulatedOvertimeThisYear > 200;
```

8.3 Relationships between objects

Fields with reference values

If an object A has a field variable that stores the reference of another object B, then the code in object A can use object B through the field variable (see Figure 8.2). Object A can also pass the reference value to other objects that want to use object B.

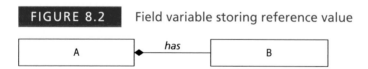

FIGURE 8.2   Field variable storing reference value

Storing reference values can be illustrated by the following analogy: I have the phone number of a taxi service (object B) in my wallet (object A), so that I can call for a taxi at any time. I can also give the phone number to others, so that they can order a taxi as well. Here the phone number acts as a reference value to the taxi service object. Regardless of how many places the phone number is stored, there is still only one taxi service.

Each employee may have a manager. Suppose we want to store this relationship in the employee object. The manager is also an employee, and can in turn have another manager. This relationship has been established by declaring the following field in the `Employee` class shown in Program 8.4:

```
Employee manager;                                                    // (1)
```

When we create an `Employee` object, the manager field at (1) is initialized to `null`. To establish a *manager-subordinate* relationship between two employees, the manager field of the subordinate object can be set to refer to the manager object. Managers are also employees, and are therefore also represented by objects of the `Employee` class.

Objects that communicate

Program 8.6 shows the use of references between objects. A company object and a user interface object are created in the main() method of the Managers class. The company object is then told to report the income difference between some of the employees in the company. The company object is defined by the SmallCompany class, and has fields that refer to four different Employee objects. The constructor of SmallCompany creates *manager-subordinate* relationship between the employees by setting the manager reference in some of the employees. Figure 8.3 shows the objects that are created by the program and the links between them.

PROGRAM 8.6 Use of the manager association

```
class SmallCompany {
  Employee president;
  Employee cfo;  // Chief financial officer
  Employee cto;  // Chief technology officer
  Employee engineer;

  TextUserInterface ui;

  SmallCompany(TextUserInterface ui) {
    this.ui = ui;

    president = new Employee("Norman", "Knuth", 37, Gender.MALE);
    cfo = new Employee("Steven", "Feynman", 30, Gender.MALE);
    cto = new Employee("Donald", "Borlaug", 32, Gender.MALE);
    engineer = new Employee("Richard", "Levy", 24, Gender.MALE);

    cfo.manager = president;
    cto.manager = president;
    engineer.manager = cto;
  }

  void reportIncomeDifferenceWithManager(Employee anEmployee) {
    Employee manager = anEmployee.manager;
    assert manager != null;
    double income_difference =
      manager.computeSalary(Employee.NORMAL_WORKWEEK)
      - anEmployee.computeSalary(Employee.NORMAL_WORKWEEK);
    ui.reportIncomeDifference(anEmployee, manager, income_difference);
  }
}

public class Managers {
  public static void main(String[] args) {
    TextUserInterface ui = new TextUserInterface();              // (1)
    SmallCompany company = new SmallCompany(ui);                 // (2)
    company.reportIncomeDifferenceWithManager(company.cfo);      // (3)
    company.reportIncomeDifferenceWithManager(company.engineer); // (4)
```

```
        }
    }
```

Program output:

```
Steven Feynman earns $262.50 less than the manager Norman Knuth during a normal
work week
Richard Levy earns $300.00 less than the manager Donald Borlaug during a normal
work week
```

FIGURE 8.3   References between objects

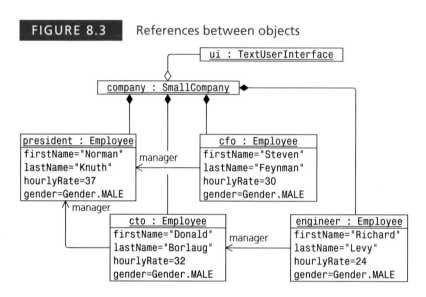

The method `reportIncomeDifferenceWithManager()` in the class `SmallCompany` finds the manager of an employee and reports the difference in income between them for a normal working week. The report is delivered to the user through a user interface that is linked to the `SmallCompany` object. The `main()` method in the `Managers` class is responsible for constructing the user interface object at (1), and passing the reference value of the user interface to the company object created at (2). The `SmallCompany` constructor stores the reference value of the user interface object in the `ui` field variable, thus establishing the relationship between the company object and the user interface object.

Object ownership

To manipulate an object we need its reference value. If the desired reference value is not available locally, it must be obtained from another object or class. In Program 8.6 the `main()` method obtains the reference values of `Employee` objects from the `SmallCompany` object at (3) and (4). The `SmallCompany` object has the main responsibility of maintaining references to the `Employee` objects. This is a case in which the relationship denotes *ownership*: the `SmallCompany` object owns the `Employee` objects referenced by its field variables.

The *association* between an employee and their manager is *not* an ownership relationship. It is obvious that the subordinate `Employee` object does not own the `Employee` object representing the manager. If the manager had references to all their subordinates, then we could perhaps call it ownership. But that would be strange, since if a manager is removed from an organisation, it does not automatically follow that all the subordinates are also removed.

Figure H.2 on page 360 shows the notation used for different kinds of association relationships. All the UML diagrams later in this chapter use this notation.

Generally, the owner of an object has the main responsibility of maintaining a reference to the object. A Java object will remain available as long as at least one reference to the object is maintained. If all references are lost, there is no way of getting hold of the object. In the following program code, the sole reference to an `Employee` object is removed:

```
Employee salesperson = new Employee("Maria", "Jensen", 25.0,
                                    Gender.FEMALE);
salesperson = null;  // Removes the only reference to the Employee object
```

Objects that are no longer used may be garbage collected by the JVM.

One-to-one and one-to-many associations

The `SmallCompany` class has four `Employee` reference fields, which means that for each `SmallCompany` object there will be four `Employee` objects. This relationship is called a *one-to-many association*.

Figure 8.4 shows the associations between the classes `SmallCompany`, `TextUserInterface` and `Employee`. This UML diagram shows the relative number of objects that take part at each end of an association. In the *employs* association between the classes `SmallCompany` and `Employee` there are four `Employee` objects for each `SmallCompany` object. Each `Employee` object may belong to a `SmallCompany`, but this is not mandatory (indicated by 0..1). It is always possible to construct an `Employee` object without linking it to a `SmallCompany` object. Table H.1 on page 360 shows typical *multiplicity* values that can occur in associations between classes.

FIGURE 8.4   Associations between classes

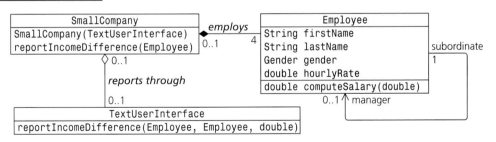

In Program 8.6 exactly four employees are referenced from one `SmallCompany` object. In the real world companies do not employ a fixed number of people. It is possible to make an association in which a variable number of employees can take part. Program 8.7 defines a `PersonnelRegister` class that maintains such an association. The responsibility of gathering gender statistics, which we decided did not belong to the `Employee` class, has also been given to the new `PersonnelRegister` class. Since the `PersonnelRegister` class, unlike the

8

Employee class, manages several Employee objects, it makes sense to place this responsibility here. Note that static fields are no longer required now that the gender statistics are stored in PersonnelRegister objects.

The class PersonnelRegister uses an array of employees to keep track of who is employed, (1). Figure 8.5 shows how the association between PersonnelRegister and Employee can be denoted in a UML diagram.

FIGURE 8.5   Association between **PersonnelRegister** and **Employee** classes

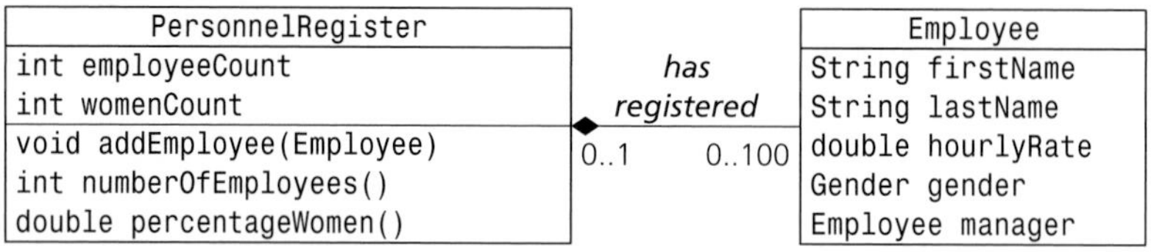

PROGRAM 8.7   One-to-many association in company with personnel register

```java
class PersonnelRegister {
  Employee[] allEmployees;
  int employeeCount;
  int womenCount;

  PersonnelRegister() {
    allEmployees = new Employee[100];                          // (1)
  }

  void addEmployee(Employee newEmployee) {
    allEmployees[employeeCount] = newEmployee;
    employeeCount++;
    if (newEmployee.gender == Gender.FEMALE) {
      womenCount++;
    }
  }

  int numberOfEmployees() {
    return employeeCount;
  }

  double percentageWomen() {
    return 100.0 * womenCount / employeeCount;
  }
}

public class NewCompany {
  public static void main(String[] args) {
    TextUserInterface ui = new TextUserInterface();
    PersonnelRegister register = new PersonnelRegister();
```

```
  do {
    Employee newEmployee = ui.inputEmployee("employee", true);
    register.addEmployee(newEmployee);
  } while (ui.requestYesNoAnswer("Are there any more employees?"));

  ui.reportPercentageWomen(register.numberOfEmployees(),
        register.percentageWomen());
  }
}
```

Excerpt from running the program:

```
Input information about employee:
- First name: Amy
- Last name: Lightman
- Hourly rate: 29
- Is this a woman? (y/n): y
- Are there any more employees? (y/n): y
Input information about employee:
- First name: Dimitri
...
- Are there any more employees? (y/n): n
The company has 5 employees, 40.0% of which are women.
```

Suggestions for further development

The structure of Program 8.7 and the classes it uses are now fairly well designed, but there is room for improvement:

- The program fails with an InputMismatchException if the hourly rate provided by the user is not a valid number. The program should use the hasNextDouble() method from the Scanner class to check for invalid numbers, and give the user another chance to enter a valid number.

- The answers given to the *Yes/No* questions are not examined properly. The program assumes the answer is *No* as long as the exact answer given was not "y". The program should verify the validity of the answer that was given.

- Even though the PersonnelRegister class can manage a variable number of employees, there is still an upper limit of one hundred employees. Since the class does not check whether this limit has been reached, the program will fail when the number of employees exceed one hundred.

- The PersonnelRegister class does not provide any way of removing employees.

8.4 Method overloading

Program 7.8 on page 190 defines the EmployeeV7 class, which has three constructors with the same name but with different parameter lists. This means that the constructors have different signatures, and that the constructor name "EmployeeV7" is *overloaded*. Which constructor is used to construct a particular object depends on the actual parameter list that is used with the new operator when creating the object.

Just as it is possible to overload constructors, it is also possible to overload method names. Within a class it is possible to define several methods with the same name, as long as they have different parameter lists. When the compiler encounters a method call using an overloaded method name in the source code, it determines to which method declaration the call actually refers. The compiler will choose the method declaration that matches the signature of the method call. This decision is made at compile time, and determines which method body will actually be executed at runtime.

We want to look up employees in the register and retrieve reference values of Employee objects. We want to be able to look up an employee, either by the index value, or by their name. Let's define two new methods, both called "getEmployee" in the PersonnelRegister from Program 8.7. This is allowed, since the method declarations will have different parameter types.

```java
Employee getEmployee(int employeeIdNumber) {
  return allEmployees[employeeIdNumber];
}

Employee getEmployee(String firstName, String lastName) {
  for (int i = 0; i < employeeCount; i++) {
    Employee anEmployee = allEmployees[i];
    if (firstName.equals(anEmployee.firstName) &&
        lastName.equals(anEmployee.lastName))
      return anEmployee;
  }
  return null;
}
```

The signature of the first method is getEmployee(int) and the signature of the second method is getEmployee(String, String). When the compiler translates a method call, it looks at the method name and the types of the actual parameters to find the method that has the corresponding signature.

```java
getEmployee(0);                    // Calls getEmployee(int)
getEmployee("Phil", "Green");      // Calls getEmployee(String, String)
```

8.5 Documenting source code

To help maintenance and further development, it is important that programs are easy to understand. Good documentation makes a program easier to understand.

An important form of documentation is comments written in the source code that explain how a program works. Other types of documentation include user manuals, UML diagrams and algorithm descriptions. This book focuses on documenting source code using comments and documenting algorithms using pseudocode.

Multi-line comments

All the code examples so far have used single line comments starting with "//". To write a comment spanning multiple lines, the "//" prefix can be used on multiple consecutive lines, like this:

```
// This text is an example of a comment in the Java programming
// language that spans multiple source code lines.  Each line needs
// to be prefixed when using this syntax.
```

The Java language also provides an alternate syntax for writing multi-line comments:

```
/* This text is an example of a comment in the Java programming
   language that spans multiple source code lines.  Only the
   start and end of the comment needs to be marked when using this
   syntax. */
```

Everything from the character sequence "/*" up to the character sequence "*/" is ignored by the compiler.

Documenting classes and members

The Java language provides a standardised way of documenting fields, methods and classes. To document one of these language constructs, a special type of comment is placed immediately preceding the construct. These special comments start with the character sequence "/**" and end with the character sequence "*/". Notice the extra asterisk (*) at the start of the comment compared to normal multi-line comments. Here is an example of a comment that describes a field variable:

```
/**
 * The price of the product, not including tax.
 */
double price;
```

These special comments are called *Javadoc comments*, named after the javadoc tool in the JDK. This tool can generate documentation that collects information written in these special comments, as well as extra information that the tool is able to extract by analysing the source code. The tool will automatically extract type descriptions of classes, fields, methods and method parameters.The javadoc tool recognizes specific markup tags within the Javadoc comments and uses these to present the information in a structured layout. Table 8.1 show the most common markup tags used for documenting methods.

TABLE 8.1	Javadoc markup tags for methods
Markup tags	**Purpose**
@param *parameter-name description*	Describes a formal parameter of a method.
@return *description*	Describes the return value from a method.

8

Hiding internal methods and fields

Some methods and fields are only meant for internal use in the class in which they are defined. The Java language provides a way to mark these methods and fields as unsuitable for use by other classes. By adding the modifier keyword private to the declaration of a class member, the compiler ensures that the member is not accessible, and will refuse to compile any code outside the class that tries to use the member. Code inside the class will still be able to use the member.

The modifier keyword public can be used in declarations of members to indicate that the member should not be hidden from external code. By default, the javadoc tool will only generate documentation for members that are declared public.

A fully-documented Java class

Program 8.8 shows the fully-documented source code for the PersonnelRegister class. Figure 8.6 on page 229 shows the HyperText Markup Language (HTML) document generated by the javadoc tool from the source code for the PersonnelRegister class in Program 8.8.

The fields allEmployees, employeeCount and womenCount, and the method addEmployeeTo-Statistics() are declared private and are not included in the generated documentation. The methods addEmployee(), getEmployee(), numberOfEmployees() and percentageWomen() are declared public and therefore included in the generated documentation.

PROGRAM 8.8   The complete and documented **PersonnelRegister** class

```
/**
 * A personnel register maintains a collection of employees.  A company
 * can use a personnel register to keep track of who is employed in the
 * company.
 *
 * The personnel register collects gender statistics for all the
 * employees that are added to the register.  These statistics reflect
 * the gender of each employee at the time the employee is added.  The
 * statistics will not reflect any gender change done later.
 *
 * The personnel register has some major limitations: the register will
 * stop working if the number of employees exceeds 100, and there is no
 * way to remove employees from the register, once they are added.
 */
public class PersonnelRegister {
  static final int MAXIMUM_NUMBER_OF_EMPLOYEES = 100;
  private Employee[] allEmployees;
  private int employeeCount;
  private int womenCount;

  public PersonnelRegister() {
    allEmployees = new Employee[MAXIMUM_NUMBER_OF_EMPLOYEES];
  }
```

```java
/**
 * Stores another employee in the register and updates the gender
 * statistics.  Only an employee with known gender can be added
 *
 * @return The ID number assigned to the employee that was added.
 */
public int addEmployee(Employee newEmployee) {
  assert newEmployee.gender != Gender.UNKNOWN
    : "Gender must be known before registration.";
  assert employeeCount < allEmployees.length;

  int employeeIdNumber = employeeCount;
  allEmployees[employeeIdNumber] = newEmployee;
  addEmployeeToStatistics(newEmployee);
  return employeeIdNumber;
}

private void addEmployeeToStatistics(Employee newEmployee) {
  employeeCount++;
  if (newEmployee.gender == Gender.FEMALE) {
    womenCount++;
  }
}

/**
 * Retrieves a stored employee with a specific ID number.
 *
 * @param employeeIdNumber The ID number of the employ to retrieve.  A
 *      valid ID number must be non-negative and less than the number
 *      returned by numberOfEmployees().
 */
public Employee getEmployee(int employeeIdNumber) {
  return allEmployees[employeeIdNumber];
}

/**
 * Retrieves a stored employee with a specific name.
 *
 * @param firstName The first name of the employee.
 * @param lastName The last name of the employee
 * @return the employee, or null if no employee with that name was
 *      found.
 */
public Employee getEmployee(String firstName, String lastName) {
  for (int i = 0; i < employeeCount; i++) {
    Employee anEmployee = allEmployees[i];
    if (firstName.equals(anEmployee.firstName) &&
        lastName.equals(anEmployee.lastName)) {
      return anEmployee;
```

```
        }
      }
      return null;
    }

    /**
     * @return The total number of employees that have been added to
     *            this register.
     */
    public int numberOfEmployees() {
      return employeeCount;
    }

    /**
     * @return The percentage of women employees in the register.  Since
     *        the register only keeps track of men and women added to the
     *        register, it is possible to calculate the percentage of men
     *        using this formula: 100 - women_percentage.
     */
    public double percentageWomen() {
      return 100.0 * womenCount / employeeCount;
    }
}
```

The syntax for generating documentation using the Javadoc tool from the command line is:

> **javadoc PersonnelRegister.java**

This generates HTML files that contain the documentation for the program based on the comments in the source code file PersonnelRegister.java. Just like the javac compiler, the javadoc tool requires the exact name of the source code file. The documentation that is shipped with the JDK describes other Javadoc comment markup tags and command line options that the javadoc tool understands.

How to document programs

Many code examples in this book are documented line by line, for the sole purpose of explaining the language constructs of Java. Under normal circumstances a programmer is already familiar with the language constructs, and the documentation should therefore focus on explaining aspects of the implementation.

BEST PRACTICES

Give priority to the non-obvious aspects of a program when documenting it. Don't spend time documenting single lines of code, unless of course a single line of code is difficult to understand. Refactor the code rather than providing a lengthy explanation.

Outside the context of a book on programming, a comment such as the following is meaningless and should be avoided:

```
t = t*2 + a;   // doubles t and adds a
```

The calculation described by this comment is self-explanatory. What is not explained, is the purpose of the calculation. Choosing meaningful variable names helps to make the purpose clear.

FIGURE 8.6   Generated Javadoc documentation

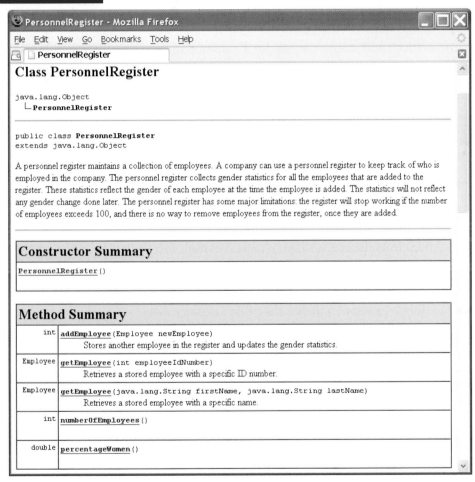

Several limitations and improvements for Program 8.7 were discussed at the end of Section 8.3. Pay attention to such limitations when documenting a program. If a program does *not* work under certain circumstances, this should be documented. The Javadoc comment at the beginning of Program 8.8 clearly states that the class only works as long as there are no more than a hundred employees. The documentation for a method should explain what assumptions the method makes about its parameter values.

Assertions can also be used to explain to the reader what assumptions the code makes:

```
assert newEmployee.gender != Gender.UNKNOWN
  : "Gender must be known before registration.";
assert employeeCount < allEmployees.length;
```

These assertions from the addEmployee() method explain that the gender of the employee that is being added needs to be known, and that it is not permitted to add any more employees if the register is already full. Another benefit of using assertions is that the assumptions they document can be checked automatically at runtime. Trying to run the following code, for example, will cause the first assertion above to fail:

```
PersonnelRegister register = new PersonnelRegister();
register.addEmployee(new Employee("Kris", "Epicene", Gender.UNKNOWN));
```

8.6 Review questions

1. The properties and behaviour defined for a class determine what _____ the class has, and what _____ objects of this class can fulfil.

2. Given a user-defined class `Egg` and a method that has the signature `void boilEgg(Egg)`, which of these statements are true?

   a The `boilEgg()` method receives a copy of the `Egg` object that is passed as parameter.

   b The `boilEgg()` method receives an `Egg` object as a parameter.

   c The `boilEgg()` method receives a reference value as parameter. It refers to an `Egg` object.

   d The `boilEgg()` method may change the state of the `Egg` object, so that the `Egg` object may have a different state after the method call completes.

3. In Java an object can ask another object to do something by _____ a _____ of the other object.

4. An association between two classes can be established by one or both of the classes declaring a _____ _____ in order to store a _____ _____ of an object of the other class.

5. An association in which a `Car` object owns four `Tire` objects is called a _____-to-_____ association.

6. If a method name is overloaded, when will the decision on which method body to execute be made?

   a When compiling the method call statement.

   b When the program is started.

   c When the method call is executed.

8.7 Programming exercises

1. In New York State there is a sales tax of 8 cents per dollar. The tax is not charged for certain products, such as fruits, vegetables, meat and dairy products. Write a `Product` class that represents products that can be sold. A product should have a name, a base price and should be marked whether or not it is exempt from sales tax. A product object should provide an easy way to determine how much a customer must pay to buy the product.

2. Write a class that represents the selection of products a grocery store provides. Name this class "`GroceryStoreSelection`", and create a one-to-many association between this class and the `Product` class in Exercise 8.1. The `GroceryStoreSelection` class should provide methods to add products to the selection and retrieve products by their product name.

8

3. Write a program that has a text-based menu that allows the user to register new products, and which finds the sale price of products that have already been registered. The program should use the classes from Exercise 8.1 and Exercise 8.2. To register a new product, the user should enter the name of the product, the base price of the product, and whether the product is tax exempt. To find the sale price of the product the user should only need to specify the name of the product.

4. Write a class that represents individual playing cards from a standard deck of Anglo-American cards, and a class that represents a whole deck of fifty-two cards. Each card can have one of thirteen ranks (2–10, Jack, Queen, King and Ace) and one of four suites (Spades, Hearts, Diamonds and Clubs.) What factors should be considered when designing the classes? Consider how the classes will be used in different types of card games, e.g. poker and blackjack.

5. We want to create a program that implements a simple card game for two players, with the following rules:
   1 A deck of 52 cards is shuffled.
   2 Each player is given a card.
   3 Each player gets the opportunity to replace their card with a new card from the deck, if they so choose.
   4 The player that has the card with the highest value wins.

   In this game cards 2 through 10 are worth their face value, and the Jack, Queen, King and Ace are worth 11, 12, 13 and 14 respectively. The program should communicate with both players via the terminal window. What classes and methods are needed in the program?

   Write a complete program that will play a single round of the game. The dialogue between the players and the program should look like this:

   ```
   A simple card game:
   Creating deck of cards.
   Creating player 1.
   Enter name of new player: Ron
   Creating player 2.
   Enter name of new player: Veronica
   Shuffling the deck of cards.
   Giving each player a card.
   Allowing players to change their card.
   Ron, you have the card 10 of Diamonds.
   Do you want to change your card, Ron (y/n)? n
   Veronica, you have the card 6 of Spades.
   Do you want to change your card, Veronica (y/n)? y
   Giving Veronica a new card.
   Ron has the card 10 of Diamonds.
   Veronica has the card Jack of Hearts.
   Veronica won.
   ```

PART THREE

Program Building Blocks

CHAPTER 9

Sorting and searching arrays

LEARNING OBJECTIVES

By the end of this chapter you will understand the following:

- **The meaning of natural order for values in a data type.**

- **The use of relational operators for comparing values of primitive data types.**

- **How to sort values using the selection sort and insertion sort algorithms.**

- **Why developing pseudocode prior to coding is useful.**

- **How to search for a value using linear search and binary search algorithms.**

- **How to write a method that defines the natural order of objects for your own class.**

INTRODUCTION

Sorting and searching are needed for many purposes, for example ranking the candidates after an election, or when looking up phone numbers in an electronic phone book. This chapter explains a few basic sorting and searching algorithms, and demonstrates their use when data is stored in arrays. The main steps of each algorithm are defined using a structured language called *pseudocode*, which is used to refine the problem at hand into successively smaller parts until each part is simple enough to be implemented in a programming language. Inserting the pseudocode as comments in the source code is used as a technique to help understand how the various steps are implemented, resulting in source code that is well documented.

9.1 Natural order

Values of numerical primitive data types have a *natural order*, allowing a *relational operator* to be used to determine the ranking of two values. This means that we are always able to compare two values, say a and b, to determine whether a is smaller than, equal to, or larger than b. This relationship holds for all numerical primitive data types, i.e. `byte`, `short`, `int`, `long`, `float` and `double`, as well as for characters (of type `char`). The only primitive data type that does not have a natural order is `boolean`. While it makes sense to compare two Boolean values for equality, it has no meaning to state that `true` is smaller than or larger than `false`.

Many types of objects also have a natural order. We have compared two strings several times in this book and chosen one of them based on their lexicographical order. The `String` class defines this natural order for strings. Later in this chapter we will look at how a class can define a natural order for its objects.

Relational operators for primitive data types

Table 9.1 shows relational operators that are predefined for operands of numerical data types and characters. The relational operators always return a `boolean` value, indicating whether the test succeeded (`true`) or failed (`false`).

TABLE 9.1	Relational operators for primitive data types
Operator	Tests whether
$a == b$	a is equal to b.
$a < b$	a is less than b.
$a > b$	a is greater than b.
$a <= b$	a is less than or equal to b.
$a >= b$	a is greater than or equal to b.

Understanding relational operators

Program 9.1 shows a simple way to test your understanding of relational operators. It uses assert statements to formulate assumptions as Boolean expressions that should be `true`. If all the assertions are correct, as in Program 9.1, the program will run without any runtime error messages. If not, the program will terminate and the JVM will print an error message. Remember to turn on the assertions by specifying the "`-ea`" flag:

```
> java -ea TestRelationalOperators
```

Had the last assertion been incorrect in Program 9.1, for example:

```
assert 'x' < 'p';
```

the JVM would have printed an error message such as the following:

```
Exception in thread "main" java.lang.AssertionError
    at TestRelationalOperators.main(TestRelationalOperators.java:17)
```

identifying the source code file (TestRelationalOperators.java) and line number (17) where the error occurred. This makes it easy to look up the statement in a text editor and make the necessary modifications to the code.

PROGRAM 9.1   Using relational operators to compare primitive values

```
// Using assertions to understand relational operators.
public class TestRelationalOperators {
  public static void main(String[] args) {
    // Tests for integers.
    assert 1 == 1;
    assert 1 < 2;
    assert 1 <= 1;
    assert 3 > 2;
    assert 3 >= 3;
    // Tests for decimal numbers.
    assert 1.0 < 1.01;
    assert 1000.0 > 999.99;
    // Test for characters.
    assert 'x' == 'x';
    assert 'x' < 'y';
    assert 'x' <= 'z';
    assert 'x' > 'p';
    System.out.println("All assertions are true.");
  }
}
```

Program output:

```
All assertions are true.
```

Comparing floating-point values

Note that the equality operator == should be used with care when comparing floating-point values for equality, as certain floating-point values cannot be represented exactly in computer memory. While for most practical purposes the values 0.333333333333 (with twelve decimals) and 1.0/3.0 can be considered equal, the assertion at (1) in the code below will not succeed:

```
final double ONE_THIRD = 0.333333333333;
double ratio = 1.0/3.0;
assert ratio == ONE_THIRD :                                  // (1)
    "ERROR: " + ratio + " is different from " + ONE_THIRD;
```

Executing this code (with the "-ea" flag) will result in an error message similar to the following:

```
Exception in thread "main" java.lang.AssertionError:
  ERROR: 0.3333333333333333 is different from 0.333333333333
  at TestDecimalEquality.main(TestDecimalEquality.java:7)
```

Although we could circumvent the problem above by defining the constant `ONE_THIRD` to be the result of the expression 1.0/3.0, the problem with using the == operator to compare floating-point values persists. A better solution is to test whether the first value is within a range of ± *epsilon* of the second value, where *epsilon* is some small value:

```
...
double epsilon = 1.0E-12; // 0.000000000001
assert Math.abs(ratio - ONE_THIRD) <= epsilon
    "ERROR: " + ratio + " is different from " + ONE_THIRD;
```

9.2 Selection sort

Sorting means ordering a set of primitive data values or objects in ascending or descending order based on the natural order defined by their data type. How can we sort the numbers drawn in this week's national lottery, or all members in a local sports club? To answer this question, we'll look first at sorting a set of integer values stored in an array.

The *selection sort* algorithm works by finding the smallest (or largest) value in the unsorted part of the array, and swapping this value with the value at the beginning of the unsorted part. In this way, the beginning of the array gradually becomes sorted and the remaining unsorted part contains one less element to sort for each pass over the array. This procedure is repeated until there is only one element left in the unsorted part. The values will be sorted in ascending order if the smallest value is picked in each pass, and in descending order if the largest value is picked in each pass.

Sorting an array of integers

Consider the following array:

```
int[] numbers = { 8, 4, 2, 6, 1 };
```

We want to sort this array in ascending order using the selection sort algorithm. Figure 9.1 illustrates what happens during the first pass. The array is searched for the *smallest* number, which is then swapped with the first element in the array. After the first pass, we have a sorted part of the array consisting of *a single value* placed correctly in the first element of the array.

In each of the subsequent passes, the smallest of the remaining values will be swapped with the value in the first position of the unsorted part of the array. In this way the sorted part of the array expands by one element placed correctly per pass, yielding a sorted array after the final pass. Figure 9.2 shows the array after each pass. Note that in Figure 9.2 the smallest value and the value in the first position of the unsorted part are identical in passes three and four.

FIGURE 9.1 First pass of an integer array during selection sort

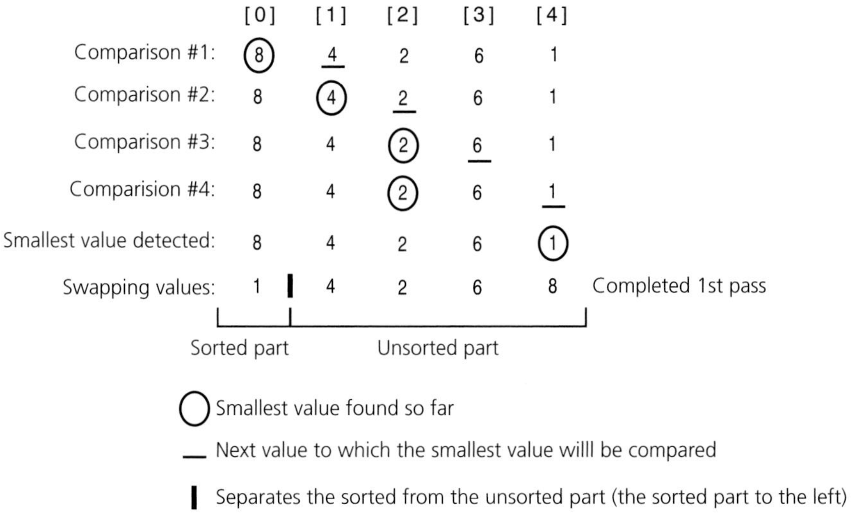

	[0]	[1]	[2]	[3]	[4]
Comparison #1:	(8)	4	2	6	1
Comparison #2:	8	(4)	2	6	1
Comparison #3:	8	4	(2)	6	1
Comparision #4:	8	4	(2)	6	1
Smallest value detected:	8	4	2	6	(1)
Swapping values:	1	4	2	6	8	Completed 1st pass

Sorted part   Unsorted part

○ Smallest value found so far

— Next value to which the smallest value willl be compared

| Separates the sorted from the unsorted part (the sorted part to the left)

FIGURE 9.2 The main steps of selection sort in an array of integers

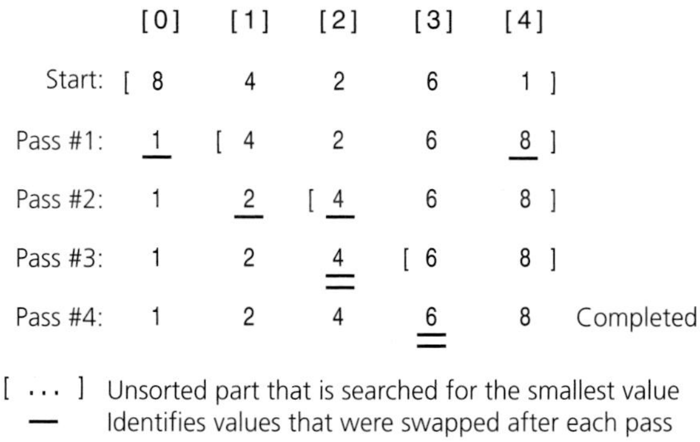

	[0]	[1]	[2]	[3]	[4]
Start:	[8	4	2	6	1]
Pass #1:	1	[4	2	6	8]
Pass #2:	1	2	[4	6	8]
Pass #3:	1	2	4	[6	8]
Pass #4:	1	2	4	6	8	Completed

[...] Unsorted part that is searched for the smallest value
— Identifies values that were swapped after each pass

Pseudocode for the selection sort

We can now formalise the steps in the selection sort algorithm using pseudocode:

For each pass:
    Find the smallest value in the unsorted part of the array
    Swap the smallest value with the first element of the unsorted part

This algorithm will sort the array in *ascending* order. If we need to sort the array in *descending* order, the algorithm must find the *largest* value in each pass, and swap this value with the value in the first position of the unsorted part of the array.

Pseudocode emphasises readability and simplicity, but cannot be compiled into an executable program in the way that Java source code can be. You can think of pseudocode as a recipe; it describes what steps are needed to prepare, say, Coq au vin, but it does not actually cook it for you. Still, the recipe is important, because chances are you will not end up with the desired results without it. Similarly, pseudocode helps you think through the problem at hand, and identifies the steps that are needed to solve it, before writing any code. The pseudocode can also be copied into the source code as comments, making it easier to relate the steps defined in the algorithm to the code that actually implements them.

Pseudocode is commonly used to develop and document algorithms, and is written in natural language. However, some statements begin with keywords that are used to indicate flow of control, such as "For each" to indicate the start of a repetition (i.e. loop), or "If" to indicate selection among alternative actions (i.e. starting a selection statement). In addition, indentation is used to show the grouping of operations, where statements at the same indentation level belong to the same block (i.e. a compound statement).

Coding the selection sort

Program 9.2 shows the implementation of the selection sort algorithm described above. The program uses two nested loops, at (1) and (2). The loop variable next in the outer loop runs from index 0 to index numbers.length-1. The loop variable current in the inner loop runs through the unsorted part of the array, i.e. from index next+1 to index numbers.length. Swapping the smallest value found in each pass with the first element in the unsorted part of the array is done at (3), each time the inner loop has completed (cf. Figure 9.2).

PROGRAM 9.2 Sorting by selection in an array of integers

```
// Utility class for sorting and searching arrays of integers.
class Utility {
  static void sortBySelection(int[] numbers) {
    // For each pass:
    for (int next=0; next < numbers.length-1; next++) { // (1) outer loop
      // Find the smallest value in the unsorted part of the array
      // Note that we need to find the position of the smallest value
      // in order to swap values later.
      int smallest = next;
      for (int current = next+1;
           current < numbers.length;
           current++) {                                 // (2) inner loop
        if (numbers[current] < numbers[smallest]) {
          smallest = current;
        }
      }

      assert smallest > next && smallest < numbers.length :
        "Index for smallest value " + smallest +
        " should have been between " + (next+1) +
        " and " + numbers.length;

      // Swap the smallest value with the first element
      // of the unsorted part
      int temp = numbers[smallest];                     // (3)
```

```
      numbers[smallest] = numbers[next];
      numbers[next] = temp;

      printArray("Pass #" + (next+1) + ": ", numbers);
    }
  }

  static void printArray(String prompt, int[] array) {
    System.out.print(prompt);
    for (int value : array) {
      System.out.print(value + " ");
    }
    System.out.println();
  }
}

// Sorting an array using the selection sort algorithm.
public class SortingBySelection {
  public static void main(String[] args) {
    int[] numbers = { 8, 4, 2, 6, 1 };
    Utility.printArray("Unsorted array: ", numbers);
    Utility.sortBySelection(numbers);
    Utility.printArray("Array sorted by selection sort: ", numbers);
  }
}
```

Program output:

```
Unsorted array: 8 4 2 6 1
Pass #1:1 4 2 6 8
Pass #2:1 2 4 6 8
Pass #3:1 2 4 6 8
Pass #4:1 2 4 6 8
Array sorted by selection sort: 1 2 4 6 8
```

Analysing the amount of work required by a selection sort

Let's take a step back and review the amount of work involved in sorting an array using selection sort. For an array of n elements, the outer loop in Program 9.2 is always executed $n-1$ times, placing one element in the correct position at each pass. For each pass, the algorithm compares the current element with all elements left in the unsorted part of the array. The number of comparisons made will be $n-1$ in the first pass, $n-2$ in the second, and so on, until only *one* comparison is made in the last pass. Even if the number of comparisons are reduced by one for each pass, the total number will be proportional to the number of elements in the array. Thus, the amount of work needed by this algorithm will be proportional to n^2. The algorithm is therefore said to be of order n^2, denoted by $O(n^2)$.

> **BEST PRACTICES**
>
> Use pseudocode to divide complex operations into smaller, manageable operations. Refine the operations until they are easier to understand and implement. Include the pseudocode as comments in your source code. This approach will document how your solution works, and help in debugging your implementation.

9.3 Insertion sort

In an array we can define a conceptual *subarray*, which consists of one or more consecutive elements inside an array. A subarray can be sorted even if the entire array is not sorted.

Let's assume we have a sorted subarray. To place a new value in the correct position in the subarray, we first shift the values of all elements that are larger than the new value one position towards the end of the array. We then place the new value in the correct position, resulting in a subarray that is still sorted and which now contains one more element. This procedure is repeated until all values have been inserted at their correct positions. Not surprisingly, this algorithm is called an *insertion sort*.

Sorting an array of integers using an insertion sort

Let's return to the array we sorted in the previous section:

```
int[] numbers = { 8, 4, 2, 6, 1 };
```

We now want to sort it using the insertion sort algorithm described above. Figure 9.3 illustrates how the insertion sort algorithm will successively expand the sorted subarray until the whole array is sorted.

Pseudocode for the insertion sort

Sorting by insertion can be described by the following pseudocode:

For each pass:
    Store the next element to be inserted in an auxiliary variable
    Iterate backwards through the sorted subarray
    If the current element is larger than the next element
        Shift the current element value one position towards the end of the array
    Insert the next element in the vacant position in the array

This will sort the array in ascending order. Writing pseudocode for the insertion sort algorithm that sorts the array elements in descending order is left as an exercise.

FIGURE 9.3   The main steps of insertion sort

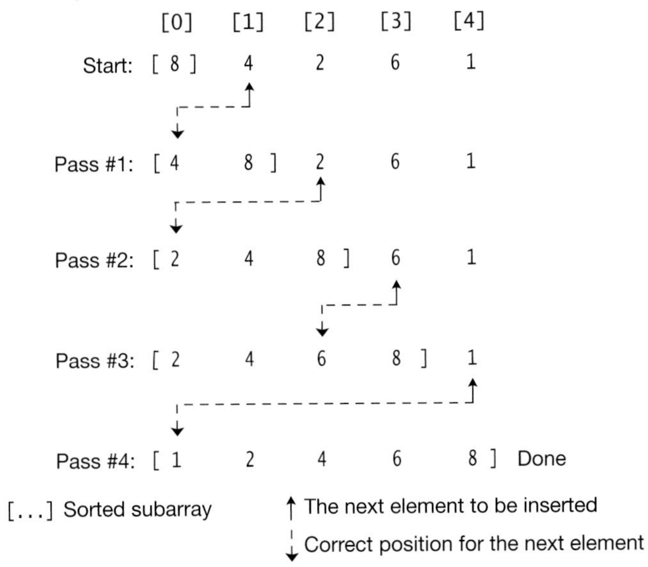

	[0]	[1]	[2]	[3]	[4]
Start:	[8]	4	2	6	1
Pass #1:	[4	8]	2	6	1
Pass #2:	[2	4	8]	6	1
Pass #3:	[2	4	6	8]	1
Pass #4:	[1	2	4	6	8] Done

[...] Sorted subarray   ↑ The next element to be inserted

                                 ↓ Correct position for the next element

Coding the insertion sort

Program 9.3 shows the implementation of sorting by insertion for an array of integers. The program uses two nested loops, at (1) and (2). The loop variable next in the outer loop runs from index 1 to index numbers.length-1. In the inner loop, which runs backwards, the element values are shifted towards the end of the array until the correct position for the next element is found (cf. Figure 9.3).

PROGRAM 9.3   Sorting by insertion in an array of integers

```
// Utility class for sorting and searching arrays of integers.
class Utility {
  static void sortByInsertion(int[] numbers) {
    // For each pass:
    for (int next = 1; next < numbers.length; next++) { // (1) outer loop
      // Store the next element to be inserted in an auxilliary variable
      int temp = numbers[next];
      // Pass through the sorted subarray backwards
      //    If the current element is larger than the next element
      //      Shift the current element one position towards the end of the array
      int current;
      for (current = next;
           current > 0 && temp < numbers[current-1];
           current--) {                            // (2) inner loop
        numbers[current] = numbers[current-1];     // (3) shift backwards
      }

      assert current == 0 || numbers[current] < temp :
```

```
                    "Index for insertion " + current +
                    " should have been between 0 and " + (numbers.length-1);

                // Insert the next element in the vacant position in the array
                numbers[current] = temp;                          // (4)

                printArray("Pass #" + next + ": ", numbers);
            }
        }

        // other methods...
    }


    // Sorting an array using the insertion sort algorithm.
    public class SortingByInsertion {
        public static void main(String[] args) {
            int[] numbers = { 8, 4, 2, 6, 1 };
            Utility.printArray("Unsorted array: ", numbers);
            Utility.sortByInsertion(numbers);
            Utility.printArray("Array sorted by insertion sort: ", numbers);
        }
    }
```

Program output:

```
Unsorted array: 8 4 2 6 1
Pass #1: 4 8 2 6 1
Pass #2: 2 4 8 6 1
Pass #3: 2 4 6 8 1
Pass #4: 1 2 4 6 8
Array sorted by insertion sort: 1 2 4 6 8
```

Analysing the amount of work required by an insertion sort

The insertion sort algorithm will pass through the array n-1 times, where n is the number of elements in the array. In the first pass, up to n-2 comparisons and element value shifts are made. In the second pass, up to n-3 comparisons and element value shifts are made, and so on, until only one comparison and at the most one element value shift is made in the last pass. Assuming that the array is not partially sorted when the algorithm starts, the maximum number of comparisons and element value shifts are found by adding (n-2) + (n-3) + ... + 2 + 1. This amounts to a number proportional to n. Even if the array is sorted beforehand, every comparison still has to be performed. Thus, insertion sort also requires an amount of work proportional to n^2, and is said to be of order $O(n^2)$.

9.4 Sorting arrays of objects

Comparing objects: the `Comparable` interface

In Chapter 4 we compared objects for reference equality using the == operator, and used the `equals()` method to compare objects for value equality. This allowed us to compare two objects for equality only. In Java, the `java.lang.Comparable` interface defines the method needed for ranking objects according to their natural order. This interface specifies a single method called `compareTo`.

For two objects t1 and t2 of class T, the method call `t1.compareTo(t2)` returns a value:

- == 0 if the objects are equal according to the same criteria as for the `equals()` method.
- < 0 if t1 is smaller than t2, i.e. t1 comes before t2 in the natural order for class T.
- > 0 if t1 is larger than t2, i.e. t1 comes after t2 in the natural order for class T.

Every class that needs to represent a data type with a natural order must adhere to the `Comparable` interface by implementing a `compareTo()` method in accordance with the natural order of its objects. The Javadoc documentation for this interface states that the natural order for a class T should be consistent with its implementation of the `equals()` method. The expression `(t1.compareTo(t2) == 0)` should therefore yield the same `boolean` value as `t1.equals(t2)` for all possible objects t1 and t2.

Many classes in the Java standard library implement the `Comparable` interface. We can, for example, compare two `String` objects by calling the `compareTo()` method:

```
String name1 = "Smith";
String name2 = "Jones";
int status = name1.compareTo(name2);
if (status == 0) {
  System.out.println("Participants have the same last name.");
} else if (status < 0) {
  System.out.println(name1 + " comes before " + name2);
} else {
  System.out.println(name1 + " comes after " + name2);
}
```

The `compareTo()` method in the `String` class compares strings based on the Unicode value of the characters at corresponding positions in the two strings. A sort based on method this will order strings in lexicographical order, which is the commonest way of ordering text strings, for example the names in a telephone directory.

All numerical wrapper classes also implement the `Comparable` interface. The natural order of such objects is given by arithmetic comparison of their values, i.e. using the relational operators predefined for numerical data types. See *Relational operators for primitive data types* on page 236. The simple example in Program 9.4 compares two `Integer` objects with values -10 and 10, respectively. The result is what one would expect.

```
// Testing the natural order for wrapper objects that hold integers.
public class TestWrapperComparison {
  public static void main(String[] args) {
    Integer number1 = -10;
    Integer number2 = 10;
    int status = number1.compareTo(number2);

    if (status == 0) {
      System.out.println("EQUAL Integer objects: " + number1 +
                          " and " + number2);
    } else if (status < 0) {
      System.out.println("Integer object " + number1 +
                          " is smaller than " + number2);
    } else {
      System.out.println("Integer object " + number1 +
                          " is larger than " + number2);
    }
  }
}
```

Program output:

```
Integer object -10 is smaller than 10
```

Implementing the natural order for time objects

Let's implement the natural order for objects of the Time class introduced in Chapter 7 (see Program 7.10 on page 195). This class defines the time of day as two integers, hours (0–23) and minutes (0–59). Objects of the Time class can obviously be ordered chronologically. We can use this order as the natural order for Time objects.

The compareTo() method implemented by the Time class must return an integer value:

- < 0 if the time represented by t1 comes before that of t2.
- > 0 if the time represented by t1 comes after that of t2.
- == 0 if the Time objects represent the same time of day.

Given two Time objects t1 and t2, we can determine their natural order by comparing their respective hours and minutes values. If the hours are different, the hour values determine the order. If the hours are the same, but the minutes are different, the minute values determine the order. If both the hours and minutes are the same, the two Time objects represent the same time of the day.

The following pseudocode describes the steps for determining the natural order of two Time objects t1 and t2:

```
If the hours are different
    Natural order is determined by the natural order of the hour values
Else if the minutes are different
    Natural order is determined by the natural order of the minute values
Else
    The two Time objects represent the same time of day
```

We need to refine the pseudocode above to determine what value the compareTo() method should return. The problem boils down to determining the natural order of two integers, representing either hours or minutes. We note that for two integers i1 and i2, their difference (i1 - i2) is positive if i1 is greater than i2, negative if i1 is less than i2, and 0 if i1 and i2 are equal. The difference is exactly what the compareTo() method needs to return. We can now refine the pseudocode above:

```
If the hours are different
    Return the difference between the hour values
Else if the minutes are different
    Return the difference between the minute values
Else
    Return 0
```

The pseudocode above can be further refined if we take into consideration that the *total number of minutes* (i.e. hours*60 + minutes) represented by each time of day are also in chronological order, but this is left as an exercise.

Program 9.5 shows how the revised Time class implements the Comparable interface. The implements clause has to be included in the class declaration, as shown in (1). The compareTo() method must have the signature shown in (2):

```
class Time implements Comparable {              // (1)

    public int compareTo(Object o2) {           // (2)
        // implementation of natural order for Time objects
    }
}
```

The compareTo() method is passed a Time object which is referenced by the parameter o2 of type Object. The construct (Time) at (3) is called a *cast*. It tells the compiler that the obj2 reference passed as parameter will refer to an object of class Time at runtime. We cast the parameter to a Time reference t2 at (3) so that we can access the time values of the Time object passed as parameter. The rest of the implementation of the compareTo() method is based on the pseudocode developed earlier in this subsection.

Note that both the toString() and compareTo() methods need to be declared as public methods. These visibility constraints are enforced by the Object class and the Comparable interface respectively.

Program 9.5 tests the compareTo() method with Time objects that represent different times.

```
// Time is given as hours (0-23) and minutes (0-59).
class Time implements Comparable {           // (1)

  // Fields for the time.
  int hours;
  int minutes;

  /** Constructor */
  Time(int hours, int minutes) {
    assert (0 <= hours && hours <= 23 && 0 <= minutes && minutes <= 59) :
            "Invalid hours and/or minutes";
    this.hours = hours;
    this.minutes = minutes;
  }

  /** String representation of the time, TT:MM */
  public String toString() {
    return String.format("%02d:%02d", hours, minutes);
  }

  /** Comparing Time objects */
  public int compareTo(Object obj2) {      // (2)
    Time t2 = (Time) obj2;                 // (3) Cast required, as we are
                                           //     comparing Time objects
    // Check if the hours are different
    if (this.hours != t2.hours) {
      // Order is determined by which of the hours is greater
      return this.hours - t2.hours;
    }
    // Have the same hours. Check if the minutes are different.
    if (this.minutes != t2.minutes) {
      // Order is determined by which of the minutes is greater
      return this.minutes - t2.minutes;
    }
    // Both hours and minutes have the same values.
    return 0;                              // Objects represent the same time
  }
}

// Testing the natural order for Time objects.
public class TestTimeComparison {
  public static void main(String[] args) {
    Time time1 = new Time(6, 30);    // 06:30
    Time time2 = new Time(15, 5);    // 15:05
    Time time3 = new Time(20, 45);   // 20:45
    compareTimeObjects(time1, time2);
    compareTimeObjects(time3, time2);
```

```
      compareTimeObjects(time1, time1);
  }

  static void compareTimeObjects(Time t1, Time t2) {
    int status = t1.compareTo(t2);
    if (status == 0) {
      System.out.println("EQUAL start and end times " + t1 +
                         " - CHECK YOUR WATCH!");
    } else if (status < 0) {
      System.out.println("Started working " + t1 + " before ending " + t2
                         + " - OK.");
    } else {
      System.out.println("Ended working " + t1 + " before starting " + t2
                         + " - YIKES!");
    }
  }
}
```

Program output:

```
Started working 06:30 before ending 15:05 - OK.
Ended working 20:45 before starting 15:05 - YIKES!
EQUAL start and end times 06:30 - CHECK YOUR WATCH!
```

Sorting arrays of comparable objects

Program 9.6 provides an alternative implementation of the sortBySelection() method first introduced in Program 9.2. The new method in the GenericUtility class can be used to sort arrays of Comparable objects.

The sortBySelection() method takes an array of Comparable objects, as shown in (1). It uses two nested loops, (2) and (3), as before. The loop variable in the outer loop (next) runs from index 0 to index objects.length-2, while the loop variable in the inner loop (current) runs through the unsorted part of the array, i.e. from index next+1 to index objects.length-2. Elements are compared using the compareTo() method at (4). The swap at (5) is done for each pass of the inner loop, using the auxiliary variable temp of type Comparable.

Program 9.6 defines an array with six Time objects, which are Comparable, and sorts them using the revised selection sort algorithm, printing the sorted array to the terminal window.

In Program 9.6, the array of Time objects is already sorted after the fourth pass. However, the selection sort algorithm has no means of detecting this, and will always perform n-1 passes for an array with n elements. For each pass, all elements in the unsorted part are compared to find the next value. The amount of work is therefore proportional to n^2.

We can use our implementation of the sortBySelection() method to sort *any* array of Comparable objects, not just Time objects. The String class and the numerical wrapper classes all implement the Comparable interface, so we use our sortBySelection() method to sort arrays with objects of these classes as well.

PROGRAM 9.6   Sorting arrays of **Comparable** objects

```java
class GenericUtility {
  static void sortBySelection(Comparable[] objects) {      // (1)
    // For each pass:
    for (int next = 0; next < objects.length-1; next++) {// (2) outer loop
      // Find the smallest value in the unsorted part of the array
      int smallest = next;
      for (int current = next+1;
           current < objects.length;
           current++) {                                    // (3) inner loop
        if (objects[current].compareTo(objects[smallest]) < 0) { // (4)
          smallest = current;
        }
      }

      assert smallest > next && smallest < objects.length :
        "Index for smallest value " + smallest +
        " should have been between " + (next+1) +
        " and " + objects.length;

      // Swap the smallest value with the first element of the usorted part
      Comparable temp = objects[smallest];                 // (5)
      objects[smallest] = objects[next];
      objects[next] = temp;

      printArray("Pass #" + (next+1) + ": ", objects);
    }
  }

  // other methods...

  static void printArray(String prompt, Comparable[] array) {
    System.out.print(prompt);
    for (Comparable element : array) {
      System.out.print(element + " ");
    }
    System.out.println();
  }
}

// Program that sorts an array of Time objects using selection sort
public class SortingObjects {
  public static void main(String[] args) {
    Time[] times = { new Time(10, 0),  // 10:00
                     new Time(12, 30), // 12:30
```

```
                new Time(6, 30),   // 06:30
                new Time(6, 56),   // 06:56
                new Time(1, 44),   // 01:44
                new Time(15, 5)    // 15:05
            };
    GenericUtility.printArray("Unsorted array: ", times);
    GenericUtility.sortBySelection(times);
    GenericUtility.printArray("Array sorted by selection sort: ", times);
    }
}
```

Program output:

```
Unsorted array: 10:00 12:30 06:30 06:56 01:44 15:05
Pass #1: 01:44 12:30 06:30 06:56 10:00 15:05
Pass #2: 01:44 06:30 12:30 06:56 10:00 15:05
Pass #3: 01:44 06:30 06:56 12:30 10:00 15:05
Pass #4: 01:44 06:30 06:56 10:00 12:30 15:05
Pass #5: 01:44 06:30 06:56 10:00 12:30 15:05
Array sorted by selection sort: 01:44 06:30 06:56 10:00 12:30 15:05
```

9.5 Linear search

We often need to look up a value in an array. If the array is not sorted, we are forced to check every element until the value sought is found, or until we have exhausted all elements in the array. This searching technique is called *linear search*, and the value we want to look up is referred to as the *search key*.

Linear search can be described by the following pseudocode:

Repeat while elements are left to compare in the array:
    If current element equals the search key
        Return the index of the current element
If the search key is not found after searching the entire array
    Return a negative index to indicate that the key was not found

Program 9.7 implements the linear search algorithm for an array of integers (type int). The method linearSearch() returns the index of the key value if it is found in the array. If the given key is not found, an invalid index, -1, is returned. The loop at (1) runs through the array until the entire array is searched or the key is found.

Because the array is not sorted in advance, the worst-case scenario is for the search to run through the entire array comparing every element to the key. The amount of work needed in linear search is therefore proportional to the number of elements in the array. The algorithm is therefore said to be of $O(n)$, i.e. of order n.

Note the use of an assert statement in Program 9.7 to verify that the algorithm has either exhausted all the elements of the array, or that the key has been found. Methods in later programming examples in this chapter use the `assert` statement in a similar way to verify that the algorithm behaves as expected.

Note that if *multiple* array elements contain the search key, Program 9.7 only reports the index of the *first* element that has the key. The program can be extended to report indices of all elements containing the key. This extension is left as an exercise.

PROGRAM 9.7   Linear search in an array of integers

```
// Utility class for sorting and searching arrays of integers.
class Utility {
  static int linearSearch(int[] numbers,  int key) {
    boolean found = false;
    int i = 0;
    // Repeat while more elements in array:
    while (i < numbers.length && !found) {  // (1)
      // If the current element contains the key:
      //   Return the index of the current element
      if (numbers[i] == key) {
        found = true;       // Found!
      } else {
        i++;                // Move to next element
      }
    }
    assert (i >= numbers.length || found) : "Error in linear search.";
    if (found)
      return i;             // The key is in element numbers[i]
    else
      return -1;            // The key is not found
  }

  // other methods...
}

// Using linear search
import java.util.Scanner;
public class LinearSearch {
  public static void main(String[] args) {
    int[] numbers = { 18, 15, 5, 2, 12, 17, 21, 3, 6, 25, 22, 1, 10 };
    Utility.printArray("Array (unsorted): ", numbers);

    Scanner keyboard = new Scanner(System.in);
    System.out.print("Enter the search key [integer]: ");
    int key = keyboard.nextInt();

    int index = Utility.linearSearch(numbers, key);
    if (index > -1)  {
      System.out.println("Linear search found the number " + key
                       + " in element with index " + index);
```

```
    } else {
      System.out.println("The number " + key + " is not in the array!");
    }
  }
}
```

Program output when the given key exists in the array:

```
Array (unsorted): 18 15 5 2 12 17 21 3 6 25 22 1 10
Enter the search key [integer]: 17
Linear search found the number 17 in element with index 5
```

Program output when the given key is not found:

```
Array (unsorted): 18 15 5 2 12 17 21 3 6 25 22 1 10
Enter the search key [integer]: 32
The number 32 is not in the array!
```

9.6 Binary search

If values in an array are already sorted, we can use a more efficient search algorithm than linear search. For example, the phone directory is sorted according to last name, and it would clearly be a waste of time to start at the beginning of a phone directory to look up a person whose last name is "Smith".

When an array is already sorted, we can start by comparing the search key with the middle element in the array. (We assume that the array is sorted in ascending order.) If the middle element is *less* than the key, we know that the key has to be in the upper half of the array, if it exists in the array at all. Analogously, the key must be in the lower half of the array if the middle element is *greater* then the key. We then repeat this procedure in the relevant half of the array. With this approach, the number of elements to be searched is halved in each step. The algorithm either finds the key or runs out of elements to compare with the key. This search algorithm is called *binary search*.

Assuming that the array is already sorted in ascending order, we can formulate the binary search algorithm as follows:

Repeat while there are elements to compare in the array:
    If the middle element is equal to the key
        Return the index of the middle element
    If the middle element is smaller than the key
        Continue search in the upper half
    If the middle element is larger than the key
        Continue search in the lower half

Figure 9.4 shows the steps for binary search in an array of integers when the search key is 17. We start by comparing the key to the middle element, which in this case contains the value 12. The middle element is less than the key, so we know that the key can only be in the upper half of the array. We repeat the procedure in the interval of the array defined by the variables lower and upper, and thus determine an even smaller part of the array that can contain the key. Note how the variables lower and upper are updated to indicate the interval for the search. After repeatedly halving the array, we end up with a middle element whose value is equal to the search key, 17. The search stops and returns the index of the middle element, as the key has been found.

If the array does not contain the key, the algorithm will stop when it runs out of elements to compare with the key, i.e. when the interval in which to search becomes empty. In this case an invalid index (-1) is returned, indicating that the key was not found.

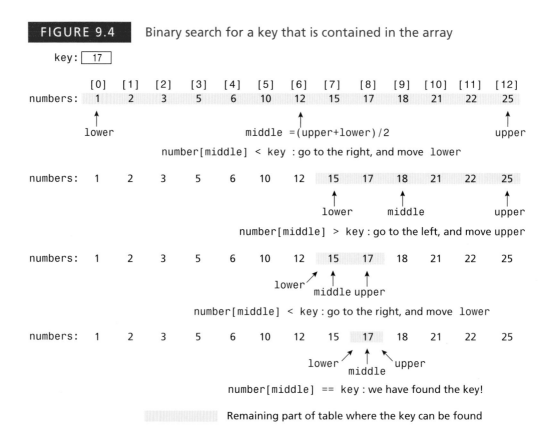

FIGURE 9.4   Binary search for a key that is contained in the array

Program 9.8 implements binary search for arrays of int values. The loop at (1) ensures that the number of remaining elements to search is halved until the key is found, or until there are no more elements left to search. The index of the middle element is computed at (2). As long as the lower limit is less than or equal to the upper limit, the search interval is not empty. See the if statement at (3). Note how the interval limits lower and upper are updated at (4) and (5). In order to search in the *upper* half, the lower limit is incremented. In order to search in the *lower* half, the upper limit is decremented. Program 9.8 tests the algorithm with different keys.

For each pass, the number of elements that needs to be compared with the search key is halved. If n is the number of elements in the array, the amount of work is proportional to the natural logarithm of n, $\log_2(n)$. For an array with $1\,048\,576$ (2^{20}) elements, the binary search algorithm will, in the worst case scenario, require only twenty comparisons to determine the result.

Binary search in arrays of integers

```java
// Utility class for sorting and searching arrays of integers.
class Utility {
  static int binarySearch(int[] numbers,  int key) {
    int lower = 0;                    // Lower limit of the search interval
    int upper = numbers.length-1;     // Upper limit of the search interval
    int middle = -1;                  // Index of middle element
    boolean found = false;            // Indicates whether the key is found
    boolean moreElements = true;      // Indicates whether there are
                                      // more elements to search

    // Repeat while more elements in array:
    while (moreElements && !found) { // (1) Main loop
      middle = (lower + upper)/2;     // (2) Middle element in this interval
      if (lower > upper) {            // (3) Determine if interval is empty
        moreElements = false;         // No more elements left to search
      } else if (numbers[middle] == key) { // Key is in the middle element
        found = true;
      } else if (numbers[middle] < key) {
        lower = middle + 1;           // (4) Search in upper half
      } else {
        upper = middle - 1;           // (5) Search in lower half
      }
    }
    assert (!moreElements || found) : "Error in binary search.";

    if (found) {
      return middle;  // The key is in element numbers[middle]
    } else {
      return -1;      // The key is not found
    }
  }

  // other methods...
}

// Looking up a search key in an array of integers using binary search.
import java.util.Scanner;
public class BinarySearch {
  public static void main(String[] args) {
    int[] numbers = { 1, 2, 3, 5, 6, 10, 12, 15, 17, 18, 21, 22, 25 };
    Utility.printArray("Array (sorted): ", numbers);

    Scanner keyboard = new Scanner(System.in);
    System.out.print("Enter the search key [integer]: ");
    int key = keyboard.nextInt();

    int index = Utility.binarySearch(numbers, key);
```

```
      if (index > -1)
        System.out.println("Binary search found the number " + key
                        + " in element with index " + index);
      else
        System.out.println("The number " + key + " is not in the array!");
    }
}
```

Program output when the given key exists in the array:

```
Array (sorted): 1 2 3 5 6 10 12 15 17 18 21 22 25
Enter the search key [integer]: 17
Binary search found the number 17 in element with index 8
```

Program output when the given key does not exist:

```
Array (sorted): 1 2 3 5 6 10 12 15 17 18 21 22 25
Enter the search key [integer]: 32
The number 32 is not in the array!
```

9.7 Sorting and searching using the Java standard library

The java.util.Arrays class in the Java standard library offers a number of methods for
sorting and searching arrays. A small subset of these methods are shown in Table 9.2. The
binarySearch() method requires that the elements are already sorted in *ascending natural
order*. The sort() methods require that elements of an array of objects implement the
Comparable interface in order to sort them.

Program 9.9 shows sorting and searching an array of integers using the methods from the
Arrays class. The method printArray() from Program 9.2 is used to print array values in
order to verify that the sorting algorithm behaves as expected.

TABLE 9.2   Selected methods from the **Arrays** class

java.util.Arrays

static int binarySearch(
  elementTypeName[] array,
  elementTypeName key)
	Uses binary search to look up the given key in the array.
	Returns the index to the key in the array, if the key exists.
	If not, a negative index is returned, corresponding to (-insertionpoint)-1, where insertionpoint is the index of the element where the key would have been if it had been in the array.
	
	The array elements must already be sorted in *ascending natural order*, otherwise the result is undefined.
	Permitted element types include byte, char, double, float, int, long, short and Object.

java.util.Arrays	
static void sort(elementTypeName[] array)	Sorts an array of elements with type *elementTypeName* in *ascending natural order*.

static void sort(
  elementTypeName[] array,
  int fromIndex,
  int toIndex)
	Only elements from the index fromIndex (inclusive) and the index toIndex (inclusive) are sorted, if these limits are specified. Permitted element types are byte, char, double, float, int, long, short and Object.

	Elements in an array of objects must implement the Comparable interface.

PROGRAM 9.9   Sorting and searching using methods in the **Arrays** class

```java
// Using the Java standard library for sorting and searching arrays.
import java.util.Arrays;
public class SortingByArrays {
  public static void main(String[] args) {
    int[] numbers = { 8, 4, 2, 6, 1 };
    Utility.printArray("Unsorted array: ", numbers);
    Arrays.sort(numbers);
    Utility.printArray("Array sorted by Java library: ", numbers);
    int key = 4;
    int index = Arrays.binarySearch(numbers, key);
    System.out.println("Key " + key + " has index " + index);
    key = 5;
    index = Arrays.binarySearch(numbers, key);
    System.out.println("Key " + key + " has index " + index);
  }
}
```

Program output:

```
Unsorted array: 8 4 2 6 1
Array sorted by Java library: 1 2 4 6 8
Key 4 has index 2
Key 5 has index -4
```

9.8 Review questions

1. Values of all numerical data types in Java, such as `int` and `double`, have a _____
_____. The Java programming language also defines a set of _____ operators
that can be used to compare numerical values.

2. The only primitive data type in Java whose values cannot be compared is _____.
Values of this data type can only be compared for _____.

3. What will be the output from statements (1) to (6) below, given that the program is
run with the following command:

```
> java -ea ComparePrimitiveValues

// Compare values of primitive data types.
public class ComparePrimitiveValues {
  public static void main(String[] args) {
    // Tests for negative integers.
    assert -10 == -10;          // (1)
    assert -10 <= -9;           // (2)
    assert -10 < -9;            // (3)
    assert -10 > -11;           // (4)
    assert -10 >= -11;          // (5)
    assert -10 >= -9;           // (6)
  }
}
```

4. Write at least three assertions verifying that the letter 'a' comes before the letter 'z'
according to the lexicographical order of characters defined by Java.

5. Write an assertion verifying that the Unicode standard defines an equal number of
lowercase and uppercase letters in the English alphabet. The first and last lowercase
and uppercase letters are 'a' and 'z', and 'A' and 'Z', respectively.

Hint: you will need to use both arithmetic and relational operators in the assertion.

6. Write an assertion that verifies that a test score is between 0 and 100. Assume that
the score is kept in a variable called `testScore`, and that the score limits are defined
as constants names `MIN_SCORE` and `MAX_SCORE` respectively. Let your `assert` statement
print a explanatory message if it fails.

7. To enable comparison of two *objects*, their class has to implement the _____
interface, which defines the _____ method used to compare objects.

8. A simple class for CDs is defined as follows:

```
// A simple CD class that can be ordered by title and # of tracks.
class CD {
  // Declaration of field variables
  String title;
  int    noOfTracks;
```

```
        // Creates a new CD with given title and # of tracks.
        CD(String title, int noOfTracks) {
          this.title = title;
          this.noOfTracks = noOfTracks;
        }

        // Prepares a string representation of the CD.
        public String toString () {
          return "The CD entitled '" + title + "' has " + noOfTracks + " tracks.";
        }
      }
```

The objects of this class can be ordered by their titles (lexicographically) and, if two titles are the same, by the number of tracks. In this case the CD with the highest number of tracks is considered the "largest".

Which of the code snippets below provides a correct implementation of the natural order of CD objects? How must the class header for the CD class be modified?

```
a  public int compareTo(CD otherCD) {
       if (title == otherCD.title) {
          return noOfTracks - otherCD.noOfTracks;
       } else {
          return title.compareTo(otherCD.title);
       }
   }
```

```
b  public int compareTo(Object otherCD) {
       if (title.equals(otherCD.title)) {
          return noOfTracks - otherCD.noOfTracks;
       } else {
          return title.compareTo(otherCD.title);
       }
   }
```

```
c  public int compareTo(Object obj) {
       CD otherCD = (CD) obj;
       if (title.equals(otherCD.title)) {
          return noOfTracks - otherCD.noOfTracks;
       } else {
          return title.compareTo(otherCD.title);
       }
   }
```

9. The revised CD class from Exercise 9.8 is used in the following program:

```
        // Sorting a CD selection.
        import java.util.Arrays;
        public class CDSorter {
          public static void main(String[] args) {
            CD[] newCDs = { new CD("Java Jive", 5),
                            new CD("T Cup Blues", 7),
```

```
                        new CD("Another cup of Joe", 6),
                        new CD("T Cup Blues", 8) };
        System.out.println("CD list:");
        for (CD nextCD : newCDs) { System.out.println(nextCD); }
        Arrays.sort(newCDs);
        System.out.println("Sorted CD list:");
        for (CD nextCD : newCDs) { System.out.println(nextCD); }
    }
}
```

What will be the output from this program?

10. Which of the following statements are true?

   a All objects whose fields have a natural order can be ordered using the relational operators offered by Java.

   b An array of objects whose fields have a natural order can be sorted by the sort() method provided by the java.util.Arrays class.

   c An array of objects whose class implements the Comparable interface can be sorted using the sort() method in the java.util.Arrays class.

   d Only an array of objects whose class implements the Comparable interface can be sorted using the sort() method in the java.util.Arrays class.

11. Which of the following statements are true?

   a Selection sort will run faster if the array is partially sorted in advance.

   b Insertion sort will run faster if the array is partially sorted in advance.

   c Selection sort requires fewer comparisons per pass than insertion sort.

   d Selection sort requires fewer assignment operations per pass than insertion sort.

9.9 Programming exercises

1. We want to sort an array of integers in *descending* order. Write pseudocode for a selection sort algorithm that does this.

   Simulate by hand on a piece of paper how the algorithm will work for the first pass on the following array:

   { 7, 2, 6, 1, 3, 4, 10, 8 }

   Simulate sorting of the array after each pass.

2. Implement a sortBySelectionDescending() method in the Utility class, based on the pseudocode from Exercise 9.1. Test your program on the following array:

   { 7, 2, 6, 1, 3, 4, 10, 8 }

   Verify that the program behaves as expected by printing the array after each pass. You can use the printArray() method of the Utility class to print the array values.

3. Extend the program from Exercise 9.2 to allow the user to enter the values for an array of integers.

Example of user dialogue:
```
Sorting an array of integers in descending order
Enter the number of values in the array [integer]: 6
Enter element value #1: 11
Enter element value #2: 7
Enter element value #3: 23
Enter element value #4: 1
Enter element value #5: 16
Enter element value #6: 15
Unsorted array: 11 7 23 1 16 15
Pass #1: 23 7 1 11 16 15
Pass #2: 23 16 1 11 7 15
Pass #3: 23 16 15 11 7 1
Pass #4: 23 16 15 11 7 1
Pass #5: 23 16 15 11 7 1
Array sorted by selection sort: 23 16 15 11 7 1
```

4. Extend Program 9.2 to allow the user to enter the values for the array. The user should also be able to specify the number of elements in the array.

Example of user dialogue:
```
Sorting an array of integers
Enter the number of values in the array [integer]: 6
Enter element value #1: 11
Enter element value #2: 7
Enter element value #3: 23
Enter element value #4: 1
Enter element value #5: 16
Enter element value #6: 15
Unsorted array: 11 7 23 1 16 15
Pass #1: 1 7 23 11 16 15
Pass #2: 1 7 23 11 16 15
Pass #3: 1 7 11 23 16 15
Pass #4: 1 7 11 15 16 23
Pass #5: 1 7 11 15 16 23
Array sorted by selection sort: 1 7 11 15 16 23
```

5. Write a new program that allows the user to enter the values for an array of integers, and select between sorting in ascending or descending order. The new program should use the sorting algorithms from Exercise 9.3 and Exercise 9.4.

Example of user dialogue:
```
Sorting an array of integers
Enter the number of values in the array [integer]: 6
Enter element value #1: 11
Enter element value #2: 7
Enter element value #3: 23
Enter element value #4: 1
```

```
Enter element value #5: 16
Enter element value #6: 15
Enter sorting order [A for ascending, D for descending]: A
Unsorted array: 11 7 23 1 16 15
Pass #1: 1 7 23 11 16 15
Pass #2: 1 7 23 11 16 15
Pass #3: 1 7 11 23 16 15
Pass #4: 1 7 11 15 16 23
Pass #5: 1 7 11 15 16 23
Array sorted in ascending order: 1 7 11 15 16 23
```

6. The following pseudocode for selection sort is meant to sort an array in descending order:

> For each pass:
> > Find the largest value in the unsorted part of the array
> > Swap the largest value with the last element in the unsorted part

Simulate by hand on a piece of paper how this algorithm will work for the following array:

> { 7, 2, 6, 1, 3, 4, 10, 8 }

Modify the pseudocode so that it correctly sorts the array in descending order.

7. Implement the algorithm for insertion sort from Exercise 9.6. Verify that it sorts the array in descending order by writing a client program that uses the algorithm to sort the same array that was used in the hand simulation.

8. A sorting algorithm called *bubble sort* works by letting smaller values *bubble* up towards the beginning of the array, while larger values *sink* towards the end of the array. Figure 9.5 illustrates how bubble sort works during the first pass of the array

> { 8, 4, 2, 6, 1 }

The algorithm makes the largest element sink all the way down to the end of the array, by comparing pairs of neighbouring values. It swaps the values in a pair if they are not in correct order.

The pseudocode for the bubble sort algorithm is given below. Use this pseudocode as a starting point for implementing the algorithm.

Pseudocode for bubble sort (in ascending order):

> For each pass of the array:
> > For each pair of neighbouring values in the unsorted part of the array:
> > > If values in the pair are in the wrong order
> > > > Swap the values in the pair

FIGURE 9.5   Sorting an array of integers using bubble sort

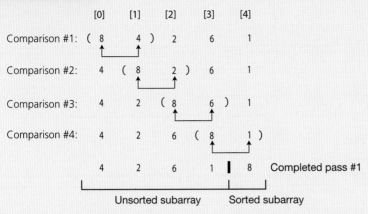

| | Separator between the sorted and unsorted subarray (sorted to the right)

(8   4) Neighbouring values to be compared

       Swap

9. Modify the Time class in Program 9.5 so that the fields hours and minutes are declared as Integer references. Show how we can we use this fact in the implementation of the compareTo() method.

10. Refine the compareTo() method for the Time class in Program 9.5 by taking into consideration that the *total number of minutes* (hours*60 + minutes) represented by each time of the day are also in chronological order.

11. In Scrabble, each player has a set of pieces with a letter on each piece. The pieces are used to make words on a game board. If a player for example has the pieces 'e', 'c', 's', 't', 'k' and 'a', they can make the word "cake" by using four of their pieces. Alternatively, they can make the word "steak" by using all but one piece. When playing Scrabble it may be helpful to sort the pieces beforehand to make it easier to find letters that can be used to form new words. Write a client that reads the letters on the pieces, sorts them and prints them out in the terminal window. Use the data type char for the letter on each piece. Select a suitable number of pieces for this purpose.

    Hint: read the characters as a string using the Scanner class, then loop through the string to extract individual characters.

12. Assume that a linear search for the value 4 is performed on the following array using the linear search algorithm in Program 9.7.

    { 2, 6, 4, 3, 7, 4 }

    Which index is returned by the algorithm in Program 9.7?

    Write pseudocode for an extended version of the linear search algorithm that reports indices of *all* elements that are equal to the search key. Modify Program 9.7 to report indices of all elements equal to the search key. Run the revised program using 4 as the search key again, and verify that it behaves as expected. Also, run the program with a key that only occurs once in the array, and with keys that are not in the array.

13. Extend the program from Exercise 9.12 to allow the user to specify an array of values and the search key from the keyboard.

An example of a dialogue for reading the array length and the element values can be found in Exercise 9.4.

14. Extend the program in Exercise 9.4 to allow binary search in the sorted array.

Example of user dialogue:
```
Sorting and searching an array of integers
Enter the number of values in the array [integer]: 6
Enter element value #1: 11
Enter element value #2: 7
Enter element value #3: 23
Enter element value #4: 1
Enter element value #5: 16
Enter element value #6: 15
Unsorted array: 11 7 23 1 16 15
Pass #1:1 7 23 11 16 15
Pass #2:1 7 23 11 16 15
Pass #3:1 7 11 23 16 15
Pass #4:1 7 11 15 16 23
Pass #5:1 7 11 15 16 23
Array sorted by selection sort: 1 7 11 15 16 23
Enter the search key [integer]: 11
Binary search found the number 11 in element with index 2
```

15. Based on the EmployeeV7 class from Chapter 7, implement the natural order for employees in a small company, where the criteria for determining their order is their last and first names respectively. Use the new EmployeeV7 class to sort the following array:

```
Employee[] salesmen = {
    new Employee("Bart", "Simpson", 20.55, Employee.MALE),
    new Employee("John", "Doe", 16.23, Employee.MALE),
    new Employee("Jane", "Doe", 12.95, Employee.FEMALE),
    new Employee("Peggy", "Sue", 13.42, Employee.FEMALE),
};
```

Select a sorting method of your choice from the GenericUtility class, and use the printArray() method to print both the unsorted and sorted EmployeeV7 array in the terminal window.

16. Implement a simple lottery game that does the following:

    a Randomly selects seven numbers out of a set of integers ranging from one to thirty-four.

    b Allows the user to enter their ticket numbers (with only one game) and compare it to the drawn lottery numbers. Assume that the numbers entered and the numbers drawn are sorted in ascending order.

    c Reports whether the user has won first prize or not. Winning first prize requires that all seven numbers match.

    Before you start programming, write pseudocode that defines the steps needed to solve the problem.

    Hint: You can use the `java.util.Random` class to generate the lottery numbers.

17. Make the program in Exercise 9.16 more realistic by allowing the user to enter their lottery ticket numbers in any order. The program should sort both the drawn numbers and the user ticket numbers before comparing the two number series. Extend the pseudocode from Exercise 9.16 to clarify the changes that are needed to incorporate the new features before writing any new code. Be sure to include your updated pseudocode in the source code, to document your program.

CHAPTER 10

Text file I/O and simple GUI dialogs

LEARNING OBJECTIVES

By the end of this chapter, you will understand the following:

- **Organising values in data records for storing in text files.**

- **Writing string representations of primitive values and objects to text files.**

- **Reading characters from text files and converting them to appropriate values.**

- **Using basic exception handling to deal with error situations during program execution.**

- **Designing simple GUI dialogues using the `JOptionPane` class.**

- **Creating message dialog boxes to present information to the user.**

- **Creating input dialog boxes to acquire data from the user.**

- **Creating confirmation dialog boxes to get confirmation from the user.**

INTRODUCTION

A program must communicate with its environment to obtain the data it requires and to publish the results it computes. Data that a program reads is called *input*, and the data a program writes is called *output*. Input is read from a *source*, and output is written to a *destination* (or *sink*). In the examples so far, the keyboard has functioned as the source and the terminal window has been the destination for data.

This chapter discusses how data can be written to and read from text files, and how to create simple graphical dialog boxes to exchange information between the program and the user.

Appendix E contains customised classes for reading values from the terminal window and creating simple GUI dialog boxes.

10.1 File handling

Data that a program manipulates is no longer available after the program terminates, unless the data is stored somewhere and can be read again by the program. Data files can be used for this purpose. A data file offers persistent storage of data and can function as both a source and destination for data.

A *file* refers to a specific storage area on media where data can be stored, for example on a hard drive. Data in a file is stored as a sequence of *bytes* (i.e. an information unit of 8 *bits*), but can be interpreted in different ways during reading and writing. If the data in a file is interpreted as a *sequence of bytes*, the file is called a *binary file*. If the data is interpreted as a *sequence of characters*, the file is called a *text file*.

In general the way in which primitive data values are stored is platform-specific. It is not at all certain that a binary file created on one platform can be moved to another and be interpreted correctly. Java solves the problem of moving binary data by defining the *size* of primitive data types. The size specifies how many bytes are needed to represent values of a particular primitive data type (see Table 10.1). A binary file containing such values will be interpreted correctly by a Java program on any platform.

A char value in a Java program always occupies two bytes, but this might not be the case when the character is stored in a text file. How many bytes a character occupies in a file depends on the *character encoding* used to store the characters in the file. Java provides classes that facilitate reading and writing characters from text files and take into account the encoding used for storing the characters.

A text editor will interpret the contents of a text file as a sequence of characters. The compiler javac interprets the contents of a Java source file as a long string of characters, but creates a binary file that contains the resulting Java byte code. Some character encodings are quite common, for example UTF-8 and ISO 8859-1, so that text files are usually interpreted correctly when moved between platforms.

TABLE 10.1 Default size of primitive data types

Primitive data type	Size in bytes
boolean	1
char	2
int	4
long	8
float	4
double	8

Data records

A company wants to store information about their employees in a text file so that the information can be reused. The class `Employee` is shown at (1) in Program 10.1. We would like to store the following information about an employee in a text file:

```
String firstName;      // Field variable 1
String lastName;       // Field variable 2
double hourlyRate;     // Field variable 3
Gender gender;         // Field variable 4
```

It is quite common to store information as data records. A *record* consists of one or more data fields. A *data field* in a record usually contains a primitive value, but we allow a string literal as well. A data record for an employee will consist of four data fields, as illustrated in Figure 10.1, corresponding to the four field variables in the `Employee` class. Note that the string representation of an enum constant is its name, as depicted for the gender field in Figure 10.1.

Program 10.1 also shows the class `PersonnelRegister` at (2), which uses an array to keep track of all employees. In the next section we use the classes from Program 10.1 to write information in the `Employee` object as records in a text file, to read back records from the text file, and to create appropriate `Employee` objects from the records read.

FIGURE 10.1   Data records

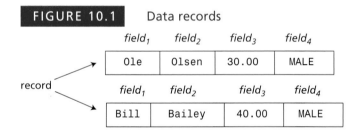

PROGRAM 10.1   Registering employees

```
// Constants to represent gender
enum Gender {FEMALE, MALE};

// Class representing an employee
class Employee {                                          // (1)

  // Static variable
  final static double NORMAL_WORKWEEK = 37.5;

  // Field variables
  String firstName;
  String lastName;
  double hourlyRate;
  Gender gender;
```

```java
    // Constructors
    Employee() { }
    Employee(String firstName, String lastName,
             double hourlyRate, Gender gender) {
      this.firstName  = firstName;
      this.lastName   = lastName;
      this.hourlyRate = hourlyRate;
      this.gender     = gender;
    }

    // Determines whether an employee is female.
    boolean isFemale() { return (this.gender == Gender.FEMALE); }

    // Computes the salary of an employee, based on the number of hours
    // worked during the week.
    double computeSalary(double numOfHours) {
      assert numOfHours >= 0 : "Number of hours must be >= 0";
      double weeklySalary = hourlyRate * Employee.NORMAL_WORKWEEK;
      if (numOfHours > Employee.NORMAL_WORKWEEK) {
        weeklySalary += 2.0 * hourlyRate * (numOfHours - NORMAL_WORKWEEK);
      }
      return weeklySalary;
    }

    // Return string representation of the field values of an employee.
    public String toString() {
      return String.format(
        "First name: %-6s Last name: %-8s Hourly rate: %6.2f Gender: %-6s",
        this.firstName, this.lastName, this.hourlyRate, this.gender);
    }
  }

// Personnel register of employees
class PersonnelRegister {                                          // (2)

    final static int MAX_NUM_EMPLOYEES = 100;

    // Fields
    Employee[] employees;
    int        numOfEmployees;
    int        numOfFemales;

    // Default constructor
    PersonnelRegister() {
      employees = new Employee[MAX_NUM_EMPLOYEES];
    }

    // Create a personnel register from an array of employees.
    PersonnelRegister(Employee[] suppliedEmployeeArray) {
```

```
    employees = new Employee[MAX_NUM_EMPLOYEES];
    for( int i = 0; i < suppliedEmployeeArray.length; i++) {
      registerEmployee(suppliedEmployeeArray[i]);
    }
  }

  // Create a personnel register with field values from parameters.
  PersonnelRegister(Employee[] employees, int numOfEmployees,
                          int numOfFemales) {
    this.employees = employees;
    this.numOfEmployees = numOfEmployees;
    this.numOfFemales = numOfFemales;
  }

  // Register an employee in the employee array.
  void registerEmployee(Employee newEmployee) {
    assert numOfEmployees != employees.length:
          "No room for more employees.";
    employees[numOfEmployees] = newEmployee;
    numOfEmployees++;
    if (newEmployee.gender == Gender.FEMALE) {
      numOfFemales++;
    }
  }


  // Selectors
  int getNumOfEmployees()     { return numOfEmployees; }
  int getNumOfFemales()       { return numOfFemales; }
  Employee[] getEmployeeArray() { return employees; }

  // Return employee with specified index.
  Employee getEmployee(int index) {
    assert 0 <= index && index <= numOfEmployees :
          "Index not valid";
    return employees[index];
  }

  // Replace an employee at index with another employee.
  void replaceEmployee(int index, Employee newEmployee) {
    assert 0 <= index && index <= numOfEmployees :
          "Index not valid";
    employees[index] = newEmployee;
  }

  // Compute percentage of females in the company.
  double getFemalePercentage() {
    assert numOfEmployees > 0 : "Personnel register is empty.";
    return 100.0 * numOfFemales / numOfEmployees;
  }
```

```
// Returns statistics about the company.
public String toString() {
  return String.format("The company has %d employees," +
                        " where %.2f%% are women.",
                        getNumOfEmployees(), getFemalePercentage());
}
}
```

10.2 Text files

A text file contains lines of text. Each *text line* consists of a sequence of characters and is terminated by a *line terminator string*. This line terminator string is platform-specific. For example, it is the string "\r\n" in Windows, but consists of a single character '\n' in Unix. However, the methods for file handling in Java ensure that the line terminator string is interpreted correctly.

The java.io package provides extensive support for reading data from various sources and writing data to various destinations. Here we concentrate on one approach to reading and writing text files. Essentially, there are four steps to file handling, which we will discuss in detail in subsequent subsections:

1 We need to *open* the file, thereby creating a connection between the program and the file.

2 We need to choose the appropriate class to convert the values, depending on whether we are reading from or writing to a file.

3 Data can now be written to or read from the designated file.

4 We *close* the file when we are finished with it, thereby freeing any resources that were used for handling the file.

We would like to store information about employees in a text file. Information about an employee is stored as a data record consisting of the field values in an Employee object, translated to a sequence of characters, and each record is terminated by the line terminator string. When reading, we can read a text line that corresponds to a record, and create an employee with the extracted field values.

Writing to text files

We need the following classes to write to a text file (see Figure 10.2):

● The class java.io.FileWriter opens the file and ensures that the characters are stored in the default character encoding for the platform.

● The class java.io.PrintWriter provides methods for converting values to their respective string representations.

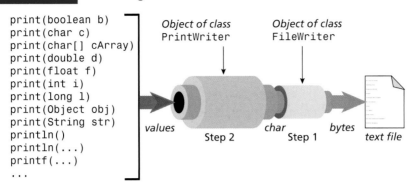

FIGURE 10.2   Writing to a text file

```
FileWriter  textFileWriter = new FileWriter(textFileName);   // Step 1
PrintWriter textWriter     = new PrintWriter(textFileWriter); // Step 2
```

Here's how the four steps for file handling apply to writing to text files. The procedure for writing string representations of values to text files is illustrated by Figure 10.2 and Program 10.2:

1 Create a `FileWriter` object to open the file for writing:

```
FileWriter textFileWriter = new FileWriter(dataFileName);     // (5)
```

The constructor accepts the name of the file. If a file with the designated name does not exist, a new file with this name is created. If the file with the designated name exists, it is reset, meaning that the writing will start at the beginning of the file and any previous content will be overwritten. The call to the `FileWriter` constructor can throw an `IOException` if the file cannot be opened for some reason. (The next section explains exception handling.)

The class also provides a constructor that allows appending to an existing file:

```
FileWriter textFileWriter = new FileWriter(dataFileName, append);
```

If the `boolean` value of the parameter append is true, this constructor will open the file for appending. Otherwise writing will start from the beginning of the file.

2 Create a `PrintWriter` object that is connected to the `FileWriter` from step 1:

```
PrintWriter textWriter = new PrintWriter(textFileWriter);     // (6)
```

Now the `PrintWriter` delivers characters to the `FileWriter`, which in turn ensures that the characters it receives are correctly stored as bytes in the file, using the default character encoding for the platform.

The class `PrintWriter` also provides a constructor that accepts a file name as parameter:

```
PrintWriter textWriter = new PrintWriter(dataFileName);
```

This constructor creates the underlying file writer to encode the characters for storing in the specified file. This constructor also creates the file if necessary, and always opens it for writing from the beginning of the file.

3 Write text representations of values using the print methods of the `PrintWriter` class. For example, the method `writeEmployeeData()` at (10) in Program 10.2 uses

the printf() method in the PrintWriter class to write the values of the different fields in an Employee object:

```
textWriter.printf(

    "%s" + FIELD_TERMINATOR + "%s" + FIELD_TERMINATOR +
    "%.2f" + FIELD_TERMINATOR + "%s%n",
    employee.firstName, employee.lastName,
    employee.hourlyRate, employee.gender);
```

Since all primitive values are written as characters, it is important to mark the *end* of each field in the record, so that the values can be interpreted correctly when read from the file. We terminate all fields with the field terminator character, except for the last field, which is terminated by the line terminator string. The format specification "%n" in the format string ensures that the correct platform-specific line terminator string is printed.

We have used comma (,) as the field terminator character in a record. This format is called the *Comma Separated Values* (CSV) *file format*. It is quite popular, and is used by many spreadsheet programs to import and export values.

4 Finish by closing the file. This is done by calling the close() method of the Print-Writer:

```
textWriter.close();                                           // (9)
```

Calling the close() method is strongly recommended, as this ensures that not only is the connection between the program and the file closed, but also that any resources that were used for handling the file are freed and that no data is lost.

Program 10.2 uses the classes from Program 10.1, and at (2) calls the method writeAllE-mployeesToTextFile() to write the employee information to the specified file. The method creates the necessary writer objects at (5) and (6), as explained above. The method first writes the number of records to be stored in the text file at (7), and at (8) calls the method writeEmployeeData() to write the information about each employee. The method writeEmployeeData() at (10) writes this information as explained in step 3 above. The file employeeFile.txt will contain the following four text lines, which can be verified by opening it in a text editor:

```
3
Ole,Olsen,30.00,MALE
Bill,Bailey,40.00,MALE
Liv,Larsen,50.00,FEMALE
```

The contents of the file are read into a personnel register at (3), and subsequently the contents of the personnel register are printed to the terminal window.

PROGRAM 10.2   Text files

```
import java.io.IOException;

public class CompanyAdmin {

    public static void main(String[] args) throws IOException {      // (1)
        // Create an array of employees.
```

```java
        Employee[] employeeInfo = {
            new Employee("Ole",  "Olsen",  30.00, Gender.MALE),
            new Employee("Bill", "Bailey", 40.00, Gender.MALE),
            new Employee("Liv",  "Larsen", 50.00, Gender.FEMALE)
        };

        // Create a personnel register.
        PersonnelRegister register = new PersonnelRegister(employeeInfo);
        // Create a company.
        CompanyUsingTextFiles company = new CompanyUsingTextFiles(register);

        // Print employee info in personnel register to a text file.
        company.writeAllEmployeesToTextFile("employeeFile.txt");        // (2)

        // Read employee info from a text file.
        System.out.println("Read from text file.");
        company.readAllEmployeesFromTextFile("employeeFile.txt");       // (3)

        // Print employee info to the terminal window.
        company.printAllEmployeesToTerminalWindow();
        company.printReport();
    }
}

import java.io.BufferedReader;
import java.io.FileReader;
import java.io.FileWriter;
import java.io.IOException;
import java.io.PrintWriter;

class CompanyUsingTextFiles {

    final static char FIELD_TERMINATOR    = ',';  // Comma

    // Field
    private PersonnelRegister register;

    // Constructors
    CompanyUsingTextFiles() {
        register = new PersonnelRegister();
    }

    CompanyUsingTextFiles(PersonnelRegister register) {
        this.register = register;
    }

    // Print statistics
    void printReport() {
        System.out.println(register);
    }
```

```
void printAllEmployeesToTerminalWindow() {
  Employee[] employees = register.getEmployeeArray();
  int numOfEmployees = register.getNumOfEmployees();
  System.out.println("Number of employees: " + numOfEmployees);
  for (int i = 0; i < numOfEmployees; i++) {
    System.out.println(employees[i]);
  }
}

void writeAllEmployeesToTextFile(String dataFileName)
    throws IOException {                                        // (4)

  FileWriter textFileWriter = new FileWriter(dataFileName);     // (5)
  PrintWriter textWriter = new PrintWriter(textFileWriter);     // (6)

  // Write the number of employees in the register.
  int numOfEmployees = register.getNumOfEmployees();
  textWriter.println(numOfEmployees);                           // (7)

  // Write info about each employee.
  Employee[] employees = register.getEmployeeArray();
  for (int i = 0; i < numOfEmployees; i++) {
    writeEmployeeData(textWriter, employees[i]);                // (8)
  }

  textWriter.close();                                          // (9)
}

void writeEmployeeData(PrintWriter textWriter,
                       Employee employee) {                     // (10)
  // Fields separated by a field terminator character.
  textWriter.printf(
      "%s" + FIELD_TERMINATOR + "%s" + FIELD_TERMINATOR +
      "%.2f" + FIELD_TERMINATOR + "%s%n",
      employee.firstName, employee.lastName,
      employee.hourlyRate, employee.gender);
}

void readAllEmployeesFromTextFile(String dataFileName)
    throws IOException {                                        // (11)

  FileReader textFileReader = new FileReader(dataFileName);     // (12)
  BufferedReader textReader = new BufferedReader(textFileReader);// (13)

  // Read how many employees are in the text file.
  String firstLine = textReader.readLine();                    // (14)
  int totalNumOfEmployees = Integer.parseInt(firstLine);

  // Create a personnel register.
```

```
    register = new PersonnelRegister();

    // Read info about all employees in the file.
    for (int i = 0; i < totalNumOfEmployees; i++) {
      // Read an employee.
      Employee employee = readEmployeeData(textReader);          // (15)
      // Register the employee.
      register.registerEmployee(employee);
    }

    textReader.close();                                          // (16)
  }

  Employee readEmployeeData(BufferedReader textReader)
          throws IOException {                                   // (17)
    // Read a record, i.e. a text line.
    String record = textReader.readLine();                       // (18)

    // Find the index of the field terminator characters in the record.
    int fieldTerminatorIndex1 = record.indexOf(FIELD_TERMINATOR);  // (19)
    int fieldTerminatorIndex2 = record.indexOf(FIELD_TERMINATOR,
                                      fieldTerminatorIndex1 + 1);
    int fieldTerminatorIndex3 = record.indexOf(FIELD_TERMINATOR,
                                      fieldTerminatorIndex2 + 1);

    // Extract the values of the fields from the data record.
    String firstName = record.substring(0, fieldTerminatorIndex1); // (20)
    String lastName = record.substring(fieldTerminatorIndex1 + 1,
                                      fieldTerminatorIndex2);

    String doubleStr = record.substring(fieldTerminatorIndex2 + 1,
                                      fieldTerminatorIndex3);
    double hourlyRate  = Double.parseDouble(doubleStr);          // (21)

    String genderStr = record.substring(fieldTerminatorIndex3 + 1);
    Gender gender;
    if (genderStr.equals(Gender.MALE.toString())) {             // (22)
      gender = Gender.MALE;
    } else {
      gender = Gender.FEMALE;
    }

    return new Employee(firstName, lastName, hourlyRate, gender);
  }
}
```

Program output:

```
Number of employees: 3
First name: Ole    Last name: Olsen    Hourly rate:  30.00 Gender: MALE
First name: Bill   Last name: Bailey   Hourly rate:  40.00 Gender: MALE
```

```
First name: Liv    Last name: Larsen    Hourly rate:  50.00 Gender: FEMALE
   The company has 3 employees, where 33.33% are women.
```

Basic exception handling

A program should be able to handle error situations that might occur at runtime. Error situations can be divided into two main categories:

1 *Programming errors.* For example, using an invalid index to access an array element, attempting to divide by zero, calling a method with illegal arguments, or using a reference with the null value to access members of an object.

2 *Runtime environment errors.* For example, opening a file that does not exist, a read or write error when using a file, or a network connection going down unexpectedly.

Programming errors are error situations that occur because of *logical errors* in the program, while runtime environment errors are errors over which the program has little control. A program must be able to handle both kinds of errors. Ideally, programming errors should not occur, and the program should handle runtime environment errors gracefully.

Checked exceptions

An *exception* in Java signals that an error or an unexpected situation has occurred during execution. We say that *an exception has been thrown*. Normal program execution is suspended, and if the program does not take any appropriate action to deal with the exception, the program execution stops and information about the exception is printed to the terminal window.

Java defines some special exceptions that a program must take a stand on. Such an exception is called a *checked exception*, because the compiler will complain if the method in which it can occur does not deal with it explicitly. When a checked exception can be thrown by the code in a method, the method must either *catch* the exception or explicitly *throw it again*. Checked exceptions force the code in which they can occur to take explicit action to deal with them, thus making programs *robust*, i.e. being able to handle error situations appropriately.

For our purpose here it is sufficient to look at how an exception can be rethrown by a method. Rethrowing an exception is analogous to "passing the buck". If no method deals with the exception and they all rethrow it, the exception finally reaches the `main()` method that started the program execution. If the `main()` method also rethrows the exception, the outcome is the same as before: the program's execution is terminated and information about the exception is printed to the terminal window.

The throws clause

At (5) in Program 10.2 the constructor call in the `writeAllEmployeesToTextFile()` method can throw an `IOException`. This is an exception that cannot be ignored, i.e. it is a checked exception. The method is therefore declared with a `throws` clause in its header:

```
void writeAllEmployeesToTextFile(String dataFileName)
        throws IOException {                                    // (4)
    ...
    FileWriter textFileWriter = new FileWriter(dataFileName);   // (5)
    ...
}
```

The `throws` clause can specify a list of comma-separated exceptions. If any exception on the list occurs during execution of the method body, then that exception is rethrown.

Since the `main()` method calls the `writeAllEmployeesToTextFile()` method, the `main()` method *must* also deal with the `IOException` that can result from the call to the `writeAllEmployeesToTextFile()` method. The `main()` method also uses the `throws` clause to rethrow the exception:

```
public static void main(String[] args) throws IOException {      // (1)
    ...
    company.writeAllEmployeesToTextFile("employeeFile.txt");     // (2)
    ...
}
```

If an `IOException` is thrown in the `writeAllEmployeesToTextFile()` method at runtime, it will be passed to the method that called the `writeAllEmployeesToTextFile()` method. In Program 10.2, this is the `main()` method. This method rethrows the exception, resulting in the JVM having to deal with it, stopping program execution and printing information about the exception to the terminal window. Removing any of the `throws` clauses in the two methods above will result in a compile time error.

There is a lot more to be said on the subject of exception handling, but the approach we have outlined above will suffice for simple programs.

Reading from text files

We need the following classes to read from a text file (see Figure 10.3 on page 281):

- The class `java.io.FileReader` opens the file and ensures that the bytes in the file are interpreted correctly as characters, according to the default character encoding for the platform.
- The class `java.io.BufferedReader` provides the ability to read a whole line of text, rather than a character at a time. We can achieve a significant improvement in the performance of our program if it is possible to store characters temporarily in memory, and move several characters at a time from the external media to this temporary storage. This approach minimises the number of accesses necessary to read characters from the external media. Such a temporary storage is called a *buffer*, and it is used by the `BufferedReader` class.

The procedure for reading text from files and converting it to values of appropriate data types is outlined below (see also Figure 10.3, Figure 10.4 and Program 10.2):

1 Create a `FileReader` object to open the file for reading:

```
FileReader textFileReader = new FileReader(dataFileName);        // (12)
```

The constructor accepts the name of the file to open. If a file with the designated name does not exist, an exception is thrown. If the file with the designated name exists, reading will start at the beginning of this file.

The call to the `FileReader` constructor will also throw an `IOException` if for some reason the file cannot be opened.

2 Create a `BufferedReader` object that is connected to the `FileReader` from step 1:

```
BufferedReader textReader = new BufferedReader(textFileReader);// (13)
```

The `BufferedReader` class provides the method `readLine()` for reading a whole line of text efficiently, as explained above. The `FileReader` reads the bytes in the file as characters, and the `BufferedReader` can be used to read these as lines of text.

3 Read one text line at a time using the `readLine()` method of the `BufferedReader` class. This method returns a `String` object:

```
String record = textReader.readLine();                          // (18)
```

Each successive call to the `readLine()` method reads the next line of text in the file. The `readLine()` method returns a `null` when there are no more characters to read, i.e. when we have reached the *end of the file* (often abbreviated as *EOF*).

If it is not the end of file, the string returned will contain the current line of text. The line terminator string at the end of each text line is *not* a part of the returned string.

The `readLine()` method can throw an `IOException` if it cannot read from the file.

In our case, the returned string corresponds to a record. We can now extract the characters that comprise each field value from the record, as shown in Figure 10.4. Since each field is terminated by the field terminator character, we first find the index of this character in the record (step 1 in Figure 10.4):

```
int fieldTerminatorIndex1 = record.indexOf(FIELD_TERMINATOR);  // (19)
```

Given this index, we can extract the substring that comprises the characters in the field (step 2 in Figure 10.4):

```
String firstName = record.substring(0, fieldTerminatorIndex1); // (20)
```

If the field value is an integer or another type of value, we must convert the substring to the corresponding value. Examples below show how we can convert a string to a `double` value or to an enum constant (step 3 in Figure 10.4):

```
String doubleStr = record.substring(fieldTerminatorIndex2 + 1,
                                    fieldTerminatorIndex3);

double hourlyRate = Double.parseDouble(doubleStr);             // (21)

String genderStr = record.substring(fieldTerminatorIndex3 + 1);

Gender gender;

if (genderStr.equals(Gender.MALE.toString())) {               // (22)
  gender = Gender.MALE;
```

```
    } else {
        gender = Gender.FEMALE;
    }
```

An alternative solution for reading field values is given in Exercise 10.1.

4 Close the file. This is done by calling the close() method of the BufferedReader class:

```
    textReader.close();                                          // (9)
```

The call ensures that all resources connected with reading from the file are freed. The close() method will throw an IOException if it cannot close the file.

FIGURE 10.3 Reading from a text file

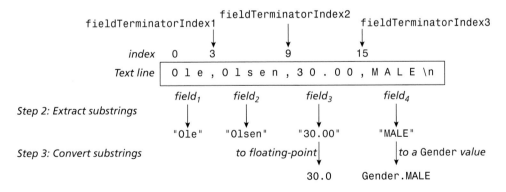

```
FileReader       textFileReader = new FileReader(textFileName);         // Step 1
BufferedReader textReader       = new BufferedReader(textFileReader);  // Step 2
```

FIGURE 10.4 Reading records and converting fields to appropriate values

Step 1: Find the index of the field terminator characters

```
                       fieldTerminatorIndex2
       fieldTerminatorIndex1        |            fieldTerminatorIndex3
                     |              |                    |
       index    0    3             9             15
   Text line  | O l e , O l s e n , 3 0 . 0 0 , M A L E \n |
              field₁      field₂         field₃         field₄
```

Step 2: Extract substrings

```
              "Ole"     "Olsen"      "30.00"        "MALE"
```

Step 3: Convert substrings   to floating-point   to a Gender value

```
                                      30.0         Gender.MALE
```

Program 10.2 on page 274 illustrates reading from a text file. The main() method in the CompanyAdmin class calls the method readAllEmployeesFromTextFile() in the CompanyUsing-TextFiles class at (2), passing it the name of the file as parameter. This method creates the necessary reader objects at (12) and (13), as explained in steps 2 and 3 above. At (14), the method reads the number of records stored in the text file:

```
String firstLine = textReader.readLine();                    // (14)
int totalNumOfEmployess = Integer.parseInt(firstLine);
```

At (15), the `readAllEmployeesFromTextFile()` method calls the `readEmployeeData()` method to read the information about each employee. The `readEmployeeData()` method declared at (17) reads the record of an employee from the text file and extracts the field values to create an `Employee` object, as explained in step 4 above. To verify the information read from the text file, the `main()` method prints it to the terminal window.

Note that the data is written sequentially from the beginning of the file, and must also be read sequentially from the beginning of the file. That is why such files are called *sequential files*. The interpretation of the characters as different types of values when reading from the file is the responsibility of the program.

Exception handling when reading from a text file

Exception handling for reading from a text file is analogous to that for writing to a text file. Calls to the method `readLine()` at (18) can throw an `IOException`, therefore the method `readEmployeeData()` is declared with a `throws` clause to deal with this checked exception:

```
Employee readEmployeeData(BufferedReader textReader)
        throws IOException {                                  // (17)
    ...
    String record = textReader.readLine();                   // (18)
    ...
}
```

The `readAllEmployeesFromTextFile()` method has several lines of code that can throw an `IOException`, and is therefore declared with a `throws` clause:

```
void readAllEmployeesFromTextFile(String dataFileName)
    throws IOException {                                      // (11)
    ...
    FileReader textFileReader = new FileReader(dataFileName); // (12)
    ...
    Employee employee = readEmployeeData(textReader);        // (15)
    ...
    textReader.close();                                      // (16)
}
```

Since the `main()` method calls the `readAllEmployeesFromTextFile()` method at (3), the `main()` method must also be declared with a `throws` clause:

```
public static void main(String[] args) throws IOException {  // (1)
    ...
    company.readAllEmployeesFromTextFile("employeeFile.txt"); // (3)
    ...
}
```

Note the following chain of calls: the main() method calls the readAllEmployeesFromText-File() method, which in turn calls the readEmployeeData() method. They all have to deal with any IOException. Removing any of the throws clauses will result in a compile time error.

10.3 Simple GUI dialogue design

The java.swing.JOptionPane class is useful for creating simple graphical user interfaces (GUIs). This section presents examples of how this class can be used for this purpose.

Overview of the **JOptionPane** class

The java.swing.JOptionPane class provides predefined simple GUI dialog boxes that can be customised for exchange of input and output with the user.

We will look at the designing of dialog boxes for three purposes, using the JOptionPane class:

1 How information can be presented to the user.
2 How the user can enter input required by the program.
3 How the program can ask the user to confirm information.

The JOptionPane class defines three static methods (see Table 10.2) that we will use to create dialog boxes for the purposes mentioned above. These methods are show*Type*Dialog, where *Type* can be replaced by Message, Input or Confirm, depending on which type of dialog box is required. These methods have many parameters in common (see Table 10.3). Some of the parameters need not be specified, in which case default values are used.

All these dialog boxes are *modal*, meaning that if a program displays such a box, all user input is directed to it. Only when interaction with the dialog box has concluded is user input directed back to the program.

Many of the examples and programming exercises in the previous chapters can be modified to use dialog boxes. Some suggestions are given as programming exercises at the end of this chapter.

Ending programs that use GUI dialog boxes

A program usually ends when the main() method has finished executing. However, when using GUI components, the JVM starts an additional task (a *thread*) to monitor the interaction between the program and the GUI. Even though the main() method has ended, this GUI task continues in the JVM and must be stopped explicitly. This is done by calling the exit() method in the System class:

```
System.exit(0);
```

This method is called when we want to stop *all* execution, usually as the last statement in the main() method. The method requires an integer value as parameter, which is passed back to the operative system to indicate whether the program executed successfully (the value 0) or not (a non-zero value).

TABLE 10.2   Summary of methods from the **JOptionPane** class

Method	Description

`static void showMessageDialog(`
`    Component parentComponent,`
`    Object message)`
 	
`static void showMessageDialog(`
`    Component parentComponent,`
`    Object message,`
`    String title,`
`    int messageType)`
	The `showMessageDialog()` method is used to present information to the user.
	
	It always shows an "OK" button.
	
	The first method uses the title `"Message"` in the title bar of the dialog box, and the message type is JOption-Pane.`INFORMATION_MESSAGE` (see Table 10.4).

`static String showInputDialog(`
`    Object message)`
 	
`static String showInputDialog(`
`    Component parentComponent,`
`    Object message)`
 	
`static String showInputDialog(`
`    Component parentComponent,`
`    Object message,`
`    String title,`
`    int messageType)`
	The `showInputDialog()` method is used to ask the user for input. Whatever is entered in the text field of the dialog box is returned as a string.
	
	It always shows an "OK" button and a "Cancel" button.
	
	If the dialog box has been cancelled, the `null` value is returned.
	
	The first and the second method use the title `"Input"` in the title bar of the dialog box, and the message type is `JOptionPane.QUESTION_MESSAGE` (see Table 10.4).

`static int showConfirmDialog(`
`    Component parentComponent,`
`    Object message)`
 	
`static int showConfirmDialog(`
`    Component parentComponent,`
`    Object message,`
`    String title,`
`    int optionType)`
 	
`static int showConfirmDialog(`
`    Component parentComponent,`
`    Object message,`
`    String title,`
`    int optionType,`
`    int messageType)`
	The `showConfirmDialog()` method is used to ask the user a question in order to confirm some information. The integer value returned by the methods indicates the action taken by the user (see Table 10.5).
	
	The first method uses the title "`Select an option`" in the title bar of the dialog box, the option type is JOption-Pane.`YES_NO_CANCEL_OPTION` (see Table 10.6) and the message type is `JOptionPane.QUESTION_MESSAGE` (see Table 10.4).
	
	The option type (Table 10.6) specifies which combination of an "OK" button, a "Yes" button, a "No" button and a "Cancel" button can be used in a confirmation dialog box.

TABLE 10.3   Common parameters for the **show*Type*Dialog()** methods

Parameter name	Description
`Component parentComponent`	If the value is `null` or no value is specified, the dialog box is placed in the middle of the screen, otherwise it is placed below the parent component.
`Object message`	Specifies what should be presented to the user, for example, a message or a prompt. Usually this object is a string. If that is not the case, the `toString()` method of the object is called to create a string representation, which is shown in the dialog box.
`String title`	Specifies the title to set in the title bar of the dialog box.
`int messageType`	This value specifies which icon should be used in the dialog box. These values are specified in Table 10.4.

TABLE 10.4   Specifying the message type in a dialog box

Message type	Description

`ERROR_MESSAGE`
`INFORMATION_MESSAGE`
`WARNING_MESSAGE`
`QUESTION_MESSAGE`
`PLAIN_MESSAGE`
	These constants in the `JOptionPane` class represent standard icons that can be used in a dialog box.

TABLE 10.5   Values returned by the **showConfirmDialog()** method

Constants	Which action the user has performed
`YES_OPTION`	Clicked on the "Yes" button.
`NO_OPTION`	Clicked on the "No" button.
`CANCEL_OPTION`	Clicked on the "Cancel" button.
`OK_OPTION`	Clicked on the "OK" button.
`CLOSED_OPTION`	Clicked on the close button of the dialog box.

TABLE 10.6   Specifying the option type in the `showConfirmDialog()` method

Constants for option buttons	Option buttons shown in the dialog box
`DEFAULT_OPTION`	"OK" button only
`YES_NO_OPTION`	"Yes" and "No" buttons
`YES_NO_CANCEL_OPTION`	"Yes", "No" and "Cancel" buttons
`OK_CANCEL_OPTION`	"Yes" and "Cancel" buttons

Message dialogs – presenting information to the user

This type of dialog box usually consists of a message to the user and an "OK" button that the user can click after having read the message. The method `showMessageDialog()` is used for such dialog boxes, as illustrated in Program 10.3. The dialog boxes created at (1) and (2) are shown in Figure 10.5.

FIGURE 10.5   Dialog windows with the `showMessageDialog()` method

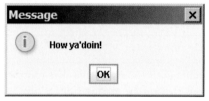

```
JOptionPane.showMessageDialog( // (1)
    null,
    "How ya'doin!");
```

(a)

```
JOptionPane.showMessageDialog( // (2)
    null,
    "You have hit the jackpot!",
    "Important Message",
    JOptionPane.WARNING_MESSAGE);
```

(b)

PROGRAM 10.3   Using the `showMessageDialog()` method

```java
import javax.swing.JOptionPane;

public class MessageDialog {
  public static void main(String[] args) {

    JOptionPane.showMessageDialog(        // (1)
        null,                             // No parent window
        "How ya'doin!"                    // Message
    );

    JOptionPane.showMessageDialog(        // (2)
        null,                             // No parent window
        "You have hit the jackpot!",      // Message
        "Important Message",              // Title in the window
```

```
        JOptionPane.WARNING_MESSAGE                    // Message type
    );

    System.exit(0);                                   // (3) Terminate the program.
  }
}
```

Input dialogs – reading data from the user

This type of dialog box usually consists of a text field where the user can enter text, and two buttons: an "OK" button and a "Cancel" button to deliver the input entered in the text field to the program, or to cancel the dialog box without supplying any input, respectively. The method `showInputDialog()` provides this functionality. Program 10.4 creates input dialog boxes at (1), (2) and (4), and they are illustrated in Figure 10.6.

The `showInputDialog()` method returns the contents of the text field as a string. This string may be explicitly converted to another type of value if necessary, as shown at (3) in Program 10.4. At (5), the input is presented to the user in a message dialog box.

FIGURE 10.6   Dialog windows with the **showInputDialog()** method

```
JOptionPane.showInputDialog( // (1)
    "Name:"
);
```
(a)

```
JOptionPane.showInputDialog( // (2)
        null,
        "Zipcode:"
    );
```
(b)

```
JOptionPane.showInputDialog(       // (4)
    null, "City:",
    "Input data", JOptionPane.PLAIN_MESSAGE);
```
(c)

Using the `showInputDialog()` method

```java
import javax.swing.JOptionPane;

public class InputDialog {
  public static void main(String[] args) {

    String name = JOptionPane.showInputDialog(      // (1)
        "Name:"                                      // Prompt
    );

    String zipcodeStr = JOptionPane.showInputDialog( // (2)
        null,                                        // No parent window
        "Zipcode:"                                   // Prompt
    );
    int zipcode = Integer.parseInt(zipcodeStr);      // (3)

    String city = JOptionPane.showInputDialog(       // (4)
        null,                                        // No parent window
        "City:",                                     // Prompt
        "Input data",                                // Title in the window
        JOptionPane.PLAIN_MESSAGE                     // Message type
    );

    JOptionPane.showMessageDialog(                    // (5) Message dialogue
        null,
        name + "\n" + zipcode + " " + city,
        "Information",
        JOptionPane.PLAIN_MESSAGE
    );

    System.exit(0);
  }
}
```

Confirmation dialogs – getting confirmation from the user

This type of dialog usually consists of a question about some fact that the user must confirm. The confirmation dialog box usually has two buttons, a "Yes" button and a "No" button, to reply to the question. The method `showConfirmDialog()` provides this functionality. Interpretation of the value returned by the method, which indicates the action taken by the user, is shown in Table 10.5 on page 285.

The `showConfirmDialog()` method can also take a parameter that specifies the *option type*. The class `JOptionPane` defines valid values for the option type that indicate what combination of "Yes", "No" and "Cancel" buttons will be used in the confirmation dialog box (see Table 10.6).

Program 10.5 provides examples of dialog boxes for confirmation of miscellaneous information at (1), (2) and (3). These dialog boxes are shown in Figure 10.7.

It is also possible to change the text that is shown on the "Yes", "No" and "Cancel" buttons, but we leave it to the reader to find the details in the Java standard library.

FIGURE 10.7   Dialog windows with the `showConfirmDialog()` method

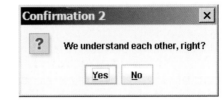

```
JOptionPane.showConfirmDialog(  // (1)
    null,
    "Are you getting married?" );
```

```
JOptionPane.showConfirmDialog( // (2)
    null,
    "We understand each other, right?",
    "Confirmation 2",
    JOptionPane.YES_NO_OPTION );
```

(a)

(b)

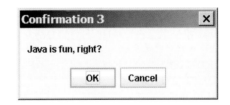

```
JOptionPane.showConfirmDialog( // (3)
    null,
    "Java is fun, right?",
    "Confirmation 3",
    JOptionPane.OK_CANCEL_OPTION,
    JOptionPane.PLAIN_MESSAGE);
```

(c)

PROGRAM 10.5   Using the `showConfirmDialog()` method

```java
import javax.swing.JOptionPane;

public class ConfirmDialog {
  public static void main(String[] args) {

    int answer1 = JOptionPane.showConfirmDialog( // (1)
        null,                             // No parent window
        "Are you getting married?"        // Prompt
    );                                    // YES, NO and CANCEL buttons
    String answerStr1 = null;
    switch (answer1) {
      case JOptionPane.YES_OPTION:
        answerStr1 = "Congratulations!";
```

```
      break;
    case JOptionPane.NO_OPTION:
      answerStr1 = "All right.";
      break;
    case JOptionPane.CANCEL_OPTION:
    case JOptionPane.CLOSED_OPTION:
      answerStr1 = "Sorry I asked.";
      break;
    default:
      assert false;
}
JOptionPane.showMessageDialog(null, answerStr1);

int answer2 = JOptionPane.showConfirmDialog( // (2)
    null,                                 // No parent window
    "We understand each other, right?", // Prompt
    "Confirmation 2",                   // Title in the window
    JOptionPane.YES_NO_OPTION            // YES and NO buttons
);
String answerStr2 = null;
switch (answer2) {
    case JOptionPane.YES_OPTION:
      answerStr2 = "Good!";
      break;
    case JOptionPane.NO_OPTION:
    case JOptionPane.CLOSED_OPTION:
      answerStr2 = "All right.";
      break;
    default:
      assert false;
}
JOptionPane.showMessageDialog(null, answerStr2);

int answer3 = JOptionPane.showConfirmDialog(     // (3)
    null,                                 // No parent window
    "Java is fun, right?",              // Prompt
    "Confirmation 3",                   // Title in the window
    JOptionPane.OK_CANCEL_OPTION,        // OK and CANCEL buttons
    JOptionPane.PLAIN_MESSAGE            // Message type
);
String answerStr3 = null;
switch (answer3) {
    case JOptionPane.OK_OPTION:
      answerStr3 = "We agree!";
      break;
    case JOptionPane.CANCEL_OPTION:
    case JOptionPane.CLOSED_OPTION:
      answerStr3 = "Pity you won't confirm.";
      break;
    default:
```

10

```
        assert false;
    }
    JOptionPane.showMessageDialog(null, answerStr3);

    System.exit(0);
  }
}
```

10.4 Review questions

1. Which of these files would you characterise as a text file?

   a A file with Java byte code.
   b A file with Java source code.
   c A file with image data.
   d A file with audio data.
   e A file with HTML (Hypertext Markup Language) content.

2. Which statements about sequential files are true?

   a When we open a sequential file for writing, we can specify whether writing will start immediately after the contents that are already in the file, or that the previous contents can be overwritten.
   b When we open a sequential file for reading, and the file does not exist, an unchecked error is thrown.
   c We can open a sequential file for both reading and writing operations.

3. Which code lines will ensure that writing will start immediately after the contents that are already in the file?

   a `FileWriter textFileWriter = new FileWriter(dataFileName);`
   b `FileWriter textFileWriter = new FileWriter(dataFileName, true);`
   c `FileWriter textFileWriter = new FileWriter(dataFileName, false);`

4. Which classes have a constructor that accepts a file name as a parameter?

   a `FileWriter`
   b `PrintWriter`
   c `FileReader`
   d `BufferedReader`

5. What methods are found in the `PrintWriter` class for writing string representations of primitive data values?

   a `printInt(int i)`
   b `print(char i)`
   c `println(int i)`

d `printIntln(int i)`

6. What value does the method `readLine()` in the class `BufferedReader` return when it comes to the end of file?

    a It returns the `null` value.

    b It returns the string `"EOF"`.

    c It returns the value `-1`.

    d It throws a checked exception.

7. Assume that the variable `textReader` refers to an object of the class `BufferedReader`, which is connected to a text file. Which code will you choose to read from the file? Why?

    a Use a `do-while` loop to read from the file.

    ```
    String line = null;
    do {
       line = textReader.readLine();
       System.out.println(line);
    } while (line != null);
    ```

    b Use a `while` loop to read from the file.

    ```
    String line = textReader.readLine();
    while (line != null) {
       System.out.println(line);
       line = textReader.readLine();

    }
    ```

8. What is the recommended way of closing the file, given the following declarations:

    ```
    FileWriter textFileWriter = new FileWriter(dataFileName);
    PrintWriter textWriter = new PrintWriter(textFileWriter);
    ```

    a `textFileWriter.close();`
    `textWriter.close();`
    b `textFileWriter.close();`
    c `textWriter.close();`
    d `textWriter.close(textFileWriter);`

9. A method can specify exceptions it will rethrow in a _____ clause in the method header.

10. Which statement about checked exceptions is true?

    a Checked exceptions that can be thrown in a method must be listed in a `throws` clause if the exceptions are not caught and dealt with in the method body.

    b A method that calls another method that has a `throws` clause with checked exceptions need not deal with these exceptions.

    c A method that calls another method that has a `throws` clause with checked exceptions must explicitly deal with these exceptions.

11. Which methods must specify a throws clause with an IOException in order for the following code to compile?

```java
class Writing {
   public static void main(String[] args) {
     PrintWriter textWriter = openFileForWrite("preciousData.txt");
     writeToFile(textWriter);
     closeWriteFile(textWriter);
   }

   static PrintWriter openFileForWrite(String dataFileName) {
     FileWriter textFileWriter = new FileWriter(dataFileName);
     PrintWriter textWriter = new PrintWriter(textFileWriter);
     return textWriter;
   }

   static void writeToFile(PrintWriter textWriter) {
     textWriter.println("To file or not to file.");
   }

   static void closeWriteFile(PrintWriter textWriter) {
     textWriter.close();
   }
}
```

a main(), openFileForWrite()

b main(), openFileForWrite(), writeToFile()

c main(), openFileForWrite(), writeToFile(), closeWriteFile()

12. Which methods must specify a throws clause with an IOException in order for the following code to compile?

```java
class Reading {

   public static void main(String[] args) {
     BufferedReader textReader = openFileForRead("preciousData.txt");
     readFromFile(textReader);
     closeReadFile(textReader);
   }

   static BufferedReader openFileForRead(String dataFileName) {
     FileReader textFileReader = new FileReader(dataFileName);
     BufferedReader textReader = new BufferedReader(textFileReader);
     return textReader;
   }

   static void readFromFile(BufferedReader textReader) {
     System.out.println(textReader.readLine());
   }

   static void closeReadFile(BufferedReader textReader) {
```

```
        textReader.close();
      }
    }
```

a main(), openFileForRead()

b main(), openFileForRead(), readFromFile()

c main(), openFileForRead(), readFromFile(), closeReadFile()

13. Which statements are true about the following methods in the JOptionPane class?

   a The method showMessageDialog() always shows an "OK" button.

   b The method showInputDialog() always shows an "OK" button and a "Cancel" button.

   c The method showConfirmDialog() can show any combination of an "OK" button, a "Yes" button, a "No" button and a "Cancel" button.

14. Which statements are true about the following constants in the JOptionPane class?

   a The message type constants specify which icon is used in the dialog box.

   b The option type constants specify which combinations of an "OK" button, a "Yes" button, a "No" button and a "Cancel" button can be used in a confirmation dialog box.

   c The return value constants indicate which button the user clicked in a confirmation dialog box.

15. Which statement will show the following dialog box?

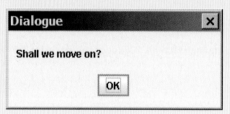

a JOptionPane.showMessageDialog(
       null,
       "Shall we move on?",
       "Dialog",
       JOptionPane.PLAIN_MESSAGE
   );

b JOptionPane.showConfirmDialog(
       null,
       "Shall we move on?",
       "Dialog",
       JOptionPane.DEFAULT_OPTION,
       JOptionPane.PLAIN_MESSAGE
   );

10.5 Programming exercises

1. Write a new version of the method readEmployeeData() in the class CompanyUsingTex-tFiles from Program 10.2 on page 274 that uses the Scanner class to extract the values from an employee record.

    The example below shows how we can use a Scanner to read a record and extract the field values that are terminated by the ' , ' character, i.e. CSV format. Note how the field terminator character ' , ' is specified by the delimiter string "\\," when using the Scanner.

    ```java
    import java.util.Scanner;

    class UsingScanner {
        public static void main(String[] args) {
            // The input record:
            String record = "123,45.67,false,1949,786,BERGEN";
            // Scanner takes the record as input string:
            Scanner lexer = new Scanner(record);
            // Uses the specified delimiter string,
            // which represents the character ',' in this case:
            lexer.useDelimiter("\\,");

            // Read values sequentially using appropriate next() method:
            int     field1 = lexer.nextInt();
            double  field2 = lexer.nextDouble();
            boolean field3 = lexer.nextBoolean();
            int     field4 = lexer.nextInt();
            long    field5 = lexer.nextLong();
            String  field6 = lexer.next();
            System.out.printf("%5d%6.2f%8s%5d%4d%8s",
                              field1, field2, field3, field4, field5, field6);

            // Close Scanner when done:
            lexer.close();
        }
    }
    ```

    Output from the program:

    ```
    123 45.67    false 1949 786  BERGEN
    ```

2. Given two text files each containing a sorted sequence of integers in ascending order, write a program that merges the sequences into one sorted sequence in a third file. You can assume that the input file contains one integer per line. The output file should also be written with one value per line. The program should not store any of the sequences in memory. It should be possible to run the program with the following command:

    ```
    > java Merge file1 file2 destinationFile
    ```

    Be sure to write the pseudocode for the main steps of the program.

3. Write a program that reads a sequence of integers from a text file and prints a report of how many times each digit from 0, 1, ... 9 occurs in the sequence. You can assume that the text file contains one integer per line, for example:

```
2006
786
1949
1972
. . .
```

The program should write the frequency of each digit to the terminal window, for example:

```
0    19
1    23
2     8
3     5
. . .
9    16
```

4. Modify the program from Exercise 10.3 so that the frequency of each digit is written to a result file.

5. Write a new version of Program 6.4 on page 140 that reads the values of the two-dimensional array weeklyData from a text file. Choose a suitable data record format for storing the values of the two-dimensional array weeklyData in the text file.

6. Write a new version of Exercise 6.1 and Exercise 6.2 on page 157 so that the sequence of digits is read from a text file and the histogram shown in a dialog box.

7. Write a new version of Exercise 3.7 on page 69 in which the student ID and the number of points are read from a text file. Choose a suitable data record format for storing the values in the text file. The program should print a list with student ID and grade to the terminal window.

8. Write a new version of Program 9.2 on page 240 to read the integers from a text file.

9. Write the following programs for handling text files. The programs should read and check the program arguments from the command line before executing any operations on the files.

    a A program that counts the number of lines and characters in a file:

    > **java LineCounter myFile**

    b A program that reads from a text file and prints the average length of the text lines in the file.

    > **java AverageLineLength sourceFile**

    c A program that copies a text file to another file:

    > **java CopyFile sourceFile destinationFile**

    d A program that splits a file. The text lines in the source file should be split among several files depending on the number of text lines in the source file. The maximum number of text lines allowed in each file should be specified as a program argument. Choose appropriate names for the new files, for example, file1.txt, file2.txt and so on.

```
> java SplitFile 100 sourceFile
```

e A program that concatenates the contents of two files to a destination file, i.e. the destination file should contain the contents of the first file, followed by the contents of the second file:

```
> java ConcatFiles sourceFile1 sourceFile2 destinationFile
```

Extend the program to concatenate any number of files to a destination file.

f A program that prints those lines in a file that containing a specified string (see the method indexOf(String substring) in the String class):

```
> java FindString searchString sourceFile
```

g A program that replaces a string in a file with another string (see the method replaceAll(String oldStr, String newStr) in the String class):

```
> java ReplaceString oldSt newStr sourceFile destinationFile
```

h A program that removes space and tab characters at the beginning and end of each text line in a file and writes the result to a new file (see the method trim() in the String class):

```
> java TrimLines sourceFile destinationFile
```

i A program that replaces all sequences of space and tab characters with a single space in each text line of a file:

```
> java ShrinkFile sourceFile destinationFile
```

10. Write a program that encrypts and decrypts a file.

For example, the following command should encrypt the source file using the specified code file, and placing the encrypted text in the destination file:

```
> java Crypto -C codeFile sourceFile destinationFile
```

The following command should decrypt the source file using the specified code file, creating the original text in the destination file:

```
> java Crypto -D codeFile sourceFile destinationFile
```

The code file is a text file in which each line consists of two characters. The first character is replaced by the second character during encrypting, and vice versa during decrypting. The coding information can, for example, be represented by two arrays of characters, in which the same index in both arrays indicates the pair of characters that can replace each other. Assume that the characters in each array are unique, i.e. the first character is unique for all pairs, as is the second character.

11. Write a program that converts the temperature from the Celsius scale to the Fahrenheit scale. Use the following formula, where fTemp and cTemp represent the temperature in degrees Fahrenheit and Celsius respectively:

```
fTemp = (9.0/5.0) * cTemp + 32.0;
```

The program should use dialog boxes for all interaction with the user.

12. Modify the program from Exercise 5.6 on page 120 to read the temperature interval using dialog boxes and present the result in a message box.

13. Modify the programs from Exercise 10.9 so that they use dialog boxes for input from the user.

14. Modify the program from Exercise 3.1 on page 67 to read the duration of a time interval in seconds from an input dialog box and present the result in a message dialog box.

15. Modify the program from Exercise 4.3 on page 97 to read the text from an input dialog box and present the result in a message dialog box.

16. Modify the program from Exercise 5.3 on page 120 to read the text from an input dialog box and present the result in a message dialog box.

17. Modify the program from Exercise 9.14 on page 264 to read the integers from a text file, to specify the key in an input dialog box, and to present the result in a message box.

18. Write a program that keeps track of items in a museum. Each item (class Item) has the following information:

   ● A unique reference number for the item
   ● Name of the item
   ● Description of the item

The program should let the user execute the following operations in the museum (class Museum):

   ● Register a new item in the museum
   ● Change the information about an existing item in the museum
   ● Delete an item from the museum collection

First write pseudocode for the operations that can be performed, then implement the operations.

The collection of items should be stored in a suitable data structure during execution, for example in an array.

All interaction between the program and the user should be through a text-based user interface (class TextBasedMuseumInteraction). The part of the program that implements the text-based interaction should be separate from the rest of the program. All other classes must be independent of the text-based interaction. It should be possible to replace the text-based interaction of the program with, for example, a graphical user interface without having to modify any of the other classes.

The program should store the collection of items in the museum in a text file. When the program starts it should read any information about existing items from a file, if such information exists. Before the program quits, information about items should be written out to a file. Choose an appropriate record format to represent an item in the file.

19. Implement a simple GUI dialog-based user interface (class `GUIBasedMuseumInteraction`) to replace the interaction between the program and the user in Exercise 10.18.

10

PART FOUR

Appendices

Answers to review questions

A.1 Getting started

1. Program 1.1 has seven comments.

2. A computer has a *central processing unit (CPU)* that executes low-level platform-specific instructions and makes the computer work.

3. *Source code* is a high-level description of the tasks the computer should perform, which are written in a high-level *language* and stored in text files.

4. (a), (c), (d).

    Compilers and virtual machines are off-the-shelf programs.

5. We specify the set of common properties we want a group of objects to share by defining a *class*.

6. All Java programs have a *method* called *main*, where the execution of the program starts.

7. (b).

8. Program 1.1 has a class called *SimpleProgram* and a method called *main*.

9. The command "javac TestProgram.java" can be executed on the command line to compile a source code file called TestProgram.java.

10. The command "java -ea TestProgram" can be executed on the command line to run a Java program consisting of a primary class called TestProgram.

11. (a) Source code. The source code can be translated to other forms.

12. (c) Only Dog.java is valid.

A.2 Basic programming elements

1. The code prints:

   ```
   10+10 is 20
   10+10 is 1010
   40
   ```

2. A variable identifies a memory location that can hold a value of a specific data type. A local variable is created during the execution of a method, and will only exist in memory while the method is being executed.

3. `int numberOfPoints = 35;`

   A value written directly in the source code is called a literal.

4. A constant is a variable whose value cannot be changed after initialization. We define a constant using the modifier `final`, as shown in the following line of code:

   `final int NUMBER_OF_POINTS = 35;`

5. (a) `minimum-Price`: The name is invalid because it contains a hyphen, (-).

   (b) `minimumPrice`: The name is valid because all letters are allowed in variable names. The name conveys its purpose.

   (c) `XYZ`: The name is valid, but it does not convey its purpose.

   (d) `xCoordinate`: This is a valid name, as it only contains letters. The name conveys what the variable stores: an x-coordinate to a point or another geometric primitive.

   (e) `y2k`: Both letters and digits are allowed in variable names. The name is valid, but not very meaningful.

   (f) `isDone`: The name is valid and easy to read. It indicates that the variable will hold a Boolean value that conveys whether a specific condition is satisfied. The name may be too general.

   (g) `numberOfDaysInALeapYear`: This is a very long variable name, and hard to read, as it contains many words, but it is a valid name.

   (h) `JDK_1_6_0`: This is also a valid name, since underscore (_) is allowed in a variable name. On the other hand, the purpose of the name is not clear. It may also be mistaken for a constant, as we have defined its name in all uppercase letters.

6. A data type is defined by a set of valid values and the operations that can be performed on these values.

   A primitive data type is a data type defined by the programming language, which we can use directly by specifying its type name in the source code. Many languages offer primitive data types, to provide support for integers and floating-point values, for example.

A

7.   (a) An arithmetic expression can consist of *operators* and operands.

      (b) Multiplication (*) requires *two* operands, and is thus a *binary operator*.

      (c) The operator - in the expression -4 is a *unary* operator, while the operator - in the expression 5 - 4 is a *binary* operator.

8.   The operands in an expression in Java are always evaluated from *left* to *right*.

      If two operators with different *precedence* are next to each other in an expression, the operator with the *highest precedence* will be evaluated first.

9.   If two operators with the same precedence are next to each other in a expression, *associativity* rules are used to determine which operator will be evaluated first.

      The operator - (unary minus) is left-associative and groups from *left* to *right*, while the - (subtraction) is right-associative and groups from *right* to *left*.

10.   (a) 3 + 2 - 1 → (3 + 2) -- 1 → 5 - 1 → 4. Addition and subtraction have the same precedence, and are left-associative.

      (b) 2 + 6 * 7 → 2 + (6 * 7) → 2 + 42 → 44. Multiplication has higher precedence than addition, and is thus evaluated first. Both operators are left-associative.

      (c) - 5 + 7 - - 6 → (-5) + 7 - (-6) → ((-5) + -7) - (-6) → 2 - (-6) → 8. Unary operators have higher precedence than binary, and are right-associative.

      (d) 2 + 4 / 5 → 2 + (4 / 5) → 2 + 0 → 2. Division has higher precedence than addition. Integer division where the denominator is less than the numerator yields 0 as the result.

      (e) 5 * 2 - - 3 * 4 → 5 * 2 - (-3) * 4 → (5 * 2) - (-3) * 4 → 10 - ((-3) * 4) → 10 - (-12) → 2. Unary operators have higher precedence than binary. Multiplication has higher precedence than subtraction. Both multiplication and subtraction are left-associative.

      (f) 10 / 0 → An exception will be thrown and the program will terminate.

      (g) 2 + 4.0 / 5 → 2 + (4.0 / 5.0) → 2 + 0.8 → 2.0 + 0.8 → 2.8. Division has higher precedence than addition. When one of the operands of a division operation is a floating-point value, the other operand is automatically converted to a floating-point value before the division is performed.

      (h) 10 / 0.0 → 10.0 / 0.0 → Infinity. The integer 10 is converted to the floating-point value 10.0 because the denominator is a floating-point value. Floating-point division is performed, giving the result Infinity, since the denominator is 0.0.

      (i) 4.0 / 0.0 → Infinity. Floating-point division where the denominator is 0.0 always gives the result Infinity.

      (j) 2 * 4 % 2 → (2 * 4) % 2 → 8 % 2 → 0. Multiplication and modulus operators have the same precedence. Both operators are left-associative.

11. Possible format strings and parameter values to the printf() method are shown below. See also Appendix C.

a `System.out.printf("%+6d%n", 123456); // positive integer`
`System.out.printf("%+6d%n", -654321); // negative integer`

b `System.out.printf("%e%n", 123456789.3837);`
`System.out.printf("%g%n", 123456789.3837);`

c `System.out.printf("We are 100%% motivated to learn Java!%n");`

d `System.out.printf("%08d%n", 1024);`

A.3 Program control flow

1. A Boolean expression can only evaluate to one of two values, true or false. The value of such an expression can be assigned to a boolean variable.

2. A relational operator compares the value of two operands. For example, the == operator compares its operands for equality.

   A logical operator negates or combines the values of Boolean expression. For example, the ! operator negates the value of a Boolean expression.

3. (a) 2 < 3 is a Boolean expression. When evaluated, the resulting value (true) can be assigned to a Boolean variable.

   (b) 2 + 3 < 1 - - 5 is a Boolean expression. When evaluated, the resulting value (true) can be assigned to a Boolean variable.

   (c) This is not a valid Boolean expression. The string "true" cannot be converted to a Boolean value.

   (d) The Boolean literal false can be assigned to a Boolean variable.

4. The expression is evaluated to true && !(false) || !(true) == true, then to true && true || !(true) == true, and finally to true || (!(true) == true).

5. Selection and loop statements offer two mechanisms for controlling the *flow of execution*. Such statements enable us to *select between* alternative actions, or to *repeat* an action a given number of times.

6. Line (1): false.

   Line (2): The expression numMen = numWomen is not a valid Boolean expression, since the operator used, =, is the assignment operator, and not the equality operator, ==. If we replace the = operator with the == operator, the expression will be valid, and it will return the value false.

   Line (3): This is a valid Boolean expression. Since the multiplication operator (*) has higher precedence than the relational operators, the value of the expression is false.

   Line (4): This is also a valid Boolean expression, whose value is false.

7. The Java operators ! (negation), && (conditional And), and || (conditional Or) expect operands of type boolean.

8. (a) true. (b) false. (c) true. (d) true. (e) true. (f) false.

9. Rewrite the Boolean expressions using De Morgan's laws:

    (a) !(b1 || b2) → !b1 && !b2

    (b) !(b1 == b2 && b2) → !(b1 == b2) || !b2 → b1 != b2 || !b2

    (c) !(!b2 || b1 == true) → !!b2 && !(b1 == true) → b2 && b1 == false

    (d) (!b1 == b2 || b2) → !(b1 == b2 && !b2)

    (e) !(b1 == b2) || !(b2 == b1)) → !((b1 == b2) && (b2 == b1)) → !((b1 == b2) && (b1 == b2)) → !(b1 == b2) (The second to last simplification follows from the fact that the order of operands to the == operator has no impact on the evaluation, i.e. b1 == b2 is identical to b2 == b1. The last simplification follows from the fact that the two operands of the conditional And have the same value.)

10. A selection statement and the remainder operator can be used to determine whether the variable numPoints has a value that is an even or an odd number:

```
if (numPoints % 2 == 0)
    System.out.println("Number of points (" + numPoints + ") is even.");
else
    System.out.println("Number of points (" + numPoints + ") is odd.");
```

11. A repetition statement is often called a *loop*. The condition for repeating the *loop body* is specified as a *Boolean* expression.

12. The difference between the two types of loops are as follows: in a while loop, the condition is tested *before* the loop body is executed. This means that if the condition is not satisfied when control flow enters the loop, the loop body will not be executed at all. In a do-while loop, the condition is not tested until *after* the loop body has been executed. This means that the loop body is executed at least once in a do-while loop.

13. An assert statement specifies a *Boolean* expression, and (optionally) a *string*. The *string* is printed to the terminal window if the expression evaluates to false, and the execution is *aborted*.

14. (a) False. Assertions are only executed if the program is run with the "-ea" (or the equivalent "-enableassertions") option. (b) False. (c) True.

A.4 Using objects

1. A class specifies the *properties* and *behaviour* of objects that can be created from the class.

2. Instance variables represent *properties*, and instance methods represent the *behaviour* of objects that can be created from a class.

3. (a), (c), (f), (g).

4. False. The code line is a declaration. It only declares a reference variable called myCD of reference type CD. No object is created by this declaration.

5. A declaration requires the type and the variable name, and object creation requires the use of the new operator with a constructor call:

```
CD cd1 = new CD();
CD cd2 = new CD();
CD cd3 = new CD();
CD cd4 = new CD();
CD cd5 = new CD();
```

6. Only one, and cd1 and cd2 are aliases to this object.

7. We can use the dot notation to call a method or access a field in an object:

```
referance.methodName();
value = referance.fieldName;
```

8. (a), (d).

   (b) and (e) are not valid, because the class name cannot be used to access instance members. (c) is not valid because a method call requires the specification of a parameter list even if there are no parameters.

9. 'z' is a character literal, while is "z" is a string literal. A character literal is represented by its Unicode value, whereas a string is represented by a String object that stores the characters in the string.

10. If (str1==str2) is true, it means that str1 and str2 are aliases and refer to the same String object. The method call str1.equals(str2) will always return true, because the String object is compared with itself. If two String objects have the same state, i.e. the character sequence in both strings are identical, the expression (str1==str2) will return true. But the reference values in str1 and str2 are different, because the references refer to two different String objects.

11. The statements will print:

```
2002
2050
20002
```

(1) calculates (2000 + 2), (2) calculates (2000 + 50), where the character '2' has the code number 50. (3) concatenates the strings "2000" and "2".

12. (b).

13. (f).

In (f), the value 12 is auto-boxed into an `Integer` object. However, the reference value of an `Integer` object cannot be assigned to a reference of type `Double`.

A.5 More on control structures

1. We can use any of the following statements:

```
i = i + 1;
i += 1;
i++;
++i;
```

2. Output:

```
4
6
6
4
4
```

3. One would choose a `for(;;)` loop, since it is appropriate for implementing a counter-controlled loop when the number of iterations is known beforehand.

4. All parts (initialization, loop condition, updating) in the `for(;;)` loop header can be omitted. No loop condition implies that the loop condition is true. No initialization or updating corresponds to the empty statement, which does nothing.

5. (a), (b), (d).

The loop body is never executed if the loop condition is `false` when control enters the loop for the first time.

6. Here is one possible `for(;;)` loop that is equivalent to the code in the question:

```
int sum = 0;
for (int i = 10; i >= 5; i -= 2) {
   sum += i;
}
```

Here we will also mention that the initialization part can be a list of declarations, separated by a comma. The loop above can also be written as follows:

```
for (int i = 10, sum = 0; i >= 5; i -= 2) {
    sum += i;
}
```

The `for(;;)` loop is executed three times.

7. In (a) the loop is executed five times, and the variable i has the value 10 after the loop has completed. In (b) the loop is executed four times, and the variable i has the value 12 on termination of the loop, but the variable is not accessible outside the loop.

8. (b).

   In (a) the loop executes three times but it does not print anything because an empty statement (;) comprises its loop body. The string "Move it!" is printed only once after the loop has completed.

9. (b), (c).

10. (b).

    A `default` label is optional in a `switch` statement. A string literal cannot be used as a case label. A `break` statement is not part of a `switch` statement. Boolean values and floating-point values cannot be specified as `case` labels.

11. Rewriting the code using a `switch` statement:

```
switch(i) {
    case 10: case 20:
        System.out.println("10 or 20");
        break;
    case 15:
        System.out.println("15");
        break;
    default:
        System.out.println("Not valid");
}
```

12. (d), (f), (g).

    Boolean `switch` expressions and `case` labels are not permitted, as in (d). The value of the `switch` expression cannot be `double`, as in (f). The `switch` expression cannot be `boolean`, as in (g). The `case` label values must be unique, which is not the case in (g).

A.6 Arrays

1. An array has a public field called `length`, whose value is the number of elements stored in the array. Given that the reference `row` refers to an array, the number of elements in the array is returned by the expression `row.length`.

2. The `[]` notation can be used to declare an array reference:

```
String[] arrayRef;
```

The `[]` notation can be used to create an array:

```
arrayRef = new String[10]; // Array can store 10 elements.
```

The `[]` notation can be used to access an array element:

```
arrayRef[2] = "Name: " + arrayRef[0];
```

3. (f).

(a) declares `age` as a reference to an array of integers; no array is created. (b) is missing the `new` operator for creating an array. (c) declares `age` as a variable of type `int`, and not as a reference to an array. Both (d) and (e) are missing the correct specification of the length of the array. Only (f) is correct.

4. (b), (d).

There is no method called `length()` for arrays. The first element in the array is given by `arrayRef[0]`.

5. (a), (d), (e), (f).

Block notation, `{}`, is used to create and initialize an array in a declaration. It cannot be used in an assignment statement as in (b) and (c).

6. (b).

The index value must be a non-negative integer value that satisfies the relation 0 ≤ index value < array length.

7. `twoDimArrayName` has the type `String[][]`, i.e. a reference to an array of array of `String` objects, which is a two-dimensional array of `String` objects.

`twoDimArrayName[1]` has the type `String[]`, i.e. a reference to an array of `String` objects.

`twoDimArrayName[1][2]` has the type `String`, i.e. a reference to a `String` object.

8. (a), (d), (e), (f)

Block notation, `{}`, is used to create and initialize an array in a declaration. It cannot be used as an assignment statement, as in (b) and (c). The delimiter in block notation is a comma (,) and not a semicolon (;), as in (g).

9. (a), (b)

The loop body is not executed if the collection is empty, and changing the value of the element variable does not change the values in the collection.

10. (b), (c), (d).

The element variable must be declared in the header of the for(:) loop. Changing the value of the element variable in the loop body is allowed, but that does not change any values in the collection.

11. (d).

The value stored in each element is its index value plus 1.

12. (c).

The values in the elements are not affected by the first loop. They remain initialized to the default value for int type (0).

13. (a), (b), (c).

In (d) the two hotels will share the same floors and rooms. In (b) enough storage is allocated for the rooms. In all cases we have to be consistent with what the different indices represent. In (a), (b) and (c) all the rooms will be initialized to the default value for type int (0).

14. (c).

Arrays have a public field named length, and String objects have a method named length. Not the other way around, as in the code.

15. (b), (d), (e).

The method call nextInt(n) will always return an integer in the interval [0, n-1], inclusive, where integer n is the upper bound on the random number returned.

A.7 Defining classes

1. Static variables in the class Counter:

MAX_VALUE, description

Static methods in the class Counter:

getDescription

Instance variables in the class Counter:

value

Instance methods in the class Counter:

getCounter, setCounter, incrementCounter, decrementCounter, resetCounter

2. *Instance members* belong to objects, while *static members* belong to the class.

3. Values of all the field variables in an object comprise its *state*.

4. The initial state of an object is the state immediately after it is created using the `new` operator.

5. The default value of any reference variable is always the `null` literal.

6. Field variables in the class `RectangleV2`, which are initialized with default values:

    length, breadth

    Field variable in the class `RectangleV2`, which is initialized with an initial value:

    area

    When an object of the class `RectangleV2` is created, the fields `length` and `breadth` are initialized to `0.0`, and afterwards the field `area` is initialized to `0.0` (`length *` `breadth`).

7. (a).

8. Class names in the class `ClientA`:

    Counter, System

    Local variables in the method `main()`:

    numOfCars, carCounter

    Names of methods called in the method `main()`:

    incrementCounter, println, getCounter

    Formal parameters to the method `main()`:

    args

    An actual parameter is specified in the call to the `println()` method. The value of this actual parameter is the value returned by the method call `carCounter.get-Counter()`.

9. Printout:

    ```
    k + d is equal to 2
    k + d is equal to 3
    k + d is equal to 12
    k + d = 12
    ```

    Note that the formal parameter `d` in method `doIt()` shadows the field `d`. The variable `k` at (1) refers to the local variable `k` that is declared in the `for` loop. The variable `k` at (2) and (3) refers to the field `k`.

10. (b), (c).

A

The method signature does not include the return type. A void method cannot return a value. The return value from a method need not be assigned to a variable.

11. (a) Yes. This is called method overloading.

(b) Yes. The actual parameters are evaluated in the method call and their values are assigned to formal parameters that are local variables in the method declaration.

(c) Yes. But a `return` statement in a void method cannot return a value.

12. There are many ways to implement methods for the situations in this question. Here are some suggestions:

(a) A non-void method that returns a Boolean value. The return value (`true` or `false`) indicates whether a person has reached retirement age or not.

(b) A `void` method, if the method does not need to return a value.

(c) A non-void method that returns an `int` value.

(d) A non-void method that returns the `int` value entered by the user.

(e) A `void` method that updates the field with the value passed as parameter.

(f) A non-void method that returns the reference value of the array containing `Counter` objects. The return type is `Counter[]`.

(g) A non-void method that returns the reference value of the two-dimensional array containing `String` objects. The return type is `String[][]`.

(h) A non-void method that returns the reference value of the two-dimensional array containing `int` values, representing the sales of newspapers. The return type is `int[][]`. Note that the array length is not specified in the return type. The first index from the left represents a week in a four-week period, and the second index represents a day in the week.

13. Printout:

```
Before method call: counter value is equal to 1 and number of times is 5
After method call: counter value is equal to 6 and number of times is 5
```

Actual parameter values are not changed after the method call. For actual parameters that are references to objects, the object state can have changed, as we can see from the printout above.

14. Printout:

```
Before swapping: counter1 is 10 and counter2 is 20
After swapping: counter1 is 10 and counter2 is 20
```

Actual parameter values are not changed after the method call. This also applies to actual parameters that are references. They refer to the same objects as they did before the call.

15. (b), (c), (d), (e), (f).

The type list of the formal parameters is (`Counter`, `Counter[]`), i.e. the actual parameter list must comprise a reference to a `Counter` object and a reference to an array of `Counter` objects. All alternatives, except (a) and (g), have a type list that is compatible with the type list of the formal parameters.

(a) is not valid because the actual parameter `counterArrayA[]` is not an array reference. It is a reference, but to a `Counter` object.

(g) is not valid because the type list of the actual parameters is (`Counter[]`, `Counter[][]`).

16. Using the `this` reference in the class:

```
class Counter {
    final static int MAX_VALUE = 100;
    static String description = "This class creates counters.";
    int value;

    Counter() { this.value = 1; }
    Counter(int initialValue) { this.value = initialValue; }

    int getCounter() { return this.value; }
    void setCounter(int newValue) { this.value = newValue; }
    void incrementCounter() { ++this.value; }
    void decrementCounter() { --this.value; }
    void resetCounter() { this.value = 0; }

    static String getDiscription() { return description; } // No this

}
```

17. (a), (c), (d), (e), (g), (h).

(b) and (f) are not valid, because instance members cannot be accessed using the class name.

18. (c), (d).

Overloaded constructors have different formal parameter lists. A constructor is not a method, and it cannot have a return type. A constructor is invoked on the object created by the `new` operator, and can therefore refer to this object using the `this` reference in the constructor body.

19. Printout if we use (a): 0

Printout if we use (b): 600

Printout if we use (c): 50

In (c), the constructor overwrites the initial values that the field variables were assigned in their declarations.

20. (a): (1) is valid, since the implicit default constructor is called. (2) is not valid, since there is no non-default constructor declared.

(b): (1) is valid, since the explicit default constructor is called. (2) is not valid, since there is no non-default constructor declared.

(c): (1) is not valid, since the explicit default constructor is not declared. (2) is valid, since the non-default constructor is called.

(d): (1) is valid, since the explicit default constructor is called. (2) is valid, since the non-default constructor is called.

21. The following lines will result in a compile time error: (3), (10), (15), (16), (18), (20).

(3), (10) and (18) are not valid, because instance members cannot be accessed by using the class name. (15) and (16) are not valid, because we cannot access instance members inside a static method, with or without the `this` reference. (20) is not valid, because the `this` reference is not available in a static method.

22. (f). It is not possible to create objects of an enumerated type using the `new` operator, but we can declare variables of an enumerated type.

23. (a), (b), (c), (d), (e).

(a): The name of the enumerated type must be used together with the name of the enum constant.

```
colour = LightColour.GREEN;
```

(b): We must create an array containing the enum constants by calling the `values()` method before we can iterate over the constants.

```
for (LightColour colour : LightColour.values()) {
    System.out.println(colour);
}
```

(c): The name of the enumerated type should not be specified in the `case` label.

```
switch(colour)
    case RED: System.out.println("STOP!"); break;
    case GREEN: System.out.println("GO!"); break;
    case YELLOW: System.out.println("CAREFUL!"); break;
    default: assert false: "UNKNOWN COLOUR!";
}
```

(d): The name of the enumerated type must be used together with the name of the enum constant.

```
boolean b = colour.equals(LightColour.GREEN);
```

(e): Cannot assign to an enum constant as it is `final`.

A.8 Object communication

1. The properties and behaviour defined for a class determine what *responsibilities* the class has, and what *roles* objects of this class can fulfil.

2. (c), (d).

   Only reference values of objects are passed, and the called method may change the object state.

3. In Java an object can ask another object to do something by *calling* a *method* of the other object.

4. An association between two classes can be established by one or both of the classes declaring a *field variable* in order to store a *reference value* of an object of the other class.

5. An association in which a Car object owns four Tire objects is called a *one*-to-*many* association.

6. (a).

   The compiler selects the method body that will be executed during compilation of the code by examining the signatures of the method declarations.

A.9 Sorting and searching arrays

1. Values of all numerical data types in Java, such as int and double, have a *natural order*. The Java programming language also defines a set of *relational* operators that can be used to compare numerical values.

2. The only primitive data type in Java whose values cannot be compared is boolean. Values of this data type can only be compared for *equality*.

3. There will be no output from statements (1) to (5), as their assertions are all valid. The output from statement (6) will be a message from the Java Virtual Machine stating that an AssertionError occurred during execution. The file name, as well as the line number that caused the error, will be reported:

   ```
   Exception in thread "main" java.lang.AssertionError
           at ComparePrimitiveValues.main(ComparePrimitiveValues.java:10)
   ```

4. Some possible ways to verify that the letter 'a' precedes the letter 'z' are:

   ```
   assert 'a' < 'z';
   assert 'a' <= 'z';
   assert 'z' > 'a';
   assert 'z' >= 'a';
   assert ('z' - 'a') > 0;
   ```

5. The following `assert` statement verifies that the Unicode standard defines as many lowercase as uppercase letters in the English alphabet:

   ```
   assert ('z'-'a') == ('Z'-'A');
   ```

6. One suggestion for an assertion:

   ```
   assert testScore >= MIN_SCORE && testScore <= MAX_SCORE :
       "Reported test score " + testScore + " is outside valid range " +
       MIN_SCORE + " to " + MAX_SCORE;
   ```

7. To enable comparison of two objects, their class has to implement the `Comparable` interface, which defines the `compareTo()` method used to compare objects.

8. (c) provides the correct implementation of the `compareTo()` method. For (a), the method signature is incorrect, as the parameter to `compareTo()` must be of type `Object`. Method (a) also compares the two title fields for reference equality, instead of object equality. In method (b) the signature is correct, but the input parameter is not cast to type `CD`, which is required to access the `title` and `noOfTracks` fields. The `Object` class has no such fields.

   The class declaration must be modified as follows: (modification in italics)

   ```
   class CD implements Comparable {
   ```

9. The `CDSorter` program produces the following output:
   ```
   CD list:
   The CD entitled 'Java Jive' has 5 tracks.
   The CD entitled 'T Cup Blues' has 7 tracks.
   The CD entitled 'Another cup of Joe' has 6 tracks.
   The CD entitled 'T Cup Blues' has 8 tracks.
   Sorted CD list:
   The CD entitled 'Another cup of Joe' has 6 tracks.
   The CD entitled 'Java Jive' has 5 tracks.
   The CD entitled 'T Cup Blues' has 7 tracks.
   The CD entitled 'T Cup Blues' has 8 tracks.
   ```

10. (c).

    Objects cannot be ordered using relational operators. These operators are only defined for values of the primitive data types. That every individual field of an object has a natural order is not a sufficient criteria for sorting using the `sort()` method of the `java.util.Arrays` class. The class of the object must implement the `Comparable` interface, defining the natural order of its objects. The `sort()` method of the `java.util.Arrays` class is also capable of sorting arrays containing values of primitive data types such as `int` and `double`.

11. (d).

    Neither the selection sort nor insertion sort algorithms are able to detect a partially-sorted array. The algorithms will compare the current element in each pass with *every* element in the remaining unsorted part and sorted subarray respectively. Both algorithms perform the same number of comparisons per pass. Thus, statements (a),

(b) and (c) are all false. However, selection sort only performs three assignments per pass, for swapping the smallest (or largest) value in the unsorted part with the first element of the unsorted part. In contrast, insertion sort shifts up to *n*-2 element values per pass, each shift requiring one assignment operation.

A.10   Text file I/O and simple GUI dialogs

1.   (b), (e).

Only (b) and (e) are text files. The others are binary files.

2.   (a), (b).

3.   (b).

(a) and (c) are equivalent.

4.   (a), (b), (c).

5.   (a), (c).

6.   (a).

7.   (b).

Alternative (b) will avoid printing `"null"` when the end of file is reached.

8.   (c).

(c) will ensure that all other connected resources are freed.

9.   A method can specify exceptions it will rethrow in a `throws` clause in the method header.

10.   (a), (c).

11.   (a).

The statements in the `writeToFile()` and `closeWriteFile()` methods do not throw an `IOException`. A call to the `FileWriter` constructor in the `openFileForWrite()` method can throw an `IOException`. The `openFileForWrite()` method must specify an `IOException` in a `throws` clause, and so must the `main()` method, as it calls the `open-FileForWrite()` method.

12.   (c).

The `main()` method calls the other three methods, which all contain code that can throw an `IOException`. All *four* methods must specify an `IOException` in a `throws` clause.

13.   (a), (b).

The showConfirmDialog() method can only show combinations specified by the following constants in the JOptionPane class: DEFAULT_OPTION (i.e. "OK" button), YES_NO_OPTION, YES_NO_CANCEL_OPTION, OK_CANCEL_OPTION.

14. (a), (b), (c).

15. (a), (b).

However, (a) will not return any value to indicate which button the user clicked.

A

Language reference

B.1 Reserved words

Keywords are reserved words in the Java programming language. These words have a predefined meaning and therefore cannot be used for other purposes in the source code than that which is defined in the Java language specification. Incorrect use will be reported by the compiler.

Table B.1 shows all the keywords that are defined in Java. In addition, three reserved words are used as literals (Table B.2). Table B.3 shows reserved words that are not used in the current version of Java (version 6.0), but may be used in future versions. All reserved words in Java are written in lowercase letters.

TABLE B.1 Keywords in Java

abstract	default	if	private	this
assert	do	implements	protected	throw
boolean	double	import	public	throws
break	else	instanceof	return	transient
byte	enum	int	short	try
case	extends	interface	static	void
catch	final	long	strictfp	volatile
char	finally	native	super	while
class	float	new	switch	
continue	for	package	synchronized	

TABLE B.2   Reserved words for literals

null	true	false

TABLE B.3   Reserved words for future use

const	goto

B.2 Operators

How an expression is evaluated depends on the precedence of the operators it uses. In the case of adjacent operators with different precedence, the operator with highest precedence is applied first. Adjacent operators with the same precedence are evaluated according to associativity rules: either operators are grouped with operands from left to right (for left-associative operators), or from right to left (for right-associative operators). Parentheses, "()", can always be used to overrule operator precedence and associativity rules. It is a good idea to use parentheses to emphasise how an expression is evaluated.

The index can be used to find where the different operators are explained and used in program examples.

Table B.4 gives a overview of the operators defined in Java. Note the following about the operators shown in Table B.4:

- The operators are arranged in decreasing order of precedence from the start of the table. Thus the assignment operators have the lowest precedence.
- Operators in the same row have the same precedence.
- All operators that are not listed either as *unary* (i.e. demanding one operand) or *ternary* (i.e. requiring three operands), are *binary* (i.e. demanding two operands).
- All binary operators except for assignment operators associate with operands *from left to right*.
- All unary operators, except for unary post-decrement and post-increment operators, all assignment operators, and the ternary conditional operator, associate *from right to left*.

TABLE B.4   Operators in Java

Operator	Operation	Example
[]	Indexing in arrays	args[0]
.	Accessing class members	System.out.println()
(*parameters*)	Actual parameters in method calls	str.indexOf('%', 10)
++	Unary post-increment	i++
--	Unary post-decrement	j--

Operator	Operation	Example
++	Unary pre-increment	`++i`
--	Unary pre-decrement	`--j`
+	Unary plus	`+x`
-	Unary minus	`-y`
~	Unary bitwise complement	`~flag`
!	Unary Boolean negation	`!done`
new	Unary object creation	`new Integer(2007)`
(*type*)	Unary type conversion operator	`(int) 3.14`
*	Multiplication	`9 * 2`
/	Integer division	`9 / 2`
	Floating-point division	`9.0 / 2.0`
%	Modulus (remainder of division)	`9 % 2`
+	Addition	`9 + 2`
	String concatenation	`"July" + 2006`
-	Subtraction	`9 - 2`
<<	Bitwise left shift	`i << 4`
>>	Bitwise right shift with sign extension	`j >> 4`
>>>	Bitwise right shift with 0 extension	`k >>> 4`
<	Less than	`a < b`
<=	Less than or equal to	`a <= b`
>	Greater than	`a > c`
>=	Greater than or equal to	`a >= c`
instanceof	Type comparison for objects	`str instanceof String`
==	Equal to: primitive values	`i == j`
	Equal to: reference values	`str1 == str2`
!=	Not equal to: primitive values	`i != j`
	Not equal to: reference values	`str1 != str2`
&	Logical AND	`(i > 0) & (i <= 10)`
	Bitwise AND	`i & 0277`
^	Logical exclusive OR	`overLimit ^ belowLimit`
	Bitwise exclusive OR	`i ^ 0277`
|	Logical OR	`found | finished`
	Bitwise OR	`i | 0277`
&&	Conditional AND	`washed && ironed`
||	Conditional OR	`washed || cleaned`
? :	Ternary conditional expression	`(i < 0) ? -i : i`

Operator	Operation	Example
	Assignment of:	
=	primitive value	`i = 2`
	reference value	`str1 = str2`
	Assignment *after*:	
+=	addition	`i += 2`
	string concatenation	`str1 += "2002"`
-=	subtraction	`i -= 2`
*=	multiplication	`i *= 2`
/=	integer division	`i /= 2`
	floating-point division	`x /= 2.0`
%=	calculation of remainder	`i %= 2`
<<=	bitwise left shift	`i <<= 2`
>>=	bitwise right shift with sign extension	`i >>= 2`
>>>=	bitwise right shift with 0 extension	`i >>>= 2`
&=	logical AND	`flag &= found`
	bitwise AND	`i &= 0277`
^=	logical exclusive OR	`flag ^= found`
	bitwise exclusive OR	`i ^= 0277`
|=	logical OR	`flag |= found`
	bitwise OR	`i |= 0277`

B.3   Primitive data types

Table B.5 shows the range for the predefined primitive data types in Java. The minimum and the maximum values for each primitive data type are defined by the constants *Wrapper*.MIN_VALUE and *Wrapper*.MAX_VALUE of the corresponding wrapper class respectively.

TABLE B.5   Primitive data types in Java

Data type	Width (bits)	Minimum value, maximum value	Wrapper class
`boolean`	not applicable	true, false (no ordering implied)	`Boolean`
`byte`	8	-2^7 (-128), 2^7-1 (+127)	`Byte`
`char`	16	0x0 (Unicode value \u0000), 0xffff (\uffff)	`Character`
`double`	64	4.94065645841246544e-324, 1.79769313486231570e+308	`Double`

Data type	Width (bits)	Minimum value, maximum value	Wrapper class
float	32	1.401298464324817e-45f, 3.402823476638528860e+38f	Float
int	32	-2^{31} (-2147483648), 2^{31}-1 (+2147483647)	Integer
long	64	-2^{63} (-9223372036854775808L), 2^{63}-1 (+9223372036854775807L)	Long
short	16	-2^{15} (-32768), 2^{15}-1 (+32767)	Short

B.4 Java modifiers

Table B.6 summarises the accessibility of classes and interfaces when placed inside a Java package. Table B.7 shows additional modifiers for classes and interfaces, while Table B.8 shows accessibility modifiers for *members* of a class, i.e. its fields and methods.

TABLE B.6 Accessibility modifiers for classes and interfaces

Modifier	Top-level classes and interfaces
default (no modifier specified)	Accessible in the package (package accessible).
public	Accessible from everywhere.

TABLE B.7 Other modifiers for classes and interfaces

Modifier	Classes	Interfaces
abstract	The class can contain abstract methods, and therefore cannot be instantiated.	Implied. It is not possible to create an instance of an interface type.
final	The class cannot be extended (i.e. it cannot be subclassed).	Not possible.

TABLE B.8 Access ability modifiers for class members

Modifier	Members
public	Accessible from everywhere.
protected	Accessible by all classes in the same package as its class, and accessible by subclasses of its class in other packages.

B

Modifier	Members
default (no modifier)	Only accessible by classes, including subclasses, in the same package as its class (package access ability).
private	Only accessible in its own class.

B

Formatted values

INTRODUCTION

The Java programming language offers the ability to format values. This appendix gives an overview of some commonly used methods from the Java standard library.

C.1 Syntax for format strings

Table C.1 gives an overview of the methods for the Java standard library that can be used for formatting values. All methods accept a *format string* as their first parameter, followed by zero or more parameters (given by the syntax `Object... args`).

TABLE C.1 Methods for formatting values

Method	Description

`String format(`
    `String formatString,`
    `Object... args`
`)`
	Found in the `String`, `PrintStream` and `PrintWriter` classes. Returns the resulting string with formatted values.

`PrintStream printf(`
    `String formatString,`
    `Object... args`
`)`
	Found in the `PrintStream` class. Generates a string, with formatted values, and prints the string to the current `PrintStream`. Returns the reference value of the current `PrintStream`. In particular, the `PrintStream` object referred to by the reference `System.out` prints to the terminal window by default.

`PrintWriter printf(`
    `String formatString,`
    `Object... args`
`)`
	Found in the `PrintWriter` class. Generates a string with formatted values and prints the string to the current `PrintWriter`. Returns the reference value of the current `PrintWriter`.

A format string can contain one or more *format specifications*. A format specification comprises a set of *conversion flags* and a *conversion code*. The methods in Table C.1

construct a string from the format string by replacing each format specification with the string representation of the corresponding parameter.

A format specification has the general form:

"%[*argumentIndex*$][*flags*][*width*][.*precision*]*code*"

All the elements in square brackets are optional. A format specification is always initiated by the character '%'. The optional *argumentIndex* is used to indicate which of the parameters that follow the format string will be formatted. The first parameter after the format string `format` has index 1 and is identified with "1$", the second parameter with "2$", and so on (see Table C.9). If no argument index is given, the parameters after the format string are used in the sequence they are listed in the call to the `format()` or `printf()` method. Thus the first parameter after the format string is converted using the first format specification, the second parameter is converted using the second specification, and so on.

The optional conversion flags, `flags`, are used to control the conversion for different types of values. Which flags are allowed is determined by the mandatory conversion code, `code`, always placed at the end of the format specification. The optional width specifies the minimum number of characters the printout must have, while the optional precision specifies the maximum number of characters to print. For floating-point values, the precision indicates how many decimals will be printed (for conversion code "%f") or the total number of significant digits (for conversion code "%g"). Note that the dot character '.' separates the width and precision flags. The last element in the format specification is the mandatory conversion code, which determines the type of conversion to be applied to a value.

C.2 Conversion codes and types

Table C.2 describes how the value of a parameter p is converted to a string by different conversion codes, e.g. through the call `printf("%code", p)`. If the parameter p cannot be converted to a value of the type defined by the code, an exception is thrown and the program terminated.

Uppercase conversion codes will generate a printout containing only uppercase letters.

Java also offers a set of conversion flags to control the conversion of values to strings. A subset of these flags is listed in Table C.3.

Table C.4 shows which conversion flags and codes can be combined for each parameter type.

TABLE C.2	Formatting parameter **p** with different conversion codes
Conversion code	Description
%	Results in the character literal '%' being inserted into the resulting string.
a, A	The value of p is converted to a hexadecimal floating-point number, formatted in exponential form.
b, B	If p is a Boolean variable, a string representation of its value is generated by calling the method `String.valueOf()`. This results in the string `"true"` for the value `true`, and the string `"false"` for the value `false`. For reference types, this conversion results in the string `"false"` if p has the value `null` and the string `"true"` otherwise.
c, C	Results in a string containing a single Unicode character.
d	The value of p is converted to an integer, which is formatted as a string where the integer is represented in the decimal numeral system (see Appendix F).
e, E	The value of p is converted to a floating-point number, formatted in scientific notation.
f	The value of p is converted to a floating-point number with base 10 and without an exponent.
g, G	The value of p is converted to a floating-point number, given either in scientific notation or decimal notation depending on the size of the exponent.
h, H	If p is equal to `null`, the result is the string `"null"`. Otherwise, the hash code is generated and converted to a string as a hexadecimal number.
n	Results in the platform-specific line terminator string being inserted into the resulting string.
o	The value of p is converted to an octal integer (see Appendix F).
s, S	If p is equal to `null`, the result is the string `"null"`. If the class of p implements the `java.util.Formattable` interface, the value of p is converted to a string through the method call `p.formatTo()`. Otherwise, the result of the conversion is given by the method call `p.toString()`.
x, X	The value of p is converted to a hexadecimal integer (see Appendix F).

C

TABLE C.3   Conversion flags

Conversion flag	Description
-	The result is left-justified, positioned within the width defined in the format specification. If this flag is not specified, the converted value is right-justified within the defined field width.
#	The result is prefixed with "0", "0x" or "0X" for integer values. For all other types of values, the formatting depends on the definition of the java.util.Formattable interface.
+	The result will always contain a sign, either '+' for positive values or '-' for negative values.
space (i.e. ' ')	The result will include a space character for positive values.
0	The result will be left-filled with the digit 0 to fill the defined width.
,	The result will include a separator character that is determined by the locale that is set when the program is run.
(	Negative values will be enclosed in parentheses.

TABLE C.4   Combinations of conversion flags and codes

Desired formatting	Conversion flag	Conversion code	Parameter type
Decimal number	-, +, 0, ,, (	d	Integer.
Octal number	-, #, 0	o	Integer.
Hexadecimal number	-, #, 0	x or X	Integer.
Floating-point number	-, #, +, 0, ,, (	d	Integer or floating-point number.
Floating-point number with scientific notation or as decimal number	-, #, +, 0, ,, (	g or G	Integer or floating-point number.
Floating-point number with scientific notation	-, #, +, 0, ,, (	e or E	Integer or floating-point number.
Percent character	*none*	%	
Newline character	*none*	n	

C

C.3 Examples

The tables below illustrate how different types of values are formatted with different combinations of conversion codes and flags.

TABLE C.5 Formatting of integer values

Value	"%d"	"%+d"	"%8d"	"%-8d"	"%08d"	"%,d"
0	"0"	"+0"	" 0"	"0 "	"00000000"	"0"
1024	"1024"	"+1024"	" 1024"	"1024 "	"00001024"	"1,024"
-999	"-999"	"-999"	" -999"	"-999 "	"-0000999"	"-999"
1650237	"1650237"	"+1650237"	" 1650237"	"1650237 "	"01650237"	"1,650,237"

TABLE C.6 Formatting of integer values (cont.)

Value	"%(d"	"%+-,11d"	"%x"	"%#x"	"%o"	"%,#o"
0	"0"	"+0"	"0"	"0x0"	"0"	"00"
1024	"1024"	"+1,024"	" 400"	"0x400"	"2000"	"02000"
-999	"(999)"	"-999"	"fffffc19"	"0xfffffc19"	"37777776031"	"037777776031"

TABLE C.7 Formatting of floating-point values

Value	"%f"	"%.2f"	"%7.2f"	"%07.2f"	"%4g"	"%.4e"
0.0	"0.000000"	"0.00"	" 0.00"	"0000.00"	"0.000"	"0.0000e+00"
0.3	"0.300000"	"0.30"	" 0.30"	"0000.30"	"0.3000"	"3.0000e-01"
1.0	"1.000000"	"1.00"	" 1.00"	"0001.00"	"1.000"	"1.0000e+00"
1.5	"1.500000"	"1.50"	" 1.50"	"0001.50"	"1.500"	"1.5000e+00"
-1.5	"-1.500000"	"-1.50"	" -1.50"	"-001.50"	"-1.500"	"-1.5000e+00"
678.9	"678.900000"	"+678.90"	" 678.90"	"0678.90"	"678.9"	"6.7890e+02"
1234.567	"1234.567000"	"1234.57"	"1234.57"	"1234.57"	"1235"	"1.2346e+03"

TABLE C.8 Formatting of strings

Value	"%s"	"%10s"	"%-10s"	"%.2s"	"%7.2s"	"%7.0s"	"%.3s"
"Hello!"	"Hello!"	" Hello!"	"Hello! "	"He"	" He"	" "	"Hel"

TABLE C.9 Using the argument index

Argument list	"%1$d-%2$d-%3$d"	"%3$d-%2$d-%1$d"	"%2$d-%3$d-%1$d"
2006, 12, 23	"2006-12-23"	"23-12-2006"	"12-23-2006"

The Unicode character set

INTRODUCTION

This appendix presents a selection of Unicode characters and their code values.

D.1 Excerpt from the Unicode character set

Table D.1 shows some characters from the Unicode character set, along with their decimal value and their char literal representation. The characters in Table D.1 are also a part of the ASCII character set, except for the '€' character.

The character codes for the characters in the groups consisting of uppercase letters, lowercase letters and digits occur consecutively in the character set. For example, if we know that the character code for the character A is 'A', i.e. 65, then the character code for character B is 'A' + 1, i.e. 66 or 'B'.

TABLE D.1   Selected values from the Unicode character set

Decimal value	Char literal	Character	Decimal value	Char literal	Character	Decimal value	Char literal	Character
32	\u0020	space	64	\u0040	@	96	\u0060	`
33	\u0021	!	65	\u0041	A	97	\u0061	a
34	\u0022	"	66	\u0042	B	98	\u0062	b
35	\u0023	#	67	\u0043	C	99	\u0063	c
36	\u0024	$	68	\u0044	D	100	\u0064	d
37	\u0025	%	69	\u0045	E	101	\u0065	e
38	\u0026	&	70	\u0046	F	102	\u0066	f
39	\u0027	'	71	\u0047	G	103	\u0067	g

Decimal value	Char literal	Character	Decimal value	Char literal	Character	Decimal value	Char literal	Character
40	\u0028	(	72	\u0048	H	104	\u0068	h
41	\u0029	)	73	\u0049	I	105	\u0069	i
42	\u002a	*	74	\u004a	J	106	\u006a	j
43	\u002b	+	75	\u004b	K	107	\u006b	k
44	\u002c	,	76	\u004c	L	108	\u006c	l
45	\u002d	-	77	\u004d	M	109	\u006d	m
46	\u002e	.	78	\u004e	N	110	\u006e	n
47	\u002f	/	79	\u004f	O	111	\u006f	o
48	\u0030	0	80	\u0050	P	112	\u0070	p
49	\u0031	1	81	\u0051	Q	113	\u0071	q
50	\u0032	2	82	\u0052	R	114	\u0072	r
51	\u0033	3	83	\u0053	S	115	\u0073	s
52	\u0034	4	84	\u0054	T	116	\u0074	t
53	\u0035	5	85	\u0055	U	117	\u0075	u
54	\u0036	6	86	\u0056	V	118	\u0076	v
55	\u0037	7	87	\u0057	W	119	\u0077	w
56	\u0038	8	88	\u0058	X	120	\u0078	x
57	\u0039	9	89	\u0059	Y	121	\u0079	y
58	\u003a	:	90	\u005a	Z	122	\u007a	z
59	\u003b	;	91	\u005b	[	123	\u007b	{
60	\u003c	<	92	\u005c	\	124	\u007c		
61	\u003d	=	93	\u005d	]	125	\u007d	}
62	\u003e	>	94	\u005e	^	126	\u007e	~
63	\u003f	?	95	\u005f	_	8364	\u20ac	€

D.2 Lexicographical order and alphabetical order

The `compareTo()` method of the `String` class compares two strings lexicographically according to the Unicode values of the characters in the strings. In many languages characters are not typically ordered according to their Unicode values. Table D.2 shows some character used in the Norwegian language ordered according to their character codes: Å, Æ, Ø, å, æ, ø. However, when sorting Norwegian text, the lexicographical order should be: Æ, Ø, Å, æ, ø, å. A `java.text.Collator` and a `java.util.Locale` provide the solution for sorting text in Norwegian order:

```
Collator norwayCollator = Collator.getInstance(new Locale("no"));
System.out.println(norwayCollator.compare("øl", "ål") < 0); // true
```

TABLE D.2   Characters used in Norwegian

Decimal value	Char literal	Character	Decimal value	Char literal	Character	Decimal value	Char literal	Character
197	\u00c5	Å	216	\u00d8	Ø	230	\u00e6	æ
198	\u00c6	Æ	229	\u00e5	å	248	\u00f8	ø

D

Console I/O and simple GUI dialog boxes

INTRODUCTION

This appendix presents two classes for reading values from the terminal window and for creating simple GUI dialog boxes.

E.1 Support for console I/O

The Console class in Program E.1 provides read*Type*() methods for reading integers, floating-point numbers and strings entered via the keyboard, where *Type* can be Int, Double and String respectively. In addition, it provides the method readToEOL() to read the remaining input on the current line, i.e. effectively emptying the current line of any input. The class allows multiple values to be entered on a line.

To use the Console class with your program, copy the file Console.java and compile it in the source code directory of your program.

Program E.2 uses the Console class. The program finds the largest integer entered on the keyboard. Note how the user is prompted to re-enter a value in case of error.

PROGRAM E.1   Console I/O

```
import java.util.InputMismatchException;
import java.util.Scanner;

/**
 * Class reads values from the console.
 */
public final class Console {
  private Console() {}; // Cannot create objects of this class.

  /** Scanner object connected to System.in. */
  private static Scanner keyboard = new Scanner(System.in);

  /**
```

```
   * Reads an int value from the keyboard.
   * @return Next value as int
   */
  public static int readInt() {
    while (true)
      try {
        return keyboard.nextInt();
      } catch (InputMismatchException ime) {
        reportError();
      }
  }

  /**
   * Reads a double value from the keyboard.
   * @return Next value as double
   */
  public static double readDouble() {
    while (true)
      try {
        return keyboard.nextDouble();
      } catch (InputMismatchException ime) {
        reportError();
      }
  }

  /**
   * Reads a string from the keyboard.
   * The returned string will not contain any white space.
   * @return Next value as string.
   */
  public static String readString() {
    while (true)
      try {
        return keyboard.next();
      } catch (InputMismatchException ime) {
        reportError();
      }
  }

  /**
   * Reads to the end of line (EOL).
   * @return Remaining input as string.
   */
  public static String readToEOL() {
    while (true)
      try {
        return keyboard.nextLine();
      } catch (InputMismatchException ime) {
        reportError();
      }
```

```
  }

  /**
   * Empties the current line, and prints an error message
   * to the terminal window.
   */
  private static void reportError() {
    keyboard.nextLine(); // Empty the line first.
    System.out.println("Error in input. Try again!");
  }
}
```

PROGRAM E.2   Using console I/O

```
// Using Console class
public class ConsoleDemo {

  public static void main(String[] args) {
    System.out.println(                                    // (1)
        "Program finds the largest number in a sequence of numbers" +
        " entered at the console.\n" +
        "A negative number signals end of the sequence.");
    int maxValue = 0;
    while (true) {
      System.out.print("Enter an integer: ");
      int n = Console.readInt();                           // (2)
      if (n < 0) {
        break;
      }
      if (n > maxValue) {
        maxValue = n;
      }
    }
    System.out.println("Largest number: " + maxValue);
  }
}
```

Compiling and running the program:

```
> javac ConsoleDemo.java Console.java
> java ConsoleDemo
```

```
Program finds the largest number in a sequence of numbers entered at the console.
A negative number signals end of the sequence.
Enter an integer: 123
Enter an integer: 2006
Enter an integer: zero
Error in input. Try again!
9
```

```
Enter an integer: 2007
Enter an integer: -1
Largest number: 2007
```

E.2 Support for simple GUI dialog boxes

The GUIDialog class in Program E.3 provides request*Type*() methods for reading integers,
floating-point numbers and strings using a GUI dialog box, where *Type* can be Int, Double
and String respectively. Each method allows a prompt to be passed as parameter, which
is shown in the input dialog box. In addition, it provides the method confirmInfo() to
confirm information passed as parameter, as well as the method prompt() to display a
message to the user.

To use the GUIDialog class with your program, copy the file GUIDialog.java and compile
it in the source code directory of your program. Remember to end your program with the
following statement to stop all execution:

```
System.exit(0);
```

Program E.4 uses the GUIDialog class. The program finds the largest integer in a sequence
of integers entered via dialog boxes. Figure E.1 shows the interaction with the user. Note
how the user is prompted to re-enter a value in case of error.

PROGRAM E.3 GUI dialog boxes

```java
import javax.swing.JOptionPane;

/**
 * This class provides methods for reading integers, floating-point
 * numbers and strings via simple GUI dialogue boxes.
 * Remember to stop all execution by using this statement in your program:
 *    System.exit(0);
 */
public final class GUIDialog {
  private GUIDialog() { };  // Cannot create objects of this class.

  /**
   * Reads an int value.
   * @return An int value
   */
  public static int requestInt(Object prompt) {                        //(1)
    String input = "";
    while (true)                                                        //(2)
      try {
        input = JOptionPane.showInputDialog(null, prompt, "Input",      //(3)
                                    JOptionPane.PLAIN_MESSAGE);
        return Integer.parseInt(input);                                 //(4)
```

```
        } catch (NullPointerException exception) {                  //(5)
            prompt("\"" + input + "\"" + " is not a valid integer.");
        } catch (NumberFormatException exception) {                 //(6)
            prompt("\"" + input + "\"" + " is not a valid integer.");
        }
}


/**
 * Reads a double value.
 * @return A double value
 */
public static double requestDouble(Object prompt) {                 //(7)
  String input = "";
  while (true)
    try {
      input = JOptionPane.showInputDialog(null, prompt, "Input",
                                  JOptionPane.PLAIN_MESSAGE);
      return Double.parseDouble(input);
    } catch (NullPointerException exception) {
        prompt("\"" + input + "\"" +
               " is not a valid floating-point number.");
    } catch (NumberFormatException exception) {
        prompt("\"" + input + "\"" +
               " is not a valid floating-point number.");
    }
}


/**
 * Reads a non-empty string.
 * @return A string
 */
public static String requestString(Object prompt) {                 //(8)
  String input = "";
  while (true)
    try {
      input = JOptionPane.showInputDialog(null, prompt, "Input",
                                  JOptionPane.PLAIN_MESSAGE);
      if (input == null || input.length() == 0) {
        throw new IllegalArgumentException();
      }
      return input;
    } catch (IllegalArgumentException exception) {
        prompt("\"" + input + "\"" + " is not a valid string.");
    }
}


/**
 * Prints a message.
 */
public static void prompt(Object message) {                         //(9)
```

```java
        JOptionPane.showMessageDialog(null, message, "Message",
                              JOptionPane.WARNING_MESSAGE);
    }


    // Return values from the method confirm()
    public static final int YES = JOptionPane.YES_OPTION;
    public static final int NO = JOptionPane.NO_OPTION;
    public static final int CANCEL = JOptionPane.CANCEL_OPTION;


    /**
     * Confirms information.
     * @return YES, if YES button was clicked.
     * @return NO, if NO button was clicked.
     * @return CANCEL, if CANCEL button was clicked.
     */
    public static int confirmInfo(Object information) {                //(10)
        return JOptionPane.showConfirmDialog(null, information, "Confirm",
                              JOptionPane.YES_NO_CANCEL_OPTION);
    }
}
```

PROGRAM E.4   Using GUI dialog boxes

```java
// Using GUIDialog class
public class GUIDialogDemo {

    public static void main(String[] args) {
        GUIDialog.prompt(                                            // (1)
            "Program finds the largest number in a sequence of numbers.\n" +
            "A negative number signals end of the sequence.");
        int maxValue = 0;
        while (true) {
            int n = GUIDialog.requestInt("Enter an integer: ");      // (2)
            if (n < 0) {
                break;
            }
            if (n > maxValue) {
                maxValue = n;
            }
        }
        GUIDialog.prompt("Largest number: " + maxValue);             // (3)
        System.exit(0);
    }
}
```

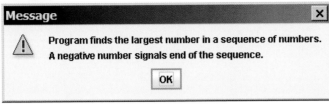

(a)

(b)

(c)

(d)

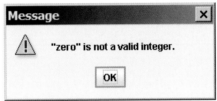

(e)

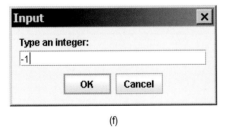

(f)

(g)

E

Numeral systems and representation

INTRODUCTION

This appendix gives an overview of different numeral systems and how we can specify numbers in them. The appendix also gives an introduction to integer representation using 2's compliment, which is the way integers are represented in Java. In addition, an example illustrates how methods from the Java standard library can be used to print a string representation of integers in the different numeral systems.

F.1 Numeral systems

Decimal numeral system

We are used to the *decimal numeral system*. This numeral system uses the digits from 0 to 9 to specify numbers (see Table F.1). This numeral system has ten digits and is also called the *base 10 numeral system*. Each digit that occurs in a number contributes to the value of the number depending on its position in the number, starting with position 0 for the digit that is right-most in the number. Each digit has a *positional value* in the number. For example, the value of the number 123 can be rewritten as follows:

$$123 = 1*10^2 + 2*10^1 + 3*10^0 = 1*100 + 2*10 + 3*1 = 100 + 20 + 3$$

It is the position and the base value that determines the weight of each digit in the number. The left-most digit contributes the most to the value of the number, and is therefore called the *most significant digit*. Conversely, the right-most digit is called the *least significant digit*.

There are numeral systems that are not based on this principle. For example, in the Roman numeral system, the digit V has the value 5, regardless of its position in a Roman numeral.

TABLE F.1   Numeral systems

Binary (base 2)	Octal (base 8)	Decimal (base 10)	Hexadecimal (base 16)
0	0	0	0
1	1	1	1
10	2	2	2
11	3	3	3
100	4	4	4
101	5	5	5
110	6	6	6
111	7	7	7
1000	10	8	8
1001	11	9	9
1010	12	10	a
1011	13	11	b
1100	14	12	c
1101	15	13	d
1110	16	14	e
1111	17	15	f
10000	20	16	10

Binary numeral system

Computers use the *binary numeral system* (also known as the *base 2 numeral system*) to store and handle data. This numeral system uses the digits 0 and 1 only (see Table F.1). This numeral system thus has two different digits, and therefore has the *base* 2. A number in this numeral system consists of a sequence of zeros and ones in which each 0 and 1 is called a *bit*. The number 1111011_2 is a binary number. Since it can also be a number in the decimal numeral system, we use the subscript 2 to indicate that it is a number in the binary numeral system.

F

We can convert a binary number to its corresponding number in the decimal numeral system by calculating the positional value of the digits. The number 1111011_2 corresponds to 123_{10} in the decimal numeral system:

$$1111011_2 = 1*2^6 + 1*2^5 + 1*2^4 + 1*2^3 + 0*2^2 + 1*2^1 + 1*2^0$$
$$= 1*64 + 1*32 + 1*16 + 1*8 + 0*4 + 1*2 + 1*1$$
$$= 64 + 32 + 16 + 8 + 0 + 2 + 1$$
$$= 123_{10}$$

We have used the base value 2 to calculate the positional value of each digit in the binary number. It is important to note that both 1111011_2 and 123_{10} represent the same value – we have just specified the value in two different numeral systems.

Octal numeral system

The bit pattern of a binary number can be long. Therefore we often use the *octal numeral system* (the *base 8 numeral system*). This uses the digits from 0 to 7 (see Table F.1). The octal numeral system has eight different digits, and thus has the *base* 8. The number 173_8 is a valid octal number. The number 180 is not, because it uses the digit 8, which is not in the octal numeral system.

We can convert an octal number to the corresponding number in the decimal numeral system by calculating the positional values of the digits, as shown for the binary number above, but using the base value 8. The number 173_8 corresponds to the number 123_{10} in the decimal numeral system:

$$173_8 = 1*8^2 + 7*8^1 + 3*8^0$$
$$= 1*64 + 7*8 + 3*1$$
$$= 64 + 56 + 3$$
$$= 123_{10}$$

The relationship between the binary numeral system and the octal numeral system is explained in Section F.2.

Hexadecimal numeral system

Numbers can be specified even more compactly by using the *hexadecimal numeral system* (the *base 16 numeral system*). This numeral system has sixteen different digits, and thus has the *base* 16. The first nine digits are the same as those in the decimal numeral system, i.e. from 0 to 9. The remaining seven digits consist of the letters from *a* through *f*, which represent the values from 10_{10} to 15_{10}. For example, the number 7b is a hexadecimal number. A digit between *a* and *f* can be replaced by the corresponding uppercase letter between *A* and *F*. The number $7B_{16}$ is equivalent to the number $7b_{16}$.

We can convert a hexadecimal number to the corresponding number in the decimal system by using the base value 16. The number $7b_{16}$ is equivalent to the number 123_{10}:

$$7b_{16} = 7*16^1 + b*16^0$$
$$= 7*16 + 11*1$$
$$= 112 + 11$$
$$= 123_{10}$$

F

The relationship between the binary numeral system, the octal numeral system and the hexadecimal numeral system is explained in Section F.2.

The procedure above can be generalised for converting any number to the decimal numeral system from a numeral system in the base R. Given a number $PQ...VW_R$ with $k+1$ digits, it can be converted to the corresponding number in the decimal numeral system as follows:

$$PQ...VW_R = P*R^k + Q*R^{k-1} + ... + V*R^1 + W*R^0$$

F.2 Conversions between numeral systems

Table F.1 shows that it requires at the most three bits to represent a digit in the octal numeral system. We also see that it requires at the most four bits to represent a digit in the hexadecimal numeral system. We can use this observation to convert between the binary, octal and hexadecimal systems (see Figure F.1).

The procedure for converting from the octal to the binary numeral system is shown by the arrow (a) in Figure F.1. The following calculation shows that the procedure of replacing each octal digit with a 3-bit binary number is correct:

$$
\begin{aligned}
173_8 &= 1*8^2 + 7*8^1 + 3*8^0 \\
&= 1*(2^3)^2 + 7*(2^3)^1 + 3*(2^3)^0 \\
&= 1*2^6 + 7*2^3 + 3 \\
&= (001_2)*2^6 + (111_2)*2^3 + (011_2) \qquad\qquad (1) \\
&= (0*2^2+0*2^1+1*2^0)*2^6 + (1*2^2+1*2^1+1*2^0)*2^3 + (0*2^2+1*2^1+1*2^0) \\
&= \qquad\quad 1*2^6 \qquad + \qquad 1*2^5+1*2^4+1*2^3 \qquad + \qquad 1*2^1+1*2^0 \\
&= 1*2^6 + 1*2^5+ 1*2^4 +1*2^3 + 0*2^2 + 1*2^1 + 1*2^0 \\
&= 1111011_2 \qquad\qquad (2)
\end{aligned}
$$

The result in (2) above is the same as the one we get by replacing each octal digit with its equivalent 3-bit sequence in (1) above. Analogously, we can convert from the hexadecimal to the binary numeral system by replacing each hexadecimal digit with the equivalent 4-bit sequence (arrow (b) in Figure F.1).

The procedure for converting from the binary to the octal numeral system is to reverse the procedure shown by the arrow (a) in Figure F.1. The arrow (c) in Figure F.1 shows this procedure. It groups bits in 3-bit sequences from right to left and replaces each 3-bit sequence with its equivalent octal digit. This is equivalent to doing the calculation at (1) in reverse. Analogously, the arrow (d) in Figure F.1 shows how we can convert from the binary to the hexadecimal numeral system.

Figure F.1 also shows how we can convert an octal number to its representation in the hexadecimal numeral system via the binary numeral system: arrows (a) and (d). Analogously, we can convert a hexadecimal number to it representation in the octal numeral system: arrows (b) and (c).

F

Conversion between decimal, octal and hexadecimal numbers

Represents each digit in an octal number with three bits.

173_8 = 001 111 011

= 1111011_2

(a)

(c)

Bits in a binary number are grouped in three-bit sequences from right to left. Each three-bit sequence corresponds to an octal digit.

1111011_2 = 1 111 011

= 1 7 3

= 173_8

Binary Number System

Represents each digit in a hexadecimal number with four bits.

$7b_{16}$ = 0111 1011

= 1111011_2

(b)

(d)

Bits in a binary number are grouped in four-bit sequences from right to left. Each four-bit sequence corresponds to a hexadecimal digit.

1111011_2 = 0111 1011

= 7 b

= $7b_{16}$

Hexadecimal Number System

F.3 Conversions from decimal numeral system

We can convert a decimal number to a binary number by reversing the procedure for converting from a binary number to a decimal number (see *Decimal numeral system* on page 345). The procedure involves dividing the quotient repeatedly with the base value 2, until the quotient is equal to 0. Division by the base value is implicit in the following steps:

123_{10} = 61*2 + 1
61_{10} = 30*2 + 1
30_{10} = 15*2 + 0
15_{10} = 7*2 + 1
7_{10} = 3*2 + 1
3_{10} = 1*2 + 1
1_{10} = 0*2 + 1
123_{10} = 1111011_2

The last step above assembles the remainders with the last remainder first. We get the binary number 1111011_2, which is equivalent to 123_{10}. We can prove this by substituting the quotients into the equations above:

123_{10} = 61*2 + 1 = (30*2 + 1)*2 + 1 = ((15*2 + 0)*2 + 1)*2 + 1
= (((7*2 + 1)*2 + 0)*2 + 1)*2 + 1
= ((((3*2 + 1)*2 + 1)*2 + 0)*2 + 1)*2 + 1
= (((((1*2 + 1)*2 + 1)*2 + 1)*2 + 0)*2 + 1)*2 + 1
= ((((((0*2 + 1)*2 + 1)*2 + 1)*2 + 1)*2 + 0)*2 + 1)*2 + 1
= ((((((0*2 + 1)*2 + 1)*2 + 1)*2 + 1)*2 + 0)*2 + 1)*2 + 1
= $1*2^6 + 1*2^5 + 1*2^4 + 1*2^3 + 0*2^2 + 1*2^1 + 1*2^0$
= 1111011_2

F

Analogously, we can convert a decimal number to an octal number by repeatedly dividing the quotient with the base value 8:

$$123_{10} = 15*8 + 3$$
$$15_{10} = 1*8 + 7$$
$$1_{10} = 0*8 + 1$$
$$123_{10} = 173_8$$

Finally, we show how we can convert a decimal number to a hexadecimal number by repeatedly dividing the quotient with the base value 16:

$$123_{10} = 7*16 + 15 = 7*16 + b$$
$$7_{10} = 0*16 + 7$$
$$123_{10} = 7b_{16}$$

F.4 Integer representation

In this section we look at how integer values are represented in memory. We will not discuss floating-point numbers here: details can be found in the comprehensive IEEE-754 standard that Java uses to represent floating-point numbers.

TABLE F.2   Representation of **byte** value with 2's compliment

Decimal value	Binary representation (8 bits)	Octal value with prefix 0	Hexadecimal value with prefix 0x
127	01111111	0177	0x7f
128	01111110	0176	0x7e
...	...	...	...
123	01111011	0173	0x7b
...	...	...	...
2	00000010	02	0x02
1	00000001	01	0x01
0	00000000	00	0x0
-1	11111111	0377	0xff
-2	11111110	0376	0xfe
...	...	...	...
-123	10000101	0205	0x85
...	...	...	...

Decimal value	Binary representation (8 bits)	Octal value with prefix 0	Hexadecimal value with prefix 0x
-127	10000001	0201	0x81
-128	10000000	0200	0x80

Table F.2 shows the representation of values in the byte primitive data type. Values of type byte are represented by eight bits in memory. With eight bits we can represent 2^8 or 256 integer values. Integer representation in Java uses *2's compliment*, which allows both positive and negative integers to be represented in memory. For the byte type, it means we can represent values from -128 (i.e. 2^7) to +127 (i.e. 2^7-1).

Before we can understand 2's compliment, we need to understand *1's compliment*. The 1's compliment of a binary number is obtained by changing the value of each bit in the number. For example, 1's compliment of 1111011_2 is 0000100_2. We use the notation $\sim N_2$ to denote the 1's compliment of a binary number N_2. 2's compliment is defined in terms of 1's compliment:

$$-N_2 = \sim N_2 + 1 \qquad\qquad (1)$$

In the equation above, we calculate 2's compliment, $-N_2$, of a binary number N_2 by adding 1 to 1's compliment, $\sim N_2$. If binary number N_2 is a positive number, 2's compliment will be the corresponding negative number, and vice versa. For example, given the positive number 1111011_2, we can calculate 2's compliment as follows:

```
N₂  = 01111011 =   123₁₀
~N₂ = 10000100
+1  =          1
-N₂ = 10000101 = -123₁₀
```

Analogously, we can calculate 2's compliment of a negative number:

```
N₂  = 10000101 = -123₁₀
~N₂ = 01111010
+1  =          1
-N₂ = 01111011 =  123₁₀
```

Adding a number and its 2's compliment always gives the result 0 (zero):

```
 01111011 =    123₁₀
+10000101 = +(-123₁₀) = -123₁₀
─────────────────────
 00000000 =      0₁₀
```

The *carry bit* from the left-most bit is ignored. The example above also shows that subtraction is calculated as addition with 2's compliment:

```
N₂ - M₂ = N₂ + (-M₂)
```

For example, the expression $(123_{10} - 2_{10})$ is calculated as follows, giving the correct result 121_{10}:

$$
\begin{array}{rcl}
123_{10} & = & 01111011 \\
+ \quad (-2_{10}) & = & +11111110 \\
\hline
121_{10} & = & 01111001
\end{array}
$$

In the binary representation, the left-most bit is called the *most significant bit*, and the right-most bit is called the *least significant bit*. Table F.2 shows that the most significant bit has the value 0 for positive integers and the value 1 for negative numbers.

Values of the primitive data types short, int and long are also represented by 2's complement with the number of bits 16, 32 and 64, respectively.

F.5 String representation of integers

In Java it is possible to specify integer values in the decimal, octal and hexadecimal numeral systems:

```
int i = 123;        // Decimal: no prefix.
int j = 0173;       // Octal: prefix 0 (zero) required.
int k = 0x7b;       // Hexadecimal: prefix 0x required.
```

It is *not* possible to specify integer values in the binary numeral system.

The wrapper classes Integer and Long provide methods that return a string representation of integers in the different numeral systems. A selection of these methods from the Integer class for int values (32 bits) is shown in Table F.3. The class Long provides analogous methods for long values (64 bits).

Program F.1 uses all the methods from Table F.3 to print the string representation of int values in the different numeral systems. Note that the prefix 0 and the prefix 0x for octal and hexadecimal notations are *not* a part of the string representation. The prefix can be printed by specifying the appropriate format conversion code when calling the printf() method provided by the PrintStream class (see Appendix C).

TABLE F.3   Methods for different string representations of integers

java.lang.Integer	
static String toBinaryString(int i) static String toOctalString(int i) static String toHexString(int i)	Returns the string representation of the integer value in the parameter i depending on the method called, either in the binary, octal or hexadecimal numeral system respectively. The string representation is for an unsigned integer without leading zeros.

F

java.lang.Integer	
static String toString(int i)	Returns the string representation of the integer value in the parameter i as defined in the decimal numeral system, with the sign '-' as the first character if the integer is less than 0.

PROGRAM F.1   String representation of integers

```
// Writes different string representations of integers.
public class IntegerRepresentation {
  public static void main(String[] args) {
    int i = Integer.parseInt(args[0]);
    System.out.println("String representation for integers: " + i);
    System.out.println("Decimal:     " + Integer.toString(i));
    System.out.println("Binary:      " + Integer.toBinaryString(i));
    System.out.println("Octal:       " + Integer.toOctalString(i));
    System.out.println("Hexadecimal: " + Integer.toHexString(i));
  }
}
```

Running the program:

> **java IntegerRepresentation 123**

```
String representation for integers: 123
Decimal:    123
Binary:     1111011
Octal:      173
Hexadecimal: 7b
```
> **java IntegerRepresentation -123**
```
String representation for integers: -123
Decimal:    -123
Binary:     11111111111111111111111110000101
Octal:      37777777605
Hexadecimal: ffffff85
```

Programming tools in the JDK

INTRODUCTION

This appendix describes some commonly used tools for developing and running Java pr ograms.

G.1 Programming tools

Sun Microsystems, Inc. offers a toolkit for Java called the Java Development Kit (JDK). This toolkit contains all necessary tools for writing and running Java programs. The latest version of the JDK can be freely downloaded from `http://java.sun.com/downloads/`. The most important tools in the JDK are:

- `javac`: the Java compiler. Translates source code to byte code.
- `java`: the Java Virtual Machine (JVM). Provides the runtime environment for executing Java byte code.
- `javadoc`: a documentation tool. Generates HTML documentation from source code.

G.2 Commands

The tools in the Java JDK are stand-alone applications that can be run from the command line. All the tools accept a command line option `-help` that provides a summary of how to use the tool.

Compiling source code: `javac`

The `javac` compiler reads class and interface declarations written in the Java programming language and compiles these to Java byte code class files.

```
> javac PersonnelRegister.java
```

This command will compile the source code in the file named "`PersonnelRegister.java`", and create byte code for all the classes and interfaces defined in this file. If the source code contains the declaration of a class called `PersonnelRegister`, a byte code file named

"PersonnelRegister.class" will be generated. If the given source code file uses other classes and/or interfaces that have not yet been compiled, the compiler will try to compile these as well. For example, if the source code in the file named "PersonnelRegister.java" uses a class called Employee, and this class has not yet been compiled, the javac compiler will attempt to compile a file named "Employee.java".

Table G.1 shows some of the parameters accepted by the javac compiler.

TABLE G.1   A subset of options for **javac** in JDK

Command line options	Description
-d *directory*	Places all generated class files in *directory*.
-Xlint	Turns on all warnings that are recommended by Sun Microsystems, Inc. There are several similar options that only provide specific types of warnings during compilation. Use option -X to get a complete list of -Xlint options.
-encoding utf8	Source code files are usually interpreted using the default character encoding for the operating system. This may cause problems if your source code files are created using another encoding scheme. The UTF-8 encoding scheme is commonly used to support non-English characters in source code. If UTF-8 is not the default character encoding for the operating system you use, you can specify the character encoding with this option.

The following command will compile the files named "PersonnelRegister.java" and "Company.java" using UTF-8 character encoding, and place the generated byte code files in the ../../my_classes directory:

```
> javac -Xlint -encoding utf8 -d ../../my_classes
        PersonnelRegister.java Company.java
```

The command must be executed as a single command, even though it is shown on two lines above.

Running the program: **java**

The java interpreter is used to run Java applications. It starts the runtime environment of Java and loads the class specified on the command line:

```
> java -ea Company
```

This command loads the class Company from the byte code file named "Company.class", and executes the main() method of the class. The interpreter will print an error message if a file named "Company.class" is not available, or if the Company class does not have a valid main() method.

Execution of assertion statements must be explicitly turned on using the option given in Table G.2.

TABLE G.2 Option for turning on assertion checking

Command line options	Description
`-enableassertions` or `-ea`	Turns on execution of `assert` statements in the program. This will cause the program to terminate if any of the assertions evaluates to `false`.

Generating documentation: `javadoc`

The `javadoc` tool reads declarations and documentation comments in the source code and generates HTML pages describing classes, interfaces and members:

```
> javadoc PersonnelRegister.java
```

This command will generate a file named "PersonnelRegister.html" with documentation for the class `PersonnelRegister` that is defined in the file named "PersonnelRegister.java".

TABLE G.3 A subset of options for `javadoc` in the JDK

Command line options	Description
`-encoding utf8`	Allows non-English characters (as for `javac`).
`-d` *directory*	Places the generated documentation in *directory*.

The following command generates documentation for all source code files in the current working directory and places the documentation in the subdirectory `doc`. The source code files are assumed to be stored in the UTF-8 character encoding.

```
> javadoc -encoding utf8 -d doc *.java
```

Section 8.5 on page 224 shows an example of the use of the `javadoc` tool.

G.3 Configuring the CLASSPATH

The tools in a standard installation of the JDK know where to find the byte code files for all classes in the Java standard library. The tools will also look for byte code files in the current working directory. In most cases this set-up will be sufficient to run the program.

However, sometimes it is necessary to instruct the JDK tools to look for byte code files in other directories as well. For examples, when we want to:

- Install additional libraries that must be made available to all Java programs.
- Start a compiled program that resides in a directory different from the current working directory.

By specifying a *class path* it is possible to augment the list of directories that are searched for byte code files. A class path can be specified by the -classpath option of the java tool, or by defining the environment variable CLASSPATH. Both techniques will work for all tools described in this appendix.

A class path consists of the paths to one or more directories where byte code files reside. Multiple paths are separated by the character ":" (colon) under Posix/Linux, and with ";" (semicolon) under Microsoft Windows.

Under Windows, the following commands will first compile the class Company in the file named "Company.java", placing the byte code files in the C:\my_classes\ directory, and then run the program:

```
> javac -classpath C:\my_classes -d C:\my_classes Company.java
> java -ea -classpath C:\my_classes Company
```

The -classpath option specifies the path of the classes used by the Company class.

Libraries can be made available as Java archive (JAR) files. Such archives can contain a large number of byte code files. To get the Java JDK tools to look for classes in these archives, the full path to the archive must be specified in the class path.

A system administrator for a Unix system who wants to make the library console.jar available for all users of the system, for example, can do the following:

1 Place the archive file, "console.jar", in a shared directory, e.g. /usr/share/java/.
2 Set the environment variable CLASSPATH for all users to /usr/share/java/console.jar.

Environment variables are set in different ways under different operating systems. Check the documentation for the operating system you are using to find out how this is done. Further information on how classes are found, and how to configure the environment variable CLASSPATH, is available at:

http://java.sun.com/j2se/1.5.0/docs/tooldocs/findingclasses.html

Introduction to UML

INTRODUCTION

The *Unified Modelling Language* (UML) is a standard modelling language for object-oriented analysis and design. UML has a graphical notation that can be used to make diagrams that specify, visualise and document various aspects of object-oriented systems. This appendix gives a short introduction to basic elements in UML diagrams.

H.1 Class diagram

A *class diagram* shows static structures in program design. Such diagrams can be used to illustrate the relationships between classes and interfaces. Figure H.1 shows a class diagram for a program that controls street lights in a city.

FIGURE H.1 Class diagram

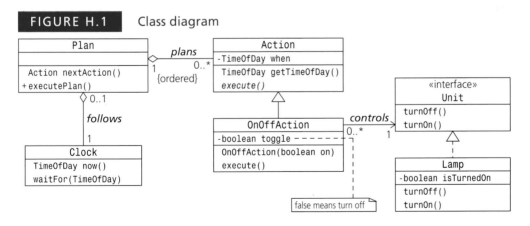

The rectangles describe *types* that are either classes or interfaces. A rectangle can consist of several compartments that describe different aspects of the type:

1 *Name.* The name of the type is always placed in the top compartment. In Figure H.1, the type Unit has also been tagged with the *stereotype* «interface», which specifies that Unit is an interface. The other types shown in the diagram are classes.

2 *Attributes.* The second compartment describes the attributes of a type. This corresponds to field variables in Java. This compartment can be left empty if you don't need to show the attributes of a class. The attributes of the `Plan` class are not shown in Figure H.1.

3 *Operations.* The third compartment describes the operations of a type. In Java, this corresponds to methods.

Attributes and operations can be marked with symbols that specify their visibility. The most important symbols are + (plus) and - (minus), which denote the `public` access modifier and the `private` access modifier, respectively.

The lines and arrows between the rectangles describe associations between the types. A triangular arrow with a solid line represents *inheritance*. In Figure H.1, the `OnOffAction` class inherits from the `Action` class. A triangular arrow with a dashed line represents implementation of an interface. In Figure H.1, the `Lamp` class implements the `Unit` interface.

Figure H.2 shows how different types of associations are depicted in UML. Associations can specify a *multiplicity* defining the number of objects at each end of the association. Table H.1 shows some typical multiplicities between types in associations. For example, the association between `Plan` and `Clock` in Figure H.1 shows that every `Plan` object has exactly one `Clock` object associated with it (multiplicity 1 at the association end connected to the `Clock` class), but that a `Clock` object need not be associated with a `Plan` object (multiplicity 0..1 at the association end connected to the `Plan` class).

A *note* can be included in a UML diagram, and can be attached to any element. Figure H.1 includes a note attached to the `toggle` field of the `OnOffAction` class, explaining how its value should be interpreted. *Constraints* on associations can be given in curly brackets, for example, the constraint {ordered} shown in Figure H.1.

FIGURE H.2   Associations

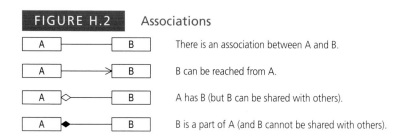

TABLE H.1   Multiplicity

Multiplicity	Description
1	Only one object can fulfil the association. A `Plan` object has exactly one `Clock` object.
0..1	Zero or one object can fulfil the association. A `Clock` object can be associated with 0 or 1 `Plan` object.

Multiplicity	Description
0..*	Any number of objects can fulfil the association. A `Plan` object has zero or more `Action` objects.
n	Only n objects can fulfil the association, where $n > 1$.
0..n	Up to and including n objects can fulfil the association, where $n > 1$.

H.2 Object diagrams

An *object diagram* shows the relationship between objects and their state. These diagrams can be used to show data structures and the state of a program at any given time during execution.

The notation for objects is similar to that used for classes, but the name of an object has the form *objectName:className* and can be underlined. The compartment for the attributes shows the state of the object, while the compartment for operations is seldom used in object diagrams. Figure H.3 shows a plan for turning street lights on at 17:30 and off at 23:45.

FIGURE H.3 Object diagram

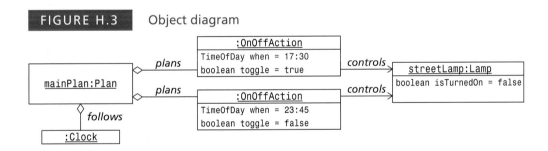

H.3 Sequence diagrams

A *sequence diagram* shows the interaction between objects, i.e. how the objects communicate during program execution. These diagrams show the *lifelines* of a set of objects, and the method calls between them. Time flows downwards in sequence diagrams.

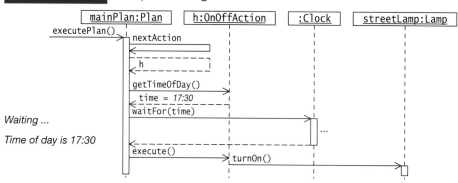

FIGURE H.4   Sequence diagram

Method calls are shown by solid arrows, and return values as dashed arrows. The first method called in Figure H.4 is `executePlan()` in the `Plan` object referred to by the reference `mainPlan`. The method calls are shown in sequence from top to bottom. The objects at the top of the diagram have lifelines that extend downwards along the time axis. The narrow rectangles on the lifeline show time intervals when an object is *active*, i.e. executing a method. Supplementary notes are given to the left of the diagram. It is a good idea to provide such additional information in sequence diagrams.

H.4 Activity diagrams

An *activity diagram* shows how an operation can be broken down into smaller steps, the order in which these steps (or *activities*) can be carried out, and alternative paths that can be followed to complete the operation. Figure H.5 shows an example of an activity diagram for managing street lights. This type of diagram can be seen as the object-oriented equivalent of the data flow diagrams that are often used in structured programming.

Each step is shown as a rectangle with rounded corners, and the action to be carried out is described using natural language. The transition from one step to the next is shown as a solid line arrow (or *activity edge*), which can be marked with a condition (or *guard*) that must be satisfied to allow the transition to take place. Such conditions are written in square brackets, [*condition*], again using natural language (see Figure H.5).

At some point the execution can reach a *decision point* where different courses of action can be selected. A decision point is shown as a diamond in the UML diagram. Any number of activity edges can exit from a decision point, each edge marked with the condition that must be satisfied for the edge to be traversed. (An edge without a condition is always traversed once the activity it originates from has completed.)

The *starting point* of the operation is marked with a filled circle, while the *endpoint* is modelled by a filled circle enclosed in a border. All activity diagrams need a starting point, and it is common to place this at the top of the diagram in Western cultures, reflecting the normal reading direction from top to bottom. A diagram may have more than one endpoint. For continuous operations it may also make sense not to have an endpoint at all.

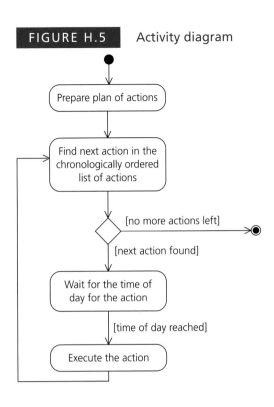

H

default 113, 321
do 60, 62, 321
double 25, 26, 27, 36, 92, 236, 321, 324
else 54, 321
enum 192, 321
extends 321
false 46, 322, 324, 329
final 24, 321, 325
finally 321
float 92, 236, 321, 325
for 102, 321
goto 322
if 50, 54, 321
implements 247, 321
import 34, 321
instanceof 321, 323
int 20, 25, 27, 92, 236, 254, 321
int class 325
interface 321
long 92, 236, 321, 325
native 321
new 78, 321, 323
null 90, 322, 329
package 321
private 226, 321, 326, 360
protected 321, 325
public 3, 9, 226, 247, 321, 325, 360
return 174, 321
short 92, 236, 321, 325
static 9, 321
strictfp 321
super 321
switch 112, 321
synchronized 321
this 173, 321
throw 321
throws 321
transient 321
true 46, 322, 324, 329
try 321
void 9, 165, 321
volatile 321
while 59, 60, 61, 62, 63, 103, 321
keywords in pseudocode 240
kitchen 7

L

language
    construct 1, 3, 6, 7, 9, 11
    structure 7
    syntax 7
large program 9
Latin-1 268
layout of source code 8
least significant bit 352
left associative operator 322
left associativity 29
left margin 8

left-justified output 31, 330
lending date 7
length of
    array 124
    string 5, 11, 87
letter
    lowercase 3
    uppercase 24
lexicographical order 85, 236, 245, 258, 259, 335
library
    loan 7
    user 7
lifeline 361
line
    command 4
    printing 10
line terminator string 272, 329
line-by-line documentation 228
linear search 251
    amount of work 251
    extended version 263
    implementation 251
    pseudocode 251
literal 17
    character 81
    string 19, 83
loan 7
local variable 20, 105, 175, 208, 217
    initialization required 22
locale 31, 88
Locale class 335
localised output 330
logical error 23, 278
    infinite loop 61
logical operator 48
    ! 48
    && 48
    || 48
    associativity rules 48
    precedence rules 48
long 236, 321, 325
Long class 325
longValue() 94
look up employees 224
loop 50, 59
    backwards 106
    body 51, 59, 60, 102
    break statement 108
    condition 51, 59, 60, 102
    conditional 102
    continue statement 108
    counter-controlled 102
    debugging 112
    for(:) loop 143
    for(;;) 103, 139
    header 102
    infinite 61, 104, 110
    initialization 102
    inner 63

iteration 59
local variable 105
nested 63, 106, 139, 240, 243, 249
optimizing 111
outer 63
post-test 60
pre-test 59, 104
sentinel value 61
while 103
lottery game 265
low-level
    language 11
    machine code 12
lowercase letters 3, 6, 82, 333

M

machine code 12
    instructions 11
    level 12
main() 6, 7, 9, 19, 356
    program arguments 184
maintaining references 220
manager 218
managing several objects 222
manipulating field variables 213
markup tag 225, 228
Master Mind 158
meaningful variable names 229
member
    static 212
memory 10
merging sequences 295
message dialog box 286
method 7, 10
    body 11
    call 10, 11, 78, 213, 224
    declaration 7
    execution 9
    helper 210
    implementation 80
    name 7, 9, 10
    overloading 223
    same name 223
    versatility 218
method call 167
    actual parameter 167
    argument 167
    call-by-value 169
    invoke methods 173
    parameter passing 168
method declaration 164
    formal parameter 165
    method name 164
    non-void method 165
    parameter passing 168
    return type 164
    returning array 177
    signature 165
    void method 165
method execution 174, 176

method name 164
milk bottle 7
minimizing duplication 212
modal dialog box 283
modern computers 1
modifier
    `private` 226
    `public` 226
modulus 26
most significant bit 352
multi-line comment 225
multi-selection statement 112
multidimensional array 136, 143
multiple-choice quiz 158
multiplication 26
multiplicity 221, 360

N

naive solution 208
name overloading 223
named location 10
naming
    conventions 24
    rules 3, 24
    source code files 3
`NaN`
    see Not a Number
narrower data type 27
`native` 321
natural order
    objects 236, 246, 259
    primitive values 235
nested loop 63, 139, 240, 243, 249
    inner 63, 240, 243, 249
    outer 63, 240, 243, 249
nested selection statement 55
nesting language constructs 8
`new` 78, 125, 321, 323
New Zealand 14
newline 82, 330
`nextDouble()` 34, 36, 38
`nextInt()` 34, 35, 37
`nextLine()` 38
non-default constructor 187
non-obvious program aspects 228
non-tangible concepts 7
Norwegian 335
Not a Number
note 360
`null` 90, 131, 322, 329
`NullPointerException` 90, 131
number
    decimal 330
    floating-point 330
    hexadecimal 330
    octal 330
number of characters 2
number representation 345
numeral system 345, 346
    binary numeral system 346

    conversions between decimal, octal
      and hexadecimal numeral systems
      348, 349
    decimal numeral system 329, 345
    hexadecimal numeral system 347
    octal numeral system 347
    string representation of integers 352
numerator 29
numerical data type 25, 236
numerical value 10
    printing 20

O

object 6, 162
    `==` 90
    automatic garbage collection 179
    availability 221
    communication 217, 219
    comparing 90, 245
    comparing type 323
    creating 78
    current object 173
    `equals()` 90
    initial state 163
    interaction 213
    model 75
    natural order 236, 245
    ownership 220
    primitive values as 92
    property 7
    relationships 218
    set state 216
    state 80, 163
    string 11
    type 7
`Object` class 247
object diagram 361
    compartment 361
    state of object 361
object-based programming 7
objects in arrays 124, 126
OBP 7
octal
    integer 329
    number 330
octal numeral system 347
    converting to binary 348
    converting to decimal 347
    converting to hexadecimal 348
off-the-shelf programs 1
omelette 6
one statement per line 8
one-dimensional arrays 136
one-off errors 110
one-to-many association 221, 222
one-to-one association 221
open a file 272, 273, 280
operating system 3, 4
operation 6, 7
operator

`!` negation 323
`!=` not equal to 323
`%` modulus (remainder) 323
`%=` assignment after modulus 324
`&` bitwise AND 323
`&` logical AND 323
`&&` conditional AND 323
`&=` assignment after bitwise AND
    324
`&=` assignment after logical AND
    324
`*` multiplication 323
`*=` assignment after multiplication
    324
`+` addition 323
`++` increment 322, 323
`+=` assignment after addition 324
`-` subtraction 26, 323
`--` decrement 322, 323
`-=` assignment after subtraction 324
`/` division 323
`/=` assignment after division 324
`<` less than 245, 246, 323
`<<` bitwise left shift 323
`<<=` assignment after bitwise left
    shift 324
`<=` less than or equal to 236, 323
`=` assignment 324
`==` equal to 236, 237, 245, 246, 323
`>` greater than 245, 246, 323
`>=` greater than or equal to 236, 323
`>>` bitwise right shift with sign ex-
    tension 323
`>>=` assignment after bitwise right
    shift with sign extension 324
`>>>` bitwise right shift with 0 exten-
    sion 323
`>>>=` assignment after bitwise right
    shift with 0 extension 324
`? :` ternary conditional operator
    323
`^` bitwise exclusive OR 323
`^` logical exclusive OR 323
`^=` assignment after bitwise exclu-
    sive OR 324
`^=` assignment after logical exclusive
    OR 324
`|` bitwise OR 323
`|` logical OR 323
`|=` assignment after bitwise OR 324
`|=` assignment after logical OR 324
`||` conditional OR 323
`~` bitwise complement 323
arithmetic operator 26
binary operator 26, 322
left-associative 322
precedence 322
relational operator 46, 235
right-associative 322
ternary operator 322

unary minus 27
unary operator 27, 322
unary plus 27
option type 288
order
ascending 238
descending 238
natural 235
out of scope 53
outer loop 63, 240, 243, 249
output 10, 267
overloaded 189
overloading method names 223
overwriting variables 22
owner of objects 220

P

package
default accessibility 325
`public` accessibility 325
`package` 321
package accessibility 325
parameter 9, 10, 78
declaration 9
list 223
reference value 211
type 224
parameter list 164
parameter passing 168
parentheses 20
`parseInt()` 94
partially-filled array 147
passing parameters 10
percent sign 328, 330
personal information 7
personnel register 221
physical machine 11
plain text 3
platform independence 12
play a role 207
positional value 345
see also numeral system
post-decrement operator (x--) 101, 322
post-increment operator (x++) 101, 322
post-test loop 60
pre-decrement operator (--x) 101, 323
pre-increment operator (++x) 101, 323
pre-test loop 51, 59, 104
precedence 322
precedence rules 28
predefined class 161
primary class 3, 9
primitive data type 25, 324
`boolean` 46, 236
`character` 236
comparing 236, 237
natural order 235
numerical 236
primitive value 95
as objects 92

principle amount 43, 70
print
report 208
values to file 273
`print()` 17, 35
`printArray()` 256
`printf()` 30, 31
printing
boolean values 48
formatted output 30
numerical values 20
strings 19, 20
text 10
to terminal window 10, 17, 30
`println()` 17, 19
`private` 226, 321, 326, 360
program 1, 9
code 7
control flow 50
entry point 9
execution 8, 9, 10
form 1
large 9
logic 56
output 10
representation 12
robust 278
small 9
testing 2
translation 2
validation using assertions 64
program argument
`main()` 184
program design 207
programmer 12
programming 1, 12
errors 12, 278
language 1, 6, 12
promoting operands 27
prompt 34
proper indentation 9
property 7, 207, 209
combining 208
`protected` 321, 325
proverb 2
provision-based salary 41
pseudo-random numbers 149
distance 150
offset 149
range 149
pseudocode 224
as comments 240
document algorithms 240
implementation 240, 243
indentation 240
insertion sort 242
keywords 240
linear search 251
selection sort 239, 260, 262
`public` 3, 9, 226, 247, 321, 325, 360

R

radius of circle 41
ragged array 141
`Random` class
`nextInt()` 149
see also pseudo-random numbers
random numbers
see pseudo-random numbers
ranking two values 235
read a text line 280
reading
from text file 279, 281
record 281
reading input
error handling 37
floating-point numbers 36
from keyboard 34
multiple values per line 37
prompt 34
reading integers 35
skipping rest of line 38
syntactic validation 37
recompiling 12
record 269, 295
field 269
reading from file 281
using `Scanner` 295
writing to file 274
refactoring 217
for clarity 228
reference
assigning to 89
declaration 77
equality 86, 245
type 77, 89
value 77, 125
variable 77
reference value 168
as actual parameter 171
as parameter 211
referring to variable 10
refrigerator 6
register of employees 213
related behaviour 209
related properties 209
relational operator 46, 235
character 236
numerical data type 236
precedence rules 46
relationships
between classes and interfaces 359
between objects 218
reliable execution 1
repeating code 210
report 208
required initialization 22
responsibility 207, 212
clear 217
focus 213
splitting sensibly 218